THE BERRYHILL FAMILY
IN
AMERICA

Compiled by
Virginia (Thompson) Brittain
Pasadena, Texas

Southern Historical Press, Inc.
Greenville, South Carolina

SOUTHERN HISTORICAL PRESS, INC.
PO BOX 1267
Greenville, SC   29601

ISBN #0-89308-293-7

Printed in the United States of America

VIRGINIA (THOMPSON) BRITTAIN

SPECIAL NOTICE

Each year on the *1st Sunday of May,* at the *Berryhill Family Cemetery* in Marion County, Alabama about five miles from *Winfield, Alabama* a memorial is held at the cemetery, and then a family reunion and lunch on the lawn is held at the Church nearby the cemetery.

All Berryhill descendants are cordially invited. Take a picnic lunch you can spread on outside tables.

In this *Berryhill* cemetery, you will find the graves marked for the *Alexander Berryhill* b. 1760 (approx.) in North Carolina who earned a free Revolutionary War marker. Also the grave of *William Berryhill Sr.,* b. 1780 (approx.) in Gerogia who earned a free War of 1812 marker.

I want to express my appreciation for all those who so kindly answered my request for the various family information. Several went even further to help me gather their whole families information.

You will find some errors in the spelling of names, as well as dates, as I often find when getting information maybe from two out of one family, that they give me a different date or spelling of a name. But we hope it is as nearly accurate as is humanly possible in handling so many thousands of names. It is only if you have attempted to do this yourself that you realize what a job it is to get names and addresses to try to contact each and every family.

But we honestly tried to not leave out a single person who connected to our family, and if we did, it was either an over-sight, or impossible to get an address on you.

I hope you will continue to send me new marriages, new births, new deaths, etc. as I would like to keep my book as up to date as possible in event someday in the future a revised supplement can be made to add to your books.

Anyone who has a Confederate soldier who does not have a marker, I will be happy to help you fill out a form to apply for his a free marker to be placed at his grave. My permanent address will be:

Mrs. Otis Brittain
1105 Pampa Road
Pasadena, Texas 77504

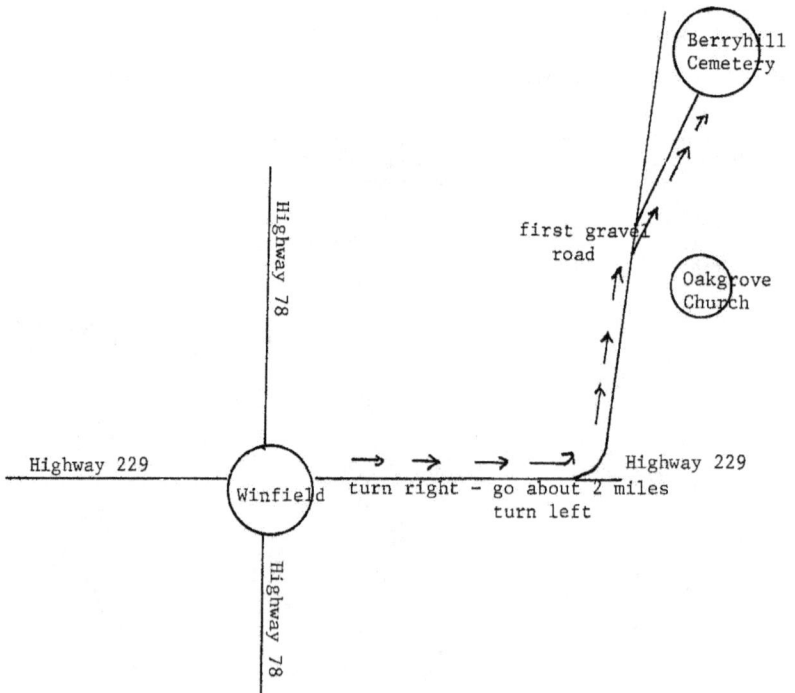

Berryhill
Cemetery

Oakgrove
Church

first gravel
road

Highway 78

Highway 229   Highway 229

Winfield   turn right – go about 2 miles
                             turn left

Highway 78

In 1981 contact was made with Mrs. Otis (Tommie) Brittain of Pasadena, Texas in regard to the Brittain Family History she had published, and during the conversation she mentioned to me about her other book on the Berryhill Family and asked me if I would be interested in reprinting this in an updated version. I was very excited at the prospect of this, and upon seeing a copy of the book, I realized that I was kin to a majority of the Berryhill descendants in Fayette and Marion Counties, Alabama.

Later, I sent out a letter to a list of perspective purchasers that was supplied by Mrs. Brittain, and word of mouth carried the news to other Berryhill descendants far and wide. We solicited updated information on their respective families, as well as any photographs they might be able to furnish us to use in this updated and expanded edition.

In the meantime, we found that another Berryhill descendant had reprinted Mrs. Brittain's book several years after its original publication, and the person who did this added new material to update some of the lines in that edition. Our job was to consolidate the new information being sent to us from the various descendants, together with the information that had been added to the original edition, and try not to omit anyone or any family that data was available on. This was a far more difficult task than we had anticipated, and as a result slowed the job down considerably. We also added a full-name index to the book to facilitate the finding of individual persons quickly, and this also caused additional delay in getting the book out based on our original schedule.

We have done the best we could with the information furnished to us, and as with any book once it is done we all realize there was much that should have been added and other information that should have been changed. We want to encourage any Berryhill descendants to send us any updated material regarding their respective families, so that if the book should be reprinted again in the future, that material can be added.

I mentioned my relationship to many of the Berryhill kin; and for those who might be curious, I am the son of Silas Emmett Lucas, Sr., of Birmingham, Alabama, and the grandson of Silas Watts Lucas, born 1852 and died 1935, and his wife Essie Gabriella Dodson, born 1953, died 1921 and buried at Old Union Primitive Baptist Church Cemetery near Bluff. Silas Watts Lucas was the son of John Lucas and his wife Jane Walters, and Essie G. Dodson Lucas was the daughter of Lemuel Dodson and his wife Jane Catherine Reed. Many of the Berryhills are descended from both of these families, but more especially from the Dodson family, as Lemuel Dodson was one of fifteen chidren who came with his parents, William and Sara (Pyles) Dodson, to Fayette County in 1817.

The Rev. Silas Emmett Lucas, Jr.
Publisher

Winfield Public School, Winfield, Alabama. 1916

T. H. SMITH & SON, Winfield, Alabama

T.H. Smith and his son Frank, (married to Emmie White) had this store. To the left was the Post Office and the postmaster's name was Whitehead. To the left of the Post Office was Span's store.

L. to R.   made approx. 1901

1. John Hodge
2. Levi Vaughn
3. unidentified
4. young boy, unidentified
5. Frank White
6. unidentified
7. unidentified
8. Otis Aston
9. John Haney
10. Preacher Self
11. Vester Bostick
12. boy - Houston Haney
13. Jonathan Jones
14. unidentified
15. Esquire "Squire" Loden
16. unidentified
17. Dr. Marcus Hill, Dentist
18. Jack Mazing
19. Newton S. Whitehead, Postmaster
20. unidentified
21. Hezzie Caddell
22. John Weeks
23. Forrest White
24. unidentified
25. lady, unidentified
26. Arch Aston
27. Fred Smith
28. unidentified
29. boy, Carey Wade
30. Dr. Seay

The two oxen are named Blue & Nig

CONTENTS

1

ADDENDA

This section contains additional data found on some of the various
Berryhills mentioned elsewhere.

3

The name BERRYHILL, according to one genealogist, originated from people living on a location by that name. There are several places named Berryhill listed in the county directory of Scotland. Warder Crow's account states several centuries ago a family by the name of HILL lived in Scotland. This family moved to Ireland and became a part of that remarkable family known as Scotch-Irish. In North Ireland one member of the family was a grower of berries. He became known as BERRY - HILL and his descendents came to America at various times around 1685 to 1720.

ALEXANDER BERRYHILL was born in Scotland in 1661, went to London and married Lady Jane Cartwright. Four of his sons: John, William, Samuel, and Andrew came to America. They helped found the Scotch-Irish Presbyterian settlement in a part of Lancaster Co., later became Dauphin Co., Pa., near the present site of Harrisburg, Pa.

One historian, writing in 1845 of these Scotch-Irish in Dauphin Co., said "they possessed all the indespensable qualities to make good pioneer settlers; dauntless and valorous were they." Educated as Presbyterians they had strong hopes of becoming the undisturbed possessors of the lands to some extent occupies by the tawny sons of the woods: this they did, but at the cost of many a helpless child, an endeared bosom companion, a father, mother or some friend or relative: for during the French and Indian Wars from 1755 to 1763, many fell victims to the cruel savages then maurauding the frontier settlements.

WILLIAM BERRYHILL, born 1689, was killed by Indians in a massacre, which resulted in the killing and scalping or adduction, of at least seven men, seven women and eleven children. This was 15 November 1755.

SAMUEL BERRYHILL was killed and scalped by Indians in 1760, and his wife made an almost miraculous escape by mounting a horse and swimming the Susquehanna River, when it was at a very high stage in spring. A Mr. Marcus Hulings, his wife and child made a similar escape with her, which was regarded as almost unbelievable.

Another source stated that ANDREW BERRYHILL, born 1693, was killed by Indians in 1756. He was married in Lancaster County, Pennsylvania.

As early as March 14, 1742, we find records of land warrants and surveys to WILLIAM BERRYHILLs, and on down through the Revolution well into the nineteenth centry we find records of marriages, land transfers, and tax lists of a number of Berryhill's in Pa. They were among the founders of Paxton Presbyterian Church in 1720, and later were prominent in the establishment of the Revolution by the state of Pa. the BERRYHILL name appears more than forty-five times. Names appearing in these records are Captain William Berryhill, Alexander Berryhill, Alexander Berrhill, Jr., Ensign Andrew Berryhill, Andrew Berryhill, Jr., Ensign Samuel Berryhill, Sergeant Samuel Berryhill, and Gilbert Berryhill. Some of them participated in the campaigns around Philadelphia, in New Jersey and on Long Island.

From Pa. it seems the Berryhill's began coming on down into N. Car. and we find ours in Mecklenburg Co., N.C. Later they came on into Ga., and on into Ala. and after the Civil War, they began venturing into all the U.S.A., where today, we find descendents in almost every state.

Will of JOSEPH BERRYHILL
dated 22 May 1781 - Meckleburg Co., N.C.

In the name of God, Amen, I, JOSEPH BERRYHILL of the county of Mecklenburg and the state of N.C. being very sick and weak in body, but of
perfect mind and memory, thanks be given unto God for the same, calling
unto mind the mortality of my body and knowing it is appointed unto all
men once to die, do make and ordain this my last Will & Testament in
form and manner following, that is to say:

Principally and first of all being penitent and sorry from the heart for
all my aggrivated sins and heinous transgressions, most humbly knowing
and trusting that the merits of Christ for pardon and forgiveness, I
recommend to the earth to be burried in a decent Christian burial at the
discretion of my loving wife and executors hereafter named. Nothing
doubting but at the general resurrection I shall receive the same again
by the mighty power of God. And as touching such worldly estate where-
with it has pleased God to bless me in this life.

I give and demist and dispose of the same in the following manner and
form. I give and bequeath unto my well beloved wife HANNA as her right
and property, my negro wench named DOLL, my bay mare named KATE, a good
featherbed, bedstead, and furniture there unto belonging, three good cows
with three calves vis: a certain cow named DAN, a brindle cow named
BRINDLE, a black and white cow named FLECK, a chest, the griddle, the
half of what pewter belongs to the dresser, 2 iron post, the wooden
vessels, tables and chairs, at the same time confirming her right to her
saddle, wearing apparel and whatever else was understood to be her own
property whether by gift, dowery, or otherwise, and to remain in the
enjoyment and possession of my dwelling house, tenaments and improvements
these unto belonging, except these improvements hereafter mentioned, and
bequeath to my son SAMUEL, upon condition of her endeavoring to take the
parental care of my family while under age, that I trust her natural
affection and love to them and me will obligate her unto.

To well beloved son SAMUEL, I give and bequeath my young negro boy named
JACK, my little gray horse, commonly his own here unto by the name of
LITTLE GRAY, at the same time confirming his title and claim to his own,
while horse saddle, wearing apparel and whatsoever was always understood
to be his, whether by gift, purchase, or otherwise. Also certain plow
called his own, beat chains, double tree and chains, one bed and furniture, two cows and calves vis: a certain named BLAZE and LIDDY, and 140
acres of land containing improvements of the lower field and meadow and
adjoining to him his heirs and assignes and to their proper use and
behoof for wearables the half of my wearing apparel and my large Bible.

To my dauther, JANE, married to Thomas Williams, to her child SARAH, I
bequeath a certain young cow and calf named BROWNY at the same time
confirming to said daughter JANE all and singular whatsoever I have
already given her within at or before her marriage the above legacy and
no more in consequence of my love and good will to her said child.

To my beloved daughter MARY, married to David Rea, I give a certain white
cow named RED and no more confirming in right and title all and singular
whatsoever I have formerly bestowed upon her whether by gift, dowery or
otherwise.

To my kind and affectionate son ANDREW, I give and bequeath a certain
black mare conveniently denominated as his own. A gun and a plow, claimed by him. Likewise two pairs of chains, double tree and chains, two
cows and a certain cow bought from William McCummins together with her
calf, a colt three years old, bed and furniture, 140 acres of land join-
ing Robert McKnight and Andrew Herrons line to be surveyed in such a
manner as not to injure that part belonging and adjacent to my dwelling
house and improvements in regard to timber. Also through the other half
of my wearing apparel and iron bound chest.

To my loving daughter SARAH, I give and devise a certain black horse, a
certain mooled (??) cow and yearling, mare colt, a certain 2 yr. heifer,

bed and furniture, her own wearing apparel and saddle to be given her
from the produce of what is hereafter mentioned as left for the support
and maintance of my family in their connected status, also one half the
???? of my d__? furniture. (Cannot read where question marks are. V.B.)

To my beloved daughter BETTY, I bequeath a certain heifer bought from
William Wishart, a certain black filly, two years old, and bed and
furniture? ? as aforesaid from the produce of my farm, other half of the
reminer of my d__?? furniture.

To my beloved daughter HANNAH, I give a certain yearling heifer had of
WILLIAM BERRYHILL and one fourth of present value of my negro man,
waggon and white horse hereafter mentioned.

To my beloved son WILLIAM, I give a certain yearling brown colt commonly
called BROWNIE, his and a certain red heifer and of WILLIAM BERRYHILL
together with bed and furniture as aforesaid, also to him I give my rifle
gun.

To my beloved son JOSEPH, I give, and bequeath all the remaining part of
my lands, viz: belonging and adjacent to my dwelling house and improvements thereunto belonging together all tenaments and buildings thereunto
belonging or anywise appertaining and in case of death before he comes to
the actual enjoyment thereof the said promise with their appertances to
dewcent to his brother JAMES hereafter named.

To my several children: HANNAH, MARGARET, THOMAS and JAMES, I bequeath my
negro man AMBROSE my waggon B__??_ land and one pair of chains together
with my white horse aforementioned, these to be valued at their present
full value and equally divided among them when they become of age, these
aforementioned articles together with the while of my stock of sheep all
the wool and flax upon land to be kept for the applied to the support and
maintance of my family while they keep together in a family connected ???,
also all the implements of husbandry, farming and which to me belonged or
in ??? ??? appertained and not particularly disposed of by this my last
WILL and testament to the same use and purpose, also all the grain of the
present or any ensuing crop that may be raised on said farm except so
much as will be necessary to defraud the expenses of schooling and other
necessary education of my children who need the same, and pay my just
debts I owe to others, Which I shall that they be faithfully and honestly
paid without injuring or dependancy, also I will that three of my young
cattle not here disposed of and most fit for the same be applied for
summer crops of the support of my family aforesaid, who I cheerfully
resign up to his guardian care and protection who gave them and who has
promised to a father to the fatherless and judge of the widow.

I constitute, make and ordain Col. Robert Irwin, Esquire, and my son
SAMUEL, the sole executors of this my last Will & Testament, all and
singular my lands ???m??? and tenants, debt and moveable effects, my
whole estate, natural and personal hereby giving the full power of
authority and solemnly charging them to dispose of the same according to
the aforesaid manner and form and I do hereby utterly disallow make and
disannual by these presents all and various other former testament &
testaments, will and wills, legacies, bequest, and exectrs. heretofore
by me in any wise forenamed, will or bequeathed either by word or
writing. Retifying and confirming this and no other to be my last Will
& Testament in witness whereof I have hereunto affixed my hand to seal
the 22nd day of May Anno Domini 1781.

Signed in his presence by   JOSEPH BERRYHILL
Robert Hunter
James Tagert
Moses Sharply

Found in Mecklenburg Co., NC. in Will Book A, pages 79 thru '82

MISSISSIPPI CONFEDERATE SOLDIERS

A.E. BERRYHILL - Rankin Co., Miss. Private, Co. B. 6 Miss Inf.; 15 Miss.Inf.

A.J. BERRYHILL - Yazoo & Warren Co., Miss. Private, Co. E, 46 Miss Inf.

G.W. BERRYHILL - Choctaw Do., Miss. Co. H, 3 Miss. Inf. State Troops.

G.W. BERRYHILL - Wilkinson, Amite, Pike & Franklin Co., Miss. Private,
     Co.I, 4 Miss. Cav.

G.W. BERRYHILL - County unknown. Private, Co. B, 31 Miss. Inf.

H.A. BERRYHILL - Zazoo County, Miss. Private, Co. K. 10 Miss. Inf.

J.C. BERRYHILL - Calhoun Co., Miss. Private, Co. D, 31 Miss. Inf.

M.V. BERRYHILL - Marshall Co., Miss. Private, Co. K, 9 Miss. Inf.

M.V. BERRYHILL - Marshall Co., Miss. Private, Co. K, 10 Miss. Inf.

GEORGE W. BERRYHILL - Private, Co. D, 43 Miss. Inf.

JOHN BERRYHILL - Private, Co. A, 9 Miss. Inf.

JOHN BERRYHILL - County unknown, Private, Co. E-A, 17 Battl. Miss. Cav.

JOHN W. BERRYHILL - County unknown, 1st Sgt. Co. K, 1 Miss. Cav. Reserves

JOHN W. BERRYHILL - Oktibbeha Co., Miss. Private, Co. K, 15 Miss. Inf.

THOMAS BERRYHILL - Lafayette Co., Miss. Private, Co. K, 22 Miss Inf.

WILLIAM H. BERRYHILL - Possibly Webster Co., Miss. 1st Lt., Co. D, 43
     Miss. Inf.

ALABAMA CONFEDERATE SOLDIERS - BERRYHILL'S

ALFORD BERRYHILL - Co. E. 1st Ala. Heavy Artillery Battalion

ALFRED BERRYHILL- Co. F. 13th Ala. Infantry Regiment. Private, age 21,
     Enlisted Montgomery, Ala. 19 July 1861. Born in Ga. Occupation
     Wheelwright.

CAROLINE BERRYHILL - Ala. Pension no. 32587. Widow of C. W. Berryhill.

CHARLES WILLIAM BERRYHILL - Co. D. 10th Reg. Ala. later transferred to
     Co. D. 10th Ala. Cavalry.

CHARLES W. BERRYHILL - Co. K. 16th Ala. Inf. Reg. Private, age 18 years,
     Enlisted Countland, Ala. 19 August 1861.

NEWTON T. BERRYHILL - Co. K. 16th Ala. Inf. Reg. Private, age 21 years,
     Enlisted Courtland, Ala. 19 August 1861.

THOMAS BERRYHILL, Jr. - Co. F. 1st Ala. Inf. Reg. Musician. Killed at
     Port Hudson, La 27 May 1864, by a musket, shot through the head.

THOMAS J. (or F.) BERRYHILL - Co. J., 16th Ala. Inf. Private, age 17
     years, Enlisted 16 August 1861 at Courtland, Ala.

E.D. BERRYHILL - Ala. Pension no. 14702 - Lawrence Co., Ala. Private,
     Co. D. 16 Regt. Ala. Enlisted 10 August 1861 at Courtland, Ala.

HENRY BERRYHILL - Co. J. "Clayton's Guards", 1st Ala. Regt. Vol.
     Private, enlisted Bargour Co., Ala. age 21 years. Henry J. W.
     Berryhill of Clayton, Ala.

JOHN B. BERRYHILL - Pensioner no. 12672 - Fayette Co., Ala. Private,
     Co. H. 26th Regt. Ala. Enlisted July 1861 at Wright's Store in
     Marion Co., Ala. Wounded at Richmond, Va.

JOHN R. BERRYHILL - Ala. Pension no. 36471 - Lawrence Co., Ala. Private,
     Co. D. 5th Regt. Ala. Enlisted October 1862, at Tuscumbia, Ala.
     Wounded at Hunts Mill, Ala.

7

JOHN J. BERRYHILL - Co. L. 16th Ala. Inf. Regt. Private, age 20 years, Enlisted at Courtland, Ala. 19 August 1861.

JOHN RILEY BERRYHILL - 4th Ala. Reg. Co.A. changed to Co. D. Born 7 March 1846 in Marion Co., Ala. Enlisted fall of 1862, at Tuscumbia and continued until paroled at Columbus, Miss. May 1865. Address Kino, Ala. in Lawrence Co.

LEVY H. BERRYHILL - Co. H. 16th Ala. Inf. 2nd Sgt. Enlisted 16 August 1861, age 32, Muster in Roll dated Courtland, Ala. 16 August 1861.

ROBERT A. BERRYHILL - Co.K 16th Ala. Inf. Reg. Private, age 20 years, Enlisted at Courtland, Ala. 19 August 1861.

T.J. BERRYHILL - Ala. Pension no. 15952 - Marion Co., Ala., Private, Co. D. 10th Ala. Regt. Enlisted September 1862 at Astons Store, Ala. Discharged April 1865.

DRUSILLA BERRYHILL - Ala. Pension no. 37804 - Marion Co., Ala. Widow of Thomas Berryhill, Private, Co. K. 22nd Regt. Miss.

T.N. BERRYHILL - Capt. J. Falkner's Co. - Randolph Cp. Militia, Home Guards. Private, age 61 years, blue eyes, gray hair, height 5'8", complexion dark. Born Jasper Co., Ala. Millwright by trade. Muster in Roll dated 13 September 1864.

THOMAS J. BERRYHILL - 5th Ala. Cav. Powell's Co. H., Private, born 27 January 1840 in Ala. Enlisted at Cherokee Co., Ala and continued until 1864. Transferred to 10th Ala. Cav. Co. D. and paroled in 1865. Address: Guin, Ala. Census Tax Assessor, Marion Co., Ala. 1907.

WILLIS H. BERRYHILL - Co. K. 16th Ala. Inf. Regt. Private, age 22 years, Enlisted at Courtland, Ala. 19 Aug 1861.

MARRIAGE RECORDS

FAYETTE COUNTY, ALABAMA

John Berryhill & Mariah Weeks	22 March	1891
M.J. Berryhill & Mrs. M.J. Platt	16 July	1893
Celia E. Berryhill & Columbus G. Weeks	16 July	1893
William Clay Berryhill & Miss M. V. Yancy Berryhill	29 June	1896
William Silas Berryhill & Allie T. Henderson	29 December	1897
Della Berryhill & Ben Ward	14 November	1901
Laura Ann Berryhill & J. T. Lee	17 September	1903
Nora Berryhill & Marvin Thomas Couch	10 January	1904
Drucilla Berryhill & James H. Estes	28 November	1870
John Berryhill & Elizabeth Tucker	2 February	1872
Jefferson D. Berryhill & Nancy Chaffin	23 January	1884
Benjamin F. Berryhill & Laura Justice	29 January	1884
Mary Jane Berryhill & Alexander Weeks	31 January	1886
Margaret M. Berryhill & Thomas T. Platt	2 May	1886
Miss M. F. Berryhill & A. W. Perry	1 September	1888
Mrs. M. M. Berryhill & James K. Gann	29 July	1904
Minnie Berryhill & Curtis Anthony	14 May	1907
Wilford Berryhill & Susan Head	10 March	1907
Thomas E. Berryhill & Cora Crews	22 July	1907
John Walter Berryhill & Rosa Whitley	24 December	1908
Jennie Berryhill & W. L. Brombloe	6 June	1909
Jennie Berryhill & Monroe Head	13 September	1910
Rastus Floyd Berryhill & Julia Henderson	4 October	1912
Exie Berryhill & Jess S. Strecklean	23 May	1923
Mertie Bell Berryhill & J. A. Barnett	14 January	1913

MARION COUNTY, ALABAMA

M.E. Berryhill & William A. Henderson	24 January	1891
William Houston Berryhill & Missouri Kuykendall	22 February	1893
Homer L. Berryhill & Sarah A. Frederick	13 October	1894
J. R. Berryhill & Savannah Wates	24 November	1895
William Silas Berryhill & Mrs. Mary E. Williams	6 June	1903
Samuel R. Berryhill & Ada M. Smith	5 October	1905
D. W. Berryhill & Dora Lee Richardson	16 January	1904
Charity Berryhill & Elec G. Homer	17 September	1904
Nancy M. Berryhill & H. W. Miller	15 October	1899
Charley Berryhill & Bettie Vickery	23 September	1900
J. W. Berryhill 7 Julia Hankins	30 December	1900
John R. Berryhill & Zora Williams	1 November	1901
Nola Berryhill & William McDonald	25 December	1901
William L. Berryhill & Mattie K. O/Mary	13 December	1902
Susie Berryhill & Walter Taylor	2 November	1906
Willis A. Berryhill & Martha Collins	23 May	1907
Henry Berryhill & Dovey Burleson	7 August	1907
Thomas A. Berryhill & Jettie Pyron	8 January	1908
Viola Berryhill & J. A. Bozeman	3 December	1908
Lulla Berryhill & Walter Northcutt	2 January	1910
Zora Berryhill & J. L. Perry	26 August	1911
Eli C. Berryhill & Susie Perry	31 August	1911
Jesse N. Berryhill & Beulah May	18 October	1912
Wanda Berryhill & Robert R. Robbins	5 October	1916
H. L. Berryhill & Ida Thompson	3 September	1915
Fred L. Berryhill & Annie Mae Carter	1 November	1916

ST. CLAIR COUNTY, ALABAMA

Elizabeth Morris Berryhill & James Parker	22 September	1828

MARRIAGE RECORDS (Continued)

ADAMS COUNTY, MISSISSIPPI

George Berryhill & Amey Brown   11 October   1910

ALCORN COUNTY, MISSISSIPPI

James Berryhill & Mary B. Harris   26 November   1852
L. M. Berryhill & Georgie Mays (or Mayo)   26 June   1881

CHICKASAW COUNTY, MISSISSIPPI

Olin Berryhill & Vera Westbrook   7 October   1911
CHOCTAW COUNTY, MISSISSIPPI

C. H. Berryhill & Cora Bell Cummins   3 March   1912

DESOTO COUNTY, MISSISSIPPI

Andrew Berryhill & Ada Bouldin   2 October   1888
J. W. Berryhill & Vellie Stephens   4 September 1904
Joseph J. Berryhill & Mary Imes   29 January   1869
M. C. Berryhill & Annie Mae Stevens   9 December   1904

HINDS COUNTY, MISSISSIPPI

Margaret E. Berryhill & John T. Akins   21 February 1867
A. C. Berryhill & Miss Lizzie Fulgham   12 February 1870
James N. Berryhill & Evie Cornelius Moler   24 December 1919
James Thomas Berryhill & Bettie Jane Jackson   30 November 1914
W. D. Berryhill & Miss E. H. May   22 December 1880
A. C. Berryhill & Georgia Salmons   27 January   1881
A. C. Berryhill & Mrs. T. J. Shirg   29 June   1871
A. E. Berryhill & Mrs. Hattie Laura Stringer   22 September 1919
A. L. Berryhill & Mrs. E. J. Brock   5 January   1881
A. E. Berryhill & Miss A. L. Goodrum   28 September 1890
Bennie D. Berryhill & Miss V. G. Hartwig   8 June   1919
Charlie M. Berryhill & Juanita Inabennett   27 November 1889
Ernest L. Berryhill & Nettie E. Cain   27 July   1904
Hugh Berryhill & Ruby Mae Newsom   24 October   1924
J. A. Berryhill & Sussie Goodrum   23 January   1895
James Martin Berryhill & Sallie Beasley   1 July   1888
John T. Berryhill & Caroline Weeks   15 April   1877
Robert A. Berryhill & Mary Emma Anding   22 February 1894
Samuel Newton Berryhill & Miss E. F. Beasley   2 May   1886
Willis H. Berryhill & Frances E. Davis   23 January   1896
Mrs. Minnie Berryhill & R. B. Dickson   28 December 1919
Jimmie R. Berryhill & Mable Cox   18 July   1922

ITAWAMBA COUNTY, MISSISSIPPI

A. L. Berryhill & Annie Lee Vickery   29 March   1926
C. C. Berryhill & Vergie Rollins   12 February 1905
J. C. Berryhill & Velma Ward   27 January   1925
Luther Berryhill & Icy Bank Guin   11 June   1926
W. H. Berryhill & Mollie L. Hammons   15 January   1880

LAFAYETTE COUNTY, MISSISSIPPI

Burie Berryhill & Miss Mandy Henry   16 May   1915
Burie Berryhill & Eula Franklin   22 January   1905
Charley Berryhill & Verna Stewart   8 January   1914
James H. Berryhill & Sarah E. Berryhill   22 February 1883
John Berryhill & Clarey Welch   7 August   1905
John T. Berryhill & Atlanta Hodge (or Dodge)   20 September 1903
N. A. Berryhill & A. J. Bryant   28 April   1886
W. R. Berryhill & M. C. Garner   20 June   1886
   (Willis Robert Berryhill & Margaret Elizabeth Garner)

MARRIAGE RECORDS (Continued)

LEE COUNTY, MISSISSIPPI

James J. Berryhill & Martha Barten	18 June	1874
Andrew Berryhill & Mable Duncan	6 February	1916
Charley Berryhill & Della Williams	14 December	1920
J. I. Berryhill & Eva Farris	6 June	1923
R. G. Berryhill & Tempie McCormick	24 December	1924

LINCOLN COUNTY, MISSISSIPPI

D. L. Berryhill & Bessie Brashear	27 November	1924

PONTOTOC COUNTY, MISSISSIPPI

C. L. Berryhill & Mary Holley	20 June	1915

PRENTISS COUNTY, MISSISSIPPI

Arthur Berryhill & Myrtle Hill	12 April	1914
Mose Berryhill & Lila Weathers	11 October	1925
R. A. Berryhill & M. S. C. Lauderdale	13 October	1892

RANKIN COUNTY, MISSISSIPPI

Alexander Berryhill & Mary N. Tiles (or Liles)	3 March	1859

YALOBUSHA COUNTY, MISSISSIPPI

S. N. Berryhill & Sela Maulding	1 November	1895

Georgia
Jefferson County

To any Judge, Justice, of the Inferior Court, Justice of the peace or
any Minister of Gospel to whom these presents shall come greeting, you
are hereby authorized to join WILLIAM BERRYHILL and MARGARET WEEKS together in the holy estate of matrimony for which this shall be your
sufficient license. Given under my hand at Office this 24th day of
July, 1807.

Jas. Bozeman,
C.C. Or.

Joined the above couple July the 26th, 1807 by me. Abs. Fryor, J.P.
Marriage Book A, page 9.

Georgia
Jefferson County

WILLIAM BERRYHILL and wife, MARGARET, of Thomas' District in Jefferson
County, Georgia sold land in the 13th District of Baldwin County, Georgia
but now in the county of Randolph, No. 118, granted to WILLIAM BERRYHILL
of Thomas' District in Jefferson County, Georgia.

We know from census telling us that several children of William and
Margaret (Weeks) Berryhill were born in Georgia and Tennessee, that they
evidentially did move from Georgia into Tennessee before coming on to
Alabama. On 1820 Federal Census this family shows in St. Clair County,
Alabama and by 1830, in Marion County, Alabama.

Many who have worked on the various Berryhill lines have said they think
WILLIAM BERRYHILL is a brother to ALEXANDER BERRYHILL, who did not come
to Marion County, Alabama until around 1836, according to his deposition
when he applied for his Pension to be transferred from Franklin County,
Tennessee to Marion County, Alabama. But if they claim ALEXANDER BERRY-
HILL was born in Mecklenburg County, North Carolina and served in the
Revolutionary War from there, HOW can they say William is a brother?
Each time I find William on census, he showed he was born in Georgia.
The year Alexander Berryhill's father's Will was proven, in North
Carolina, was the same year William shows being born in Georgia.

My frank opinion is these two were not brothers! I do not doubt they may
have been kin, but I just find no proof that they were brothers.

1820 St. Clair County, Alabama Federal Census
WILLIAM BERRYHILL
    1 male over 21 years (William b. 1781)
    4 males under 21 years (William II b. 1811, James b. 1812, Alexander
      b. 1817, Thomas b. 1820)
    1 female over 21 years (Margaret Weeks b. 1785/1790)
    2 females under 21 years (Basheba b. 1816, Nancy b. 1819)

1830 Marion County, Alabama Federal Census
WILLIAM BERRYHILL
    1 male 10/15 years (Thomas b. 1820)
    2 males 15/20 years (James b. 1812, Alexander b. 1817)
    1 male 40/50 years (William, Sr., b. 1781)
    2 females under 5 years (1826-1830) Sarah B. 1816, Margaret b. 1829)
    3 females 5/10 (1820-1825)
    1 female 10/15 (1815-1820) (Nancy b. 1819)
    1 female 40/50 (1780-1790) (Margaret Weeks)

1830 Marion County, Alabama Federal Census
William Berryhill, II
    1 male 15/20 years (1810-1815) I cannot account for him, unless he is
      a brother perhaps of Elizabeth Gage.
    1 male 20/30 (William b. 1811)
    1 female under 5 years (Nancy E. b. 1829)
    1 female 20/30 (1800-1810) Elizabeth Gage

12

1840 Marion County, Alabama Federal Census - page 58
WILLIAM BERRYHILL, Sr.
  1 male under 5 years (1836-1840)
  2 males 10/15 years (1825-1830)
  1 male 50/60 years (1780-1790) William B. 1781
  1 female under 5 years (1836-1840)
  1 female 5/10 years (1830-1835)
  1 female 20/30 years (1810-1820) Second wife, Elizabeth ?
  This tells us Margaret Weeks is dead, and he has remarried!

WILLIAM BERRYHILL, Jr., or II - "Bill Dergin"
  1 male 30/40 (1800-1810) "Bill Dergin" b. 1811
  2 females 10/15 (1830-1835)
  1 female 20/30 (1810-1820) Elizabeth Gage

As you look at census from 1790 through 1840, this shows you how difficult it is to identify children, unless they lived until 1850, when they
began naming each person in a household. But from 1807 until 1850,
most of William's children were grown and had families of their own.
So we sometimes have trouble following the girls unless we know who they
married, but it is much easier to follow the males.

1850 Marion County, Alabama Federal Census - #9 - Beat #11
William Berryhill		65 M	Georgia	b. 1785	
Elizabeth	"	30 F	Alabama	1820	(his second wife)
Francis	"	14 M	Alabama	1836	
Catharine	"	12 F	Alabama	1838	
Isabella	"	9 F	Alabama	1841	(Perhaps first issue by Elizabeth)
John	"	8 M	Alabama	1842	
Robert	"	6 M	Alabama	1844	
Perry	"	5 M	Alabama	1845	
Infant not named		1/12 M	Alabama	1850	(1860 census tells us this is Jos.)

1860 Marion County, Alabama Federal Census - #160/166 page 24

William Berryhill		79 M	Georgia	b. 1781	
Elizabeth	"	46 F	Tennessee	1814	(Some say his third marriage But age and State born is differ-ent.)
Rachel Catherine	"	21 F	Alabama	1839	
John B. S.	"	19 M	Alabama	1841	
Pheby E.	"	16 F	Alabama	1844	(Cannot account for her unless she is John's wife, Eliz. Tucker)
Charles Robert	"	14 M	Alabama	1846	
Richard Perry	"	12 M	Alabama	1848	("Dick" was a cripple, I'm told)
Joseph J. N. C.	"	11 M	Alabama	1849	
Andrew N.	"	8 M	Alabama	1852	
George W.	"	6 M	Alabama	1854	

Some say William's third or maybe second wife was ELIZABETH WEBSTER,
sister to Alexander Berryhill's second wife, Rebecca Webster. Apparently
William, Sr., died soon after 1860 census was taken, as his wife, Elizabeth, took the younger children and moved to DeSoto County, Mississippi
before 1870 census.

WILLIAM BERRYHILL
No amount of research has come up with any proof as to who the parents
of William Berryhill were. Both census records of 1850 and 1860 show he
was born in Georgia.

From Jefferson County, Georgia marriage records we find in Book A, page 2,
a marriage for NANCY BERRYHILL, she must be a sister to William Berryhill)
to Charles Weeks on 9 January 1806, and in Book A, page 9, we find
WILLIAM BERRYHILL married Margaret Weeks on 26 July 1807.

Certainly this would suggest a brother and sister married a brother and sister in the Weeks family. It is also known the Weeks families came on into Marion County, Alabama and Hinds County, Mississippi and in fact, a family cemetery in Hinds County, Mississippi, three and one-half miles from Utica, Mississippi, where all the Weeks and Berryhill families used, is named Weeks Cemetery, often commonly called "the burying grounds for the Berryhill's of Alabama."

We find William Berryhill on the 1820 Tax List of St. Clair County, Alabama and it would suggest the ELIZABETH BERRYHILL, who married James Parker in St. Clair County, Alabama on 22 September 1828, can either be a sister to William Berryhill, Sr., or a daughter. But no proof has been found for this either.

WILLIAM BERRYHILL served in the War of 1812, from Tennessee and his Warrant for free lands was forwarded to the Honorable John D. Terrill, Probate Judge of Marion County, Alabama at Pikesville. He was given two land grants in Marion County, Alabama for his service duty.

A free marker for his service has been applied for on his service in the War of 1812.

State of Alabama, Marion County 15th January A.D. 1851 WILLIAM BERRYHILL, 70 years old, made deposition he was the same man who was in a Company Commanded by Captain Francis Jones, in 2nd Regiment of the rifle mounted volunteers from Tennessee commanded by Colonel Allen or Colonel Allcorn. That he volunteered at Winchester, Tennessee and was mustered into the service of the United States at Huntsville, Alabama on or about the fall of 1812 or 1813 for the term of three months. Discharged at Winchester, Tennessee the early part of the winter of 1813.

State of Alabama, Marion County 20th December A.D. 1855 Age 66 years, WILLIAM BERRYHILL, was in the War with the Creek Indian, volunteered in the fall of the year of 1814 for three months, and stayed 3 months and 14 days and was honorably discharged at Winchester, Tennessee in the winter of 1814 or 1815. He received a land Warrant No. 42,987 for 40 acres which he has since legally located and cannot now return. He makes declaration for the purpose of obtaining the additional bounty land to which he may be entitled under the Act approved the 3rd day of March 1855.

Witnesses: John Rea and J.M. White

Jefferson County, Georgia 20th April 1810
WILLIAM BERRYHILL and wife, MARGARET, of Thomas' District in Jefferson County, Georgia, sold land in the 13th District of Baldwin County, Georgia but now in the County of Randolph, No. 118, granted to WILLIAM BERRYHILL of Thomas' District in Jefferson County, Georgia.

This would indicate that if WILLIAM BERRYHILL sold land in Jefferson County, Georgia in 1810, and his first two sons show they were born in Georgia, and his first known child, Basheba Berryhill, shows she was born in Tennessee in 1816, that he did not remain long in Tennessee since he shows up in St. Clair County, Alabama by 1820.

WILLIAM BERRYHILL - often called "Grand Sir"
b. 1780/1781 - Georgia, possibly in Richmond Co., or Jefferson Co.
d. 1861/1864 approx. - Marion Co., Alabama
bur. Wheeler's Chapel Cemetery, Marion County, Alabama
m. MARGARET WEEKS - 26 July 1807 - Jefferson County, Georgia
   b. 1780/1790, according to census records
   d. 1845/1846 approx. - Marion County, Alabama
   bur. assumed in Wheeler's Chapel Cemetery
   dau. of. Samuel Weeks & mother's name is unknown.

1. Elizabeth Morris Berryhill (either a daughter or a sister)
   m. James Parker - 22 September 1822 - St. Clair County, Alabama
     b. 22 May 1811
     d. 31 August 1893
     bur. New River Baptist Cemetery - Fayette County, Alabama
     No marker was found for Elizabeth (Berryhill) Parker in the
     cemetery, and I am sorry no other information is available.

2. William Berryhill, Jr. - "Bill Dergin"
   b. 7 September 1811 - Jefferson County, Georgia
   m. Elizabeth Gage and 2nd m. Nancy Adeline Andleton

3. James Berryhill - "Dominicker"
   b. 1812 - Jefferson County, Georgia
   m. Patience McMinn ' "Passie"

4. Basheba Berryhill - "Bashey"
   b. 9 May 1817 - Franklin County, Tennessee
   m. Thomas Berryhill - "Tommy", son of Alexander Berryhill & Rebecca
     Webster

5. Alexander Berryhill - "Alec"
   b. 1818 - Franklin County, Tennessee
   m. Celia Weeks

6. Nancy Berryhill
   b. 1819 - Franklin County, Tennessee
   m. Edward Berryhill - "Edd", son of Alexander Berryhill & Rebecca
     Webster

7. Thomas Berryhill
   b. 1820 - Franklin County, Tennessee
   m. Rachel Gage

8. Sarah Ann Berryhill
   b. 1822 - St. Clair County, Alabama
   m. Silas L. Webb - "Sie"

9. Benjamin Franklin Berryhill
   b. 1828 - Marion County, Alabama
   m. Rebecca Vickery

10. Margaret Ann Berryhill
   b. 6 June 1829 - Marion County, Alabama
   m. Francis Marion Couch - "Frank"

11. Susan Berryhill - "Suze"
   b. 1830 - Marion County, Alabama
   m. Parten Vickery

12. Male b. 1830/1835 - Marion County, Alabama, according to census

13. Male b. 1830/1835 - Marion County, Alabama, according to census

14. Francis Berryhill
   b. 1836 - Marion County, Alabama

15. Rachel Catherine Berryhill - "Kate"
   b. 1838 - Marion County, Alabama
   m. ? Scott, according to 1880 DeSoto County, Mississippi census

16. Isabella Berryhill
   b. 1841 - Marion County, Alabama
   m. ? Gilchrist, according to 1880 DeSoto County, Mississippi census

17. John Booker Silas Berryhill - "John Gabe"
   b. 1842 - Marion County, Alabama
   m. Pheby Elizabeth Tucker

18.Charles Robert Berryhill - "Bob"
     b. 1844 - Marion County, Alabama

WILLIAM BERRYHILL, Sr.2nd m. ELIZABETH -?-
                         b. 1820 - Alabama
                         bur. Wheeler's Chapel, Marion County, Ala.
    19.Richard Perry Berryhill - "Dick"
     b. 1848 - Marion County, Ala.

WILLIAM BERRYHILL, Sr. 3rd m. ELIZABETH WEBSTER
                         b. 1814 - Tennessee
                         living 1880 DeSoto Co. Miss. census
    20.Joseph J.N.C. Berryhill - "Joe"
     b. 1850 - Marion County, Ala.
     m. Mary Imes - 29 January 1869 - Desoto Co, Miss.

    21.Andrew N. Berryhill -"Andy" (or Anderson)
     b. 1852 - Marion County, Ala.
     m. Ada Bouldwin - 2 October 1888 - DeSoto Co, Miss.

    22.George Washington Berryhill
     b. 1854 - Marion County, Ala.
     m. Elizabeth Gellispie

Family history tells us that William Berryhill, Sr. died during the
Civil War, and while John Booker Silas Berryhill was off in the War, his
family of brothers and sisters left Alabama, and went to De Soto County,
Mississippi.

    1. ELIZABETH BERRYHILL
     b. 1808/1809 - Jefferson Co. Ga, assumed bur. New River Baptist Ceme.
     m. James N. M. Parker - 22 Sept. 1828 - St. Clair Co., Ala.
        b. 22 May 1811
        d. 31 August 1893 bur. New River Baptist ceme. Fayette Co., Ala.
     No information was available on this couple, but several PARKER
     families did show in Marion & Fayette Co., Ala.

    2. WILLIAM BERRYHILL, II - "Bill Dergin"
     b. 7 September 1811 - Jefferson County, Georgia
     d. 3 June 1876 - Hinds County, Miss.
     bur. Weeks Ceme. - 3½ miles east of Utica, Miss.
     m. Elizabeth Gage - 1828 approx. - Marion County, Ala.
        b. 1814 - Tennessee
        d. 1845/1848 - Marion County, Ala.
        bur.   Marion County, Ala.

     A. Nancy E. Berryhill
        b. 1829 - Marion County, Ala.
        m. Thaddeous A. Harris & 2nd m. Silas L. Webb - "Sie"

     B. Priscilla Berryhill
        b. 1832 - Marion County, Ala.
        m. William Moss - "Bill"

     C. James Carl Berryhill
        b. 1834 - Marion County, Ala.
        m. Mary E. Harris - 26 November 1852 - Alcorn County, Miss.
        2nd m. Mrs. Frances Ann (McClung) Dodson
        3rd m. widow:

     D. Mary Isabel Berryhill
        b. 1837 - Marion County, Ala.
        m. James Lewis Lee - "Jim"

     E. Thomas Berryhill
        b. 1839 - Marion County, Ala.
        m. Drucilla Webb

     F. Newton Berryhill
        b. 1841 - Marion County, Ala.

     G. Charles Berryhill
        b. 1844 - Marion County, Alabama

H. Martha Ann Berryhill
   b. 1845 - Marion County, Ala.
   m. John E. White

"Bill Dergin" Berryhill 2nd m. Nancy Adeline Andleton - 1851 approx.
Marion County, Ala.   b. 1833 - Tennessee
                                 d. 1874 - approx. - Hinds County, Miss.
                                 bur. Weeks Cemetery Hinds County, Miss.

I. William D. Berryhill
   b. 1852 - Marion County, Ala.
   m. Emmie May

J. Alexander Berryhill
   b. 1854 - Marion County, Ala.

K. Benjamin B. Berryhill
   b. 1855 - Marion County, Ala.

L. Nathan Berryhill
   b. 1857
   m. Agnes Bryant Gains

M. Monroe Jasper Berryhill - "Tony"
   b. 24 November 1859 - Marion County, Ala.
   m. Mrs. Relia Midcalf (Bishop) Slack

N. Mary Margaret Berryhill - "Mollie"
   b. 1862 - Marion County, Ala.
   m. -?- Naudock

O. Elviria Berryhill
   b. 1864 - Marion County, Ala.
   m. Dan W. Stewart - "Bud"

P. Robert W. Berryhill - "Willis Robin"
   b. 1865 - Marion County, Ala.
   m. Margaret E. Garner

Q. M. A. Berryhill (female)
   b. 1867 - Marion County, Ala.- shows age 3 years on 1870 census

R. Polk D. Berryhill
   b. 6 September 1869 - Marion County, Ala.
   m. Susie Anner Colista Foshee & 2nd m. Cora Estella Jackson

S. Austin Berryhill
   I never found this one on census, but according to Mr. Will
   Price's record he says they had one named Austin.

```
1850 Marion Co. Ala. - William Berryhill, II - "Bill Dergin"
William Berryhill      41 M  Ga.   b. 1809 (This tells his 1st wife died)
Priscilla          "   18 F  Ala.     1832
James Carl         "   16 M  Ala.     1834
Mary               "   13 F  Ala.     1837
Thomas             "   11 M  Ala.     1839
Newton             "    9 M  Ala.     1841
Charley            "    6 M  Ala      1844
Martha Ann         "    5 F  Ala.     1845


1860 Marion Co. Ala.
William Berryhill, Jr.50 M  Ga.   b. 1810
Nancy              "   25 F  Tenn.     1835 (Nancy A. Andleton, 2nd wife)
Newton             "   18 M  Ala.     1842
Charles            "   16 M  Ala.     1844
Martha Ann         "   15 F  Ala.     1845 (Last issue by Elizabeth Gage)
William            "    8 M  Ala.     1852 (First issue by Nancy Andleton)
Alexander          "    6 M  Ala.     1854
Benjamin           "    5 M  Ala.     1855
Nathan             "    3 M  Ala.     1857
Monroe             " 8/12 M  Ala.     1859


1870 Marion Co., Ala.
William Berryhill      60 M  Ga.   b. 1810
Nancy              "   32 F  Tenn.     1838
William            "   18 M  Ala.     1852
Abram              "   16 M  Ala.     1854 (Called Alexander - 1860 census)
Berry              "   14 M  Ala.     1856 (Called Benjamin - 1860 census)
Nathan             "   13 M  Ala.     1857
Monroe             "   10 M  Ala.     1860
Mary Margaret      "    8 F  Ala.     1862
Elviria            "    6 F  Ala.     1864
Robert W.          "    5 M  Ala.     1865
M. A.              "    3 F  Ala.     1867
Polk               "    1 M  Ala.     1869

1880 Hinds County, Mississippi Federal Census
I find some of their children living there, but we know William, II. died
1876, and apparently Nancy A. (Andleton) Berryhill died before 1880
census was taken.

1850 Marion County, Alabama - 51/51
Elizabeth Andleton     39 F  Tenn. b. 1811 (mother of Nancy A. who m.
                                              William Berryhill)
Margaret           "   17 F  Tenn.     1833 (Twin of Nancy A.)
NANCY A.           "   17 F  Tenn.     1833 (Twin of Margaret)
Samuel             "   15 M  Ala.     1835
Jesse O.           "   12 M  Ala.     1838
Ellender           "   10 F  Ala.     1840
Tebitha            "    5 F  Ala.     1845
William J.         "    2 M  Ala.     1848
This tells us the father of these children died after 1848, but before
1850.

1850 Marion County, Alabama - 15/15 Beat #6
Silas L. Webb          29 M  Tenn. b. 1821
Sarah Ann          "   28 F  Tenn     1822 (Sarah Ann Berryhill- 1st wife)
Joab S.            "   12 M  Ala.     1838
William T.         "   11 M  Ala.     1839
Thadius W.         "   10 M  Ala.     1840
Hannah             "    4 F  Ala.     1846
```

18

```
1860 Marion County, Alabama   - 65/68
Silas    Webb           41 M Tenn.   b. 1819
*NANCY E.  "            29 F Ala.       1831  (This is Nancy E. Berryhill
                                               Harris - 2nd wife)
Thadius W. "            19 M Ala.       1841  (Issue by 1st wife)
Hannah     "            12 F Ala.       1848  (Issue by 1st wife)
ANDERSON HARRIS          7 M Ala.       1853  (Issue of Nancy by her 1st
                                               husband)
John     Webb            4 M Ala.       1856  (Issue of 2nd wife Nancy. He
                                               can be a Harris)
Elisha     "             2 M Ala.       1858  (Issue by 2nd wife Nancy)
Martha     "          5/12 F Ala.       1859  (Issue by 2nd wife Nancy)

1870 Marion County, Alabama
164/164 - page 23 9th August 1870, P. O. Thornhill, Alabama
Silas    Webb           47 M Ala.   b. 1823
Nancy      "            35 F Ala.       1835
John       "            19 M Ala.       1851  (If this is their John, an
                                               error on age!)
Anderson Harris         14 M Ala.       1856
Elija (Elisha) Webb     12 M Ala.       1858
Martha             "    11 F Ala.       1859
Bettie             "     8 F Ala.       1862
Jane               "     6 F Ala.       1864
Mary               "     4 F Ala.       1866
William Franklin   "     1 M Ala.       1869

1880 Hinds County, Mississippi    259/273
Silas    Webb           61 M Ala.   b. 1811
Nancy      "            49 F Ala.       1831
John       "            24 M Ala.       1856
Sarah J.   "            17 F Ala.       1863  (Jane on 1870 Marion census)
Mary       "            14 F Ala.       1866
Charley    "            12 M Ala.       1868  (Cannot account for him, but
                                               William is gone.)
Henry S.   "             7 M Ala.       1873

258/272
Elijah Webb             22 M Ala.       1858
Sarah J.   "            26 F Ala.       1854
Elzetta    "         11/12 F Miss. Nov.1879
POLK D. BERRYHILL       10 M Miss.       1870  (Nephew)
```

Some have expressed the opinion that Silas L. Webb was not married
before he married Nancy E. Berryhill, but census proves he was married
before!

19

A. NANCY ELIZABETH BERRYHILL
   b. 15 August 1831 - Marion County, Alabama
   d. 7 September 1881 - Hinds County, Mississippi
   bur.Weeks Cemetery - Hinds County, Miss.
   m. Thaddeous Anderson Harris - 1850 approx. - Marion Co, Ala.
      b. 1831 - Alabama
      Living 1850 census, but apparently died about 1853/1854.
      Son of Moses Harris & Drucilla, b. 1802 - S. C.
               b. 1793 - S. C.

   (1) Thadious Anderson Harris, II (See 1880 Hinds Co, Miss.census)
       b. 7 March 1853 - Marion County, Ala.
       d. 3 August 1886 - Hinds Co., Miss.
       bur. Weeks Cemetery
       m. Mary Virginia -?-
          b. 18 July 1857 - Ala.
          d. 1 April 1908
          bur. Weeks Cemetery
          Did she 2nd m. -?- Dodson?

       (a) Nora Harris
           b. 17 October 1873 - Hinds Co., Miss.
           d. 26 January 1875 - Hinds Co., Miss.
           bur. Weeks Cemetery Hinds co., Miss.
Nancy E. Berryhill Harris
m (2nd) Silas L. Webb - "Sie" 1855/1856 approx.
           b. 15 September 1817 - Tennessee
           d. 2 January 1898 - Hinds Co., Miss.
           bur. Weeks Cemetery
Silas L. Webb had 1st m. Sarah Ann Berryhill, dau. of William
Berryhill, Sr. and I am not sure where his children by Nancy
begins.

   (2) John Webb
       b. 1856 - Marion Co., Ala
       d. 1918
       m. Laura Davis - 18 February 1886 - Hinds Co., Miss.
          b. 25 October 1858 - Fayette Co, Ala.
          d.   1925 - Utica, Miss.
          bur:
          dau. of Robert G. Davis & Margaret -?-
             b. 15 November 1833 - Ala. b. 22 August 1836 - Ala.
             d. 29 December 1883   d. 9 November 1906-Hinds Co.
             both bur. Weeks Cemetery, Hinds Co., Miss.

       (a) Anderson Webb
           b. 1888 approx. - Hinds Co, Miss.
           m. Fannie -?-
              b. 1890 approx.
              d. 1955
              bur. Weeks Cemetery and marker says age 65, but no
                   dates.

              1.Leroy Webb
              2. Willie B. Webb m. Luther Martin
              3. Edgar Webb
              4. Robert Webb
              5. Lena Webb m. Lester Rushing
              6. Alice Webb
              7. Little Melvin Webb
                 b. 18 December 1908
                 d. 22 June 1910
                 bur. Weeks Cemetery

       (b) Charlie Winton Webb
           b. 22 January 1889 - Hinds Co., Miss.
           d. 22 October 1889 - Hinds Co., Miss.
           bur. Weeks Cemetery

   (3) Elisha Webb
       b. 1858 - Marion Co., Ala.
       d.
       bur.

```
        m. Sarah A. -?-
           b. 1854 - Ala.
           d.
           bur.

        (a) Elzetta Webb
            b. November 1879 - Hinds Co., Miss.
            m. -?- Hilton

        (b) Hattie Webb
            m. Harvis Lagrone

               1. Harvis Lagrone, Jr.

        (c) Dessie Webb
            m. Collie Barlow

        (d) Mary Webb
            single

        (e) Grace Webb
            m. Malick Joseph

               1. Armond Joseph
               2. Carolas Joseph
               3. Umphrey Joseph

        (f) Armond Webb
            m. Lorrie Hullen

        (g) Umphrey Webb
            Single.  Deceased and buried in Utica Cemetery

        (h) Collis Webb
            Single.  Deceased and buried in Utica Cemetery

 (4) Martha Ann Webb
     b. 1859 - Marion Co., Ala.
     m. John William Dodson - 12 November 1879 - Hinds Co., Miss.
        b. 7 September 1861
        d. 28 November 1892
        bur. Weeks Cemetery

 (5) Bettie Webb
     b. 1862 - Marion Co., Ala.

 (6) Sarah Jane Webb
     n. 1864 - Marion Co., Ala.
     m. Edwin Joel Fulgham

        (a) Nannie Fulgham
            m. Walter A. Dodson

 (7) Mary M. Webb
     b. 5 November 1865 - Marion Co, Ala.
     d. 13 November 1891 - Hinds Co, Miss.
     bur. Weeks Cemetery
     m. M. W. Love

 (8) William Franklin Webb
     b. 1869 - Marion Co, Ala.  Gone from his parents home by
        1880 census, so we can assume he died young.

 (9) Charley M. Webb
     b. 1868 - Marion Co, Ala.
     m. Ella Keithley

(10) Samuel Webb
     b. 25 February 1870
     d. 9 September 1879 - Hinds Co, Miss.
     b. Weeks Cemetery - Hinds Co, Miss.

(11) Henry S. Webb
     b. 1873 - Hinds Co, Miss.
     m. Addie Morgan
```

21

B. PRISCILLA BERRYHILL - "Silla"
   b. 1832 approx. - Marion Co, Ala.
   d.
   bur. Wheeler's Chapel - Marion Co, Ala.
   m. William "Bill" Moss - Marion Co, Ala.

Family history tells us that when all the Berryhill's and connecting
families began leaving Marion Co, Ala. and moving into Hinds Co, Miss.
that "Silla" refused to leave Alabama. So "Bill" Moss went on, and
evidentially later they were divorced and he is said to have remarried
and raised a family around Learned, Miss.

C. JAMES CARL BERRYHILL (Served in 38th Ala. Inf.)
   b. 20 December 1833 - Marion Co, Ala.
   d. 25 November 1917 - near Mineola, Texas
   bur. Sand Springs Cemetery - Mineola, Texas
   m. Mary E. Harris - 26 November 1852 - Alcorn Co, Miss.
      b. 1836 - Ala.
      d. 1863/1864 - Marion Co, Ala.
      bur. Unknown
      dau. of Thomas Harris & -?- (She was dead by 1850 census)
         b. 1806 - Ga.

      (1) Nancy Adeline Berryhill
          b. 17 November 1853 - Marion Co, Ala.
          d. 6 October 1944 - Hinds Co, Miss.
          bur. Utica Cemetery - Utica, Miss.
          Single

1880 Hinds Co, Miss. Federal Census
John T. Atkins   42 M Ala.   b. 1838
Margaret E.   "   37 F Ala.   1843
Lucian   "   11 M Ala.   1869
Robert E.   "   9 M Ala.   1871
Bashi   "   8 F Ala.   1872
Rufus K.   "   19 M Ala.   1861
JOHN BERRYHILL   24 M Ala.   1856 (Son of James Carl Berryhill)
James C.   "   46 M Ala.   1834 (Son of William Berryhill, Jr.)
NANCY BERRYHILL   26 F Ala   1854 (Dau. of James Carl Berryhill)
WILLIS R.   "   15 M Ala.   1865 (Son of William Berryhill, Jr.)

      (2) John Martin Berryhill
          b. 11 December 1856 - Marion Co, Ala.
          d. 24 November 1904 - Texas, and believed to be in Wood Co.
          bur.
          m. Sallie Maliessa Beasley - 1 July 1888 - Hinds Co., Miss.
             b. 27 June 1871
             d. 15 March 1934 - She deceased before him, so he took
                his children and came to Texas.
             dau. of Phillip Beasley & Hannah Webb

          (a) Florence Berryhill

          (b) Lola Berryhill

          (c) Alice Addie Berryhill

          (d) James Thomas Berryhill
              b. 25 May 1895
              d. 26 August 1861

          (e) Barney B. Berryhill

          (f) Charlie Reed Berryhill

          (g) Willie Berryhill

          (h) Emma Julia Berryhill

          (i) Walter Coleman Berryhill

          All contacts with this family seems lost. There are
          possibly other children.

22

(3) Samuel Newton Berryhill - "Newt"
   b. 21 December 1858 - Marion Co., Ala.
   d. 11 December 1904 - in Texas, possibly Wood Co.
   bur.
   m. Emma F. Beasley - 2 May 1886 - Hinds Co., Miss.
      Deceased before him, and he came to Texas with his
      children along with his brother, John Martin.

   (a) Jim Berryhill
       b. 1887 approx - Hinds Co., Miss.

   (b) Mary Berryhill
       b. 1889 approx. - Hinds Co., Miss.

   (c) Sammie Berryhill
       b. 27 January 1890 - Hinds Co., Miss.
       d. 6 February 1890 - Hinds Co., Miss.
       Marker says son of S. N. & E. F. Berryhill. So am sure
       his mother is probably buried in the same cemetery, with
       no marker.

(4) Mary Elizabeth Berryhill
   b. 24 May 1862 - Marion Co., Ala.
   d.   1864 - Marion Co., Ala.
   bur. Berryhill Cemetery - Winfield, Ala.
   It is said she was about two years old when she died.

JAMES CARL BERRYHILL
m. 2nd Mrs. Frances Ann (McClung) Dodson (widow) - 28 Dec. 1865
   b. 16 March 1839 - Fayette Co., Ala.
   d. 15 September 1887 - Hinds Co., Ala.
   bur. Weeks Cemetery - Hinds Co., Ala.
   She had 1st m. William Franklin Dodson, who died in the
   Civil War, and she had sons: Reuben Dodson b. 1865 - Ala.
                                 John Dodson b. 1859 - Ala.
                                 Franklin Dodson b. 1861 - Ala.
   Her marker says placed by her son Reuben Dodson.

(5) Mary Lula Berryhill - "Lou"
   b. 25 September 1866 - Marion Co., Ala.
   d. 21 December 1944 - Hinds Co., Miss.
   bur. Utica Cemetery
   m. Thomas Henry Price - 27 November 1884 - Hinds Co., Miss.
      b. 23 May 1859
      d. 15 March 1925 - Hinds Co., Miss.
      bur. Utica Cemetery
      son of Thomas W. Price & Elizabeth Woodard

   (a) William Henry Price - "Will"
       b. 27 April 1887
       d. 15 February 1961 - Hinds Co., Miss.
       bur. Utica Cemetery
       Single
       Mr. Price did a lot of work and research on the various
       families, and much of what we have on James Carl's
       family came from his material.

   (b) Reuben Dodson Price
       b. 5 February 1889
       d. 2 May 1962 - Hinds Co., Miss.
       bur. Utica Cemetery - Hinds Co, Miss.
       m. Mamie Owen - 1 July 1917 - Hinds Co., Miss.
          b.
          d. 10 May 1964 - Hinds Co., Miss.
          bur. Utica Cemetery
          dau. of D. A. Owen and Mary Smith

          1. Marie Lamar Price
             b. 24 July 1918 - Hinds Co., Miss.
             m. Henry Harris Gunter - 21 May 1942
                b.
                d. 15 July 1966
                bur.

23

       A. Gail Price Gunter
          b. 31 May 1946 - Columbus, Miss.
          m. James Edgar Pennington - 5 September 1964
             b.
          (1) Liza Gunter Pennington
              b. 10 August 1965
       B. Henry Harris Gunter, Jr.
          b. 5 May 1948

    2. Reuben Dodson Price, Jr.
       b. 30 January 1920
       d. 3 June 1923 - Hinds Co., Miss.
       bur. Utica Cemetery

    3. June Owen Price
       b. 6 June 1922 - Hinds Co., Miss.
       m. Sherwood Cook - 2 May 1948 - Hinds Co, Miss.
          b.
          son of Thomas L. Cook & Lillie Mayer

       A. Sherwood Price Cook
          b. 1 December 1950 - Hinds Co., Miss.

       B. Reuben Thomas Cook
          b. 12 October 1954 - Hinds Co., Miss.

       C. Sherry Lynn Cook
          b. 6 July 1963 - Hinds Co., Miss.
          d. 6 September 1963 - Hinds Co., Miss.
          bur.

    4. Reuben Dodson Price, Jr.
       b. 8 August 1927 - Hinds Co., Miss
       Single

    5. Elizabeth Patricia Price
       b. 11 July 1929 - Hinds Co., Miss
       m. James Andrew Gregory - 1 July 1956
          son of Jim Gregory & Emma Dolton

(c) Annie May Price
    b. 10 February 1892
    d. 7 November 1892 - Hinds Co., Miss.
    bur. Utica Cemetery - Hinds Co., Miss.

(d) Errol Thomas Price
    b. 1 January 1894
    b. 26 September 1955 - Hinds Co., Miss.
    bur. Utica Cemetery
    Single

(e) Linton Earl Price
    b. 24 June 1897
    d. 28 June 1964 - Hinds Co., Miss.
    bur. Utica Cemetery
    m. Josephine Jenkins - 27 September 1924
       b. 3 March 1900 - Yazoo City, Miss.
       dau. of Joseph M. Jenkins & Ella Clark
    no issue

(f) Beryl Louise Price
    b. 30 July 1899 - Hinds Co., Miss.
    m. Harry Brown Richmond - 18 February 1917
       b. 5 July 1897 - Gillsburg, Miss.
       son of Seaborn Clay Richmond & Rosie McDaniel

    1. Henry Clay Richmond
       b. 19 February 1918 - Hinds Co., Miss.
       m. Bonnie Caldwell - 5 June 1943 - Memphis, Tenn.
          b.
          dau. of

       A. Kay Price Richmond
          b. 25 May 1947 - Memphis, Tenn.
          m. James sidney Major - 10 December 1966 -
             Hattisburg, Miss.

                        24

      b.
      son of James Douglas Major &

B. Meridith Richmond
   b. 20 August 1948 - Hattisburg, Miss.

C. Bonnie Caldwell Richmond
   b. 21 May 1953 - Hattisburg, Miss.

D. Martha Elizabeth Richmond
   b. 25 October 1954 - Hattisburg, Miss.
   d. 20 August 1956 - Hattisburg, Miss.
   bur. Hattisburg, Cemetery, Hattisburg, Miss.

(g) Powell Austin Price
   b. 14 May 1903 - Hinds Co., Miss.
   d. 17 September 1954 - Hinds Co., Miss.
   bur. Utica Cemetery
   m. Irene Newman - 25 February 1923 - Hinds Co., Miss.
   b. 6 December 1906 - Newman, Miss.
   dau. of J. W. Newman & Carrie Mae Payne

1. Powell Austin Price, Jr.
   b. 24 March 1924 - Hinds Co., Miss.
   m. Katherine Templeton - 15 February 1944
      b.
      dau. of J. C. Templeton & Rosie Green

A. James Powell Price
   b. 11 December 1956

B. Betty Katherine Price
   b. 21 October 1959

2. William Newman Price
   b. 18 October 1927 - Hinds Co., Miss.
   m. Willanna Thomas - 29 May 1960 - Madden, Miss.
      b.
      dau. of Glover Thomas & Mattie Sue Selmen

A. William Newman Price, Jr.
   b. 14 March 1962 - Meridian, Miss.

B. Ray Thomas Price
   b. 11 June 1966 - Meridian, Miss.

3. Betty Jean Price
   b. 10 November 1929 - Hinds Co., Miss.
   m. William Wallace Hubbard, 4 August 1950 Hinds Co.
      b.
      son of C. W. Hubbard & Sally Dudley

A. William W. Hubbard, Jr.
   b. 24 October 1953 - Vicksburg, Miss.

B. Powell Price Hubbard
   b. 11 October 1955
   d. 15 July 1958

C. Mary Lynn Hubbard
   b. 10 June 1959

D. Pollyanna Hubbard
   b. 15 April 1961

(h) Nora Elizabeth Price
   b. 27 May 1907 - Hinds Co., Miss.
   d. 28 May 1958
   bur. Carpenter Cemetery, Carpenter, Miss.
   m. William L. Lloyd - 26 November 1930
   b. 3 March 1904 - Carpenter, Miss.
   son of W. L. Lloyd & Lizzie McKey

1. William Errol Lloyd - "Bill"
   b. 26 July 1937
   m. Alleeta Broome - 26 February 1956
      b.
      dau. of W. R. Broome & Lillian Earl Ross

    A. William Lane Lloyd
       b. 28 January 1957

    B. Stacy Lynn Lloyd
       b. 29 July 1959

    C. Errol Scott Lloyd
       b. 15 May 1961

    D. Melinda Joyce Lloyd
       b. 9 May 1963

    E. Randal Earl Lloyd
       b. 4 May 1964

(6) Charles Monroe Berryhill - "Charlie"
    b. 24 April 1868 - Marion Co., Ala.
    d. 4 February 1935 - Thrall, Williamson Co, Texas
    bur. St. Mary's Catholic Cemetery - Taylor, Texas
    m. Juanita Aloysius Inabnet - 27 November 1889 - Hinds Co.
       b. 18 July 1870 - Hinds Co., Miss.
       d. 22 February 1963 - Austin, Travis Co, Texas
       bur. St. Mary's Catholic Cemetery - Taylor, Texas
       dau. of Joseph Benson Inabnet & Urania Calloway
       gr. dau. of Baltie Inabnet & -?-

(a) Charles Prentice Berryhill
    b. 10 October 1890 - Hinds Co., Miss.
    d. 29 September 1899 - Williamson Co., Texas
    bur. Wilson Springs Cemetery - near Taylor, Texas

(b) Ruby Flora Berryhill
    b. 3 March 1892 - Hinds Co., Miss.
    d. 27 February 1962 - Wichita Falls, Archer Co., Texas
    bur. Sacred Heart Cemetery - Wichita Falls, Archer Co.
    m. Michael Hilbers - 21 April 1914 - Williamson Co.,Tex.
       b. 19 July 1890 - Williamson Co., Texas

    1. Benjamin Charles Hilbers
       b. 7 August 1915 - Archer Co., Texas
       d. 1 July 1960
       bur.   -?- Cemetery, Olney, Archer Co, Texas
       m. Evelyn Peters - 30 November 1937 - Wink, Texas
         b.

       A. Bennie Jo Hilbers
          b. 28 December 1941 - Archer Co., Texas
          m. Harold Leon Hutson - 22 September 1956
            b.

          (1) Barry Leon Hutson
             b. 15 October 1957

       B. John Charles Hilbers
          b. 8 July 1943 - Archer Co., Texas
          m. Melissa Powell - 23 August 1966
            b.
          (1) John Mark Hilbers
             b. June 1968

    2. Juanita Elizabeth Hilbers
       b. 24 February 1917 - Archer Co., Texas
       m. Lee Haynemeyer - 12 May 1954 - Pilgrims Knob, Va.
         b.

       A. James Lee Haynemeyer
          b. 1955 - Pilgrims Knob, Va.

       B. David Allen Haynemeyer
          b. 1957 - Pilgrims Knob, Va.

    3. Henry Joseph Hilbers
       b. 11 August 1918 - Archer Co., Texas
       m. Clarence Bull
       Known to live in California, and have some children

4. Linwood Theodore Hilbers
   b. 20 January 1921 - Williamson Co., Texas
   m. Anna Lee Pearce - 1951 - Wichita Falls, Texas
      b.

   A. Donald Ray Hilbers
      b. September 1952

   B. Judy Ann Hilbers
      b. February 1954

   C. Billy Joe Hilbers
      b. 1956

5. John Fred Hilbers
   b. 22 August 1922 - Williamson Co, Texas
   m. Thelma Pitts - 18 September 1954
      b.

   No issue

6. Nona Hilbers
   b. 24 January 1924 - Williamson Co., Texas
   m. Paul Miller - 1946 - Archer Co., Texas
      b.

   A. Carolyn Ann Miller
      b. 4 December 1946
      m. John Ciano - December 1966

   B. Treva Elaine Miller
      b. 27 April 1948
      m. Robert Cambell - 5 June 1965
         b.

      (1) Debbie Cambell
          b. 2 April 1966

      (2) Robert Wayne Cambell
          b. April 1968

   C. Dale Michael Miller
      b. 24 May 1949

   D. Donna Jo Miller
      b. 28 May 1959

   E. Bruce Allen Miller
      b. 7 September 1967

7. William Edwin Hilbers
   b. 27 May 1925 - Slayton, Lubbock Co., Texas
   m. Patsy Hall - 18 September 1954 - Archer Co, Tex
      b.

   A. Mary Lou Hilbers
      b. 7 September 1956

   B. Brenda Nell Hilbers
      b. January 1958

8. Ruby Thresea Hilbers
   b. 3 August 1928
   m. Ronnie McGhee - September 1967
      b. -?-   Ohio

9. Mildred Hilbers
   b. 8 November 1929 - near Decatur, Texas
   m. William Craibs - 1952
      b.

   A. Bobby Craibs
      b. June 1953 - Detroit, Mich.

   B. Charlotte Craibs
      b. 1 January 1955 - Detroit, Mich.

   C. Michael Craibs
      b. November 1960

10.Myrtle Mae Hilbers
   b. 20 November 1931 - near Decatur, Texas
   m. Eugene Martin - June 1953 - Archer Co., Texas
      b.

   A. Michael Eugene Martin
      b. 14 March 1954

   B. Susan Yvonne Martin
      b. 12 January 1955

   C. Cecilia Marie Martin
      b. 21 March 1959

   D. Bennie Joseph Martin
      b. 21 October 1963

(c) Nona Annie Berryhill
    b. 19 January 1894
    d. 26 April 1898 - Thrall, Texas
    bur. Wilson Springs Cemetery, near Taylor, Texas

(d) James Grady Berryhill
    b. 13 July 1896
    d. 5 January 1897 - Thrall, Texas
    bur. Wilson Springs Cemetery

(e) Minna Gertrude Berryhill
    b. 17 October 1897 - Thrall, Texas
    m. Stanislaus J. Budnick - 5 May 1917 - Thrall, Texas
       b. 22 October 1894 - Brenham, Texas

   1. Thomas Woodrow Budnick
      b. 20 August 1918 - Taylor, Texas
      single

   2. Theodore Malcom Budnick - "Ted"
      b. 17 August 1921 - Holland, Bell Co., Texas
      m. Viola Elsie Alford - 1942
         b. 12 April 1922 - Taylor, Texas

      A. Sharon Gail Budnick
         b. 22 February 1945 - Norman, Oklahoma
         m. Ronald E. Brooks
            b.

         (1) Laurie Ann Brooks
             b. 2 July 1962 - Harris Co., Texas

         (2) Scott Brooks
             b. 6 January 1964 - Harris Co., Texas

      B. Russell Scott Budnick
         b. 19 June 1955 - Harris Co., Texas

      C. Janet Kay Budnick
         b. 8 February 1959 - Harris Co., Texas

   3. Margaret Flonora Budnick
      b. 4 October 1923 - Holland, Bell Co., Texas
      m. Robert E. Dickerson - 29 January 1949 - Wash,DC
         b. 10 May 1921 - Jersey City, N.J.

      A. Daniel Joseph Dickerson
         b. 7 November 1949 - Santa Monica, California

      B. Francis Edward Dickerson
         b. 12 October 1952 - Santa Monica, California

      C. Richard Thomas Dickerson
         b. 8 November 1954 - Santa Monica, California

      D. Mary Ann Dickerson
         b. 21 June 1957 - Santa Monica, California

      E. Catherine Marie Dickerson
         b. 9 September 1958 - Glendale, California

      F. Robert Jay Dickerson
         b. 16 December 1963 - Arcata, California

4. Hallie Jean Budnick
   b. 30 November 1930 - Holland, Bell Co., Texas
   m. Tom Rovello, Jr. - 30 May 1953
     b. 25 November 1929 - Waco, Texas

   A. Tom Rovello, III
     b. 11 November 1954 - Dallas, Texas

   B. Jo Ellen Rovello
     b. 17 February 1959 - Austin, Texas

   C. Mary Kay Rovello
     b. 15 April 1963 - Maracaibo, Venezuela

5. Mary Genene Budnick
   b. 18 June 1936 - Taylor, Texas
   m. Stanley Oestrick "Sid" 18 July 1953, Taylor,Tex.
     b. 1 February 1934 - Austin, Texas

   A. Stanley Oestrick, Jr.
     b. 23 August 1954 - Austin, Texas

(f) Linwood John Berryhill
   b. 19 May 1900 - Taylor, Texas
   m. Nettie Stallcup - 12 December 1923
     b. 13 September 1907 - Taylor, Texas
     dau. of Samuel Stallcup & Ada Ponkney

   1. Leon John Berryhill
     b. 24 May 1925 - Thrall, Texas
     m. Jane Elizabeth Mitchell - 19 Nov. 1945 Taylor, TX

       b. 19 December 1921 - Jeffersonville, Ind.

     A. Suzie Lee Berryhill
       b. 2 September 1946 - Jeffersonville, Ind.
       m. Robert Taylor Kent - 5 January 1968
         b. 27 May 1943 - Wills Point, Texas

     B. Linda Kay Berryhill
       b. 13 July 1947 - Taylor, Texas
       m. Robert Leonard Golightly - 23 March 1968
         b. 7 June 1941 - Thoydada, Texas

   2. Arvel Dave Berryhill
     b. 2 November 1929 - Taylor, Texas
     m. Betty Ann Hertz - 31 December 1953
       b. 25 May 1938

     A. Arvel Dave Berryhill, Jr. - "Davey"
       b. 30 December 1954 - Taylor, Texas

     B. Sue Ellen Berryhill
       b. 25 December 1957 - Taylor, Texas
     C. Daniel Alan Berryhill
       b. 17 July 1960 - Taylor, Texas

(g) Myrtle Mae Berryhill
   b. 4 May 1902
   d. 19 July 1902 - Thrall, Texas
   bur. Wilson Springs, Cemetery - near Taylor, Texas

(h) Joseph Roy Berryhill
   b. 29 April 1903 - Thrall, Texas
   m. Clara Saller - 29 September 1926
     b. 10 May 1898 - San Francisco, California

(i) Hyacinth Louise Berryhill
   b. 6 February 1906 - Thrall, Texas
   m. Hal Stone Wallace, 17 June 1927
     b. 4 June 1903 - Holland, Texas
     d. 15 February 1946 - Corpus Christi, Texas
     bur. -?- Cemetery - Belton, Bell Co., Texas
     son of William R. Wallace & Viola Leslie Stone

       1. Joe Ann Wallace
          b. 13 October 1928 - Holland, Texas
          m. Charles Bingham - 23 March 1946
             b. 30 April 1924
             son of Edgar Bingham & Mary Hirrington

          A. Jack Bingham
             b. 28 August 1947

          B. Hal Edgar Bingham
             b. 21 December 1948

   Hyacinth Louise Berryhill
   m (2nd) Charles Logan Wiegmann - 23 March 1946
             b. 10 October 1924
             son of Fritz Wiegmann & Rosalee Fromme

(j) Earl John Berryhill
    b. 25 June 1908 - Thrall, Texas
    m. Helen Parkhurst - 13 April 1935 - Orange, Texas
    b. 15 September 1915 - Orange, Texas

       1. Barbara Ann Berryhill
          b. 13 November 1937
          m. John Robert Murray - 21 May 1960 - Bedford, Tex.
          b. 4 December 1925 - Boston, Mass.

          A. John Phillips Murray
             b. 3 January 1961 - Columbia, S. C.

          B. Steven Robert Murray
             b. 7 June 1962 - Toul Rosiere, France

          C. Jean Ann Murray
             b. 1 August 1963 - Rawstine, Germany

       2. Maria Elizabeth Berryhill
          b. 23 July 1950 - Cheyenne Wyoming
          m. Robert Anthony Golff, 3 April 1974 - Boulder, Colo.
          b. 12 September 1950 - Los Angeles, Ca.

          A. Marta Rachelle Golff
             b. 26 June 1979 - San Antonio, Texas

(k) Alvin Patrick Berryhill
    b. 6 March 1910 - Thrall, Texas
    m. Evelyn Kuban - 23 November 1938
    b.
    dau. of Joe Kuban & Julia -?-

       1. Alvin Patrick Berryhill, Jr.
          b. 23 June 1940 - Taylor, Texas
          m. Sandra Tyler - 11 October 1961 - Taylor, Texas

          A. Alvin Patrick Berryhill, III - "Trey"
             b. 3 July 1962 - Lake Jackson, Texas

       2. Barbara Jean Berryhill
          b. 23 September 1942 - Taylor, Texas
          m. Jay W. Smith - 24 December 1961 - San Gabriel, Tex.
          b.
          son of Jasper W. Smith & -?-

          A. Nicky Warren Smith
             b. 11 August 1963 - Sherman, Texas

          B. Steven Jay Smith
             b. 14 February 1966 - Massawa, Japan
             d. 14 February 1966 - Massawa, Japan
             bur.

          C. Aaron Jay Smith
             b. 25 September 1967 - Austin, Texas

(l) Lois Regina Berryhill
    b. 22 May 1913 - Thrall, Texas
    m. Louis Herkert Matteck - 8 November 1933 - Taylor, Tex.
    b. 21 January 1909 - Taylor, Texas
    son of John Ernest Matteck & Bertha Katherine Herkert

1. Albert Roy Matteck
   b. 12 December 1935 - Taylor, Texas
   m. Jeanette Elaine Brown - 8 July 1960 - Taylor, TX.
       b.
       dau. of

   A. Diane Elaine Matteck
      b. 24 February 1961 - Austin, Texas

   B. Albert Roy Matteck, Jr.
      b. 3 September 1962 - Austin, Texas

   C. Dawne Ellen Matteck
      b. 16 May 1964 - Austin, Texas

   D. Gregory Lynn Matteck
      b. 5 October 1967 - Austin, Texas

2. Kathie Louise Matteck
   b. 20 December 1940 - Taylor, Texas
   m. Albert Lee Hilbers - 23 June 1962 - Archer Co.
       b. 7 April 1937 - Archer Co., Texas
       son of

   A. Deborah Louise Hilbers
      b. 15 March 1963 - Wichita Falls, Texas

   B. Donald Lee Hilbers
      b. 4 June 1964 - Wichita Falls, Texas

   C. Dennis Lee Hilbers
      b. 21 November 1967 - Wichita Falls, Texas

3. Mary Beth Matteck
   b. 18 February 1947 - Taylor, Texas

(m) Herbert Hugh Berryhill
    b. 16 September 1916 - Thrall, Texas
    d. 4 August 1968 - Austin, Texas
    bur. St. Mary's Cemetery - Taylor, Texas
    Single

(7) Walter Berryhill
    b. 4 November 1870 - Hinds Co., Miss.
    d. 9 July 1873 - Hinds Co., Miss.
    bur. Weeks Cemetery - Hinds Co., Miss.

(8) Lenora Isabel Berryhill - "Nora" (twin)
    b. 27 August 1877 - Hinds Co., Miss.
    d. 23 August 1960 - Vicksburg, Miss.
    bur. Utica Cemetery - Hinds Co., Miss.
    m. Lee Wilson Shepherd - 26 December 1908 - Hinds Co., Miss.
        son of James Shepherd & Drucilla Nehrig
    No Issue

(9) Flenora Elizabeth Berryhill - "Flora" (twin)
    b. 27 August 1877 - Hinds Co., Miss.
    d. 12 November 1947 - Vicksburg, Miss.
    bur. Silver Cross Cemetery - Tallulah, La.
    m. Douglas Alvin Fortner - 3 November 1904 - Hinds Co., Miss.
        b. 31 January 1871 - Terry, Miss.
        d. 10 March 1933 - Vicksburg, Miss.
        bur. Silver Cross Cemetery - Tallulah, La.
        son of Henry Turner Fortner & Sarah Cathings

(a) Henry Douglas Fortner
    b. 13 June 1906 - Hinds Co., Miss.
    d. 11 December 1954 - Vicksburg, Miss.
    bur. Silver Cross Cemetery - Tallulah, La.
    m. Ellen Cason - 7 February 1925
        b. 1 February 1907 - Tallulah, La.
        dau. of James L. Cason & Bessie Allnutt

    1. Douglas Allnutt Fortner
       b. 8 December 1925 - Tallulah, La.
       m. Winnie Zelle Gould

                    2. James Cason Fortner
                       b. 19 April 1927 - Tallulah, La.
                       m. Gail Fleming Hall - August 1967 - Monroe, La.

                       A. James Cason Fortner, Jr.
                          b. 28 April 1968 - Monroe, La.

              (b) Nora Louise Fortner
                  b. 28 December 1911 - Hinds Co., Miss.

        JAMES CARL BERRYHILL
        m. 3rd Mrs. Frances Powell - Texas

        JAMES CARL BERRYHILL
        m. 4th Mrs. Martha Green - 1906

1860 Marion County, Alabama Federal Census 67/70
James Carl Berryhill 26 M Ala. b. 1834
Mary A.   "   24 F Ala.   1836
Nancy   "   6 F Ala.   1854
John M.   "   4 M Ala.   1856
Samuel N.   "   1 M Ala.   1859

1870 Marion County, Alabama Federal Census East Division 10 August 1870
159/159 page 23   P. O. Thornhill, Alabama
J. C. Berryhill   35 M Ala. b. 1835
Ann   " 30 F Ala.   1840 (Mrs. Frances Ann McClung Dodson)
Nancy   " 16 F Ala.   1854
John   " 15 M Ala.   1855
Samuel   " 11 M Ala.   1859
Mary   "   4 F Ala.   1866
Charles   "   2 M Ala.   1868

        D. Mary Isabel Berryhill
           b. 31 December 1836 - Marion Co., Ala.
           d. 30 October 1907 - Marion Co., Ala.
           bur. Glen Allen Meth. Cemetery - Fayette Co., Ala.
           m. James Louis Lee
              b. 3 March 1831 - Pickens Co., Ala.
              d. 24 November 1904 - Marion Co., Ala.
              bur. Glen Allen Meth. Cemetery.

           (1) Margaret Elizabeth Lee
               b. 23 January 1854 - Marion Co., Ala.
               d.
               bur. Glen Allen Meth. Cemetery
               Never Married

           (2) William Anderson Lee
               b. 20 November 1855 - Marion Co., Ala.
               d. 24 April 1921
               bur. Glen Allen Meth. Ceme.
               m. Melvina Savilla Oden - 14 November 1875 - Marion Co., Ala.
                  b. 20 April 1856
                  d. 30 March 1936
                  bur. Glen Allen Meth. Cemetery

               (a) Genva Alice Lee - "Jennie"
                   b. 13 September 1876
                   d. 13 January 1965
                   bur. Glen Allen Meth. Cemetery
                   Never Married

               (b) Mary Orlena Lee - "Lena"
                   b. 30 January 1881
                   d. 1 April 1952
                   bur. City Cemetery - Winfield, Ala.
                   m. LeRoy Hill, Physician

                       1. Roger Hill, Physician
                          married and had a son and two daughters

                                    32

(c) Henry Bascom Lee
   b. 24 January 1884
   d. 13 January 1965
   bur. City Cemetery - Winfield, Ala.
   m. DeLona McCaleb

(d) Grover Cleveland Lee
   b. 10 October 1886
   d. 18 May 1949
   bur. City Cemetery - Winfield, Ala.
   m. Minnie Mills

(e) Mittie Lou Lee
   b. 16 December 1888
   m. John Belton Hodge - 10 June 1914 - Marion Co., Ala.
      b. 2 April 1888

      1. Jean Hodge
         b. 23 October 1916 - Marion Co., Ala.

      2. Sarah Hodge

      3. Virginia Ann Hodge (crippled)

      4. Richard Henry Hodge
         b. 29 May 1915 - Marion Co.

(f) Mertie Lee
   b. 14 February 1892
   d. 24 June 1908
   bur.
   Never Married

(g) Carra Ruth Lee
   b. 11 February 1894
   m. John Wesley Curl, Rev.

(3) John Thomas Lee
   b. 6 June 1857 - Marion Co., Ala
   d. 11 May 1944
   bur. Glen Allen Meth. Cemetery
   m. Tabitha Rhoda Frances Beasley - 1882

(4) Mary Jane Lee
   b. 7 March 1859 - Marion Co., Ala.
   d. 29 December 1932
   bur. Glen Allen Meth. Cemetery
   m. Franklin Aldridge
      b. 14 February 1859
      d. 19 February 1949
      bur. Glen Allen Meth. Cemetery

   (a) Cora Aldridge
      b. 1881 approx.
      Never Married

   (b) Marion Claud Aldridge
      b. 1 November 1883 - Hinds Co., Miss.
      m. Louvenia Canterbury - 2 September 1906

         1. Davis Aldridge
            b. 1 November 1907
            m. Lemora Pitchford

            A. Davis Elbert Aldridge
               b. 25 September 1942
               m. Donna Bond

         2. Loudell Aldridge b. 3 Oct. 1910
            m. Celden Miles

            A. Nelyn Miles
               b. 11 October 1930
               m. Don Hall & Has 5 issues

            b. Joe Morris Miles
               b. 25 July 1932
               m. and has 2 issues

C. Barbara Lee Miles
   b. 13 September 1935
   m. Dick Stone and has 2 issues

3. Bowling Aldridge
   b. 23 July 1912
   m. Beatrice Ray

   A. Scott Aldridge

4. Mary Nell Aldridge
   b. 18 June 1914
   m. Elgin S. Clayton

   A. Wanda Fay Clayton
      b. 15 September 1948 - New Orleans, La.

   B. Ronald Elgin Clayton
      b. 22 July 1952

   C. Terry Lyn Clayton
      b. 22 June 1955

5. William Gray Aldridge
   b. 13 September 1915
   m. Lorane Weeks

   A. Thomas Aldridge
      b. 2 November 1937

   B. Kenneth Aldridge
      b. 10 May 1939

   C. Larry Aldridge
      b. August 1940

   D. Joe Aldridge
      b. 10 December 1941

   E. Bebe Joy Aldridge
      b. 5 December 1952

   F. Jerry Wayne Aldridge
      b. 16 June 1955

6. Ray Franklin Aldridge
   b. 26 September 1918
   m. Floy Burleson
   m. 2nd. Mannie Erwin

   A. Betty Ann Aldridge
      b. 1940
      m. Jimmy Devaney

      (1) Rhonda Lyn Devaney
         b. 20 October 1958

      (2) Lyndia Kay Devaney
   m. 2nd Mannie Erwin

   B. William Franklin Aldridge
      b. 13 April 1942
      m. Martha Elizabeth Dodson

      (1) Libby Aldridge
         b. 1962

7. Elizabeth Coy Aldridge (twin)
   b. 7 October 1921
   m. J. P. Gilstrap
   No issue

8. Marion Roy Aldridge (twin)
   b. 7 October 1921
   m. Myrtle Tucker

   A. Mary Hellen Aldridge
      b. 1951 approx.

            9. Ruby Evelyn Alldridge
               b. 3 March 1924
               m. Herbert Richard

               A. John Lee Richard

               B. Laura E. Richard

               C. Donnie Richard

               D. Lynn Richard

           10. Ellis Lee Aldridge
               b. 24 February 1926
               d. 4 October 1951 - Korea
               bur. Glen Allen, Ala. 1952
               m. Robbie Miles

               A. Lucy Hope Aldridge
                  b. 6 November 1944
                  m. Joe McCalys

               B. Ellis L. Aldridge, Jr.
                  b. 28 September 1947
                  m. -?- Smith

               C. Micky Frank Aldridge
                  b. 9 November 1948

           11. Hoyt Drew Aldridge
               b. 31 May 1930
               m. Martha Nell Mills

               A. Hoyt D. Aldridge, Jr.
                  b. 30 May 1950

               B. Robert Owen Aldridge
                  b. 1 January 1956

(5) Martha Drucilla Lee (twin)
    b. 26 April 1860
    d. 5 December 1940
    bur. New River Church of Christ - Fayette Co, Ala.
    m. John Tyler McCaleb
       b. 1849
       d. 1918

(6) Infant Male Lee (twin)
    b. and d. 26 April 1860

(7) Nancy Catherine Lee
    b. 15 April 1862
    d. 19 January 1898
    bur. Glen Allen Meth. Cemetery - Fayette Co, Ala.
    Never Married

(8) Charles Samuel Lee
    b. 14 April 1864
    d. 5 April 1955
    bur. Morris Family Cemetery - Fayette Co, Ala.
    m. Nora Cochran
       b. 1869
       d. 1899
       bur. Glen Allen Meth. Cemetery
    m. 2nd Narcie C. Morris
       b. 1879
       d. 1964
       bur. Morris Family Cemetery

(9) Rosah Adaline Lee - "Rose"
    b. 20 February 1866
    d. 4 November 1932/34
    bur. Glen Allen Meth. Cemetery
    Never Married

(10) Susan Josephine Lee
     b. 3 March 1867
     d. 15 October 1902
     bur. Glen Allen Meth. Cemetery
     m. Noah Lewis

(11) Dolley Frances Lee
     b. 3 February 1869
     d.
     bur. Glen Allen Meth. Cemetery
     m. Noah Lewis
        b. 30 January 1869
        d. 8 September 1934
        bur. Glen Allen Meth. Cemetery

(12) James Anthony Lee
     b. 1871 approx.
     d.
     bur. in Texas
     m. Rhoda Russel

(13) Emma Lee
     b. 1872 approx.
     d.   bur. Glen Allen Meth. Ceme.
     m. Foster Fowler

(14) Oscar Fee Lee
     b. 1874 approx.
     m. Lona Whitehead

THOMAS BERRYHILL
b. 1839 - Marion Co., Ala.
Confederate Record No. 37804
Application made in Marion Co., Ala. by DRUSILLA (WEBB) BERRYHILL, wife
of THOMAS BERRYHILL. He served as a Private in Co. N. 22nd Regiment of
Miss. Volunteers. He was killed, or came home and died, on or about the
20th day of July 1864.

Marion Co., Ala.
Before me, Mack Pearce, Judge of Probate, in and for said county and
State, personally appeared DRUSILLA BERRYHILL, who being by me first duly
sworn deposes and says that DRUSILLA BERRYHILL is now on the pension roll
of Marion County, in the 4th class; that she hereby makes application
under an Act approved 5th August 1907, to be placed on the Pension Roll
of the 1st class on account of her age, she, being at the time of making
application over the age of 80 years, she further states that she was
born in Marion Co., Ala. that she depends solely upon her pension for
support and maintance; that she is unable to procure any other positive
proof as to her age, as there is no one in this part of the county can
testify to her birth.

                           DRUSILLA BERRYHILL

Attest: J. C. White
Sworn to and subscribed before me this 3rd day of August, 1910.
Mack Pearce, Judge Probate

W. S. Berryhill made affadavit he had known her 48 years. A statement
signed by J. C. Johnson, M.D. also signed by S. M. Davis to the Board of
Pension Examiners for Marion Co., Ala. 3rd Aug. 1910 of Hamilton, Ala.
to State Board of Pension Examiners that DRUSILLA BERRYHILL is said to
be 85 years of age and pratically helpless. They recommend she be granted a pension and also be placed on Pension Roll in Class no. 1., because
of old age and because she is a widow of THOMAS BERRYHILL.

The above W. S. Berryhill is Drusilla's son, William Silas Berryhill,
and J. C. White, is her son-in-law, John C. White.

E. THOMAS J. BERRYHILL (Pvt. in Co. N, 22nd Miss Vol.)
   b. 1839 - Marion Co., Ala.
   d. 20 July 1864 during the Civil War. Grave site unknown, but
   a grand-daughter has applied for a marker as a memorial put up
   in the Center Cemetery. The family remembers when their father,
   William Silas Berryhill, once made a trip to contact two men who
   were supposed to have buried his father, so his mother, Drucilla
   (Webb) Berryhill could have proof to enable her to draw a
   pension.
   m. Drucilla Webb - approx. 1857/1858 - Marion Co., Ala.
      b. 1831 approx. - Marion Co., Ala.
      d. 1913
      bur. Center Cemetery - Marion Co., Ala.
      dau. of Thomas Webb & -?- Webster
                b. 1810 - Ga. and dec.d by 1850 census so name is
                   is unknown.
                m. 2nd. Nancy _/_ by 1850 census
                   b. 1825 - S.C.

   1. William Silas Berryhill -"Bill"
      b. 1858 - Fayette Co., Ala - March 1, 1858
      d. 11 November 1937 - Marion Co., Ala.
      bur. Center Cemetery
      m. Sarah Jane White - 1878 approx. - Marion Co., Ala.
         b. 1854 - Ala.
         d. 1902 approx. - Marion Co, Ala.
         bur. Center Cemetery

      (a) John Robert Berryhill
          b. 23 November 1879 - Marion Co., Ala.
          d. 3 November 1906 - Marion Co., Ala.
          bur. Center Cemetery
          m. Zora Williams - 1 November 1901 - Marion Co, Ala.
             b. 7 July 1884
             d. 26 April 1933
             bur.

          (1) Curtis Berryhill
              b. 7 August 1903 -
              d. 1950
              bur.
              m. Alice Homer
          (2) Carlie Berryhill
              b. 7 November 1905
              m. Velma Ward - 27 June 1925
                 b. 4 October 1908
                 dau. of Benjamin S. Ward & Cora Couch.

      (b) Thomas Alvin Berryhill - "Tom"
          b. 28 February 1880 - Marion Co., Ala.
          d. 12 January 1832 - Guin, Ala.
          bur. Guin Cemetery
          m. Jettie Pyron - 12 January 1908 - Marion Co, Ala.
             b. 25 October 1889
             dau. of. James Watson Pyron & -?-

          (1) Hattie Esther Berryhill
              b. 1 October 1910
              m. Gordon Webb Crawford - 12 May 1940
                 b. 14 May 1911

              A. Harriet Ann Crawford
                 b. 28 October 1943 - Jasper, Ala.

          (2) Howard Berryhill
              b. 16 December 1912
              m. Amelia Helen Miller - 1939
                 b. 5 October 1920
          (3) Lexie Mae Berryhill
              b. 12 January 1915
              m. Filmore LaFayette Stone - 12 February 1936
                 b. 1 September 1908

37

(4) Clarence Berryhill
    b. 11 November 1916
    m. Willie Louise Gingles - 26 October 1945
       b. 30 July 1919

    A. Carolyn Louise Berryhill
       b. 10 July 1947 - Fayette, Ala.
(5) Azalee Berryhill
    b. 10 March 1921
    m. Thomas Mack Williams, II - 27 December 1942
       b. 12 May 1912

    A. Thomas M. Berryhill, II
       b. 14 December 1945 - Jasper, Ala.

(c) William Alonzo Berryhill - "Lonzo"
    b. 25 November 1885 - Marion Co., Ala.
    d. 29 November 1947 - Hampton, Calhoun Co, Ark.
    bur. Camp Ground Cemetery - Hampton, Ark,
    m. Mattie Kizzar O'Mary - 14 December 1902 - Marion Co.
       b. 15 February 1883 - Ala., possibly Marion Co.
       d. 30 June 1935 - Hampton, Ark.
       bur. Camp Ground Cemetery

    (1) Minnie Belle Berryhill
        b. 7 January 1904 - Marion Co., Ala.
        d. 26 April 1963 - Cherokee, Ala.
        bur. Guin, Ala.
        m. William Kirk Cantrell
           b. 23 October 1906

        A. James Leon Cantrell
           b. 31 December 1923
           m. Alama Lea -?-
              b.

           1. Larry Cantrell
              b. February 1948
           2. Deborah Cantrell

        B. William Fay Cantrell
           b. 19 January 1925
           m. Marrianne -?-   (in Germany)

           1. son:

        C. Mattie Elsie Cantrell
           b. 16 May 1928/1929
           m. Roy Douglas Hassell

           1. Valarie Hassell
              b. 1950 approx.
           2. Connie Hassell
              b. 1952 approx.

        D. Autress Mae Cantrell   b. 27 December 1938
           m. Bob Markham
              b.

           1. Rhonda Markham
              b. 1960 approx.

        E, F, and G - All three infants died at birth

    (2) William Thomas Berryhill
        b. 17 February 1906 - Marion Co., Ala.
        m. Lottie Eason - 2 January 1934
    (3) Dewey Leroy Berryhill
        b. 11 February 1909 - Marion Co., Ala.
        m. Pearl Lea Wages - August 1929
           b.   d. Feb. 1932 - Camden, Ark. bur. Bearden, Ark.
        A. Deceased Infant b and d 1930
        B. Della Marie Berryhill b. 11 January 1932, Camden
           m. James Strickland 1946
              1. Brenda Strickland b. 11 June 1947
              2. Berlin Gee Strickland b. 27 October 1949

        1. Brenda Strickland
           b. 11 June 1947
        2. Berlin Gee Strickland
           b. 27 October 1949

     Della Marie (Berryhill) Strickland
     m. 2nd. 1956/1957 to Herman Lynn Harris
                        b.

Dewey Berryhill
m. 2nd Mary Colvin - 1958

        C. Dianna Lynn Berryhill
           b. 1960 approx.
        D. Judy Kay Berryhill
           b. November 1963

(4) Archie David Berryhill
    b. 25 May 1911 - Marion Co., Ala.
    m. Ophelia Jeffrey's - 1929
    b.

        A. Ruby Dean Berryhill
           b. 24 April 1930
           m. Ray Vickery - 1949
              b.

           1. Mike Vickery
              b. 13 January 1952
           2. Son:

        B. Doris Jean Berryhill
           b. 12 May 1932
           m. Redas Lee
              b.

           1. Reda Jean Lee
           2. Dau.

        C. Nettie Sue Berryhill
           b. 11 February 1938

        D. Max Archie Berryhill
           b. 25 September 1940
           m. and has family but information not available

        E. Charles Allen Berryhill
           b. 7 February 1950

        F. Sylvia Ann Berryhill
           b. 25 November 1953

(5) Dessie Florence Berryhill
    b. 7 November 1914 - Marion Co., Ala.
    m. Benjamin Walter Oliver - September 1934
    b.

        A. Jimmy Dale Oliver
           b. 21 August 1937
           d. May 1938
           bur.
        B. Donnie Mac Oliver
           b. 24 February 1939
           m. Carolyn Holder
              b.

           1. Terry Wayne Oliver
              b. 1962 - approx.
           2. Lisa Oliver
              b. 1964 - approx.

        C. Jerry Wayne Oliver
           b. 5 November 1944
           m. Carlene Darby
              b.
           1. Vicki Oliver   b. 1965
           2. Tena Oliver   b. 1967

    D. Teresa Ann Oliver   b.   1957

(6) Carlie Alfred Berryhill
    b. 21 November 1918 - Marion Co., Ala.
    m. Annie Mae Beasley - 28 May 1942
    b.

    A. Carlon Ann Berryhill
       b. 23 May 1943
       m. Jerry Cloud - 1963
          b.

    B. Joe Alfred Berryhill
       b. 13 July 1947
       d. 9 August 1954
       bur.   -   Cemetery - near Sparkman, Ark.

(7) Lanta Mae Berryhill
    b. 28 November 1921 - Marion Co., Ala.
    m. Wayne Meece - 17 June 1939 - Dallas Co., Ark.
    b. 28 March 1918 - Hill Co., Texas

    A. Peggy Jane Meece
       b. 14 July 1940 - Sparkman, Ark.
       m. Weldon Lamar Graves - 7 October 1957 - Dallas Co.
          b. 20 May 1938 - Kingsland, Cleveland Co, Ark.

       1. Kathy Lynn Graves
          b. 26 August 1958 - Nashville, Tenn.

    B. Infant Daughter
       b. 27 April 1942
       d. 28 April 1942
       bur. Sardis Cemetery - near Sparkman, Ark.

    C. Waynette Meece
       b. 19 April 1945 - Hampton, Ark.
       m. Oscar Kee, Jr. - 11 June 1963 - Dallas Co., Ark.
          b. 22 June 1943 - New Edinburg, Cleveland Co, "

       1. Tammy Lynn Kee
          b. 3 December 1964 - Fordyce, Ark.
       2. Michael Wayne Kee
          b. 3 November 1966 - Fordyce, Ark.

    D. Cynthia Ann Meece
       b. 20 August 1949 - El Dorado, Ark.

(d) Charity Berryhill
    b. 15 July 1889 - Marion Co., Ala.
    b. 1967 - Marion Co., Ala.
    bur. Center Cemetery
    m. Alex Golden Homer - 17 September 1904 - Marion Co.

    (1) Ellie Homer
        b. 23 October 1909
        m. Mary Howell

    (2) Elma Homer
        b. 24 September 1910
        m. Harvey Bailey

    (3) Alvie Lee Homer
        b. 30 September 1914
        m. Lonnie Foster

    Charity Berryhill
    m. 2nd. Andrew Franks

    (4) Gladys Franks
        b. 26 March 1920
        m. Owen Dickinson

    (5) Ester Franks
        b. 23 May 1924
        m. Jim Foster

        (6) Vaudell Franks
            b. 28 October 1930
            m. Leon Farris

        (7) Gatha Franks
            m. J. D. Stanley

William Silas Berryhill m. 2nd 6 June 1903 - Marion Co. Ala.
m. Mrs. Mary E. "Mollie" (Maddox) Williams
    b. 27 March 1880 - Marion Co., Ala.
    d. 23 April 1952 - Ty Ty, Ga.
    bur. Lawrence Cemetery - near Brookfield, Ga.

(e) Icie Mae Berryhill
    b. 27 April 1904 - Marion Co., Ala.
    m. Iley D. Crow - 25 October 1923
        b. 14 January 1907 - Marion Co., Ala.

    (1) Verta Mae Crow
        b. 23 August 1924 - Marion Co., Ala.
        m. Marvin Davis
            b. 26 December 1917 - Marion Co., Ala.

    (2) Jimmy D. Crow
        b. 13 November 1939 - Marion Co., Ala.
        m. Lola Mae Lynn

(f) Willie Berryhill
    b. 17 February 1906 - Marion Co., Ala.
    m. Tom Beasley
        b. 10 April 1887

    (1) William Jessee Beasley
        b. 11 July 1933
        m. Leah Elizabeth Childers
            b. 20 October 1935

        A. Jeanne Marie Beasley   b. 27 September 1956
        B. Jessica Leigh Beasley   b. 29 March 1959
        C. Thomas Allen Beasley   b. 3 June 1961
        D. Weldon Beasley   b. 14 April 1964

    (2) Garland Loden Beasley
        b. 11 March 1937
        m. Minoise Hayes

        A. Jonathan Beasley
        B. Maribeth Beasley
        C. David Garland Beasley

    (3) James Darold Beasley
        b. 15 November 1938
        m. Drucilla Gibson

        A. Jamelle Beasley
        B. Sherise Beasley

(g) Essie Lou Elma Berryhill
    b. 27 August 1908 - Marion Co., Ala.
    m. Flem Shaw
        b. 24 May 1905 - Marion Co., Ala.

    (1) Mable Lucilla Shaw
        b. 13 November 1927
        m. Jack Smith
    (2) Roland Eugene Shaw
        b. 16 December 1928
        m. Jeanette Sumner
    (3) Leon Middleton Shaw
        b. 20 January 1930
        Single
    (4) Edith Mary Shaw
        b. 11 December 1931
        m. Guy Cravey
    (5) Adele Ida Shaw
        b. 23 March 1934
        m. James Pitts

        (6) Virginia Faye Shaw
                b. 12 December 1940
                m. James Talbert

    (h) Ruby Gladys Berryhill
            b. 4 December 1911 - Marion Co., Ala.
            m. Melvin Akins

        (1) Royal Eugene Akins
                b. 7 June 1931 - Marion CO., Ala.
                m. Eva Jenaette Clark
        (2) Max Lourell Akins
                b. 13 November 1933 - Brookfield, Ga.
                m. Barbara Ann Kennedy
        (3) Richard Donald Akins
                b. 29 October 1937 - Brookfield, Ga.
                m. Annie Ruth Heard

        Ruby Gladys Berryhill
        2nd m. Amos Alexander
                b. 3 August 1914 - St Marks, Fla.

2. John Thomas Berryhill
    b. 26 April 1860 - Lafayette Co, Miss.
    d. 24 January 1934 - Anderson Co., Texas near Palestine
    bur. Olive Branch Cemetery - 3½ miles from Frankston, Texas
    m. Rachel Caroline Weeks - 15 April 1877 - Hinds Co., Miss.
        b. 1858 - Ala.
        d. 18 May 1931 - near Olive Branch Community, Anderson
        bur. Olive Branch Cemetery - Anderson Co., Texas
        dau. of John Weeks & Mariah Webster
                b. 1825 - Tenn b. 1824 - Ala.
        gr. dau. of Samuel Weeks & Prudence -?-
                b. 1804 - Ga. b. 1805 - N. C.

    (a) William Berryhill
            born after 1880 and died age 3 weeks
            bur. Harmony Grove Cemetery - Fayette Co., Ala.
    (b) Martha Yancy Virginia Berryhill
            b. 1882 - approx. - Fayette Co., Ala.
            d. 2 June 1965 - Anderson Co., Texas
            bur. Olive Branch Cemetery - near Frankston, Texas
            m. William Clayburn Berryhill - "Clay"
                b. 1878 - Fayette Co., Ala.
                d.
                bur.
                son of Charles W. "Cap" Berryhill & Caroline (Perry)
                        Dickinson

        (1) Charlie Berryhill
        (2) William Berryhill
        (3) Nolan Berryhill
        (4) Maggie Berryhill
        (5) Bankhead Berryhill
        (6) Eckford Berryhill
        (7) Croman Berryhill
        (8) Ora Berryhill
        (9) Eudean Berryhill -' "Dean"
        (10) Raleigh Berryhill
        (11) Cecil Berryhill
        (12) Douglas Berryhill
        (13) Ivory Berryhill

    (c) Florence Berryhill
            died young and buried Harmony Grove Cemetery, Fayette Co.
    (d) Charlie Berryhill
            b. 1884
            d. 1905 - Fayette Co., Ala.
            bur. Harmony Grove Cemetery - Fayette Co, Ala.

(e) Nora Brewrilla Berryhill
    b. 2 December 1886 - Fayette Co., Ala.
    m. Marion Thomas Couch - "Tom" - 10 January 1904
       b. 25 January 1875 - Fayette Co., Fayette Co., Ala.
       d. 7 October 1951 - Bristow, Okla.
       bur. Magnolia Cemetery - Bristow, Okla.
       son of John Thomas Couch & Virginia Rebecca Vickery
                 b. 21 September 1858   b. 1862 - Ala.
                 d. 17 March 1889
                 bur. Harmony Grove Cemetery - Fayette Co.

    (1) Florence Couch
        b. 14 April 1905 - Fayette Co., Ala.
        d.   May 1906 - Fayette Co., Ala.
        bur. Harmony Grove Cemetery
    (2) May Couch
        b. 14 August 1907 - Fayette Co., Ala.
        d.   May 1908 - Fayette Co., Ala.
        bur. Harmony Grove Cemetery
    (3) Deena Couch
        b. 13 February 1908 - Fayette Co., Ala.
        m. Mack Gillum

        A. Eloise Gillum
        B. Wm. Thomas Gillum
        C. Nora Belle Gillum
        D. Wanda Jean Gillum

        Deena (Couch) Gillum m. 2nd David Stanley

    (4) Clara Couch
        b. 1910 - Fayette Co., Ala.
        m. Moodie Elmer Webster
           b. 25 August 1911 - Fayette Co., Ala.
           son of Ellie M. Webster & Sarah Elizabeth Henderson

        A. Linda Webster m. "Buddy" Thorp
        B. Ronald Webster
        C. Kenneth Webster

    (5) Myrthel Wates Couch
        b. 13 April 1912 - Marion Co., Ala.
        m. Ruel Artice Cook - 27 October 1929 - Anderson, Co.
           b. 13 January 1910 - Frankston, Texas
           son of John Quincy Cook & Ida Mae Elrod

        A. Oleta Rae Cook
           b. 13 September 1930 - Anderson Co., Texas
           m. George Lee Mills - 27 October 1951

           1. George Lee Mills, Jr.
              b. 27 August 1952
           2. Steven Ross Mills
              b. 13 January 1954
           3. Mischelle Denise Mills
              b. 30 May 1958

        B. Dorothy Earnestine Cook
           b. 14 May 1932 - Anderson Co., Texas
           m. Wm. Murray Spillers

           1. Dorothy Ruth Spillers
              b. 4 April 1953 - Bethesden, Md.
           2. Clara Jean Spillers
              b. and d. 26 July 1955 - Jacksonville, Fla.
           3. Wm. Ruel Spillers
              b. 14 December 1957 - Jacksonville, Fla.

        C. Clara Dell Cook
           b. 11 June 1936 - Anderson Co., Texas
           m. Henry Lee Walker, Jr.

           1. Henry Lee Walker, III
              b. 28 August 1956 - Shreveport, La.
           2. Clara Gayle Walker
              b. 19 July 1958 - Kansas City, Mo.

(6) Arvel Elton Couch
    b. 11 November 1914 - Marion Co., Ala.
    d. 30 August 1965 - Sand Springs, Okla.
    bur. Magnolia Cemetery - Bristow, Okla.
    m. Lucille King

    A. Elton Couch
    B. Jerry Couch
    C. Tommy Couch
    D. James Neal Couch
    E. Regina Couch

(7) Cornelius Washington Couch
    b. 30 November 1916 - Anderson Co., Texas
    m. Joyce -?-

    A. Pamela Couch

(8) Margaret Melvirdie Couch
    b. 23 March 1919 - Anderson Co., Texas
    m. Birdie Amos Albert Bradford

    A. Homer Dale Bradford
       b. 11 December 1940 - Creek Co., Texas

(9) Minnie Virginia Couch
    b. 14 April 1922 - Anderson Co., Texas
    m. Benjamin Hookey

    A. Leroy Hookey
    B. Larry Hookey
    C. Mark Hookey
    D. Danny Hookey
    E. Roger Hookey
    F. Paula Hookey
    G. Dennis Hookey

(10) John Thomas Couch
     b. 29 August 1924 - Maysville, Okla.
     m. Virginia Sexton

     A. Johnny Manard Couch

(f) Minnie Nancy Jane Berryhill
    b. 27 February 1889 - Fayette Co., Ala.
    m. James Curtis Anthony - 16 May 1907 - Fayette Co, Ala.
       b. 9 June 1884 - Fayette Co., Ala.
       d. 1 April 1958 - Shannon, Miss.
       bur. Shannon Cemetery - Shannon, Miss.
       son of James Richard Anthony & Zay G. Perkins
                 b. 19 February 1858   b. 10 May 1864
                 d. 10 February 1918   d. 24 December 1924
                 both bur. Hubbertville Cemetery - Fayette Co.

    (1) Lethie Thomas Anthony
        b. 1 May 1908 - Fayette Co., Ala.
        m. Bertha C. Champion - 5 July 1930
           b. 4 April 1914 - Frankston, Texas

        A. Lloyd Thomas Anthony
           b. 19 June 1931 - Frankston, Texas
           m. Daisy Ladd - 2 July 1965
              b. 12 August 1934 - Trinity Co., Texas
        B. Marlin Harding Anthony
           b. 20 December 1938 - Tupelo, Miss.
           m. Karolyn K. Koon - 13 June 1964
              b. 2 March 1946 - Lufkin, Texas

    (2) Wilburn Lee Anthony
        b. 2 November 1911 - Fayette Co., Ala.
        m. Florine Gillentine - 9 October 1937
           b. 15 May 1916 - Lee Co., Miss.

        A. Barbara Lee Anthony
           b. 29 May 1945 - Tupelo, Miss.

44

(g) Rastus Floyd Berryhill
     b. 16 September 1895 - Marion Co., Ala.
     m. Julie Adline Henderson - 4 October 1912 - Fayette Co.
        b. 15 November 1896 - Fayette Co., Ala.
        dau. of Wm. Andrew Henderson & Rachel Louise Berryhill
                    b. 2 February 1856   b. 16 April 1858
                    d. 27 June 1916   d. 3 August 1934

   (1) Rachel Unamay Berryhill
        b. 2 October 1913 - Fayette Co., Ala.
        m. Russell Meetze

        A. Peggy Ann Meetze
           b. 23 October 1936 - Roby, Texas
           m. Ray Toney

           1. Rhonda Toney
              b. 1957 - Brownfield, Texas
           2. Ray Toney, Jr.
              b. 1960 - Brownfield, Texas

        B. Charles Russell Meetze
           b. 12 January 1940 - Roby, Texas
           m. Gail Smith

           1. Charles R. Meetze, Jr.
              b. 22 September 1964 - Oahu, Hawaii
           2. Steven John Meetze
              b. 7 October 1966 - Lovington, N. Mex.

        C. Judy Lee Meetze
           b. April 1945 - Orange, Texas
           m. Nicky Henery

           1. Nicky Floyd Henery
              b. 2 May 1963 - California
           2. Sherry Henery
              b. 1965 - Lovington, N. Mexico

   (2) Norman Lodaska Berryhill
        b. 24 November 1916 - Fayette Co., Ala.
        d.   November 1960 - Rusk, Texas
        bur. Atoy Cemetery - 10 miles SE of Rusk, Texas
        m. Homer Rogers

        A. Homer Rogers, Jr.
           b. 10 November 1935 - Roby, Fisher Co, Texas
           m. Virginia McGohey

           1. Charles Lee Rogers
              b. 25 July 1961

        Norman Lodaska Berryhill m. 2nd Benford Hughey

        B. Dennis Wayne Hughey
           b. 4 February 1938 - Roby, Texas
           m. Dorothy Ann Lusk
              b. 19 May 1942

           1. Marcella Hughey
              b. 2 March 1961 - Acton, Texas
           2. Walter Ray Hughey
              b. 19 November 1962 - Acton, Texas
        Norman Lodaska Berryhill m. 3rd William "Bill" Cox

        C. William Ammit Cox - "Buddy"
           b. June 1944 - Fort Worth, Texas

   (3) Virginia Estell Berryhill
        b. 18 January 1920 - Fayette Co., Ala.
        m. Ray White - Jacksonville, Texas

        A. Ralph Floyd White
           b. 7 June 1942 - Frankston, Texas
           m. Sandy Deets

           1. Briggett White
              b. 1963

(4) Julian Floyd Berryhill
    b. 10 September 1923 - Naches, Texas
    m. Jewell Whitehead
    A. Dennis Berryhill
       b. 5 November 1947
       m. Susan Bivins
          b. 11 May 1949
    B. Clyde Berryhill
       b. 11 May 1949
    C. Linda Berryhill
       b. June 1951

(5) Odoniel Berryhill
    b. 11 May 1926 - Palestine, Anderson Co., Texas
    m. Mary Sullivan
       b. 14 February 1929

    A. Billie Berryhill   b. 23 December 1947
    B. Barbara Berryhill   b. February 1949 d. Dec. 1952
    C. Debra Berryhill   b. 26 August 1951
    D. Travis Berryhill   b. 8 October 1952
    E. Eddie Berryhill   b. 23 June 1954
    F. Rachel Berryhill   b. 15 December 1956
    G. Norma Berryhill   b. 7 October 1961

(6) William Harry Berryhill
    b. 17 August 1928 - Anderson Co., Texas
    m. Lester Stoneman

    A. Harry Odoniel Berryhill
       b. 3 May 1952 - Brownfield, Texas
    B. Julian Elizabeth Berryhill
       b. 22 June 1955 - Dallas, Texas
    C. Mark Wayne Berryhill
       b. 1959   d. 1963
    D. Montie Lee Berryhill
       b. October 1965 - Dallas, Texas

(7) June Elizabeth Berryhill
    b. 13 June 1931 - Anderson Co., Texas
    m. W. T. Goolsbee

    A. Homer Wayne Goolsbee
       b. 16 December 1951 - Fort Worth, Texas

    June Elizabeth Berryhill m. 2nd. Robert L. Sherwin

    B. Vickie June Sherwin
       b. 8 March 1957 - Odessa, Texas

(8) Ray Arnold Berryhill
    b. 26 July 1936 - Roby, Fisher Co., Texas
    m. Sherry Stovall

    A. Kenneth Ray Berryhill
       b. 30 August 1964

(h) Mertie Bell Berryhill
    b. 19 September 1897 - Fayette Co., Ala.
    d.   1949 - Corsicana, Texas
    bur.
    m. Joseph A. Barnett - "Joe" - 14 January 1913 - Fayette Co.
       b.   d. 1915

    (1) Gertrude Barnett
        d. 4 years old below Palestine, Anderson Co., Texas
    (2) Ida Barnett
        b. 1914 - approx.
        m. -?- Blackwell

        A. Essie Blackwell

    Mertie Bell Berryhill
    m. 2nd Jim Congleton
       d. 1960 - Palestine, Texas
       bur.

            (3) Maidie Congleton
            (4) Hazel Congleton
            (5) Lawrence Congleton
            (6) Willidean Congleton
            (7) Lodaskie Congleton
            (8) T. W. Congleton
            (9) Louise Congleton
            (10) Curtis Congleton - died young

    3 Mary Ann Berryhill - "Annie"
      b. 1862 - Fayette Co., Ala.
      d.   Winfield, ala area (known to be living 29 Dec. 1933)
      bur.
      m. John C. White
         b. 1854 - Ala.
         d. after 29 December 1933
         bur.
         son of Robert White & Charity -?-
               b. 1826 - Tenn b. 1824 - Tenn.

      (a) John Y. White b. 1871 - Marion Co., Ala.
      (b) James White b. 1873 approx - Marion Co., Ala.
      (c) Jane White b. 1875 - approx. - Marion Co., Ala.
      (d) Wm. T. White b. 1877 - approx. - Marion Co., Ala.
      (e) Frances White b. 1878 - approx. d. 1969, Marion Co., Ala.
          m. John Wm. Baccus - "Rilly"
      (f) Nathan White b. 1880 approx. - Marion Co., Ala.
      (g) Travis White b. 1882 - approx. - Marion Co., Ala.
      (h) Drucilla White b. 1884 - approx. - Marion Co., Ala.
          m. John Burgess.
      (i) Cleve White   b. 1885 - approx. - Marion Co., Ala.

      I found several people who know this family, and from some
      old letters among them, we are able to put this much
      together correctly, but have been unable to make any
      contacts with the immediate family.

F. Newton T. Berryhill - "Newt"
   b. 1841 - Marion Co., Ala.
   Killed or died during the Civil War. Never married. We assume
   if he came home and died that he is buried in Berryhill Cemetery.
   Grave site is unknown. But should anyone know where he is
   buried, I will be happy to apply for him a free Confederate
   marker.

G. Charles W. Berryhill - "Charlie"
   b. 1844 - Marion Co., Ala.
   d. Was wounded in the Civil War, came home and later died.
      Never married. We assume he was also buried in the Berryhill
      Cemetery.

   Newton T. Berryhill served in "Co. K, 16th Ala. Inf. Regt. as a
   private. Age 21 years, enlisted 19 August 1861 at Courtland, Ala.

   Charles Washington Berryhill served in "Co. K. 16th Ala. Inf.
   Regt. as a Private, age 18 years old, and enlisted at Courtland,
   Ala. 19 August 1861.

   This would indicate to us that the two brothers joined together
   and it is sad we find they died for the same cause, but probably
   not together.

H. Martha Ann Berryhill - "Annie" - (ran a boarding house many
   years in Winfield)
   b. 15 April 1844 - Marion Co., Ala.
   d. 11 December 1925 - Penelope, Hill Co., Texas
   bur. Penelope Cemetery, Penelope, Hill Co., Texas
   m. John Ellis White - 1863-64 approx., Marion Co., Ala.
      b. 15 December 1841 - Marion Co., Ala.
      d. 6 August 1906 - Marion Co., Ala.
      bur. Winfield Cemetery , Marion Co., Ala.
      son of P. H. White & R. L. -?- who m. 6 December 1838
            b. 24 March 1819 b. 13 November 1817

1. William Thomas White - "Willie"
   b. 16 October 1865 - Marion Co., Ala.
   d. 21 October 1895 - Guthrie, Ark.
   bur.   Cemetery - Guthrie, Ark.
   m. Chessie Lula Reed - (m. 2nd Doc White)
      b. 28 March 1871 - Cobb Co., Ga.
      d. 17 November 1964 - Birmingham, Ala.
      bur.
      dau. of Thomas Haynes Reed & Mary Elizabeth McClesky

   (a) Bressie Forest White
       b. 4 August 1891 - Marion Co., Ala.
       m. Gracie Mae Webster
          b.
          d. 17 January 1966 - Amory, Miss.
          bur.
          dau. of

       (1) Beulah Mae White
           b.
           m. Noel Fred Myers - 7 June 1932
              b.

           A. Carol Myers   b.
              m.
                 b.

              1. Debbie Myers   b. 1958
              2. Scott Myers   b. 1961

           B. James Neal Myers
              b.

       (2) Bressie Herbert White   b.
           m. Leta Hixon - 12 June 1954
              b.

           A. Anita White   b. 1958

       (3) Houston Thomas White
           b. 1923 -
           d. 14 December 1935
           bur.
       (4) James William White   b.
           m. Rubye Clement
              b.

           A. son - b. 1964
           B. dau. - b. May 1968

   (b) Willie White
       b. 1894 - d. 1896   bur. Guthrie, Ark.

2. James N. White - "Jim"
   b. 4 October 1869 - Marion Co., Ala.
   d.   1917 - Marlon Hill Co., Texas
   bur. Mart Cemetery - Mart, Texas
   m. Nellie Stevens - 30 January 1901
      b. 14 November 1877 - Bunkie, La.
      d. 20 June 1952 - Dallas, Texas
      bur. Forest Hill Cemetery - Dallas, Texas
      dau. of George Henry Stevens & Alice Ann -?-

   (a) Gilbert Stevens White
       b. 19 November 1904 - Mexia, Limestone, Co., Texas
       m. Juliette Mable Bachemin
          b. 21 July 1913 - Harris Co., Texas
          dau. of Victor H. Bachemin & Margaret Hilda Mahne

3. Anthony Fee White
   b. 15 October 1872 - Marion Co., Ala.
   d. 28 February 1956 - Shreveport, La.
   bur. Blanchard Cemetery - Blanchard, La.
   m. Daisy Estes - 1 May 1898
      b. 1 April 1874 - Keatchie, DeSoto Parish, La.
      d. 17 December 1926 - Shreveport, La. bur. Blanchard Ceme.

(a) Arlan Fonso White
    b. 9 June 1899 - Blanchard, Caddo Parish, La.
    d. 11 June 1926 - Blanchard, Caddo Parish, La.
    bur. Blanchard Cemetery
(b) Orvis LaRue White
    b. 25 October 1906 - Blanchard, La.
    m. Gladys Neely

    (1) Martha Jane White   b. 13 February 1939 - Plano, Tex.
        m. Kenneth Miller

        A. Jerry Lyn Miller

        Martha Jane White m. 2nd Henry Clark

        Orvis LaRue White m. 2nd Mrs. Beulah Mae Hull

(c) Ouida Odell White
    b. 12 August 1911 - Blanchard, La.
    m. Harold Chadwick Butler   b.

    (1) Janice Ouida Butler
        b. 6 April 1937 - Dallas, Texas
        m. Maurice Dean Ervin   b.

        A. Jeffrey Dean Ervin
           b. 11 April 1966 - Shreveport, La.

    (2) Lynn Chadwick Butler
        b. 12 February 1940 - Dallas, Texas
        m. Carolyn Sue Carin   b.

        A. Phillip Chadwick Butler
           b. 27 September 1964 - Albany, Ga.

4. Maude Virginia White
   b. 12 February 1875 - Marion Co., Ala.
   d. 29 November 1962 - Dallas, Texas
   bur. Cottonwood Cemetery - Hill Co., Texas
   m. John Thomas Berryhill - 18 November 1900 - Caddo Parish, La
      (Something killed his wife Maude's Uncle ? White, so
      they left Ala. for Texas ?)
      b. 13 January 1868 - Marion Co., Ala.
      d. 21 October 1915 - Falls Co., Texas
      bur. Cottonwood Cemetery
      son of Benjamin Franklin Berryhill & Rebecca Vickery
         b. 17 December 1833 - Ala.   b. 1831 - Tenn.
      See more information listed under John Thomas Berryhill

   (a) Fola Berryhill
       b. 29 November 1901 - Marion Co., Ala.
       d. 11 February 1907 - Penelope, Hill Co., Texas
       bur. Cottonwood Cemetery - Hill Co., Texas
   (b) Thomas Raymond Berryhill - "Tom"
       b. 19 April 1914 - Highbank, Falls Co., Texas

5. Mary Emmie White
   b. 30 October 1880 - Hinds Co., Miss.
   d. 10 September 1956 - Oklahoma City, Okla.
   m. John Frank Smith - 17 January 1903 - Marion Co., Ala.
      b. 23 August 1873 - Marion Co., Ala.
      d. 13 June 1918 - Sulphur, Oklahoma
      bur. Winfield Cemetery - Marion Co., Ala.
      son of John Henry Smith & Martha Jane Aston

   (a) Thelma Natalie Smith
       b. 18 September 1904 - Marion Co., Ala.
       d. 23 October 1954 - Mineral Wells, Texas
       bur. Chapel Hill Memorial Gardens - Okla City, Okla.

(a) Thelma Natalie Smith (Continued)
    m. Claud Ladd - 20 June 1923
      b. 4 July 1900

    (1) Bettie Ladd
        b. 27 October 1925 - Pauls Valley, Okla.
        m. Jerome Wienckowski - 6 May 1946
    (2) Claudine Ladd
        b. 26 September 1927 - Pauls Valley, Okla.
        m. James Stoker - 4 September 1954

(b) Thomas Harry Smith
    b. 27 January 1907 - Marion Co., Ala.
    m. Gladys -?-

    (1) Betty Sue Smith (twin)
        b. 12 August 1942 - Okla. City, Okla.
    (2) Barbara Lou Smith (twin)
        b. 12 August 1942 - Okla. City, Okla.
    (3) Mary Jean Smith - (twin)
        b. 23 November 1941 - Panama Canal Zone
    (4) Joan Margaret Smith (twin)
        b. 23 November 1941 (twin) - Pamana Canal Zone

    Thomas Harry Smith m. 2nd Sadie Louise Barlow - 20 Jan 1947
                         b. 9 June 1909 - Hinds Co., Miss

    (5) Frank Carroll Smith
        b. 3 September 195 0 - Memphis, Tenn.

(c) Martha Olive Smith
    b. 11 March 1913 - Marion Co., Ala.
    m. Orville Hicks - 5 February 1938
      b. 18 October 1906 - Guthrie, Okla.
      son of Bruck Hicks and Nancy Ellison

    (1) Larry Orville Hicks
        b. 23 January 1941 - Okla City. Okla.
        m. Ellen Frances Nolan - 11 July 1964 - Colo Springs
        b.

        A. Larry Wayne Hicks
           b. 30 April 1968 - Colo. Springs, Colo.

    (2) Mary Kathryn Hicks - "Kay"
        b. 2 January 1947 - Okla City, Okla.

6. Lula Olive White
   b. 29 October 1888 - Hinds Co., Miss.
   d. 25 April 1955 - Dallas, Texas
   bur. Memorial Park Cemetery - Memphis, Tenn.
   m. Nathan Newton Harris - 1903/1904 - Marion Co., Ala.
     b. 1880 - Montgomery Co., Miss.
     d. 1923 - Memphis, Tenn.
     bur. Red Hill Cemetery - Sweatman, Miss.
     son of Elijah William Harris & Jennie Williams

(a) Ellis Elijah Harris
    b. July 1905 - Marion Co., Ala.
    d. 1926 - Duckhill, Miss.
    bur. Red Hill Cemetery - Sweatman, Miss.
    m. Delores O'Neal
    No Issue
(b) John White Harris
    b. 2 December 1909 - Marion Co., Ala.
    m. Annie Hood May - 22 December 1935 - Shelby Co, Tenn.
      b. 21 July 1914 - Shelby Co, Tenn.
      dau. of Henry Benton May & Frances Miller

    (1) John White Harris, Jr.
        b. 4 December 1941 - Shelby Co, Tenn.

7. Martha Jane Hight White
   b. 10 March 1891 - Marion Co., Ala.
   m. Geater Woodson Berryhill - 22 December 1912 - Waco, Texas
      b. 21 May 1890 - Marion Co., Ala.
      d. 1 January 1953 - Dallas, Texas
      bur. Ridgepark Cemetery - Hillsboro, Texas
      son of Jesse Burton Berryhill & Vilantia Cantrell
      gr. son of Benjamin Franklin Berryhill & Rebecca Vickery

   (a) James Terrance Berryhill
       b. 18 July 1918 - Penelope, Hill Co, Texas
       d. 30 July 1943 - Kessel, Germany. Killed in action in
          World War II.
       bur. Fort Sam Houston National Cemetery
       m. Thelma Mann

       No Issue

   (b) Reba Jean Berryhill
       b. 9 January 1921 - Penelope, Hill Co., Texas
       m. Harold P. Angel - 3 December 1940
          b. 29 September 1918

       (1) Beverly Jean Angel
           b. 6 November 1942 - Waco, Texas
           m. Douglas Averitt - 30 June 1962
              b. 28 April 1939

           A. Michael Averitt   b. 9 September 1963
           B. Steven Averitt   b. 18 October 1966
           C. Richard Averitt   b. 7 May 1968

       (2) James Terrance Angel
           b. 6 June 1945 - Waco, Texas
           m. Elizabeth Ann Wulff - 18 December 1967 - Germany
              b. 24 March 1948
       (3) Harvey Woodson Angel
           b. 6 April 1952 - Dallas, Texas
       (4) Kyp Randolph Angel
           b. 22 October 1959 - Garland, Texas

   (c) Ruby Olive Berryhill
       b. 22 August 1923 - Penelope, Hill Co., Texas
       m. Chauncey Roebuck, Jr. - 18 August 1943
          b. 18 July 1922

       (1) Chauncey Roebuck, III
           b. 18 August 1951 - Dallas, Texas

William Berryhill, Jr. - "Bill Dergin" married 2nd approx. 1851 -
m. Nancy Adeline Andleton (twin of Margaret Andleton), Marion Co., Ala.
  b. 1833 - Tenn.
  d. 1874 approx. - Hinds Co., Miss.
  bur. Weeks Cemetery - Hinds Co., Miss.
  She doesn't have a marker, but family history says she died a
  couple of years before her husband.
  dau. of -?- Andleton & Elizabeth -?-
      dead by 1850   b. 1811 - & living 1850

I. William Dee Berryhill - "Bud"
  b. 3 August 1852 - Fayette Co., Ala.
  d. 18 March 1934 - El Paso, Texas
  bur. Forest Lawn Cemetery - El Paso, Texas
  m. Emma Hutchens May - 22 December 1880 - Hinds Co, Miss.
    b. 1 July 1862 - Crystal Springs, Miss.
    d. 7 June 1935 - El Paso, Texas
    bur. Forest Lawn Cemetery - El Paso, Texas
    dau. of James May & -?- Hutchens

(1) Edgar May Berryhill
    b. 4 December 1881 - Hinds Co., Miss.
    d. 13 November 1950 - Blythe, California
    m. Lillian E. Suddath - 28 October 1906 - Abilene, Texas

    (a) Max Harold Berryhill
      b. 2 August 1908 - Abilene, Texas
    (b) W. D. Berryhill
      b. 22 May 1910 - Abilene, Texas
      m. Virginia -?-
    (c) Beatrice Virginia Berryhill
      b. 11 November 1913 - Mayer, Arizona
      m. Maurice Frank Wing - 28 March 1937 - El Paso, Texas
        b. 30 September 1912 - El Paso, Texas
        d. 23 February 1979 - Douglas, Arizona
        son of Samuel Maurice Wing & Marian Irene Browne

        1. Diane Ashley Wing
          b. 24 February 1938 - El Paso, Texas
          m. John Burdette Serage - 26 May 1957
        2. Maurice Frank Wing
          b. 1 August 1940 - Douglas, Arizona
          m. Eliza Gomez - 24 November 1966
        3. Mariam Rose Wing
          b. 7 January 1951 - Douglas, Arizona
        4. Virginia Beatrice Wing
          b. 5 December 1953 - Douglas, Arizona
          m. Robert Gordon Hartwell - 14 December 1978

    Edgar May Berryhill m. 2nd Mary Josephine Henderson

    (d) Marie Berryhill
      m. Sam Digiglia

(2) William Earl Berryhill
    b. 1 March 1884 - Hinds Co., Miss.
    d. 27 January 1961 - near San Francisco, California
    m. Tommie Obar - 11 September 1910
(3) Millard Lamar Berryhill
    b. 28 September 1885 - Hinds Co., Miss.
    d. 16 April 1963 - near San Diego, California
    m. Kate Denton

    (a) Alice Berryhill
      m. -?- Carlin
    (b) Dixie Berryhill
    (c) Lavonne Berryhill
      m. -?- Birtkise
    (d) Jackie Berryhill
    (e) Doris Berryhill
    (f) Lila Rose Berryhill
      m. -?- James

(4) Ashley Erroll Berryhill
    b. 31 July 1887 - Hinds Co., Miss.
    d. 25 March 1968 - El Paso, Texas
    bur. Forest Lawn Cemetery - El Paso, Texas
    m. Lilahrose Brown - 23 April 1910
        b. 1880 approx. - Pikesville, Tenn.
        d. 1960 -
        bur. Forest Lawn Cemetery - El Paso, Texas
    No issue
(5) Lillian Gertrude Berryhill
    b. 25 January 1892 - Jones Co., Texas
    d. 24 January 1970
    m. Jesse Neil - 23 May 1912 - Plainview, Texas

    (a) Frances Imogene Neil
        b. 12 December 1918
        d. 5 June 1980
        m. -?- Dryer
    (b) Charles E. Neil
        b. 31 January 1915
    (c) Jesse Martin "Jay" Neil
        b. 11 April 1913
        d. 13 August 1979
    (d) Ida Marie Neil
        b. 26 May 1921
        m. -?- Hancock
    (e) Mary Virginia Neil
        b. 6 March 1923
        d. 1 June 1925

(6) Erna Berryhill
    b. 6 March 1893 - Jones Co, Texas
    d. 2 July 1905 - Jones Co, Texas
    bur. O'Phantom Hill Cemetery - between Lueders & Abilene, TX
(7) Ida Mae Berryhill
    b. 11 May 1895 - Jones Co, Texas
    m. Rex O. Bounds - 21 October 1922 - El Paso, Texas

    (a) Rex Oeney Bounds, Jr.
        b. 18 July 1923 - Los Angeles, California

(8) Zuella Marie Berryhill
    b. 22 March 1897 - Jones Co, Texas
    m. Richard Nathaniel Rasmus - 1 March 1919 - El Paso, Texas
        deceased young
    Zeulla Marie Berryhill
    m. 2nd. Roy Edward Warren
    m. 3rd. Basil Barjoni

(9) Winifred Virginia Berryhill
    b. 11 October 1901 - Nugent, Texas
    d. 24 January 1968 - El Paso, Texas
    bur. Forest Lawn Cemetery - El Paso, Texas
    m. Barney Frank Camp - 17 November 1923 - El Paso, Texas
    No Issue

J. Alexander L. Berryhill - "Elac"
    b. 10 April 1853 - Marion Co., Ala.
    d. 1890 - approx. - Hinds Co., Miss.
    bur. Weeks Cemetery - 3½ miles E. of Utica, Hinds Co, Miss.
    One marker in Weeks Cemetery says:
    "Alexander Berryhill born in Alabama" and it shows no dates.
    Another marker says:
    "A. L. Berryhill b. 20 November 1854 & d. 11 July 1892."
    Another marker says:
    "Elaxandria Berryhill b. 7 March 1848 & d. 11 November 1885."
    We have absolutely no way to say which of the three markers is for
    the above Alexander, but his marriage license shows his middle
    initial was "L". Yet, we find another A. L. Berryhill in same
    county.

    But the Bible record shows "Elac" who is Otis's father was born
    10 April 1853.

J. Alexander L. Berryhill (Continued)
    m. Mrs. Eliza Jane (Weeks) Brock - 12 June 1876 - Hinds Co., Ms.
        b. 7 June 1846 - Hinds Co., Miss (marker says 20 June 1845)
        d. 12 September 1887 - Hinds Co. (marker says 18 October 1887)
        bur. Utica Cemetery - Utica, Hinds Co., Miss.
        widow of Andrew V. Brock, buried by him with a double tomb

    (1) Bernice Berryhill
        b. 17 August 1877 - Hinds Co., Miss.
        d. 1 February 1950 - Antlers, Okla.
        bur. Antlers Cemetery - Antlers, Okla. (marker says born
            14 August 1881)
    (2) Otis Berryhill (Bible spells it Otice)
        b. 19 June 1880 - Hinds Co., Miss.
        d. 21 February 1969 - Hot Springs, Ark.
        bur. Mars Hill Cemetery
        m. Susan Jane "Susie" Ledbetter - 1907 - Buda, Texas
            b. 3 November 1889 - Bauxite, Ark.
            d. 9 November 1918 - Alexander, Ark.
            bur. Mars Hill Cemetery - Bauxite, Ark.
            dau. of J. H. Ledbetter & Candace M. Satterwhite

        (a) Ernest Lee Berryhill
            b. 1 December 1909 - Buda, Hayes Co., Texas
            m. Nettie Ruth Rowland
                b. 27 December 1912 - Maplevale, Ark.
        (b) Gertrude Leloa Berryhill
            b. 1 October 1912 - Buda, Texas
            d. 26 December 1943 - Bauxite, Ark.
            bur. New Friendship Cemetery - Bauxite, Ark.
            m. Calvert Burton

            1. Inez Burton m. Tom Gill
            2. Elvin Burton m. Martha Jones

        (c) Samuel Clyde Berryhill
            b. 1 December 1914 - Buda, Hayes Co., Texas
            m. Mary Frank White
                b.

            1. Patsy Jean Berryhill
                b. 28 August 1940 - Bauxite, Ark.
            Samuel Clyde Berryhill m. 2nd. Fay Belle Robinson

            2. James Richard Berryhill
                b. 2 January 1951
            3. Ronald Raye Berryhill
                b. 15 May 1953
            4. Shelia Ann Berryhill
                b. 7 February 1956
            5. Kelley Marie Berryhill
                b. 6 February 1961

        (d) Leon Nelson Berryhill
            b. 30 September 1916 - Buda, Texas
            m. Edna Earl Weatherford - 3 June 1939
                b. 5 March 1923 - Oma, Ark.

            1. Wanda Sue Berryhill
                b. 5 January 1941
                m. Lavelle E. Foshee

                A. Laura Jean Foshee
                    b. 7 March 1961

            Wanda Sue Berryhill m. 2nd. Vernon Wright
                                        b. 20 August 1942

                B. Robert Joe Wright
                    b. 8 August 1964

            2. Norris Leon Berryhill
                b. 28 August 1943
                m. Linda Lee Faulkner
                    b. 3 March 1943

                    A. Rebecca Lynn Berryhill
                       b. 12 May 1963

              3. Judith Ann Berryhill
                 b. 30 September 1949
                 m. David Lynn Harper
                    b. 5 May 1947

                    A. Sherri Lynn Harper
                       b. 17 October 1966

    (2) Otice Berryhill m. 2nd. Mary Emily Borders
                                 b.
                                 d. 9 April 1933 - Alexander, Ark.
                                 bur. Mars Hill Cemetery, Bauxite
                                 dau. of John Wesley Borders & Nannie
                                        Elutherius Satterwhite
        (e) Infant Son
            b.   d.   bur.
        (f) Horace Wesley Berryhill
            b. 9 July 1923 - Saline Co., Alexander, Ark.
            m. Martha Marie Jones
               b. 11 March 1927 - Shreveport, La.

            1. Mary Rosa Berryhill
               b. 14 June 1946 - Little Rock, Pulaski Co., Ark.
               m. Michael John Sweeney - 22 December 1966
                  b. 31 August 1944 - Taylor, Columbia Co., Ark.
            2. Mason Otis Berryhill
               b. 24 May 1949 - Little Rock, Pulaski Co., Ark.
            3. Wesley Eugene Berryhill
               b. 16 May 1953 - Little Rock, Pulaski Co., Ark.

        (g) Jewell Grace Berryhill
            b. 16 September 1924 - Saline Co., Ark.
            m. Vadar Winfield Bretton Brown - 14 November 1942
               b. 22 August 1916 - Saline Co., Ark.

            1. Bretton Ervin Brown
               b. 19 September 1943 - Saline Co., Ark.
               m. Mildred Joyce Richey - 20 March 1962

               A. Shelley Janette Brown
                  b. 20 June 1964
               Bretton E. Brown m. 2nd. Patricia Ann Wills

               B. Davis Otis Brown
                  b. 18 July 1967

            2. Karen Lane Brown
               b. 11 December 1945 - Saline Co., Ark.
               m. John William Jones

               A. Johnna Jane Jones
                  b. 23 May 1964
               B. Debra Lynn Jones
                  b. 9 July 1967

            3. Emily Ellen Brown
               b. 12 August 1954
            4. Laura Annette Brown
               b. 11 August 1956

        (h) Edith Marie Berryhill
            b. 25 March 1926 - Bearden, Saline Co., Ark.
            m. Frank Harvey Nash - 9 January 1946
               b. 5 July 1926 - Richmond, Mo.

            1. Susan Marie Nash
               b. 22 June 1947 - Benton, Saline Co., Ark.
               m. Jerry Loyd Melton - 27 April 1963

               A. Amanda Sue Melton
                  b. 7 February 1965

                2. Martha Ann Nash
                      b. 1 February 1949 - Benton, Saline Co., Ark.
                      m. William O'Neal Simpson - 23 July 1965
                3. Loretta Mae Nash
                      b. 21 February 1953 - Benton, Saline Co., Ark.
                4. John Harvey Nash
                      b. 17 December 1957 - "   "   "
                5. Harold Joseph Nash
                      b. 3 February 1965 - "   "   "

          (i) Mary Doris Berryhill
                b. 1 October 1927 - Saline Co., Ark.
                m. Olen May - 29 May 1943
                   b. 25 December 1916 - Saline Co., Ark.

                1. Phillip Don May
                      b. 5 March 1944 - Saline Co., Ark.
                2. Nancy Carole May
                      b. 15 July 1945
                      d. 8 August 1965 - Saline Co., Ark.
                      bur. Mars Hill Cemetery - Saline Co., Ark.
                3. Wayne Edward May
                      b. 16 June 1947 - Saline Co., Ark.
                4. Phyllis Jean May
                      b. 11 January 1950 - Saline Co., Ark.
                5. David Olen May
                      b. 24 April 1951 - Pulaski Co., Ark.
                6. Janis Kay May
                      b. 12 February 1954 - Saline Co., Ark.
                7. James Otis Gary May
                      b. 23 April 1960 - Saline Co., Ark.
                8. Iris Rosella May
                      b. 24 June 1961 - Eddy Co., N. Mex.

          (j) Roberta Jean Berryhill
                b. 17 November 1928 - Saline Co., Ark.
                m. Maurice Oliver Nash - 1 March 1947
                   b. 27 July 1927 - Richmond, Mo.

                1. Robert Dale Nash
                      b. 28 January 1948 - Saline Co., Ark.
                2. Charles Keith Nash
                      b. 1 March 1950 - Saline Co., Ark.

                Roberta Jean Berryhill m. 2nd John William Bethards -
                26 November 1963

                3. Gene Edwards Bethards
                      b. 21 September 1964 - Saline Co., Ark.

          (k) Otis Paul Berryhill
                b. 15 December 1930 - Saline Co., Ark.

K. Benjamin Berry Berryhill
      b. 1855-1856 - Marion Co., Ark.
      d. 1875 approx. - Hinds Co., Miss.
      bur. Weeks Cemetery - Hinds Co., Miss.
      Was accidently killed by a wagon accident when about grown.

      Otis Berryhill can remember when his mother, or perhaps his
      father, died, he lived with "Aunt Martha Adkins."

      From Census, wedding date, & Weeks Cemetery records, I have
      pieced this family together, but I am unable to tell you HOW
      Mary E. (Berryhill) Adkins was his aunt.

      Martha E. Berryhill
      b. 1854
      d. 1913
      m. George W. Adkins - 21 January 1877 - Hinds Co., Miss.
         b. 1855 - Alabama
         d. 1939 - age 84 years - Miss.

         1. Missouri Adkins
            lived 5 months and 4 days

                                    56

```
                    2. Infant Adkins
                    3. Infant Adkins
                    4. Minnie Adkins
                       Lived 1 year, 2 months, and 7 days
                    5. Son  Adkins
                       b. 19 December 1885
                       d. 7 January 1892 (7 Years)
                    6. Alma Adkins
                       b. 11 January 1889
                       d. 24 February 1892 (3 Years)
                    7. Jim Adkins
                       Otis Berryhill can remember his Aunt Martha Adkins
                       had a son named "Jim".

1880 Hinds Co., Miss. Federal Census
Eliza J. Brock   35 F  Miss.   Ala.   Miss.  b. 1845
Holand        "  12 M  Miss.   Ala.   Miss.  b. 1868
Frank H.      "  10 M  Miss.   Ala.   Miss.  b. 1870
Elizabeth     "   8 M  Miss.   Ala.   Miss.  b. 1872
Conrad        "   4 M  Miss.   Ala.   Miss.  b. 1874


George Adkins    25 M. Ala.   Tenn.   Tenn.  b. 1855
Martha E.     "  24 F   "     Ala.     "       1856
Thomas M.     "  21 M   "     Tenn.    "       1859
Rufus         "  19 M   "      "       "       1861
Sallie Berryhill 70 F  Tenn.  Va.    N. C.     1810 (Mother-in-law)
```

There is a possibility that Sallie Berryhill came from Tenn. to Ala. and
on to Hinds Co., Miss. to join kin and we do not know who her husband was.
I even wonder can Sallie be the widow of Lensfield Berryhill of Franklin
Co., Tenn? Her age in in that favor.

```
Cornelius Goodrum 52 M.  b. 1828
Sorrey           "  36 F    1844
Clarence         "  17 M    1863
Ancy C.          "  12 F    1868
Laura J.         "  10 M    1870
Agnes L.         "   7 F    1873 (m. Arther Erastus Berryhill)
Susan M.         "   6 F    1874 (m. John Adam Berryhill)
Cora R.          "   2 F    1878
Julia W. Goodrum 2/12 F     1880
```

        L. Nathan A. Berryhill
           b. 1857 - Marion Co., Ala.
           d. August 1894 - Hinds Co., Miss.
           bur. Weeks Cemetery - Hinds Co., Miss.
           m. Agnes J. Bryant - "Aggie" - 28 April 1886 - Lafayette Co. MS
              b.
              d. 26 August 1936 - near Abbott, Ark.
              bur. -?- Cemetery - Pleasant Grove, Ark.

           (1) Harvey Oscar Berryhill
               b. 1892 - making him the second child.
               m. ?

               (a) June Berryhill
               (b) Thelma Berryhill (twin) & her twin deceased as an
                   infant.
                   m. -?- Edwards

                   1. Delores Edwards
                      b. 1930 approx.
                   2. Jackie Edwards
                      b. 1932 approx.
                   3. Jeanie Edwards
                      b. 1936 approx.

               Thelma Berryhill m. 2nd Lee Myers
               Harvey Berrhill m. 2nd. Pearl -?- (sister to his 1st wife)

               (c) Margarete Berryhill
               (d) Dorothy Berryhill m. Wonk Able

                                57
```
```

(2) Addie Viola Berryhill - "Ola"
    b. 6 April 1890 - Oxford, Miss.
    d. 8 September 1965 - Tulsa, Okla.
    bur. Greenhill Cemetery - Muskogee, Okla.
    m. Noah Adolphus Eskridge
       b. 25 September 1885 - Hackett, Ark.

    (a) Bertha Paulene Eskridge
        b. 20 June 1908 - Talihina, Okla.
        m. Dewey S. Howard
    (b) Margaret Irene Eskridge
        b. 9 November 1909 - Talihina, Okla.
        m. Irvin T. Moxley
    (c) Mildred Louise Eskridge
        b. 22 February 1913 - Ft. Smith, Ark.
        d. 27 January 1936 -
        bur. Greenhill Cemetery - Muskogee, Okla.
        m. Scott Cochran

        1. Donald Gilbert Cochran
           b. 7 April 1932

    (d) Nathan Thomas Eskridge
        b. 9 April 1919 - Muskogee, Okla.
        m. Thelma Leona Hunt - 10 July 1945
           b. 17 January 1921 - Muskogee, Okla.

        1. Paul Nathan Eskridge
           b. 19 November 1946
        2. Carolyn Joyce Eskridge
           b. 31 October 1949

    (e) Noah Adolphus Eskridge, Jr.
        b. 7 June 1924 - Muskogee, Okla.
        m. Mildred Rock
           b.   Brinkley, Ark.

        1. Ronald Eskridge
           b. 1947 - approx.
        2. Richard Eskridge
           b. 1950 - approx.
        3. Randall Eskridge
           b. 1953 - approx.

    (f) William David Eskridge
        b. 12 July 1924 - Muskogee, Okla.
        m. Evelyn (Cook) Treadwell - 9 September 1948
           b. 26 December 1926

        1. Rex (Treadwell) Eskridge
           b. 1947 - approx.
        2. Debbie Eskridge
           b. 1950 - approx.
        3. David Eskridge
           b. 1960 - approx.

(3) Nathan Basil Berryhill
    b. 17 April 1894 - Lafayette Co., Miss.
    m. Nora Ludie Hearin
       b. 28 August 1900 - Paris, Texas

    (a) Opal Venita Berryhill
        b. 27 July 1921 - Morris, Okla.
        d.   July 1943 - Russell, Kansas
        bur. City Cemetery, Russell, Kansas
    (b) Irma Christine Berryhill
        b. 13 April 1923 - Morris, Okla.
        m. Frederick Lawrence Tillotson
           b. 3 July 1913 - Battle Creek, Iowa

        1. June Ovina Tillotson
           b. 1 June 1947 - Harris Co., Texas
           m. Ronald McWatters
              b. 3 May 1946 - Atlanta, Ga.

58

            A. Christine Loraine McWatters
                b. 6 September 1966 - Atlanta, Ga.

        2. Joan Christine Tillotson
            b. 4 September 1948 - Kingsley, Iowa
            m. Bruce Wayne Standlee
                b. 13 March 1947 - Great Bend, Kansas

            A. Ronald Alan Standlee
                b. 13 February 1968 - Great Bend, Kansas

    (c) William Nathan Berryhill
        b. 20 December 1925 - Wynona, Okla.
        m. Carol Mayse Cochrun

        1. Brenda Sue Berryhill
            b. 6 September 1952 - Lucas, Kansas
        2. Donna Mae Berryhill
            b. 2 August 1954 - Lucas, Kansas
        3. Elizabeth Ann Berryhill
            b. 12 February 1956 - Lucas, Kansas
        4. James Nathan Berryhill
            b. 20 April 1958 - Lucas, Kansas

    (d) Helen Mae Berryhill
        b. 27 January 1930 - Wynonna, Okla.
        m. Kenneth Standlee - 29 June 1946
            b. 4 February 1929 - Winfield, Kansas

        1. Jerry Mitchell Standlee
            b. 25 May 1947 - Russell, Kan.
            m. Linda Ann Berger

            A. Colleen Marie Standlee
                b. 27 June 1966

        2. Curtis Alan Standlee
            b. 14 January 1952 - Hays, Kansas
        3. Ricky Len Standlee
            b. 11 April 1959 - Plainville, Kan.

    (e) Donald Ray Berryhill
        b. 27 January 1936 - McPherson, Kan.
        m. Patricia Lee - 6 April 1956
            b. 24 November 1935 - LaGrange, Oregon

        1. Christina Lee Berryhill
            b. 2 January 1957 - Sacramento, Calif.
        2. Sheri Lynn Berryhill
            b. 6 August 1958 - Roseville, Calif.
        3. Catherine Ann Berryhill
            b. 10 October 1959 - Roseville, Calif.
        4. Deborah Kay Berryhill
            b. 29 January 1961 - Roseville, Calif.

In weeks Cemetery, we find:
Nathan A. Berryhill
b. 29 January 1855
d. 11 December 1935
We hope to re-check the marker with chalk dust at a future date to see
was an error possibly make on the death date.

    M. Monroe Jasper Berryhill - "Tony"
        b. 24 November 1858 - Marion Co., Ala.
        d. 21 November 1948 - Westbrook, Texas
        bur. Lueders Cemetery - 1½ miles S. of Leuders, Texas
        "Tony" taught school in Indian Territory Oklahoma!
        m. Mrs. Relia Midcalf (Bishop) Slack - 21 July 1908 - Shackleford
            County, Texas
            b. 22 March 1877 - Palo Pinto Co, Texas
            d. 31 January 1939 - Lueders, Texas
            bur. Lueders Cemetery
            dau. of Joe Bishop & Lizzie DeRossitt

(1) Ora Odella Berryhill
    b. 5 January 1910 - Lueders, Texas
    m. Marvin Earl Casbeer - 19 June 1926 - Jones Co, Texas
       b. 13 February 1906 - Mills Co., Texas
       d. 16 November 1975

    (a) Jasper Earl Casbeer
        b. 24 November 1927 - Leuders, Jones Co., Texas
        m. Mary Katherine Lorde - 16 December 1949

        1. Dana Earl Cashbeer
           b. 20 May 1966 - Angleton, Texas

    (b) Jean Elwood Casbeer
        b. 29 September 1929 - N. Mex.
        m. John Ervin Mashburn - 13 November 1947 - Merkle, Tex.
           b. 14 May 1927
        m. 2nd. J. M. Edwards - 2 June 1961
              b. 8 July 1927 - Love Co., Okla.

        1. John Ervin Mashburn, Jr.
           b. 19 April 1949 - Colorado City, Texas
           m. Annie Ruth Green - 2 June 1980
              b. 16 January 1953
              She had a child Amy Ruth Green b. 4 September 1971
        2. Mitchell David Mashburn
           b. 11 November 1950
           m. Juhree Ann Johnson - September 21, 1974
              b. 10 May 1951

           A. John Clinton
              b. 21 September 1971
           B. Casey Casbeer
              b. 22 July 1977
           C. David Cody
              b. 20 February 1980

        3. Beverly Jean Mashburn
           b. 22 December 1951 - Tokaho, Lynn Co., Texas
        4. Brenda Kay Mashburn
           b. 10 August 1956 - San Saba, Texas
        5. Bruce Jay Edwards
           b. 11 December 1964 - Midland, Texas

    (c) Joyce Edwin Casbeer
        b. 11 March 1932 - Goldthwaite, Mills Co, Texas
        m. Barbetta Kendall - 31 July 1953 - Carson City, Nev.
           b. 19 August 1934 - Lampoc, Calif.

        1. Bob Edwin Cashbeer
           b. 5 February 1956 - Willington, Tenn.
        2. Rex Alan Casbeer
           b. 11 February 1958 - Oakland, Calif.
        3. Keith Waine Casbeer
           b. 2 November 1960 - San Jose, Calif.

    (d) Jessie Elmon Casbeer
        b. 25 January 1923 - Anson, Jones Co., Texas
        m. Viva Newman - 18 July 1953 - Abilene, Texas
        m. 2nd. Leta Aline Turner - 5 November 1955
           b. 30 October 1929 - Floydada, Texas

        1. Shelia Ann Casbeer
           b. 7 February 1954 - Glen Rose, Texas
           m. Steven Harold Klucker
              b. 12 January 1950

           A. Sarah Jean Klucker
              b. 29 November 1975
           B. Steven Michael Klucker
              b. 5 October 1980

        2. Clifton Ray Casbeer
           b. 5 August 1956 - Lubbock, Texas
           d. 25 December 1977

3. Ginger Lee Casbeer
   b. 5 October 1955
   m. -?- Miller
   m. 2nd. James C. Knight - February 1978
   A. Amanda Lee Miller
      b. 11 December 1975
   B. Keith Alan Miller
      b. 28 November 1976

   Ginger Lee Casbeer m. 2nd. James C. Knight -
   February 1978

(e) Jo-Evelyn Casbeer
    b. 21 December 1936 - Goldwaite, Mills Co., Texas
    m. Thomas Clayton Garvin - 9 October 1953 - Jones Co, TX
    son of Leon and Lessie Blackely Garvin

    1. Julia Lanette Garvin
       b. 4 July 1957 - Wurtzburg, Germany
          m. Michael Terrell - 1 August 1976

       A. Joshua Evan Terrell
          b. 5 December 1978

    2. Alisa Jo Garvin
       b. 19 October 1959
       m. David Wayne Lander - 28 December 1978

       A. Jo Nichelle Lander
          b. 25 January 1981

    3. Karen Jean Garvin
       b. 11 July 1961 - Midland, Texas
    4. Donna Alene Garvin
       b. 25 May 1964 - Midland, Texas

(f) Julia Elizabeth Casbeer
    b. 4 January 1939 - Goldwaithe, Texas
    m. Floyd Jerry Watts - 20 December 1953 - Abilene, Texas
    b. 29 November 1935 - Carpenters Gap, Texas

    1. Lance Edward Watts
       b. 15 October 1956 - Abilene, Texas
       m. Cheryl Lamar - 6 September 1980

       A. Dallas Lamar
       B. Daniel Lamar Watts
          b. 13 February 1981

    2. Juanell Devone Watts
       b. 22 March 1959 - Abilene, Texas
    3. Terry Delane Watts
       b. 5 October 1963 - Abilene, Texas
       m. Mark Watson Miller - 6 June 1981

(g) Jerry Eli Casbeer
    b. 4 March 1941 - Goldwaithe, Mills Co., Texas
    m. Betty Eula Cross - 16 October 1962 - Durant, Okla.
    b. 4 December 1943 - Okla.
    dau. of Tom Cross & Ida Branch - 1902 - 1967

    1. Mark Edward Casbeer
       b. 8 April 1963 - Stanton, Texas
       d. 1970
    2. Thomas Earl Casbeer (twin)
       b. 14 April 1964 - Midland, Texas
    3. Joseph Earl Casbeer - (twin)
       b. 14 April 1964 - Midland, Texas
       d. 15 April 1964 - Midland, Texas
    4. Jason Eldon Casbeer (twin)
       b. 17 June 1966 - Los Angeles, Calif.
    5. Belinda Elizabeth Casbeer (twin)
       b. 17 June 1966 - Los Angeles, Calif.

(2) Thomas Marshall Berryhill
    b. 28 April 1911 - Lueders, Jones Co, Texas
    m. Jessie Belle Shelley - 31 May 1939 - Jones Co., Texas
       b. 24 September 1920 - Whitney, Hill Co., Texas
       dau. of J. Earl Shelley & Fannie Mae Petty

    (a) Gary Marshall Berryhill
        b. 8 August 1941 - Stanford, Texas
    (b) Olga Bleassia Berryhill
        b. 22 March 1956 - Stanford, Texas
        m. Johnny Albert Wyatt - 1 December 1974

        1. Chris Wyatt
           b. 26 June 1976
        2. Aaron Blake Wyatt
           b. 13 April 1980

(3) Nellie D. Berryhill
    b. 22 October 1916 - Lueders, Jones Co., Texas
    m. Loyd David Walls - 4 February 1933 - Lueders, Texas
       b. 9 November 1908 - Aquilla, McClennon Co., Texas

    (a) Nellie August Walls
        b. 3 January 1934   d. 3 January 1934
    (b) Loyd David Walls, Jr.
        b. 28 February 1935 d. 1 March 1935
    (c) Glenda Faye Walls
        b. 6 March 1937 - Lueders, Texas
        m. James Ray Cox - 4 June 1955 - Lueders, Texas
           b. 13 January 1936 - Stephenville, Texas

        1. Teresa Gean Cox
           b. 30 July 1956 - Hondo, Texas
           m. Vance Roderick Talley - 19 November 1976 -
              Cleburne, Texas

           A. David Lex Lucas Talley
              b. 1 June 1978 - College Station, Texas
           B. Amelia Elizabeth Talley
              b. 5 April 1980 - Childress, Texas

        2. Darla Faye Cox
           b. 17 April 1958 - Stamford, Texas
           m. Dante Reed Frisbie - 24 September 1977 - Childress
              b. 26 August 1956

           A. Samantha Paige
              b. 27 October 1980 - Childress, Texas

        3. Lori Susanne Cox
           b. 20 December 1960 - Stamford, Texas
           m. Ted Neal Phillips - 27 December 1980 - Memphis, TX
              b. 17 July 1958
        4. Matthew Neal Cox
           b. 25 August 1976 - Cleburne, Texas
        5. Molly Ranell Cox
           b. 28 January 1979 - Childress, Texas

    (d) Arla Gean Walls
        b. 1 June 1941 - Stamford, Jones Co., Texas
        m. Marlin D. Felts - 24 January 1964 - Lueders, Texas
           b. 7 October 1938 - Lueders, Texas

        1. David Drea Felts
           b. 4 November 1965 - Stamford, Texas
        2. Marty Lance Felts
           b. 23 February 1969 - Abilene, Taylor Co, Texas
        3. Marlin Blake Felts
           b. 9 June 1972 - Abilene, Texas

Song or Poem
Found in possession of "Tony" Berryhill

Farewell, Farewell to all below
My Savior calls, and I must go
I launch my boat upon the sea
This land is not the land for me.

I've found the rugged paths of sin
A rugged way to travel in
Beyond this chilly wave I see
The land my Savior bought for me.

Oh! sinner, why will you not go
There's room enough for you I know
Our boat is sound, and passage free
And, there's a better land for thee.

That land is on the other shore
Where angels sing forever more
Where seraphs bow, and bend the knee
Oh that's the land for me.

Farewell, dear friends I may not stay
The land I seek is far away
Where Christ is not, I cannot be
Oh there's a better land for me.

No night is there, 'this always day
And God will wipe all tears away
Those pearly gates are open free
That surely is the land for me.

N. Mary Margaret Berryhill - "Mollie"
   b. 1862 - Marion Co., Ala.
   d. 1946 - Durango, Colo (living 21 November 1921 in Durango.)
   bur.
   m. Rufus B. Naudock (Naudack)

   (1). Rufus Naudock
   (2) Lester Naudock
   (3) James Naudock
   (4) Mamie Naudock m. -?- Bergerhoff & lived in Memphis, TN in 1966
   (5) Katie Naudock m. -?- Schockley & lived in Memphis, TN in 1966
   (6) Cala Willie Naudock

O. Elviria Berryhill - "Eggie"
   b. 1864 - Marion Co., Ala.
   d. 1931 - Miss.
   bur.
   m. Daniel Hubert Stewart - "Bud"
      b. 1860 - Ala.
      d. 1942 - Miss.
      bur.

   (1) Bob Stewart (I wrote him and my letter did not return, yet
       he did not reply.)
   (2) Son
   (3) Daughter
   (4) Daughter

P. Willis Robin Berryhill
   b. 7 September 1865 - Ear, Fayette Co., Ala.
   d. 22 September 1951 - Overton, Texas
   bur. Antlers Cemetery - Antlers, Okla.
   m. Margaret Elizabeth Garner - 20 June 1886 - Lafayette Co., MS.
      b. 10 April 1871 - Yalobusha Co, Miss.
      d. 10 January 1951 - Antlers, Okla.
      bur. Antlers Cemetery
      dau. of Johnithan Nance Garner & Charlotte Lewis
      Some say his name was W. Adam Nance. C. Lewis b. 19 March 1850
      Nance b. 18 August 1847 d. 11 August 1887   d. 12 Nov. 1915

   (1) Walter Berryhill
       b. 2 April 1888 - Yalobusha Co., Miss.
       d.   November 1914 - Tula, Miss area
       bur. Paris Cemetery - Tula (others say Potlochney Cemetery)
       m. Edna Binson - 12 May 1909

       (a) Willie Berryhill
           b. 1911 approx - Miss.
       (b) Johnnie Berryhill
           b. 1913 approx. - Miss.
       (c) Andrew Jackson Berryhill
           b. 1914 approx. - Miss.

       Edna came to Texas with the children after he died, and all
       contacts seem to be lost.

   (2) Charles Monroe Berryhill - "Charlie"
       b. 5 April 1890 - Lafayette Co., Miss.
       d. 7 January 1966 - Memphis, Tenn.
       bur. Memorial Park Cemetery - Memphis, Tenn.
       m. Vernor Steward - 8 January 1914 - Lafayette Co., Miss.
          b. 25 August 1896 - Moscow, Tenn.

       (a) Margaret Louise Berryhill
           b. 16 May 1919 - Antlers, Okla.
           m. John E. Hundley - 21 December 1941

           1. John Cornelius Hundley
              b. & d. 24 July 1943 - Memphis, Tenn.
              bur. Memorial Park Cemetery - Memphis, Tenn.

           Margaret L. Berryhill m. 2nd. Jess E. Carr - 29 October
           1955

    (b) Katherine Berryhill
        b. 31 March 1924 - Memphis, Tenn.
        m. Nathaniel G. Amend - 4 June 1945 - McAlester, Okla.
          b. 28 September 1924 - Antlers, Okla.

        1. Kathy Jo Amend
          b. 6 October 1956 - Memphis, Tenn.

(3) John Cecil Berryhill
    b. 9 July 1892 - Lafayette Co., Miss.
    d. 27 November 1952 - Antlers, Okla.
    bur. Antlers Cemetery
    m. Vera Steward - 9 December 1917 - Springfield, Mo.
      b. April 1898 - Moscow, Tenn.

    (a) Blois Lee Berryhill
        b. 1920 - Antlers, Okla.
        m. Mary Jo -?-

        1. Jimmy Berryhill
          b. 1949 - approx. - Calif.

    (b) Daughtrey Nell Berryhill
        b. 5 March 1925 - Antlers, Okla.
        m. Foster Calvin Berry - 30 June 1946

        1. Peggy Janet Berry
          b. 16 April 1950 - Antlers, Okla.
        2. Foster Calvin Berry, Jr.
          b. 2 May 1954
          d. 3 May 1954
        3. David Ray Berry
          b. 3 May 1961 - Antlers, Okla.

    (c) Glena Fay Berryhill (twin)
        b. 25 July 1931 - Antlers, Okla.
        m. John Huckabay

        1. Johnnie Huckabay
          b. 1957
        2. Janie Huckabay
          b. 1955

    (d) Billy Ray Berryhill (twin)
        b. 25 July 1931 - Antlers, Okla.
        m. Wanda Fay Melton - 14 October 1955 - Pushamataha Co, OK
          b. 28 October 1933 - Carter Co., Okla.

        1. Kenneth Michael Berryhill
          b. 25 October 1965 - Alameda Co., Calif.
        2. Calvin Lee Berryhill
          b. 19 February 1968 - Alameda Co, Calif.

(4) Bulah Lottie Berryhill
    b. 23 August 1894 - Lafayette Co., Miss.
    m. Carl Gossett - 4 June 1917 - Antlers, Okla.

    (a) Dorothy Carlton Gossett
        b. 12 May 1918 - Antlers, Okla.
        m. A. W. Nussbaumer

        1. Steven Nusshaumer
          d. Fall of 1968 - Viet Nam
        2. Pat Husshaumer
        3. Michelle Nusshaumer

    (b) Dehnere Clarence Gossett
        b. 27 January 1921 - Antlers, Okla.
        m. Juanita Logan
    (c) Louie Edwin Gossett
        b. 22 November 1923 - Antlers, Okla.

(5) Zula Berryhill
    b. 19 September 1896 - Yalobusha Co., Miss.
    d. 20 July 1907 - Abilene, Texas
    bur. Ft. Phantom Hill Cemetery - Jones Co., Texas

(6) Bertha Irene Berryhill
    b. 13 June 1899 - Yalobusha Co., Miss.
    m. Fred Norwood - 7 December 1917 - Fort Worth, Texas
       d. Fall of 1968

    (a) Freda Irene Norwood
        b. 10 September 1918 -
        d. 1958
        m. Howard Wright

        1. Janice Wright
           m. Billy Dee White - 1966

           A. Dee Ann White
              b. 1967

    (b) Reba LaRue Norwood
        b. 1923 approx.
        m. A. J. Tatum

        1. Jay Tatum

(7) Preston Wayne Berryhill
    b. 11 January 1902 - McIntosh Co., Okla.
    m. Exie Perrin - 9 April 1932
       b. 16 September 1905 - Sulphur Springs, Texas
       d. 23 September 1963 - Paris, Texas
       bur. Odd Fellows Cemetery - Antlers, Okla.

    (a) Betty Jane Berryhill
        b. 14 July 1938 - Paris, Texas
        d. 11 August 1940 - Paris, Texas
        bur. Odd Fellows Cemetery - Antlers, Okla.

    Preston W. Berryhill m. 2nd Eloise Redman - 3 June 1968
                            b. 26 December 1911 - Sulphur,
                               Okla.

(8) Jessie Hugh Berryhill
    b. 15 June 1904 - Hitchita, Indian Territory Oklahoma in
                      Creek Nation
    m. Venus Julia Teems - 13 October 1924

(9) Ruby Mae Berryhill
    b. 5 July 1913 - Lafayette Co., Miss.
    m. Douglas Conger - 18 April 1935
       b. 7 March 1912 - Kiowa, Okla.

    (a) Robert Douglas Conger
        b. 19 June 1944 - Merced, Calif.
        m. Shelia Mae Oliver - 2 May 1964
           b. 3 January 1946 - Merced, Calif.

        1. Sheri Lynn Conger
           b. 29 May 1966 - Merced, Calif.
        2. Robinette Louise Conger
           b. 5 May 1969 - Merced, Calif.

Q. M. A. Berryhill (female)
   b. 1867 - Fayette Co., Ala.
   Living age 3 years on 1870 census, but apparently died young
   as no one remembers her. I do wish census takers would not
   have used initials so much!

R. Polk Dallas Berryhill
   b. 6 September 1869 - Marion Co., Ala.
   d. 21 September 1955 - Hitchita, Okla.
   bur. Hitchita Lackey Cemetery - Hitchita, McIntosh Co, Okla.
   m. Susie Anner Colista Foshee
      b. 9 August 1871 - Ala.
      d. 7 September 1899 - near Hitchita, Okla. (died of German
         measles)
      bur. Hitchita Lackey Cemetery

(1) Isobenda Berryhill - "Iso"
    b. 22 November 1897 - McIntosh Co., Cemetery
    m. Waldow F. Toliver
       b. 1891
       d. 31 July 1868 - LaJolla, Calif.
       bur. Hitchita Lackey Cemetery - Hitchita, Okla.

    (a) Faron Toliver
        m. Lucille Storm

        1. Linda Toliver
        2. Tolley Toliver
        3. Terri Toliver

    (b) Fern Toliver
        m. Don Bradshaw

        1. Freddie Bradshaw

(2) Infant Daughter
    b. & d. September 1899 - McIntosh Co., Okla.
    bur. Hitchita Lackey Cemetery - Hitchita, Okla.

Polk D. Berryhill m. 2nd. Cora Estella Jackson - 12 December 1900
                   McIntosh Co., Okla.
                   b. 22 April 1884 - Wright Co., Mo.
                   dau. of Joel V. Jackson & Elizabeth Wynder

(3) Infant Daughter
    b. 16 November 1901
    d. 24 November 1901 - McIntosh Co., Okla.
    bur. Hitchita Lackey Cemetery

(4) Flossie Elvira Berryhill
    b. 22 October 1902 - McIntosh Co., Okla.
    m. W. T. "Jack" Houston

(5) Audria May Berryhill
    b. 20 May 1904 - McIntosh Co., Okla.
    d. 10 August 1907 - McIntosh Co., Okla.
    bur. Hitchita Lackey Cemetery
(6) Owen Dallas Berryhill
    b. 22 September 1907 - McIntosh Co., Okla.
    m. Mattie Allison

    (a) James Owen Berryhill
        b. 1 November 1933
        m. Betty Appleton
        1. Jamie Berryhill
           b. 30 March 1953
        2. Mary Berryhill
           b. 16 June 1959
        3. Nancy Berryhill
           b. 24 May 1962

    (b) Carolyn Sue Berryhill
        b. 14 January 1936
        m. Bill Max Geron

        1. Michael Kraig Geron
           b. 21 September 1956
        2. Timothy Brent Geron
           b. 19 April 1959

(7) Joel Alvin Berryhill
    b. 14 February 1915 - McIntosh Co., Okla.
    m. Undine Hall

    (a) Joel A. Berryhill, Jr.
        b. 5 March 1946
    (b) Jana Berryhill
        b. 17 July 1948
    (c) Bill Hall Berryhill
        b. 13 November 1951

(8) Helen Venita Berryhill
    b. 2 April 1917 - McIntosh Co., Okla.
    m. Edwin Cook
        b. 6 September 1915

    (a) Charlene Nell Cook
        b. 25 February 1939
        m. John Wesley Reynolds

        1. Dwight David Reynolds
           b. 28 August 1960
        2. Michael Kent Reynolds
           b. 12 May 1962

    (b) Edwina Lee Cook
        b. 27 January 1947

(9) Elizabeth Wynona Berryhill
    b. 19 August 1922 - Hitchita, Okla.
    m. Buford Parker
        b. 2 January 1918

    (a) Shirley Ann Parker
        b. 9 September 1937
        m. Leon Goddard

        1. Steven Leon Goddard
           b. 10 September 1959
        2. Bryan Goddard
           b. 20 October 1962
        3. LyAnn Goddard
           b. 5 February 1965

    (b) Harold Buford Parker
        b. 29 October 1938
        m. Ruth Bledsoe

        1. Sharolyn Sue Parker
           b. 16 December 1959
        2. Patricia Ruth Parker
           b. 29 November 1962
        3. Harold B. Parker, Jr.
           b. 29 July 1964

S. Austin Berryhill
   I did not find him on census, but Mr. Will Price lists him as
   dying young.
   b. 1870 approx.
   bur. Weeks Cemetery

T. Infant Son Berryhill
   b. & d. 1872 approx.
   bur. Weeks Cemetery - Hinds Co., Miss.
   It is said William Berryhill, II had 20 children between the
   two wives.

1830 Marion Co., Ala. Federal Census (taken every 10 years)
William Berryhill, II
1 male 15/20 (1810 -1815) Cannot account for him unless a brother of
                          Elizabeth Gage.
1 male 20/30 (1800-1810) William Berryhill, II
1 female under 5 years of age (Nancy E. b. 1829)
1 female 20/30 (1800-1810) Elizabeth Gage, 1st wife.

1840 Marion Co., Ala. Federal Census - page 58
William Berryhill II
1 male 30/40 (1800-1810) William Berryhill, II or "Bill Dergin"
2 females 10/15 (1830-1835)
1 female 20/30 (1810-1820) Elizabeth Gage, 1st wife

```
1850 Marion Co., Ala. Federal Census   83/84
William Berryhill, II    41 M.   Ga.    b. 1809  (Elizabeth Gage Berryhill
Priscilla        "       18 F    Ala.      1832   has deceased)
James C.         "       16 M     "        1834
Mary             "       13 F     "        1837
Thomas           "       11 M     "        1839
Newton           "        9 M     "        1841
Charley          "        6 M     "        1844
Martha Ann       "        5 M     "        1845
```

```
1860 Marion Co., Ala. Federal Census 75/78 page 11
P. O. Astons Store, Ala   14 June 1860
William Berryhill II     50 M    Ga.   b. 1810
Nancy            "       27 F    Tenn.    1833  (2nd wife, Nancy Adeline
Newton           "       18 M    Ala.     1842   Andleton)
Charles          "       16 M     "       1844
Martha A.        "       15 F     "       1845
```

Due to a fire at Marion Co., Ala. Courthouse, all old records were
destroyed, and no marriage date could be found, but we know he married
Nancy A. Andleton after the 1850 census was taken, but apparently they
married in 1851, as first issue by Nancy was born in 1852. The following
are issues by Nancy.

```
William Berryhill III     8 M    Ala.  b. 1852
Alexander        "        6 M     "       1854
Benjamin         "        5 M     "       1855
Nathan           "        3 M     "       1857
Monroe           "     8/12 M     "       1859
```

```
1870 Fayette Co., Ala. Federal Census 29/29 Page 6   3 October 1870
Township #13, Range #12, P. O. New River, Ala.
William Berryhill, II    60 M    Ga.   b. 1810
Nancy            "       37 F    Tenn.    1833
William        ", III    18 M    Ala.     1852
Abram            "       16 M     "       1854
Berry            "       14 M     "       1856
Nathan           "       12 M     "       1858
Monroe           "       10 M     "       1860
Margaret         "        8 F     "       1862
Elijah           "        6 M     "       1864
R. W.            "        5 M     "       1865
M. A.            "        3 F     "       1867
Polk             "        1 M     "       1869
```

Apparently soon after census was taken in 1870, the family moved to
Hinds County, Miss.

    3. James Berryhill - "Dominicker"
       b. 1812 - Jefferson Co., Ga.
       d. 1859/1860 - Marion Co., Ala.
       bur. Believed to be in Mulberry Hollow Cemetery, often called
       "Berryhill Buring Grounds" in Marion Co., Ala.
       m. Patience C. McMinn - "Passie" - 1831/1832 - Marion Co., Ala.
          b. 1819/1820 - S. Car. or St. Calir, Co., Ala (Both on Census)
          d. Fall of 1864/1865 - Marion Co., Ala.
          bur. Assumed in Mulberry Hollow Cemetery - Marion Co., Ala.
          dau. of William Abraham McMinn & Mary Margaret Byars

       A. Nancy Jane Berryhill
          b. 1833 - Marion Co., Ala.
       B. Mary Ann Berryhill
          b. 1834 - Marion Co., Ala.
       C. William Berryhill
          b. 1835 - Marion Co., Ala.
       D. Susan Catherine Berryhill
          b. 1837 - Marion Co., Ala.
       E. Hannah A. Berryhill
          b. 1839 - Marion Co., Ala.
       F. Sarah Elizabeth Berryhill
          b. 1841 - Marion Co., Ala.
```
```

G. Margaret Berryhill
   b. 1843 - Marion Co., Ala.
H. James K. Polk Berryhill
   b. 1845 - Marion Co., Ala.
I. Drucilla C. Berryhill
   b. 1853 - Marion Co., Ala.
J. Martha F. Berryhill
   b. 1855 - Marion Co., Ala.
K. Rachel Louise Berryhill
   b. 1858 - Marion Co., Ala.

"Passie" (McMinn) Berryhill is said to have had the longest and
most beautiful hair!

1850 Marion Co., Ala. Federal Census

James Berryhill	"	38 M	Ga.	b. 1812	Farmer $350.00
Patsey C.	"	30 F	Ala.	1820	
Nancy Jane	"	17 F	"	1833	
Mary Ann	"	16 F	"	1834	
William	"	15 M	"	1835	
Catherine	"	13 F	"	1837	
Hannah	"	11 F	"	1839	
Sarah E.	"	9 F	"	1841	
Margaret	"	7 F	"	1843	
James K. P.	"	5 M	"	1845	

1860 Marion Co., Ala. Federal Census 80/84

Patsey Berryhill		49 F	S.C.	b. 1811	(James is deceased)
Mary	"	24 F	Ala.	1836	
Susan C.	"	20 F	"	1840	
Hannah A.	"	18 F	"	1842	
Sarah E.	"	16 F	"	1844	
Margaret	"	13 F	"	1847	
James K. Polk	"	12 M	"	1848	
Drucilla C.	"	8 F	"	1852	
Martha F.	"	5 F	"	1855	
Rachel L.	"	2 F	"	1858	
William	"	23 M	"	1837	

There is a collection of family history on the family of James Berryhill
and several versions of each story. Much of this family is estimated, due
to no records of proof.

The story goes that James Berryhill acquired the nickname of "Dominicker"
because he was evidentially quite a "scraper", and a fight eventually
led to his death.

I am told when his youngest child, Rachel Louise Berryhill was about 1½
to 2 years old, her father got into a fight with Jerry Hunt at a county
store. He whipped Jerry "fair and square", but Jerry left for home and
got his gun and hid by the side of the road where he knew James Berryhill
would travel going to his home. As James Berryhill rode by Jerry Hunt
shot him. It is not known if he died immediately, but some say he crawled
and tried to get out of the woods for help, leaving a trail of blood.

Jerry Hunt is said to have taken off for Texas after the shooting, with
James Berryhill's son, James K. Polk Berryhill, vowing to find Jerry
Hunt and kill him.

I have learned from some of the Berryhill kin in Texas that one night a
cowboy rode into town where Jerry Hunt was, shot Jerry five times, and
rode on out. They say "we don't know for sure, but we believe it was
Uncle Polk."

At some point "in the game", James K. Polk Berryhill lost an eye in a
fight with another cowboy. But back in the 1870's, there seemd to be
fighting just as it is today.

There seems to be two opinions as to where, and how, the wife of James
Berryhill, Patience "Passie" (McMinn) Berryhill died and was buried.

One version is that Passie had sold out and was going to Texas with her
son Polk, and had traveled as far as Pontotoc, Mississippi, where she
died of smallpox and is buried. Another version is "a negro man had
been put off a ship with smallpox and as he traveled to his destination,
he stopped at "Passie's" well and drank water, no doubt from her dipper.
Then Passie and her daughter, Susan Catherine Berryhill both took smallpox, but were about well when they went out and picked cotton one day,
and a cold, blowing rain came up and both had complications from smallpox
and died in Marion Co., Alabama??

Much research was done on this family after I lost them after 1850 and
1860 Marion County, Alabama census. Not knowing then that James and
Passie both were dead, and it is much harder to follow the females unless
one knows who they married. Since Marion County Courthouse had suffered
a fire, all old records were lost. So by the time I had collected every
Berryhill I could find, and corresponded with, several others who were
working on the lines, I finally found a lead on this family and find
many of them live in Texas today as well as many still in Marion County,
and Fayette County, Alabama.

I am told the land owned by James and Patience (McMinn) Berryhill was
lost in some way, and that part of the town of Winfield, Alabama today
sits on the very land they once owned. About 1910 Polk Berryhill and his
sister, Nancy Jane (Berryhill) Harper came back to Alabama from Texas and
Oklahoma and entered suit trying to recover the land, but were unable to
accomplish this.

3. James Berryhill
    b. 1812 - Jefferson Co, Ga.
    d. 1859-1860 - Marion Co., Ala.
    bur. Mulberry Hollow Cemetery - Marion Co., Ala. (many believe)
    m. Patience C. McMinn -"Passie"
       b. 1819/1820
       d. Fall of 1864/1865
       bur. Assumed in mulberry Hollow Cemetery
       dau. of William Abraham McMinn & Mary Margaret Byars

    A. Nancy Jane Berryhill
       b. 1833 - Marion Co., Ala.
       d. March 1916 - Childress Co., Texas, just across from Newlin,TX
       bur. Newlin Cemetery - Newlin, Hall Co., Texas
       m. Josiah H. Harper - 1857 approx. - Marion Co., Ala.
          b. 1826 - Tenn.
          d. Before census taking time of 1870 - Marion Co., Ala.
          bur. gravesite unknown
          Is said to have been a "home guard", and made shoes for Army.
          son of Thomas Harper & Mary -?-
                  b. 1803 - VA   b. 1807 - Tenn.
                  both living in 1860 census

       (1) Mary Harper
           b. 1858 - Marion Co., Ala.
           Little is remembered of her, except she did marry and died
           very young leaving two small children.

       (2) Thomas W. Harper - "Tom"
           b. 1861 - Marion Co., Ala.
           d. 1953 approx. - near Birmingham, Ala.
           m. Georgiann Tucker

           (a) Texanna Harper
               b. 1885/1890 approx.
               m. John Tucker

               1. Beatrice Tucker
                  m. -?- Glover
                  m. 2nd. -?- Wright

           (b) Johnny Harper
           (c) Gus Harper

           No contacts could be made on this family.

(3) Rebecca Jane Harper - "Becky"
    b. 25 October 1862 - Marion Co., Ala.
    d. 3 August 1952 - Clarendon, Donley Co., Texas at home of
       her son, Woodson
    bur. Newlin Cemetery - Hall Co., Texas
    m. James Walter McDonald Dodson - "Jimmy"
       said to be 6'tall, about 200 lbs., and very handsome
       b. 24 October 1857 - Fayette Co., Ala.
       d.   October 1882 - Marion Co., Ala.
       bur. Probably in old Ireland Cemetery in Marion Co., Ala.
            6 miles W. of Haleyville, Ala.
       son of Addison Whitfield Dodson & Margaret Emeline Musgrove
                    b. 2 April 1828   b. 11 May 1829
                    d. 1862/1863 - Civil War d. 20 July 1898
                    bur. Confederate Cemetery bur. Musgrove Chapel
                         in Meridian, Miss.   in Fayette Co., Ala.
       "Jimmy Dodson had been "deputized" by Sheriff Jess Broad-
       rick to go with him to arrest Bill Sanford. Sanford had
       sent word to Dodson not to come to help arrest him as
       he would shoot him. "Becky" also begged him not to go
       as they had 2 small children and expected the third. But
       he went on, and was shot and died, and is said to have
       written his name in blood on the sheet he died on!

(a) Mary Alice Dodson
    b. 23 November 1880 - Marion Co., Ala.
    d. 25 December 1965 - Kansas, Walker Co., Ala.
    bur. Shiloh Cemetery - near Kansas, Ala.
    m. William Thomas Estes - "Tom"
       b. 23 September 1875 - Marion Co., Ala.
       son of John Estes & Ann Pratt

    1. Dempsey Estes
       b. 1 August 1897 - Marion Co., Ala.
       d. 31 August 1897 - Marion Co., Ala.
       bur. Hopewell Baptist Cemetery - Fayette Co., Ala.
    2. Bessillee Estes
       b. 17 July 1898 - Marion Co., Ala.
       m. James Posey - 16 January 1917

       A. Carmon Posey
          m. Alvin Mayben
       B. Gonez Posey
          m. Madge Thomas

    3. John Chris Estes
       b. 23 May 1901 - Marion Co., Ala.
       m. Ethel Hocket - November 1925

       A. John C. Estes, Jr.
          b. 1926 approx.
       B. Charles Estes
       C. Bobby Estes
       D. James Thomas Estes
       E. Billy Estes
       F. Johnie Nell Estes
          m. Don Palmer
       G. Frances Estes
          m. Bill Dunil
       H. Betty Estes

    4. Woodson Estes
       b. 1904 d. 1906 - Marion Co., Ala.
       bur. Hopewell Baptist Cemetery - Fayette Co., Ala.
    5. Katie Ann Estes
       b. 26 November 1906 - Marion Co., Ala.
       m. James Andrew Studdard - 1 November 1924
          b. 21 December 1897 - Fayette Co., Ala.
          son of James Jackson Studdard & -?-

       A. James Thomas Studdard
          b. 2 August 1925 - Kansas, Ala.
          m. Johnnie Ruth Pierce - 3 May 1950 -Carbon hill, Ala

         (1) Karen Dagmar Studdard
             b. 9 March 1951 - Birmingham, Ala.
         (2) Randall Thomas Studdard
             b. 5 August 1953 - Birmingham, Ala.
         (3) Sharon Gay Studdard
             b. 6 October 1955 - Birmingham, Ala.
         (4) Steven Boyd Studdard
             b. 11 February 1960 - New Orleans, La.

    6. Josie Pearl Estes
       b. 20 December 1908 - Marion Co., Ala.
       m. Lawrence Farris - 14 January 1928

       A. Jack Farris
          b. 1930 approx.
       B. Joe Farris
          b. 1932 approx.
       Josie Estes m. 2nd Alfred F. Fulton - 10 October 1953
       Fulton, Miss.

    7. Simon Peter Estes
       b. 28 July 1911 - Marion Co., Ala.
       m. Pauline Rutledge - 23 December 1933

       A. Polly Katherin Estes
          b. 1935 approx.
          m. Ray Rumford

    8. Bascom Lee Estes
       b. 6 August 1914 - Marion Co., Ala.
       m. Louise Fikes - 23 December 1939
       No issue
    9. Sampson Estes
       b.   November 1915 - Marion Co., Ala.
       d. 31 May 1916 - Marion Co., Ala.
       bur. Hopewell Baptist Cemetery - Fayette Co., Ala.
    10. Olen Young Estes
        b. 17 January 1917 - Marion Co., Ala.
        m. Mary Belle Cunningham

        A. Diana Estes
        B. Kathey Estes

    11. Ceetus Hail Estes
        b. 11 May 1920 - Kansas, Walker Co., Ala.
        m. Evelyn Fowler

        A. Alice Ann Estes
        B. Tilsia Sue Estes
        C. Tommy Estes
        D. Duane Estes

(b) Wilburn Woodson Whitfield Dodson
    b. 9 November 1881 - Marion Co., Ala.
    d.   January 1965 - Newlin, Texas
    bur. Newlin Cemetery
    m. Pearl Alexander
       dau. of Wiley Petty Alexander & Mary Vaughn
                b. Ga.   b. Ala.

    1. Herman Dodson
    2. Cecil Dodson
    3. Blanch Dodson m. -?- Fletcher
    4. Athalee Dodson
    5. Orville Dodson

(c) James Thomas Dodson - "Jimmy"
    b. 9 July 1883 - Marion Co., Ala.
    d. 9 August 1900 - Fayette Co., Ala.
    bur. Hopewell Baptist Cemetery - Fayette Co., Ala.
    Some say he died of injuries from falling from a moving
    train, while others say he died of Typhoid fever, and
    that he kept wiping blood from his nose and wrote "D" on
    his bed linen meaning he was going to die! He was born
    after his father was killed in Oct/Nov. 1882, as stated above.

                              73

(3) Becky Jane Harper Dodson (Continued)
    m. 2nd John White - Wood Co., Texas
       bur. Newlin, Texas
(4) William Jefferson Harper - "Jeff" was not a Harper, illegiti-
    mate! Father was Bill Walker - came to Wood Co., Texas in 1902
    b. 17 October 1871- Marion Co., Ala.
    d. 13 January 1964 - Sudan, Lamb Co., Texas
    bur. Newlin Cemetery - Newlin, Texas
    m. Nancy Elizabeth Glover - 1890/1891 - Marion Co., Ala.
      b. April 1872 - Jasper Co., Ala.
      d. 3 November 1965 - Muleshoe, Bailey Co., Texas
      bur. Newlin Cemetery - Newlin, Texas

  (a) Maude Electra Harper
      b. 16 August 1892 - Pierce's Mill, Marion Co., Ala.
      m. Charles Burlos Alexander
        b. 16 June 1885 - Van Zandt Co., Texas
        d. 21 February 1953 - Sudan, Texas
        bur. Sudan Cemetery

    1. Eva Mae Alexander
        b. 4 September 1909 - Hall Co., Texas
        d. 25 December 1961 - Sudan, Lamb Co., Texas
        bur. Sudan Cemetery
        m. Auther Lee Spruill

      A. Verna Lee Spruill
        m. Bill Munger

        (1) Rita Mae Munger

    2. Edith Pauline Alexander
        b. 13 February 1912 - Colgate, Okla.
        m. Clifford Williams - 8 September 1932 - Clovis, NM
        b. 29 March 1909 - Durant, Okla.

      A. LaQuite Joy Williams
        b. 29 September 1933 - Lamb Co., Texas
        m. Ivan Dale Weaver - 10 September 1953 - Lamb Co.
          b. 27 September 1933 - Lamb Co., Texas

        (1) Kathy Alane Weaver
          b. 17 August 1954 - Lamb Co., Texas
        (2) Lanita Gaye Weaver
          b. 2 May 1957 - Lamb Co., Texas

      B. Clifford Gedonne Williams
        b. 8 May 1939 - Lamb Co., Texas
        m. LaVayne Gregory - 17 March 1957 - Bailey Co.,TX
          b. 24 August 1939 - Crosby Co., Texas

        (1) Cheryl Lynette Williams
          b. 24 April 1958 - Bailey Co., Texas
        (2) Kevin Gedonne Williams
          b. 21 November 1959 - Bailey Co, Texas
        (3) Gregory Scott Williams
          b. 1 December 1962 - Bailey Co., Texas

      C. Nancy Jane Williams
        b. 20 March 1946 - Sudan, Texas
        m. Rex Foust - 26 February 1966 - Lamb Co., Texas
          b. 3 July 1943 - Lamb Co., Texas

    3. Ethel Jewel Alexander
        b. 29 January 1915 - Memphis, Texas
        m. William Allen Beale

      A. Morris Duane Beale m. Bobbie Lee Rains
      B. Bobby Charles Beale m. Kalan Han Aycock

    4. Lois Bernice Alexander
        b. 15 April 1920 - Newlin, Texas
        m. Othel Brooks Chambers

      A. Anita Sue Chambers m. Michael Sidney King

(1) Michel Shane King

B. Lois Adelia Chambers
m. James Awin Downs

(1) Michelle DeAnn Downs

5. Lillian Elizabeth Alexander
b. 15 October 1923 - Newlin, Texas
m. Willie Bailey Cook

A. Patricia Diane Cook
m. Anton Follmann Walter
B. Billie Elizabeth Cook

(b) William Clovis Harper
b. 23 June 1894 - Marion Co., Ala.
d. 29 January 1905 - Golden, Wood Co., Texas
bur. Sand Springs Cemetery - Golden, Texas
(c) Dorsey Effie Mae Harper
b. 1896 approx. - Marion Co., Ala.
(d) Wiley Felton Harper
b. 1 June 1899 - Marion Co., Ala.
m. Lucille Glover

1. Roy Lee Harper

(e) Lewis Melton Harper
b. 1901 - Marion Co., Ala.
m. Della Ethel Hemphill

1. Raymond Harper
m. Mary Helen Holtkamp

A. Donney Harper
B. Lisa Harper
C. Lory Harper
D. Dale Harper
E. David Harper

2. Edwin Harper
m. Laverne Sager

A. Brenda Harper
B. Joan Harper
C. Gregg Harper

3. Jan Harper
m. Kenneth Sinclair

A. Darla Sinclair
B. Kala Sinclair
C. Kevin Sinclair

(f) Nancy Ellen Harper
b. 23 January 1905 - Wood Co., Texas
d. 16 December 1942
bur. Newlin Cemetery - Newlin, Texas
m. Hubert Abram - 14 March 1926
b. 9 June 1902 - Ala.
d. 15 December 1940 - (car accident)
bur. Newlin Cemetery - Newlin, Texas

1. William Alton Abram
b. 17 June 1927 - Newlin, Texas
d. 28 August 1966 - (car addicent)
bur. Memphis Cemetery - Memphis, Texas
m. Nell McLean - December 1951
b. 31 May 1932

A. Sarah Alexis Abram
b. 21 June 1955 - Memphis, Texas
B. Alton Vernon Abram
b. 22 January 1958 - Memphis, Texas
C. Lesinee Abram
b. 12 August 1959

2. Roy Milton Abram
   b. 24 November 1928 - Clarendon, Texas
   m. Aleen Russell - 22 July 1951 - Clovis, N. Mex.
      b. 3 January 1931 - Estelline, Texas

   A. Lisa Anne Abram
      b. 15 February 1955 - Childress, Texas
   B. Teresa Lynn Abram
      b. 27 August 1956 - Childress, Texas
   C. Roy Milton Abram, Jr.
      b. 5 March 1959 - Childress, Texas

3. Tommy Trilton Abram
   b. 14 September 1931 - Memphis, Texas
   m. Tommie Margaret Moore
      b. 17 February 1928

   A. Robbin Michele Abram
      b. 11 August 1961 - Lubbock, Texas

(g) Rose Ella Harper
    b. 19 August 1907 - Childress Co, Texas
    m. Ivan Ben Gresham
       b. 20 February 1905 - Tyron, Beaver Co, Texas

   1. Erma Louise Gresham
      b. 7 January 1927 - Childress Co, Texas
      m. Curtis Allen Williams

      A. Curtis Ivan Williams
         b. 14 July 1952 - Floydada, Texas
      B. Betty Diann Williams
         b. 19 June 1955 - Floydada, Texas
      C. Robert Lee Williams
         b. 20 November 1961 - Silver City, N. Mex.

   2. Norma Elloise Gresham
      b. 14 December 1939 - Knox City, Texas
      m. Aubry Leon Watson
         b. 10 October 1935 - Knox City, Texas

      A. Kelly Denene Watson
         b. 15 June 1962 - Knox City, Texas
      B. Kerry Craig Watson
         b. 11 April 1965 - Knox City, Texas

   3. Euwanna Jean Gresham
      b. 25 August 1942 - Munday, Texas
      m. Durwood Ben Bruton
         b. August 1940
   4. Lynda Kay Gresham
      b. 11 March 1944 - Haskell, Texas
      m. Jerry Brown
         b. July 1940

      A. Monty Brad Brown
         b. 20 June 1965 - Haskell, Texas

(h) Stella Lee Harper
    b. 12 July 1909 - Childress Co, Texas
    m. Curtis Pope Phillips - 1 February 1930 - Hollis, Okla.
       b. 7 April 1905 - Coleman Co., Texas

   1. Pernie Lovell Phillips
      b. 17 October 1930 - Childress Co., Texas
      m. Robert Deen Elkin - 4 September 1950
         b. 4 April 1931 - Oskluse, Iowa

      A. April Sue Elkin
         b. 8 April 1951 - Oskluse, Iowa

   2. Clifton Pope Phillips
      b. 7 October 1935 - Childress Co., Texas
      m. Harlene Smith - 14 September 1958
         b. 22 August 1937 - Donley Co., Texas

    A. Mark Phillips
       b. 14 January 1959 - Donley Co., Texas
    B. Brenda Jean Phillips
       b. 24 April 1967 - Hall Co., Texas
    C. Curtis Wayne Phillips
       b. 15 February 1961 - Donley Co., Texas

 3. Jimmy Eugene Phillips
    b. 12 December 1943 - Hall Co., Texas
    m. Virginia Harred - 30 November 1962
       b. 22 January 1942 - Claude, Texas

    A. Jimmie Jo Phillips
       b. 12 December 1966 - Amarillo, Texas

 4. Connie Lee Phillips
    b. 20 June 1947 - Hall Co., Texas
    m. Bobby Jean Havers - 25 October 1963
       b. 8 August 1938 - Quale, Dickens Co., Texas

    A. Linda Dianne Phillips
       b. 28 May 1964 - Amarillo, Texas

 5. Danny Mack Phillips
    b. 13 March 1959 - Hall Co., Texas
    m. Beverly McPherison - 8 April 1967
       b. 20 August 1949 - Hedley, Donley Co., Texas

(i) Mozell Harper
    b. 7 September 1911 - Newlin, Texas
    m. Frank B. Skinner
       b. 10 October 1908 - Medills, Okla.

 1. Erma Dean Skinner
    b. 28 February 1930 - Newlin, Texas
    m. Earl Ray Meadows
       b. 9 February 1926 - Parnell, Texas

    A. Linda Rae Meadows
       b. 15 September 1947 - Amarillo, Texas
       m. Lewis Douglas Rigdon
          b. 7 February 1946 - Amarillo, Texas
    B. Danny Frank Meadows
       b. 28 October 1949 - Amarillo, Texas

 2. Rita Janelle Skinner
    b. 25 February 1934 - Newlin, Texas
    m. Robert Eugene Hopkins
       b. 28 July 1927 - Spaninaw, Okla.

    A. Larry Eugene Hopkins
       b. 18 August 1956 - Amarillo, Texas
    B. Rita Diane Hopkins
       b. 20 September 1962 - Amarillo, Texas

 3. Janice Yentona Skinner
    b. 15 September 1939 - Hall Co., Texas
    m. James Storer

    A. Deena Leann Storer
       b. 26 September 1962 - Salt Lake City, Utah
    B. James Douglas Storer
       b. 16 August 1964 - Kansas City, Mo.

(j) LaVell Harper
    b. 3 November 1914 - Hall Co., Texas
    d. September 1919 - Tenn.
    bur. near Loretta, Tenn.

(k) Dorell Harper
    b. 22 November 1916 - Hall Co., Texas
    m. Alford Odell Rawls
       b. 8 October 1915 - Fannin Co., Texas

77

1. Larry Dale Rawls
   b. 5 June 1940 - Hall Co., Texas
   m. Thelma Sue Kimbell
      b. 22 November 1941 - Quitaque, Briscoe Co., Texas

   A. Rockey Dell Rawls
      b. 25 January 1960 - Dimmitt, Castro Co., Texas
   B. Jeffrey Scott Rawls
      b. 26 August 1963 - Dimmitt, Castro Co., Texas

2. Kennith Gale Rawls
   b. 29 June 1943 - Amherst, Texas
   m. Trixie Ann Gregg
      b. 23 February 1947 - Seymour, Texas

   A. Deborah Ann Rawls
      b. 20 July 1965 - Dimmitt, Texas

3. Bobby Glynn Rawls
   b. 14 April 1946 - Pampa, Texas
   m. Judy Lee Hanks
      b. 9 February 1949 - Tulia, Texas

   A. Michael Wayne Rawls
      b. 12 December 1967 - Amarillo, Texas

(1) Jennie Bell Harper
    b. 16 March 1919 - Hall Co., Texas
    m. Vernon Phillips - 9 December 1939

    1. Kathy Phillips
       b. 16 March 1940

1860 Marion Co., Ala. Federal Census   46/46   page 6
James W. M. Dodson   22 M   Ala.   b. 1858
Rebecca   "   18 F   "   1862

1860 Marion Co., Ala.   216/224 page 32 Astons Store, Ala.
Josiah Harper   25 M   Tenn. b. 1835   Farmer $150-$200
Nancy J.   "   26 F   Ala.   1834 (Nancy Jane Berryhill)
Mary   "   2 F   "   1858
Thomas W.   "   6/12 M   "   1860
Elizabeth Berryhill   17 F   "   1843 (Sister to Nancy Jane)

210/218 page 31 21 June 1860 Astons Store, Ala.
James Harper   25 M. Tenn. b. 1835 (evidentially a twin to Josiah)
Drucilla   "   26 F   Ala.   1834 (possibly Drucilla Anthony)
Elizabeth   "   12 F   "   1848 (evidentially James' sister)
Martha   "   11 F   "   1849 ("   "   "   )
Eliza   "   9 F   "   1851 - 1st issue of James & Drucilla
Nancy Y.   "   7 F   "   1853
Thadius W.   "   5 M   "   1855
Savannah F."   2 F   "   1858

East Div. page 1 household #1/1
Thomas Harper   54 M   Va.   b. 1806 - Father of the 2 above brothers
Mary   "   30 F   Ala.   1830 - Dau. so wife,
Denton   "   18 M   "   1842 - Elisha D on 1850 census
Polk   "   16 M   "   1844
George M.   "   14 M   "   1846
Green H.   "   11 M   "   1849
Martha   "   7 F   "   1853
Nancy   "   5 F   "   1855
Malissa   "   1 F   "   1859

1850 Marion Co., Ala. Federal Census   52/53 Beat #6
Thomas Harper   47 M   "   b. 1803
Mary   "   43 F   "   1807
Mary E.   "   18 F   "   1832
Josiah H.   "   17 M   "   1833 m. Nancy Jane Berryhill
Rebecca   "   14 F   "   1837
Thomas W.   "   11 M   "   1839
Elisha D.   "   9 M   "   1841

78

Harper's (Continued from previous page)
Tenn. Polk Harper   7 M   Ala.   b. 1843
George M. D.   "   3 M   "   1847
Jasper G.   " 4/12 M   "   1850
I find a marriage for Jasper G. Harper to M. E. Hyder - 17 December 1874
in Fayette Co., Ala.

1870 Marion Co., Ala. Federal Census 199/199 East Sub. Div. Thornhill, Ala
Nancy Harper   36 F   Ala.   b. 1834 (Nancy Jane Berryhill,Josiah's
Mary   "   10 F   "   1860 widow)
Thomas   "   9 M   "   1861
Rebecca   "   7 F   "   1863

1880 Marion Co., Ala. Federal Census
Nancy J. Harper   47 F. Ala.   Ga. S.C. b. 1833
Mary   "   21 F   "   1859
Jefferson   "   8 M   "   1972
Thomas W.   "   20 M   "   1860
Lucinda   "   21 F. Ga.   1859

PA and MA

I have a great granddad whom I know as Pa,
And by his side is beloved Ma,
Pa is a little bitty man
But he wears a great big hat,
His home is out east of Newlin,
Out near Gilipin flat.

He wears a handlebar mustache
below his Roman nose,
Which is quiet in style with his old-fashioned clothes.
His gallaces go over his shoulders and cross in the back
to hold up his trousers that fit him like a sack.

Pa is a man of great will and a strong determination.
A tax-paying citizen who helped to build our nation.

The maid he chose for his wife was Nancy Elizabeth Glover.
And she did, for him, twelve children mother.
Ma's motto for a woman was modesty,
With the body full covered
To me in her long dresses
Resembles old Mother Hubbard.
And back from her face so fair,
Is pulled a bun of her snow-white hair.

Pa and Ma are pioneers of the range
And can't seem to realize how things change
On the back porch is a cistern
From which they draw their water
This makes their work much harder.

They live surrounded by a sod land
Not yet conquored by the hand of man
In this pasture land, mesquite trees grow
But these trees do not grow in a row.
Many people decided this land was too thin
But Ma and Pa worked harder to master, and win.
Even though they are drooping with age
They can still find the lost calves in the sage.

Their children played in the canyons
Where the rattlesnakes den
And the black trantuala
Could jump higher than men.
The dry flies buzz in the heat at noon.
And the coyotes howl in the light of the moon.

Prayer for quidance was their only protection.
Now with dim eye sight they gaze in higher direction.
I know if God takes Ma and Pa apart,
The other will go to - from a broken heart.

Written by a great granddaughter, Nancy Williams

B. Mary Ann Berryhill - "Poll"
   b. 1834 - Marion Co., Ala.
   d. 1910 approx. - Marion Co., Ala.
   bur. Anthony Family Cemetery - in wooded area on a hill near
      the Elm Church of Christ - Fayette Co., Ala.

   (1) James Berryhill
       b. 1862/1865 - Marion Co., Ala.
       d. 1883/1885 - around Russellville, Ala and buried there.
          Family history tells us "Jim" had gone there to visit
          some of her Berryhill kin, and that he and another
          Berryhill cousin both liked the same girl. The girl
          and the two Berryhill cousins went into the woods to
          look for wild muscadines, and that "Jim" Berryhill was
          killed and buried there in the woods because the cousin
          felt he'd lose the girl to "Jim".
   (2) Theodocey Berryhill - "Doshia"
       b. 1865 - Marion Co., Ala.
       d. December 1939 - Marion Co., Ala. around Brilliant, Ala.
       bur. Brilliant Cemetery, sometimes called Berryhill cemetery
       m. (all five children said to be of Gus Pearce)

       (a) Arthur C. Berryhill
           b. 1885 - Marion Co., Ala.
           d. 1962 - Brilliant, Ala.
           m. Alice M. Makamson
              b. 15 November 1891

           1. Audrey Berryhill
              b. 1918 approx. - Marion Co., Ala.
              m. Cleaton Ledlow
                 b. 1910 - Marion Co., Ala.
                 son of John Sidney Ledlow & Mollie Florrie May
                 Henderson (her records are in the following pages)
           2. Bradley Berryhill
              m. Josie Aldridge
           3. Delacy (Deliska) Berryhill
              m. Frank -?-
              m. 2nd -?- Bostick
           4. Roger Berryhill
           5. Daughter
              m. Danny Cotton
           6. Daughter
              m. Robert Webb
           7. Daughter
              m. Elton Cagle
           8. Olin Berryhill
              b. 10 June 1916
              m. Hattie Mae Tidwell
           9. Mary Berryhill
          10. Wannell Berryhill
              m. Buster Martin
          11. Robert R. Berryhill
              b. 4 November 1918
              d. 1 January 1942

       (b) Charles C. Berryhill - "Charlie"
           b. 1887 approx. - Marion Co., Ala.
           m. Agnes -?-

           1. Carl Berryhill
              deceased by 1969
           2. Charles Berryhill
           3. Claude C. Berryhill
              b. 27 March 1914
              d. 9 June 1965
              bur. Church of Christ Cemetery
              m. Pauline H. -?-
                 b. 6 February 1918
           4. Wallace Berryhill
              Other issues, names unknown

        (c) Angus Berryhill (served as Sheriff of Marion Co., Ala)
            b. 1889 approx & living 1969
            married but no issues
        (d) Maude Wanda Berryhill
            b. 1 September 1892 - Marion Co., Ala.
            d. 29 May 1962 - Marion Co., Ala.
            bur. Winfield City Cemetery - Winfield, Ala.
            m. Robert L. Robbins - 5 October 1916 - Marion Co., Ala.
               b. 24 July 1890 - N. C.
               d. 13 January 1962 -
               bur. Winfield City Cemetery
               son of C. N. Robbins
                      d. 1863 - N.C.   d. 21 October 1915

            1. Catherine Robbins
               b. 17 July 1917 - Marion Co., Ala.
               m. Leslie De Bruch
                  has a son
            2. Randolph Robbins
               b. 2 November 1919 - Marion Co., Ala.
            3. Melba Robbins
               b. 1920 approx.
               m. James E. Raines
                  b. 10 June 1916
                  d. 26 December 1969 - Winfield, Ala.
                  bur. City Cemetery - Winfield, Ala.
                  son of James E. Raines, Sr. & Mertal -?-
                                         b. 1893 - Ala.
                                         d. August 1970

               A. Sandra Raines m. -?- Earnest
               B. Linda Raines m. -?- Ott
               C. Marcia Raines
               D. Jimmy Raines

            4. Robert L. Robbins, Jr. -"Bob"
               b. 1921
               d. 1956
               bur. Winfield City Cemetery - Marion Co., Ala.
            5. Dorothy Robbins
               b. 1923 approx - Marion Co., Ala.
               m. James Reagh
            6. Richard Robbins
               b. 1925 approx - Marion Co., Ala.
               m. & has 4 daughters
    (3) Nancy Berryhill - "Nan"
        b. 1868/1869 - Marion CO., Ala.
        d. October 1930

        (a) Clara Berryhill m. -?- Price
        (b) Lee Berryhill
            d. 1960 - approx. in Ark.
            m. & has issues, but names unknown.

1870 Marion Co., Ala - P. O. Thornhill, Ala.   200/200
Mary Berryhill   35 F   Ala.   b. 1835
James   "   4 M   "   1866 son
Theodocey   "   3 F   "   1867 dau.
Nancy   "   1 F   "   1869 dau.
Hannah Anthony   25 F   "   1845 - sister to Mary
William Anthony   1 M   "   1869 - son of Hannah (Berryhill)
                                            Anthony

1880 Fayette Co., Ala. - 21 June 1880 - Township #13, Range #11 202/204 p25
Mary Berryhill   40 F   Ala.   b. 1840
Dosha   "   15 F   "   1865 dau.
Nancy   "   12 F   "   1868 dau.
James   "   18 M   "   1862 son

82

C. William Berryhill - "Billy"
   b. 1835 - Marion Co., Ala.
   No information is available on him except he is known to have
   married and had two little girls when his young wife died. All
   contacts seem to be lost with this family.

D. Susan Catherine Berryhill
   b. 1837 - Marion Co., Ala.
   d. 1864/1865 approx. - Marion Co., Ala.
   bur. possibly Mulberry Hollow Cemetery - Marion Co., Ala.
   She is said to have died along with her mother with smallpox.
   m. -?- Berryhill

   (1) Mary Elizabeth Berryhill
       b. 4 October 1859 - Marion Co., Ala.
          Raised by her Aunt Hannah after her mother died. Others
          say raised by the Tom Kelley family of Walker Co.
       d. 12 July 1923 - Fayette Co., Ala.
       bur. New Liberty Cemetery - Fayette Co., Ala.
       m. John Aldridge
          b. 1853 - Ala.
          d. 1928 - Fayette Co., Ala.
          bur. New Liberty Cemetery
          son of -?- Aldridge & Mary Ann Manasco
                  d. &   b. 24 November 1824
                  bur. in Ark.   d. 4 March 1919 - Fayette Co.
                  so some say   bur. New Liberty Freewill Bap. Ceme.

       (a) Mary Ann Aldridge
           b. 14 October 1881 - Fayette Co., Ala.
           d. 8 April 1951 - Fayette Co., Ala (truck ran over her)
           bur. New Liberty Cemetery
           Never married - others say she m. Rassie A. Cooper
       (b) Susie Catherine Aldridge
           b. 18 December 1885 - Fayette Co., Ala.
           d. 24 January 1924 - Fayette Co, Ala. (died of measles)
           bur. New Liberty Cemetery
           m. John William Little - 29 September 1908
              b. 6 November 1880 - Dallas Co., Ala.
              d. 1 March 1944 - Walker Co., Ala.
              bur. New Liberty Cemetery
              son of Earlie Little & Georgia Ann Brazil

           1. Alma Little
              b. 11 July 1909 - Fayette Co., Ala.
              m. William Franklin McLemore - "Bill" - 19 May 1929
                 b. 15 May 1904 - Walker Co., Ala.

              A. Hazel Ruth McLemore
                 b. 21 February 1933
                 m. Fenton Loyd Garrison - 25 April 1950
                 son of Hayes Garrison & Effie Smith b. 1924 - Ala.

                 (1) Leona Pamelia Garrison
                     b. 8 April 1951 - Fayette Co., Ala.
                 (2) Peggy Ann Garrison
                     b. 16 February 1953 - Fayette Co., Ala.
                 (3) William Loyd Garrison
                     b. 21 July 1954 - Fayette Co., Ala.
                 (4) Jerry Wayne Garrison
                     b. 24 October 1958 - Fayette Co., Ala.
                 (5) June Carolyn Garrison
                     b. 18 September 1960 - Fayette Co., Ala.
                 (6) Anthony Ray Garrison
                     b. 21 June 1965 - Marion Co., Ala.

              B. Linda Louise McLemore
                 b. 29 August 1948 - Fayette Co., Ala.

           2. Alice Little
              b. 6 January 1912 - Fayette Co., Ala.
              m. Ulas Gunter - 25 December 1925
                 b. August 1905

            A. Mary Sue Gunter
               b. 8 June 1929 - Marion Co., Ala.
            B. Betty Lou Gunter
               b. July   - Fayette Co., Ala.
            C. John William Gunter
               b. April   - Fayette Co., Ala.
            D. Evelyn Ann Gunter
               b. 8 July 1940 - Fayette Co., Ala.

         3. Thomas Alton Little
            b. 31 January 1914 - Fayette Co., Ala.
            m. Amalie Benton

            A. Sarah Catherine Little
               b. September
            B. Dorothy Little
               b. 18 July 1942
            C. Robert Little
            D. Virginia Little

         4. Eunice Lucille Little
            b. 18 June 1916 - Fayette Co., Ala.
            d. 30 October 1918 - Fayette Co., Ala.
            bur. New Liberty Freewill Baptist Cemetery

         5. John William Little, Jr.
            b. 14 May 1918 - Fayette Co., Ala.
            d. 24 December 1918 - Fayette Co., Ala.
            bur. New Liberty Freewill Baptist Cemetery

         6. Lora Lee Little
            b. 14 October 1919 - Fayette Co., Ala.
            m. James F. Miller

            A. Edwin Miller
               b. 19 September 1948

         7. Infant Daughter Little
            b. 29 July 1922 d. 31 July 1922 - Fayette Co, Ala.
            bur. New Liberty Freewill Baptist Cemetery

         8. Edward Little
            b. 4 January 1924 d. 28 January 1924 - Fayette Co.
            bur. NEw Liberty Freewill Baptist Cemetery

   (c) William A. Aldridge - "Bill"
       b. 31 December 1886 - Fayette Co., Ala.
       d. 1958
       bur. New Liberty Freewill Baptist Cemetery - Fayette Co.
       m. Cora B. Franks
          b. 25 July 1887
          d. 16 October 1914
          bur. New Liberty Freewill Baptist Cemetery

       1. George Aldridge
       2. John Wesley Aldridge
          b. 10 September 1908 -
          d. 18 July 1943
          bur. New Liberty Freewill Baptist Cemetery
       3. Bertha Aldridge
       4. Felix Aldridge

       Bill Aldridge m. 2nd. Mrs. Frances (Aldridge) Johnson
                                b. 1896
                                dau. of Prince Aldridge

       5. Edith Aldridge
       6. Berthenia Aldridge
       7. Ludia Mae Aldridge
       8. William A. Aldridge, Jr.
       9. Virgie Aldridge
      10. Willie Aldridge
      11. Jerry P. Aldridge

   (d) Felix A. Aldridge
       m. Josie Martin - 12 February 1911 - Marion Co., Ala.

                          84

1. J. D. Aldridge
(e) David Emmanuel Aldridge - "Dave"
b. 7 May 1894 - Fayette Co., Ala.
d. 29 May 1968 - Fayette Co., Ala.
bur. New Liberty Cemetery - Fayette Co., Ala.
m. Essie Lee Hawkins - 7 November 1914 - Marion Co., Ala.
b. 17 December 1893 - Marion Co., Ala.
dau. of Bud Hawkins & Mary A. Haney

1. Herman Otis Aldridge
b. 4 November 1915 - Fayette Co., Ala.
m. Mary Magdalene Odom - 9 June 1940
b. 14 September 1922 - Walker Co., Ala.
dau. of Wm Thomas Odom 7 Minnie Lee -?-

A. Mary Louise Aldridge
b. 22 May 1941 - Fayette Co., Ala.
m. Johnny Wm. Gillion - February 1957
b. 27 March 1932 - Fayette Co., Ala.
son of Herbert Sedenas Gillion & Vera -?-

(1) Infant Son
b. 4 September 1958   d. 5 September 1958 -
bur. New Liberty Cemetery - Ala.
(2) Nell Dean Gillion
b. 28 May 1959   d. 29 May 1959
bur. New Liberty Cemetery
(3) Johnnie Sue Gillion
b. 2 May 1961 - Fayette Co., Ala.
(4) Linda Lou Gillion
b. 24 May 1962 - Marion Co., Ala.
(5) Luke Gillion
b. 15 February 1963 - Marion Co., Ala.
(6) William Mark Gillion
b. 10 June 1964 - Marion Co., Ala.

B. David Ralph Aldridge
b. 24 June 1943 - Fayette Co., Ala.
d. 22 August 1947 - Fayette Co., Ala.
bur. New Liberty Freewill Baptist Cemetery
C. William Ottis Aldridge
b. 6 December 1945 - Fayette Co., Ala.
m. Judy Ann Reese - 10 September 1966
dau. of Albert Reese 7 -?-

(1) Kim Louise Aldridge
b. 10 July 1967 - Fayette Co., Ala.

D. Lester Dennis Aldridge
b. 5 November 1947 - Shelby Co., Ala.
m. Carolyn Sue Seay - 27 January 1964
b. 22 October 1945 - Coal Valley, Ala.
dau. of Columbus Otis Gray & Clemmie Seay
E. Lynda Kay Aldridge
b. 1 November 1949 - Shelby Co., Ala.
F. Billy Lamar Aldridge
b. 17 September 1952 - Shelby Co., Ala.
G. Carol Lynn Aldridge
b. 26 March 1961 - Fayette Co., Ala.

2. Coy Ralph Aldridge
b. 27 September 1917 - Fayette Co., Ala.
m. Cora Ozella Lowery - 11 December 1937
b. 7 September 1919 - Fayette Co., Ala.
dau. of James K. Polk Lowery & Donzie E. Moore

A. James Emmanuel Aldridge
b. 10 September 1938 - Fayette Co., Ala.
m. Era Lee Chandler - 19 May 1962
b. 13 March 1945 - Marion Co., Ala.
dau. of Woodie Chandler & Annie Bell Kerr

(1) Randall Lynn Aldridge
b. 25 February 1966 - Fayette Co., Ala.

B. Jerrell Ray Aldridge
   b. 5 October 1940 - Fayette Co., Ala.
   m. Miriam June Smith - 8 October 1960
      b. 25 June 1942 - Fayette Co., Ala.
      dau. of Wilburn Smith & Jalia Sawyer

   (1) Scotty Blaine Aldridge
       b. 29 August 1963 - Fayette Co., Ala.

C. Jacob Hudson Aldridge
   b. 29 April 1947 - Fayette Co., Ala.

3. Thelma Lugene Aldridge
   b. 28 December 1919 - Carbon Hill, Walker Co., Ala.
   m. Vester Madison - 31 March 1934
      b. 10 February 1916 - Fayette Co., Ala..
      son of Wm. Thomas Madison & Catherine Clemmons

   A. Marion Bradford Madison
      b. 30 July 1935 - Fayette Co., Ala.
      d. 15 October 1935 - Fayette Co., Ala.
   B. William Calvin Madison
      b. 25 April 1937 - Fayette Co., Ala.
      m. Lawanda Sue Williams - 25 February 1956
         b. 12 June 1938 - Flat Creek, Cass Co., Texas

      (1) Malinda Deneace Madison
          b. 13 February 1958 - Bessemer, Ala.
      (2) Donna Marie Madison
          b. 22 October 1960 - Bessemer, Ala.
      (3) Sharon Ann Madison
          b. 28 Spetember 1964 - Bessemer, Ala.

   C. Charles Curtis Madison
      b. 3 March 1940 - Fayette Co., Ala.
      m. Carolyn June Marlow - 20 August 1958
         b. 26 December 1938 - Northport, Ala.

      (1) Mark Elliot Madison
          b. 24 September 1956 - Jefferson Co., Ala.

   D. Joseph Loyal Madison
      b. 27 April 1942 - Fayette Co., Ala.
      m. Glenda Fay Moore - 29 September 1963
   E. Martha Lugene Madison
      b. 30 December 1943 - Fayette Co., Ala.
      m. Raymond Clay Junkin - 12 September 1963
         b. 27 February 1932 - Gordo, Pickens Co., Ala.
         son of Eaphon Virley Junkin & Edna Mae Koon
   F. David Dale Madison
      b. 24 June 1952 - Fayette Co., Ala.
   G. Phillip Nathaneal Madison
      b. 14 December 1957 - Fayette Co., Ala.

4. Ilene Aldridge
   b. 13 March 1922
   m. Charlie Kirby

   A. Charles Kirby
   B. Betty Joyce Kirby
   C. Jack Kirby
   D. Donald Kirby
   E. Wayne Kirby

5. Christine Aldridge
   b. 19 October 1924
   m. J. C. Palmer

   A. John Palmer
   B. Nancy Palmer
   C. Janet Palmer
   D. Larry Palmer

6. David Everette Aldridge
   b. 10 September 1926 - Fayette Co., Ala.
   m. Jewel Carroll - 8 May 1945
      b. 3 February 1925 - Selma, Ala.

   A. Julia Ann Aldridge
      b. 23 December 1946 - Jefferson Co., Ala.
      m. William Allen Williams
         b. 18 December 1946 - Jefferson Co., Ala.

7. Rosa Evanell Aldridge
   b. 13 January 1929 - Fayette Co., Ala.
   m. Louis Ezekiel Alexander - 8 July 1950
      b. 11 May 1929 - Walker Co., Ala.

   A. David Austin Alexander
      b. 5 June 1951 - Washington, D. C.
   B. Donna Sue Alexander
      b. 14 January 1955 - Siluria, Ala.
   C. Gary Louis Alexander
      b. 24 April 1956 - Jefferson Co., Ala.
   D. Timothy Fitzjerald Alexander
      b. 15 May 1961 - Alabastur, Ala.

8. Edrel Mae Aldridge
   b. 11 May 1934 - Fayette Co., Ala.
   m. Mack Arthur Cory - 19 December 1952
      b. 14 March 1932 - Canoe, Ala.

   A. Joye LeeAnn Cory
      b. 28 October 1954 - Chattahoochie Co, Ga.
   B. Stephen Arthur Cory
      b. 17 September 1957 - Maury Co., Tenn.

E. Hannah A. Berryhill
   b. 1839 - Marion Co., Ala.
   d. 1885/1890 approx. - Marion Co., Ala.
   bur. probably Mulberry Hollow Cemetery, Marion Co., Ala.
   m. William E. Anthony - Spring or Summer of 1860
      b. 1841 - Ala.
      dead by 1870 census taking time

   (1) William Anthony - "Bill"
       b. 1869 - Marion Co., Ala.
       d. 1888/1890 approx. - Memphis, Tenn. area
       Family history says he was working on the bridge that
       spanned the Miss. River at Memphis, when he got sick and
       died of pneumonia. He never married.

   Hannah A. Berryhill m. 2nd. Jimmy Watkins

   (2) James Watkins
       b. 1875 - Marion Co., Ala.
       No other information available on him.

   Hannah A. Berryhill m. 3rd. Cadd Mills - by 1880 census time
                            b. 1816 - Tenn.

   (3) Jerona Mills - "Romie"
       b. 1879 - Marion Co., Ala.
       d. 1902 approx. - Marion Co., Ala.
       bur. Mulberry Hollow Cemetery - called Old Russell Cemetery
       Romie was a crippled girl, probably polio, and was raised by
       her cousin Mary Elizabeth (Berryhill) Aldridge, after her
       mother died. Romie was in the field helping Mary Elizabeth
       (Berryhill) Aldridge and Susie Catherine Aldridge burn off
       some hew ground, when her clothes caught fire, and she took
       pneumonia and died from the burns.

1880 Marion Co., Ala. Census 45/45 page 5 Beat #8 - TX 13 - R11W
John Aldridge   25 M   Ala. b. 1855
Mary E.   "   19 F   Ala.   1861

87

```
1860 - Marion Co., Ala.    81/85 - page 13
Wm. E. Anthony          19 M  Ala.    b. 1841
Hannah A.     "          18 F  Ala.       1842

1870 Marion Co., Ala.   200/200 page 29 14th August 1870 - Thornhill, Ala.
Hannah Anthony          25 F  Ala.    b. 1845
William      "           1 M  Ala.       1869

1880 Marion Co., Ala.    43/43 page 5 TS13 - Rii West
J. C. Mills             64 M  Tenn.   b. 1816
Hannah      "            35 F  Ala.       1845
William Anthony         10 M  Ala.       1870 - Step-son
James       "            5 M  Ala.       1875 - Step-son
Jerona Mills             1 F  Ala.       1879
```

    F. Sarah Elizabeth Berryhill - "Bet"
       b. 27 March 1843 - Marion Co., Ala.
       d. 23 November 1923 - Fayette Co., Ala.
       bur. White Springs Cemetery - Fayette Co., Ala.
       m. James Van Buren Mills - "Van"
          b. 1843 - Ala.
          d. 1926 - Towley or Jasper, Ala.
          bur. White Springs Cemetery - Fayette Co., Ala.
          "Van" Mills served as a Pvt. in Co. H, 26th Ala. Inf. - CSA
          Was blind for sometime before he died. He married 2nd.
          Barbara Barton.

       (1) Daughter, name is unknown.
          She died when about a year old and I can find no one who
          knows where she was buried.

    G. Margaret A. Berryhill
       b. 1845 - Marion Co., Ala.
       Living at time of 1860 census, but no other information is
       available on her.

    H. James K. Polk Berryhill
       b. 1846 - Marion Co., Ala.
       d. 1919 - in Cushing, Okla.(no death certificate can be found)
       m. Mollie Lindsey - Marion Co., Ala.

       (1) Edna Berryhill
          b. 1880 approx.
          m. George W. Barlow - 15 February 1909 - Potter Co., Texas
       (2) Myrtle Berryhill
          b. 1882 approx.
          m. Warren Nottingham
       (3) Beulah Berryhill
          b. 1884 approx.
          m. Decatur Cox
       (4) Jennie Berryhill
          b. 1886 approx.
          m. -?- Cowart
       (5) Fred Berryhill
          b. 1888 approx.
       (6) Jessie Berryhill
          b. 1890 approx.
          d. 1915/1916 approx. (Was hit by a train and it killed him.)

Family history tell when Jerry Hunt shot and killed James Berryhill, Polk vowed to find Jerry Hunt and kill him. Jerry Hunt
took off from Alabama for Texas. Apparently that was the main
reason Polk left Alabama and came to Texas. It is said one
night a cowboy rode into town, shot Jerry Hunt five times, and
rode on out. It is believed that it was Polk Berryhill who
shot him.

Felton Harper of Newlin, Texas wrote this: "All I know about
Uncle Polk Berryhill is I remember he and Aunt Mollie and their
daughter, Beulah, came to our house once when I was small. Then

when Grandma Nancy Jane (Berryhill) Harper died, Uncle Polk came
by himself for the funeral. That was in 1916. I had a stag
hound pup and he wanted to buy it from me, so I gave it to him.
He shipped it from Newlin, Texas back to Oklahoma."

Polk had a glass eye, after he lost his right eye in a fight once.

I. Drucilla C. Berryhill - "Silla"
   b. 1853 - Marion Co., Ala.
   Living on 1860 census, 8 years old. I am sorry there is no
   other information available on her.

J. Martha Frances Berryhill - "Marth"
   b. 1855 - Marion Co., Ala.
   d.
   bur. Harmony Grove Cemetery - Fayette Co., Ala.
   m. Robert Mills - "Bob"
      bur. Harmony Grove Cemetery - Fayette Co., Ala.

   (1) Polk Mills
       m. Lula Alexander

       (a) David Mills
       (b) Hassie Mills
       (c) Martha Mills
       (d) Thomas Mills
       (e) Myrtle Mills
       (f) J. D. Mills

   (2) Effie Mills
       b. 1 December 1886
       d. 18 December 1963
       bur. Hawkins Cemetery - Brilliant, Ala.
       m. Jess Vickery
          b. 24 December 1883 - Fayette Co., Ala.
          d. 5 January 1972 -
          bur. Holcomb Cemetery
          son of Thomas Vickery & Mary M. Read (Reed)
                   b. 1850 - Ala.   b. 1850 - Ala.
                   (son of Elisha Vicery & Tebitha -?- (1st wife)
                            b. 1815 - Tenn. b. 1828 - Tenn.

       (a) Belton Vickery
           m. Lillie Casken - Longivew, Texas
       (b) Mennie Vickery
           m. Tompie Anderson - Brilliant, Ala.
       (c) Martha Vickery
           m. Clebbon Goodwin - Orlando, Fla.
       (d) Lander Vickery
           m. Lucille Willcutt - Winfield, Ala.
       (e) Carrie Vickery
           m. Clyde Burks -
       (f) Troy Vickery
           m. Earline Homby - California
       (g) Bertie Vickery
           m. J. C. Davis - Winfield, Ala.

   (3) Belle Mills
       m. George Olinger

       (a) Maybelle Olinger
           m. -?- Cupper
       Other issues names are unknown.

   (4) Minnie Mills
       m. Arthur Gerganus & had no issues
   (5) -?- Mills (Female)
       m. Willis Gunter

       (a) Jimmie Gunter
       (b) Arrie Gunter
           m. Demas Roden

(6) Franklin Mills
    m. Ida Hankins

    (a) Pauline Mills
    (b) Inez Mills
    (c) J. K. Mills
    (d) Bell Mills

(7) Vadis Mills
    Died about 12 years of age and
    bur. Harmony Grove Cemetery
(8) Mary Jane Mills
    b. 1874 -
    d. after 1956
    bur. Harmony Grove Cemetery
    m. Bud Hawkins - 4 September 1898 - Marion Co., Ala.
        b. 1871
        d. 10 June 1956
        bur. Harmony Grove Cemetery
        son of William T. Hawkins & "Puss" Vickery

    (a) Will Hawkins
        m. Zettie -?-
    (b) Thresa Hawkins
        m. Walter Larkhart
    (c) Zora Hawkins
        m. Glen Larkhart
    (d) Loise Hawkins
        m. Murll Berryhill
    (e) Louie Hawkins
        m. Jenisser Spillers
    (f) Mack Hawkins
        m. Mae Spillers
    (g) Dempsie Hawkins
        never married
    (h)
    (i) Twins, who were born and died in 1900 and
        bur. Harmony Grove Cemetery
    (j) Jessie Hawkins
        b. 1906
        d. 1910
        bur. Harmony Grove Cemetery
    (k) Dessmer Hawkins
        m. Raymond Bozeman

K. Rachel Louise Berryhill
    b. 16 April 1858 - Marion Co., Ala.
    d. 3 August 1934 - Frankston, Anderson Co., Texas
    bur. Olive Branch Cemetery - near Frankston, Texas (Brushey Creek)
    m. William Andrew Henderson
        b. 2 February 1856 - Fayette Co., Ala.
        d. 27 June 1916 - Fayette Co., Ala.
        bur. Harmony Grove Cemetery - Fayette Co., Ala.
        son of Jackson Henderson & Hannah Tucker

    (1) Sarah Elizabeth Henderson
        b. 27 February 1877 - Fayette Co., Ala.
        m. Ellie M. Webster - 24 February 1892 - Fayette Co., Ala.
            b. 21 February 1872
            d. 24 February 1948 - Mineral Wells, Texas
            bur. Mineral Wells, Texas
            son of Silmon Webster & Mary Angeline Martin

        (a) Chelcie Newton Webster
            b. 17 August 1893 - Fayette Co., Ala.
            d. 1963 - Mineral Wells, Texas
            m. Sophia Brown - 15 February 1914

            1. Ernest Riou Webster
            2. Daniel Voudy Webster
            3. Marion Inez Webster
               m. -?- Mabry

4. Ada Pearl Webster
   m. -?- Roberson
5. Edna Joy Webster
   m. -?- Mullonax
6. Newton Junior Webster
7. Almon Lincoln Webster

(b) Houston Andrew Webster
    b. 8 December 1895 - Fayette Co., Ala.
    d. 11 January 1911 - Fayette Co., Ala.
    bur. Harmony Grove Cemetery - Fayette Co., Ala.
(c) Wilham Fred Webster
    b. 12 August 1898 - Fayette Co., Ala.
    m. Maggie Griffin - 30 August 1919

    1. Homer Webster
    2. Clifford Freddie Webster

(d) Rilla Pearl Webster
    b. 8 June 1901 - Fayette Co., Ala.
    m. Morris Harrison Capes - 10 August 1919
(e) Lomax Webster
    b. 27 February 1906 - Fayette Co., Ala.
    m. Zelpha Rhodes

    1. Alton Webster
       d. 1963
    2. Wanda Webster
       m. -?- Silivan
    3. Elwine Webster
    4. Harral Webster
    5. Jerry Webster
    6. Carrol Webster
    7. Cathy Webster

(f) Raymon Troy Webster
    b. 9 October 1908
    d. 9 January 1911 - Fayette Co., Ala.
    bur. Harmony Grove Cemetery - Fayette Co., Ala.
(g) Samiel Vester Webster
    b. 6 December 1909 - Fayette Co., Ala.
    m. Verda Smith
(h) Moodie Elmer Webster
    b. 25 August 1911 - Fayette Co., Ala.
    m. Clara Couch
       b. 1910 - Fayette Co., Ala.
       dau. of Marion Thomas Couch & Nora Drewrilla Berryhill

    1. Linda Webster
       m. "Buddy" Thorp
    2. Ronnie Webster
    3. Kenneth Webster

(i) Ronlee Webster
    b. 15 July 1915 - Fayette Co., Ala.
    m. Mosie Walls

    1. Doyle Webster
    2. Gary Lee Webster
    3. Doris Jean Webster
       m. -?- Lewallen
    4. Scherl Webster
    5. James Webster
    6. Terry Webster

(j) Luther Jonson Webster
    b. 17 August 1919 - Garvin Co., Okla.
    m. Mary Alice Donley

    1. Loretta Jongeore Webster (twin)
       m. -?- Johens
    2. Vinetta Webster (twin)
       m. -?- Smith

(2) Virginia Isabell Henderson - "Jennie"
    b. 1879/1880 - Fayette Co., Ala.
    d. 1952 - Burk Burnett, Texas
    m. James Mills - "Jim"
       son of Franklin Mills & Sarah Ann -?-

    (a) Lorene Mills
        m. Woodrow W. Perry
    (b) Tommy Mills
    (c) Morgan Mills
    (d) Belvin Mills
    (e) Ada Mills
    (f) Troy Mills
    (g) Erie Mills
    (h) Collie Mills
    (i) Guy Mills
    (j) Harlin Mills
    (k) Virgil Mills

(3) Mollie Florrie May Henderson
    b. 2 February 1882 - Fayette Co., Ala.
    m. John Sidney Ledlow - "Sid" - Fayette Co., Ala. - July 1898
       b. 1878
       d. 1953 - Marion Co., Ala.
       bur. Mt. Olive Cemetery - Marion Co., Ala., near Guin
       son of J. M. Ledlow & Nancy M. -?-
                              b. 29 July 1851
                              d. 13 November 1909
                              bur. Madison Family Cemetery -
                                   Fayette Co., Ala.

    (a) Nina Ledlow
        b. 1899 - Fayette Co., Ala.
        m. Marvin Cook

        1. Euna Mae Cook
        2. Cecil Cook (deceased)
        3. Lisa Cook
        4. Eardeal Cook
        5. Robert Lewis Cook

    (b) Milton Ledlow
        b. 25 August 1900 - Fayette Co., Ala.
        d. 18 April 1921 - Marion Co., Ala.
        bur. Mt. Olive Cemetery - Marion Co., Ala.
    (c) Lue Annie Ledlow
        b. 26 September 1902 - Fayette Co., Ala.
        d. 5 October 1919 - Marion Co., Ala.
        bur. Mt. Olive Cemetery - Marion Co., Ala.
    (d) Elbert Ledlow
        b. 1904 - Fayette Co., Ala.
        m. Effie Graham

        1. R. L. Ledlow
        2. Gaither Ledlow
        3. Mary Lou Ledlow
        4. Robin Ledlow

    (e) Flora Ledlow
        b. 1905 - Marion Co., Ala.
        m. Otha Markham

        1. Jeraldine Markham
        2. Charlie Lee Markham
        3. Delister Markham

    (f) Cora Ledlow
        b. 1907 - Marion Co., Ala.
        m. Jeff Wilson

        1. Julia Wilson
        2. Carolyn Wilson

(g) Eula Ledlow
b. 1908 - Marion Co., Ala.
m. Tom Elliott

1. Donna Fay Elliott
2. Euline Elliott
3. Tommy Elliott
4. Johnnie Elliott (deceased)
5. Billy Elliott

(h) Cleaton Ledlow
b. 1910 - Marion Co., Ala.
m. Audry Berryhill
dau. of Arthur Berryhill & Alice Makamson
(i) Dilmos Ledlow
b. 1911 - Marion Co., Ala.
d.
bur. Center Cemetery - Marion Co., Ala.
m. Vera Waits

1. Joyce Ledlow
m. Harry -?-

(j) Jack Ledlow
b. 1912 - Marion Co., Ala.
m. Peggy Ingram

1. Sidney B. Ledlow - "Freddie"
2. Martha D. Ledlow
m. -?- Terry

(k) Grady Ledlow
b. 1915 - Marion Co., Ala.
(l) Beretta Ledlow
b. 24 March 1927 - Marion Co., Ala.
m. Arthur Geissie

1. Robert Geissie

(4) James Thomas Jackson Henderson
b. 15 September 1886 - Fayette Co., Ala.
d. 16 October 1966 - Dallas, Texas
bur. Providence Cemetery - Jacksonville, Texas
m. Thomas Weeks

(a) Earlie Henderson
(b) Sam Henderson
(c) Morgan Henderson
(d) Robert Henderson
(e) Vereda Henderson
m. Chester Couch
(f) Billy Henderson
(g) Ranie M. Henderson
b. 27 February 1908
d. 20 May 1909
bur. Harmony Grove Cemetery - Fayette Co., Ala.
(h) Dealie L. Henderson
b. 23 December 1909
d. 12 December 1910
bur. Harmony Grove Cemetery - Fayette Co., Ala.

James Thomas Henderson m. 2nd. Dorothy Taylor

(i) Raburn Henderson
(j) Preston D. Henderson
(k) Turner Henderson
(l) Joe Henderson
(m) Nell Henderson
(n) Barbara Henderson

(5) William Cay Henderson
    b. 15 July 1888 - Fayette Co., Ala.
    d. 5 May 1967 - Jacksonville, Texas
    bur. Elm Church of Christ Cemetery - Fayette Co., Ala.
    m. Mary Alma Anthony - 15 March 1907 - Fayette Co., Ala.
        b. 1889
        d. 1960 - Fayette Co., Ala.
        bur. Elm Church of Christ Cemetery - Fayette Co., Ala.
        dau. of Alexander Fanning Anthony & Sarah Catherine Webster
        (More information in McMinn Family Tree Book p. 122)

    (a) Quinton Frazier Henderson
        b. 2 February 1910 - Fayette Co., Ala.
        m. Adelle Perry
            b. 10 August 1911 - Marion Co., Ala.
            d. 20 January 1973 - Winfield, Ala.
            bur. Harmony Grove Cemetery

        1. William Charles Henderson
           b. 17 April 1931 - Fayette Co., Ala.
           m. Bettie L. Bamfortmer

           A. Rickey Henderson
              b. 21 November 1951
           B. Perry Henderson
           C. Ronda Henderson

        2. Clinton Hancel Henderson
           b. 8 September 1934 - Marion Co., Ala.
           m. Lorene Hollingsworth

           A. Scott Henderson
              b. 1957
           B. Shinel Henderson
           C. Paul Henderson
           D. Linda Jo Henderson

        3. Annie Foy Henderson
           b. 21 November 1936 - Marion Co., Ala.
           m. George Hubbert

           A. Dannie Thomas Hubbert
              b. 1958
           B. Sandra Rena Hubbert

        4. Lenora Henderson
           b. 14 November 1938 - Marion Co., Ala.
           m. Edwin D. Turner

           A. Mickey Allen Turner
           B. Timothy Glen Turner
           C. Dena Leah Turner

        5. Sara Hazle Henderson
           b. 22 December 1940 - Winfield, Ala.
           m. Alford Horlean
           m. 2nd -?- Horlean.

           A. Dona Horlean
           B. Cindy Horlean

        6. Essie Lue Henderson
           b. 11 July 1943 - Marion Co., Ala.
           m. John Price
        7. Quinton F. Henderson
           b. 3 November 1945 - Marion Co., Ala.
        8. Geraldine Henderson
           b. 14 August 1948 - Marion Co., Ala.
        9. Harold Henderson
           b. 9 September 1950 - Marion Co., Ala.
       10. Karen Elizabeth Henderson
           b. 7 March 1952 - Marion Co., Ala.
           m. -?- Hollingsworth

(b) Gasma Henderson
    b. 4 March 1911 - Fayette Co., Ala.
    m. Doc Kelley
        b. 14 November 1907
        d. 7 April 1963
(c) Roberta Henderson
    m. Malcom Vaughan
(d) Decatur Henderson
    b. 1912
    d. 1925
    bur. Elm Church of Christ Cemetery - Fayette Co., Ala.
(e) Infant Henderson
    b. 1914   d. 1914
    bur. Elm Church of Christ Cemetery - Fayette Co., Ala.
(f) Infant Henderson
    b. 1916   d. 1916
    bur. Elm Church of Christ Cemetery - Fayette Co., Ala.
(g) Hudson Henderson
    m. Betty Davis
(h) Myrl Henderson
    m. Cecil Tidwell
(i) Virginia Henderson
    m. Raymond Starks
(j) Robbie Henderson
    m. Cleophus Bagwell
(k) Augustine Henderson
    m. T. H. Sloas

    1. Jerome Sloas
        b. 1948 - Fayette Co., Ala.
        d. 5 July 1967 - Chicago, Ill.
        bur. Elm Church of Christ Cemetery - Fayette Co., Ala.

(1) W. D. Henderson
    m. Edith -?-

(6) Dosha Passie Ann Henderson
    b. 26 February 1891 - Fayette Co., Ala.
    m. Murph Webster
    m. 2nd. Henry Lonzo Underwood

    (a) Robert Velmon Underwood
        b. 22 August 1922
        m. Josephine Campbell

        1. Gaylon Lee Underwood
           m. Linda -?-
        2. Vickie Victoria Underwood
           m. Tinsley Huff
        3. Lyndon Dale Underwood
        4. Lane Underwood
        5. Elissa Jean Underwood

    (b) William Elmer Underwood
        b. 10 July 1914
        m. Jane Davis

        1. Shirley Underwood
        2. David Underwood

    (c) Lonnie Lee Underwood
        b. February 1916
        d. 1933 - Anderson Co., Texas
        bur. Olive Branch Cemetery - Brushey Creek, Anderson Co.

Dosha Passie A. Henderson m. 3rd. James Thomas Long

    (d) Myrtle Long
        b. 5 November 1919
        m. Howard Gour

        1. Murlene Gour

        Myrtle Long m. 2nd. James Scott

        2. Tony Scott

95

            3. Rickie Scott

        (e) Lucille Long
            b. August 1922
            m. Audrey Lee Collins

            1. Ruth Ann Collins
                m. Charles Duvall
            2. Edward Lee Collins

        (f) James Givins Long
            b. 10 March 1923
            m. Bessie Lillie

            1. Janie Long
            2. Harriett Long

        (g) Julian Odonall Long
            b. 1925
            m. Claudine Mackbee
        (h) Passie Evelyn Long
            b. August 1926
            m. Jimmie Richard Sipes

            1. Thomas Richard Sipes
            2. Una Faye Sipes
                m. Tracey Lee Morgan
            3. Ross Michael Sipes
            4. Jimmie Ann Sipes
            5. Tolbert Lee Sipes

        (i) Thomas Ted Long
            b. May 1950
            m. Florence Malone

            1. Danny Joe Malone (step-son)
            2. Teddy Long
            3. Timmy Long

(7) Willie Frances Henderson
    b. 2 January 1893 - Fayette Co., Ala.
    d. 1962 - Jacksonville, Texas
    bur. Providence Cemetery
    m. John William Martin

    (a) Rita Martin
        m. Lewis Bowser
    (b) Gladys Martin
        m. Holly Campbell
    (c) Kay Martin
    (d) Raymond Martin
    (e) Gilbert Martin
    (f) Meryal Martin
    (g) Hilda Martin

    Willie F. Henderson m. 2nd. Arthur Filo Anthony
                            b. 17 May 1888 - Fayette Co., Ala.
                            d. Feb. 1953 - Jacksonville, Texas
                            bur. Providence Cemetery -", Texas
                            son of James Richard Anthony &
                                Zay Perkins

    (h) Iris Eline Anthony
        b. 1930 - Anderson Co., Texas
    (i) Jerry Marlin Anthony
        b. 1932 - Anderson Co., Texas

(8) Julie Adline Henderson
    b. 15 November 1896 - Fayette Co., Ala.
    m. Rastus Floyd Berryhill - 4 October 1912 - Fayette Co., Ala.
        b. 16 September 1895 - Marion Co., Ala.
        son of John Thomas Berryhill & Rachel Caroline Weeks
        (More information in preceeding pages)

(9) Myrtle Louise Henderson
    b. 17 April 1898 - Fayette Co., Ala.
    m. Walt Guin
       b. 1890 - Marion Co., Ala.
       d. 3 February 1968 - Fayette Co., Ala.
       bur. Old Union Cemetery - Fayette Co., Ala.

    (a) Coy Guin
        b. 6 August 1914
        m. Eulice Heath

        1. Ray Guin
        2. Barbara Ann Guin
        3. Linda Guin
        4. R. B. Guin
        5. Betty Guin

    (b) Parnell Guin
        b. 6 October 1917
        m. Reben Fowler

        1. Patsy Loretta Fowler
        2. Jimmy Fowler

    (c) Lee Roy Guin
        b. 28 July 1924
        m. Loretta Celey

        1. Johnnie Lee Guin
        2. James Marlin Guin
        3. Marsha Jean Guin
        4. Anneta Sue Guin

        Lee Roy Guin m. 2nd. Shirley -?-

        5. Shirrel Dean Guin
        6. Rachel Luese Guin

    Myrtle Louise Henderson m. 2nd. James Washington Westbrook
                                    b. 17 March 1898

    (d) Etma Luedell Westbrook
        b. 8 June 1931 - Fayette Co., Ala.
        d. 22 June 1968 - Grand Bay, Ala.
        bur. White Springs Cemetery
        m. Leon Mayfield

        1. Jimmy Dail Mayfield
           b. 1953

    (e) Ramie Evelin Westbrook
        b. 24 May 1933 - Fayette Co., Ala.
        m. Odis Cowart

        1. Brenda Sue Cowart

        Ramie Westbrook m. 2nd. J. R. Miller

        2. Tommy Ray Miller
        3. Rickey Deon Miller
        4. James Edwin Miller

    (f) James Jay Westbrook
        b. 11 March 1935 - Fayette Co., Ala.
        m. Helen Miller

        1. Lisa Westbrook
           b. 1955
        2. Rita Westbrook
           b. 1958

    (g) Angus Rubon Westbrook
        b. 22 January 1937 - Fayette Co., Ala.
        m. Jimmie Nell McDuff

        1. Kathy Lynn Westbrook
           b. 1959
        2. Deborah Annese Westbrook
           b. 1961

4. Basheba Berryhill - "Bashey"
   b. 9 May 1817 - Franklin Co., Tenn. - near Winchester
   d. 6 February 1892 - Hinds Co., Miss. - near Utica
   bur. Weeks Cemetery - 3½ miles east of Utica, Miss.
        Often called the "Alabama Berryhill's Burying Ground"
   m. Thomas Berryhill - "Tommy" - approx. 1837 in Marion Co., Ala.
      b. 9 May 1815 - Franklin Co., Tenn. near Winchester
      d. 17 May 1917 - Hinds Co., Miss. near Utica
      bur. Weeks Cemetery
      son of Alexander Berryhill & 2nd wife Rebecca Webster
              b. 1760 - N. C.   b. 1785 - N. C.
              d. 3 February 1839   d. Living in 1850, but
                                                      cannot locate in 1860
   Family history says five days before his death, age 102 years
   old, "Tommy" Berryhill rode his horse the six miles from his
   home to the town of Utica.

   A. Willis H. Berryhill
      b. 4 March 1838 - Marion Co., Ala.
   B. Robert Allen Berryhill
      b. 15 April 1840 - Marion Co., Ala.
   C. Emeline Berryhill
      b. 9 May 1842 - Marion Co., Ala.
   D. Rebecca Jane Berryhill
      b. 1844/1845 - Marion Co., Ala.
   E. Alexander Berryhill
      b. 1846 - Marion Co., Ala.
   F. William Berryhill
      b. 1848 - Marion Co., Ala.

1850 Marion Co., Ala. Federal Census 16/16 Beat #11

Thomas Berryhill		35 M	Tenn.	b. 1815
Basheba	"	33 F	Tenn.	1817
Willis	"	12 M	Ala.	1838
Robert	"	10 M	Ala.	1840
Emaline	"	8 F	Ala.	1842
Rebecca J.	"	6 F	Ala.	1844
Alexander	"	4 M	Ala.	1846
William	"	2 M	Ala.	1848

17/17 Best #11

Rebecca Berryhill	65 F	N. C.	1785 Living along between her sons

1860 Marion CO., Ala. Federal Census 334/332 page 48 3 July 1860

Thomas Berryhill		45 M	Tenn.	1815
Basheba	"	43 F	Tenn.	1817
Willis H.	"	21 M	Ala.	1839
Robert A.	"	19 M	Ala.	1841
Emaline	"	16 F	Ala.	1844
Rebecca J.	"	15 F	Ala.	1845
Alexander	"	13 M	Ala.	1847

It should be notice that Rebecca (Webster) Berryhill b. 1785 is now
missing, so we can assume she has died.

Since we miss William Berryhill b. 1848, I had already supposed he had
died, before I got the 1850 Murtality List, which listed him.

1870 Hinds Co., Miss. Federal Census 147/157 p. 19. Township #3, Utica, MS.

Thomas Berryhill		53 M	Tenn.	b. 1817
Basheba	"	53 F	Tenn.	1817
Willis H.	"	32 M	Ala.	1838
Rebecca J.	"	26 F	Ala.	1844
Alexander	"	24 M	Ala.	1846

148/138 page 20

Robert A. Berryhill		30 M	Ala.	b. 1840 (son of the above couple)
Mary M.	"	24 F	Ala.	1846 (wife, Mary M. Moss)
Lorena S.	"	4 F	Ala.	1866
William A.	"	3 M	Ala.	1867
Solon N.	"	7/12 M	Ala.	Dec. 1869
Rufus A.	"	25 M	Ala.	1845 (son of Edward & Mary)
James H.	"	23 M	Ala.	1847 (son of Edward & Mary)

1880 Hinds Co., Miss. Federal Census 301/317

Thomas Berryhill		63 M	Tenn.	N.C.	N.C.	b. 1817	
Basheba	"	60 F	Tenn.	Ga.	Ga.	1820	
Willis H.	"	40 M	Ala.	Tenn.	Tenn.	1840	
Perry	"	8 M	Miss.	Ala.	Ala.	1872 - grandson
Mary A.	"	12 F	Miss.	Tenn.	Tenn.	1868 - niece
Jennie Brooks		46 F	Miss.	Miss.	Miss.	1834 - white servant

I have been unable to determine who Perry Berryhill belonged to, that he is a grandson of Thomas & Basheba Berryhill!

It is possible that Mary A. Berryhill b. 1868, niece of Thomas & Basheba Berryhill, is the daughter of Thomas' half brother, Lensfield Berryhill, who remained in Franklin Co., Tenn., when the rest of the family moved to Alabama.

1880 Hinds Co., Miss. Federal Census 262/276

Robert A. Berryhill		40 M	Ala.	Ala.	Ala.	b. 1840	
Mary M.	"	36 F	Ala.	Tenn.	Ala.	1844	
Lorena S.	"	14 F	Ala.	Ala.	Ala.	1866	
Auther	"	10 M	Miss.	Ala.	Ala.	1870	William A. -1870
John A.	"	4 M	Miss.	Ala.	Ala.	1876	census
Ernest L.	"	10/12 M	Miss.	Ala.	Ala.	Aug. 1879	

Solon N. Berryhill is missing from home. Either died young, or was missed on census, as he is too young to be gone from home. Should be 11 years old on 1880 census.

A special thanks is given to Ethel (Berryhill) Purvis for all the help he gave in working up this family.

A. Willis H. Berryhill
    b. 4 March 1838 - Marion Co., Ala.
    d. 29 January 1897 - Hinds Co., Miss.
    bur. Weeks Cemetery - 3½ miles east of Utica, Hinds Co., Miss.
    m. Frances E. Davis - 23 January 1896 - Hinds Co., Miss
        b. 17 June 1860
        d. 13 February 1904 - Hinds Co., Miss.
        bur. Weeks Cemetery
        dau. of Robert G. Davis & Margaret -?-
            b. 1833 d. 1883   b. 1836   d. 1906
B. Robert Allen Berryhill
    b. 15 April 1840 - Marion Co., Ala.
    d. 7 December 1909 - Hinds Co., Miss.
    bur. Weeks Cemetery
    m. Mary Melinda Moss - 1864/1865 - Marion Co., Ala.
        b. 3 October 1845 - Marion Co., Ala.
        d. 22 September 1892 - Hinds Co., Miss.
        bur. Weeks Cemetery
        dau. of Abram H. Moss & Nancy Harris
            b. 1816 - S.C.   b. 1821 - Ala.

    (1) Lorena S. Berryhill - "Rena"
        b. 16 September 1866 - Marion Co., Ala.
        d. 10 March 1945 - Hinds Co., Miss.
        bur. Raymond Cemetery - Hinds Co., Miss.
        m. Robert Russell
            b. 1860
            d. 1930 approx.   bur. Salem Cemetery

(a) Florence Russell
    bur. Raymond Cemetery
(b) Fred Russell
    m. Irene -?-

    1. Essie Lorena Russell
    2. Fred Russell, Jr.
    3. Maurine Russell
    4. David Russell
    5. Irene Russell
    6. Fay Russell
    7. Charles Russell

    Fred Russell m. 2nd. Pearl Alford
    8. Son Russell
    9. Son Russell
    10 Daughter Russell

(c) Robert Russell, Jr.
    d. 1954
    m. Rosa Barker

    1. Allen Russell
    2. Mabel Russell
    3. Wayne Russell
    4. Daughter Russell

(2) William A. Berryhill
    b. 2 January 1867 - Marion Co., Ala.
    d. 3 October 1870 - Hinds Co., Miss.
    bur. Weeks Cemetery
(3) Solon N. Berryhill
    b. December 1869 - Marion Co., Ala. according to 1870 census
    d. by 1880 census, so we can assume he died young
(4) Arthur Erastus Berryhill
    b. 1870 approx. - Hinds Co., Miss.
    d. 1923/1924 - Hinds Co., Miss.
    bur. Salem Cemetery - Hinds Co., Miss.
    m. Agnes Louise Goodrum - 28 September 1890 - Hinds Co., Miss.
      b. 30 August 1872
      d. 25 December 1914 - Hinds Co., Miss.
      bur. Salem Cemetery
      dau. of Cornelius Goodrum & -?-

    (a) Bennie Durard Berryhill
        b. 17 April 1892
        d. 18 September 1949 - Hinds Co., Miss.
        bur. Salem Cemetery
        m. Emma Veola Hartwig - 3 June 1919 - Hinds Co., Miss.
          b. 20 October 1897
        No issue
    (b) Robert Berryhill
        b. 24 December 1893 - Hinds Co., Miss.
        m. Lillian Hindeman
          b. 1909 approx.
        No issue
    (c) Rufus Berryhill - "Ruffie"
        b. 1894 approx.
        d. 1904 approx. - Hinds Co., Miss.
        bur. Salem Cemetery
    (d) Agnes Louise Berryhill
        b. 1898 approx. - Hinds Co., Miss.
    (e) Mattie Mae Berryhill
        b. 23 January 1901 - Hinds Co., Miss.
        m. Percy Boone - 20 September 1921
          b. 30 September 1899 - Winston Co., Miss.

        1. Mary Agnes Boone
           b. 3 July 1922
           d. 6 November 1951 - Hinds Co., Miss.
           bur. Raymond Cemetery - Hinds Co., Miss.
           m. -?- Lick - October 1942

        A. Betty Jean Lick
           b. 17 February 1944
        B. Georgia Frances Lick
           b. 19 September 1946
        C. Billy Jor Lick
           b. 27 November 1947

     2. J. W. Boone
        b. 1 March 1924
        d. 28 December 1938
        bur. Salem Cemetery - Hinds Co., Miss.

(f) Eula Lee Berryhill
    b. 11 October 1903 - Hinds Co., Miss.
    m. Luther L. Loften - 20 December 1919 - Hinds Co., Miss.

     1. Agnes Louise Loften
        b. 4 July 1922 - Capiah Co., Miss.
        m. William B. Jones - 18 July 1941 - Brandon, Miss.
           b. 29 September 1921 - Jones Co., Miss.
           son of W. M. Jones & Annie Mae Campbell

        A. Sandra Lee Jones
           b. 3 March 1948 - Hinds Co., Miss.
           m. Ralph J. Shows - 17 October 1966 - Rankin Co, MS
              b. May 1944
        B. Shelia Mae Jones
           b. 12 October 1949 - Hinds Co., Miss.
           m. James Clyde Quinn - 21 February 1966 - Rankin Co.
              b. 5 October 1948 - Hinds Co., Miss.

     2. James Luther Loften
        b. 15 July 1924
        m. Eula Mae Broome
           b. 17 June 1926

        A. Ricky James Loften
           b. 16 November 1946
        B. Deborah Kaye Loften
           b. 23 November 1949

(g) Edna Berryhill
    b. 1907
    d. 1937 - Hinds Co., Miss.
    bur. Salem Cemetery
    m. -?- Wilson

     1. Ralph Wilson - "Sonny"

(h) Matthew Pool Berryhill
    b. 6 February 1909
    d. 9 September 1961 - Hinds Co., Miss.
    bur. Salem Cemetery
    m. Margaret Hughes

     1. Edna Earline Berryhill
        m. Russell Earl Edwards

        A. Russell E. Edwards, Jr.
           b. 1961 - Texas
        B. Leslie Renia Edwards
           b. 1963 - Bossier City, La.

    Matthew P. Berryhill m. 2nd Ada Mae Herrin - 24 Oct. 1944

     2. Charlotte Fay Berryhill
        b. 19 July 1945 - Scott Co., Miss.
        m. Douglas Edward Dean - 8 February 1963
     3. Tommy Ray Berryhill
        b. 8 September 1947 - Scott Co, Miss.
     4. Matthew P. Berryhill, Jr.
        b. 1 July 1952 - Scott Co., Miss.
     5. Danny Berryhill
        b. 20 September 1955 - Hinds Co., Miss.

Arthur E. Berryhill m. 2nd. 22 September 1919 - Hinds Co., MS
m. Hattie Laura Stringer
(5) S. L. Berryhill
b. 30 September 1872 & d. 10 November 1872 - Hinds Co., MS
bur. Weeks Cemetery
(6) Little Babe Berryhill
b. 1 September 1873   & d. 10 October 1873 - Hinds Co., MS
bur. Weeks Cemetery
(7) A. Y. Berryhill
b. 2 May 1875 & d. 10 September 1875 - Hinds Co., Miss.
bur. Weeks Cemetery
(8) John Adam Berryhill
b. 10 August 1876 - Hinds Co., MS
d. 12 March 1958 - Tahoka, Texas
bur. Tahoka Cemetery - Tahoka, Texas
m. Sussie Goodrum - 23 January 1895 - Hinds Co., MS
b. 1874 approx.
d. 1902 approx. - Hinds Co., Miss
bur. Utica Cemetery - Utica, Miss.
dau. of Cornelius Goodrum & -?-
m. 2nd. Bessie Campbell - 1903 approx. - Texas
b. 28 February 1881 - Hunt, Texas
d. 30 September 1938
bur. Tahoka Cemetery - Tahoka, Texas

(a) Allen Campbell Berryhill
b. 10 February 1904 - Jones Co., Texas
m. Nera Walldon - 17 October 1925 - Ellis Co., Texas
b. 30 September 1908 - Ellis Co., Texas
1. Nera Mae Berryhill
b. 12 December 1926 - Ellis Co., Texas
m. Ferrell Daniel - 19 December 1943
b. 25 May 1924 - Briscoe Co., Texas

A. Deryel Gene Daniel
b. 2 January 1945 - Terry Co., Texas
B. Shelia Dianne Daniel
b. 6 October 1949 - Terry Co., Texas

2. John William Berryhill
b. 5 November 1928 - Ellis Co., Texas
m. Betty Jean Baker - 30 April 1949
b. 4 March 1934 - Hardman Co., Texas

A. Eddie Wayne Berryhill
b. 10 November 1950 - Terry Co., Texas
B. Glenna Jean Berryhill
b. 18 April 1958 - Terry Co., Texas
C. Chris Allen Berryhill
b. 8 August 1961 - Terry Co., Texas

3. Robert Allen Berryhill
b. 15 May 1930 - Ellis Co., Texas
m. Janie Brown - 28 May 1954
b. 1 July 1936 - Terry Co., Texas

A. Pamela Sue Berryhill
b. 25 September 1955 - Terry Co., Texas
B. Cindy Kay Berryhill
b. 17 September 1957 - Terry Co., Texas
C. Angela Terese Berryhill
b. 12 December 1962 - Terry Co., Texas
D. Regina Robin Berryhill
b. 20 February 1965 - Terry Co., Texas

4. Jimmie Earl Berryhill
b. 7 February 1933 - Terry Co., Texas
m. Esta Mae Beavers - 17 March 1955
b. 11 December 1934 - Childress Co., Texas

A. Natalie Beth Berryhill
b. 30 November 1958 - Terry Co., Texas
B. James Alan Berryhill
b. 7 June 1961 - Gaines Co., Texas

5. Ernest Lynnwood Berryhill
    b. 2 July 1935 - Terry Co., Texas
    m. Tommie Ruth Arp - 7 August 1953
       b. 15 May 1935 - Wichita Co., Texas

    A. Ricky Lynn Berryhill
       b. 12 September 1954 - Terry Co., Texas
    B. Rebecca Elaine Berryhill
       b. 30 December 1956 - Terry Co., Texas

(b) Infant Berryhill
    b. 1905   d. 1905 - Jones Co., Texas
(c) Violet Berryhill
    b. 29 January 1906 - Texas
    m. Walter Jackson Reed - 29 July 1929
       b. 23 August 1907 - Howard Co., Texas
       d. 10 January 1961 - Big Springs, Texas
    bur. Big Springs Cemetery

    1. Carroll Lynn Reed
       b. 23 August 1934 - Big Springs, Texas
       m. Vista Jean Estes - 31 May 1956
          b. 3 January 1938 - Holdenville, Okla.

       A. Laura Lynne Reed
          b. 8 May 1957 - Bartlesville, Okla.
       B. Bradley Scott Reed
          b. 8 April 1959 - Bartlesville, Okla.
       C. Judith Ellen Reed
          b. 24 November 1062 - Harris Co., Texas

(d) James Ervin Berryhill
    b. 18 March 1908 - Howard Co., Texas
    Single
(e) Mary Jewell Berryhill
    b. 1 August 1910 - Tarrant, Texas
    m. R. L. Upchurch - 5 August 1931
       b. 22 February 1904 - Canton, Van Zandt Co., Texas

    1. Mary Lou Upchurch
       b. 21 March 1934 - Terry, Texas
       m. Courtney Hankins - November 1950
          b. 8 December 1933

       A. Carolyn Hankins
          b. 29 July 1951 - Tarrant Texas
       B. Kathy Hankins
          b. 4 November 1953 - Lubbock, Texas

    2. George Brandon Upchurch
       b. 14 June 1932 - Ellis Co., Texas
       m. Sue Seay - 1 August 1953

       A. Mickie Sue Upchurch
          b. 23 June 1954 - Lubbock, Texas
       B. Brenda Kay Upchurch
          b. 9 May 1956 - Lubbock, Texas

    3. James Upchurch
       b. 16 December 1941 - Ellis Co., Texas
       m. Rosemary Graves - 12 July 1963

       A. Michael Upchurch
          b. 28 December 1964 - Lubbock, Texas

(f) Johnnie Lynnwood Berryhill
    b. 5 July 1913 - Tarrant, Texas
    d. 21 March 1960 - Howard Co., Texas
    bur. Big Springs Cemetery - Big Springs, Texas
    m. Dollie Marie Carter - 7 March 1942

    1. Janette Ruth Berryhill
       b. 1944 approx.
       m. W. Hugh Kirby

        2. Vanette Kay Berryhill
           b. 1946 approx.
           m. Willie Harris

    (g) Goldie Berryhill
        b. 27 July 1918 - Johnson Co., Texas
        d. 7 February 1936 - Tahoka, Texas
        bur. Tahoka Cemetery - Tahoka, Texas

John Adam Berryhill m. 3rd. 1943
m. Mrs. Nannie (Cain) Puckett
    b. 1880
    d. 1962 - Jackson, Miss.
    bur. Cedarlawn Cemetery - Hinds Co.
    dau. of John Chesterfield Cain & Rebecca VaNamen

(9) Ernest Lynwood Berryhill
    b. 29 August 1879
    d. 18 April 1968 - Hinds Co., Miss.
    bur. Lakewood Cemetery - Hinds Co., Miss.
    m. Nettie Ethel Cain - 27 July 1904 - Hinds Co., Miss.
       b. 15 March 1882
       dau. of John Chesterfield Cain & Rebecca VaNamen

    (a) Earnest Lamar Berryhill
        b. 10 May 1905 - Hinds Co., Miss.
        m. Elizabeth Hammett - 1934 - Hinds Co., Miss.
           b. 3 December 1912 - Warren Co., Miss.

        1. Betty Lucille Berryhill
           b. 16 June 1935 - Hinds Co., Miss.
           m. Sidney Unsworth - August 1967

           A. Sidney Unsworth, Jr. (from his former marriage)
              b. 13 June 1955
           B. Madolyn Unsworth (from his former marriage)
              b. 21 May 1959
           C. Tammie Unsworth (from his former marriage)
              b. 1 July 1963

        2. Ernest Lamar Berryhill
           b. 26 March 1937 - Hinds Co., Miss.

    (b) Herman Leroy Berryhill
        b. August 1907 - Hinds Co., Miss.
        m. Winnifred Lou Thompson - 27 December 1937
           b. 1 January 1911 - Dermott, Ark.

        1. David Leroy Berryhill
           b. 24 April 1948

    (c) Alice Lucille Berryhill
        b. 13 October 1908 - Hinds Co., Miss.
        m. Robert Thomas Alliston - 21 August 1938 - Hinds Co.
           b. 19 March 1913 - Rankin Co., Miss.
        No issue
    (d) John Robert Berryhill - "Robin"
        b. 17 February 1913 - Harrison Co., Miss.
        d. 15 March 1914
        bur. Wiggins Cemetery - Wiggins, Miss.
    (e) Rebecca Yvonne Berryhill
        b. 12 December 1914 - Stone Co., Miss.
        m. Clifton L. Magee - 1946 - Hinds Co., Miss.
           b. 2 November 1898
           d. 21 February 1952
           bur. Lakewood Cemetery - Hinds Co., Miss.

        1. Deborah Yvonne Magee
           b. 5 March 1947 - Hinds Co., Miss.
           m. Kim Kimbrough - 6 June 1968 - Hinds Co., Miss.

        Rebecca Yvonne Berryhill m. 2nd 1964 - Hinds Co., Miss.
        m. P. M. Cox
           d. January 1967 - Hinds Co., Miss.
           bur. Lakewood Cemetery

(f) Hugh Wilson Berryhill
   b. 20 January 1917 - Stone Co., Miss.
   m. Fannie Louise Bates - 1946 - Hinds Co., Miss.
      b. 19 January 1923 - Carroll Co., Miss.
(g) Ethel Lorrine Berryhill (twin)
   b. 14 October 1922 - Stone Co., Miss.
   m. Ottis Johnson Purvis - 17 September 1944 - Hinds Co.
      b. 30 August 1918 - Jones Co., Miss.

   1. Ottis Jack Purvis
      b. 29 June 1945 - Hinds Co., Miss.
   2. Nettie Joan Purvis
      b. 29 December 1947 - Hinds Co., Miss.
   3. Alice Marion Loraine Purvis
      b. 9 February 1949 - Hinds Co., Miss.
   4. Kathy Lyn Purvis
      b. 23 January 1953 - Hinds Co., Miss.

(h) Nettie Corinne Berryhill (twin)
   b. 14 October 1922 - Stone Co., Miss.

(10) Little Babe Berryhill
   b. 19 August 1881
   d. 28 August 1881 - Hinds Co., Miss.
   bur. Weeks Cemetery - Hinds Co., Miss.
(11) Maggie M. Berryhill
   b. 2 February 1883
   d. 18 January 1884 - Hinds Co., Miss.
   bur. Weeks Cemetery
(12) Alma Stella Berryhill
   b. 6 June 1885 - Hinds Co., Miss.
   d. 26 November 1962 - Hinds Co., Miss.
   bur. Raymond Cemetery - Raymond, Hinds Co., Miss.
   m. Eugene Allison McGee - 15 January 1903 - Hinds Co., Miss.
      b. 29 January 1874 -
      d. 9 November 1933 - Hinds Co, Miss.
      bur. Raymond Cemetery

(a) Sweet Maruine McGee
   b. 1904
   d. 1906 - Hinds Co., Miss.
   bur. Salem Cemetery - Hinds Co., Miss.
(b) Mary George McGee
   b. 25 October 1906 - Hinds Co., Miss.
   m. Vincent Anthony Canizaro - 12 Feburary 1930

   1. Alma Josephine Canizaro
      b. 12 June 1931
      m. Robert Louis Ranft - 22 January 1953

      A. Rene' Lorraine Ranft
         b. 13 March 1954
      B. Rebecca Ranft
         b. 18 August 1955
      C. Mary Michaele Ranft
         b. 24 May 1958
      D. Paul Vincent Ranft
         b. 27 June 1959
      E. David Louis Ranft
         b. 11 November 1961

   2. Mary Vincent Canizaro
      b. 17 February 1937
      m. Stanley Darrell Marquardt - 17 May 1954

      A. Stanley D. Marquardt, Jr.
         b. 24 February 1955
      B. Donald Lee Marquardt
         b. 2 September 1956
      C. Darrell Lynn Marquardt
         b. 3 September 1957
      D. Christine Ann Marquardt
         b. 13 October 1958

```
                    E. Mary June Marquardt
                       b. 18 August 1959
                    F. Barbara Particia Marquardt
                       b. 1 June 1961
        (c) Beatrice Beard McGee
            b. 29 May 1908 - Hinds Co., Miss.
            m. Homer Lane Ford - 26 September 1935
               b. 10 April 1895
               d. 18 July 1951

            1. Frances Alice Ford
               b. 2 July 1931
               m. Howard William Seibert - 22 August 1953
                  b. 3 March 1930

               A. William Lane Seibert
                  b. 18 December 1955
               B. Eric John Seibert
                  b. 4 July 1959
               C. Susan Alice Seibert
                  b. 22 August 1960
               D. Lane Allison Seibert
                  b. 24 May 1966

            2. Lane Allison Ford
               b. 2 March 1938 - Warren Co., Miss.
               m. William Graham Smart, Jr. - 16 August 1958
                  b. 15 July 1933

               A. Elizabeth Lane Smart
                  b. 18 May 1959
               B. William G. Smart, III
                  b. 4 January 1963
               C. Thomas Ford Smart
                  b. 26 January 1964
               D. Ellen Lucile Smart
                  b. 13 January 1968

        (d) Vivian Dangerfield McGee
            b. 10 January 1914 - Hinds Co., Miss.
            m. Orley Mason Hood - 9 May 1942 - Warren Co., Miss.
               b. 30 December 1915

            1. Howard Allison Hood
               b. 9 February 1943
            2. Catherine Nelson Hood
               b. 11 January 1945
               m. Cary Alton Phillips - 26 June 1965 - Warren Co.
                  b. 2 April 1943

               A. Cary Allison Phillips
                  b. 4 November 1967

            3. Orley Mason Hood, Jr.
               b. 28 November 1948

        (e) Catherine Cain McGee
            b. 25 December 1917 - Hinds Co., Miss.
            m. James Claude Ryan - 20 May 1935
               b. 1908
               d. 4 September 1958

            1. John Robert Ryan
               b. 26 March 1936
               m. Barbara Marie Coates - 29 August 1958 - Hinds Co.
                  b. 12 June 1936

               A. Wendy Marie Ryan
                  b. 17 September 1960
               B. John Coates Ryan
                  b. 22 March 1964
```

                2. Catherine Eugenia Ryan
                   b. 10 June 1938
                   m. H. M. Walker - 30 December 1956 - Warren Co., Miss.
                      b. 17 December 1933

                   A. Theresa Gwin Walker
                      b. 11 December 1957
                   B. Catherine Lynn Walker
                      b. 13 February 1959
                   Catherine E. Ryan m. 2nd. 5 January 1964 - Warren Co.
                   m. Graham William Tucker
                      b. 10 March 1929

                   C. Patricia Allison Tucker
                      b. 18 August 1964
                   D. Margaret Michaelle Tucker
                      b. 15 October 1966

                Catherine C. McGee - m. 2nd - 2 November 1956 - Warren Co.
                m. John Thomas Ryan
                   b. 27 January 1918 - Warren Co., Miss.

            (f) Eugene Allison McGee, Jr.
                b. 8 October 1922
                d. 2 November 1942
                bur. National Military Cemetery - Vicksburg, Miss.

     Robert Allen Berryhill m. 2nd - 22 February 1894 - Hinds Co.
     m. Mary Emma Anding
        b. 22 September 1860
        d. 25 March 1949
        bur. Lebanon Presbyterian Cemetery - Hinds Co., Miss.

     (13) James Robert Berryhill - "Jimmy"
          b. 31 January 1895 - Hinds Co., Miss.
          m. Maybel Cox - 18 July 1922 - Hinds Co., Miss.
             b. 26 May 1904 - Hinds Co., Miss.

          (a) Mary Lee Berryhill
              b. 21 December 1923 - Hinds Co., Miss.
              m. Harvey Elmo Nail, Jr. - 8 September 1942 - Rankin Co.
                 b. 7 October 1922

              1. Jack Stephen Nail
                 b. 13 December 1950 - Hinds Co., Miss.
              2. Larry Phillips Nail
                 b. 26 October 1958 - Hinds Co., Miss.

          (b) Evelyn Berryhill
              b. 5 February 1925 - Hinds Co., Miss.
              m. Howard Hennington - 18 April 1943 - Hinds Co., Miss.
                 b. 31 October 1920

              1. Michael Wayne Hennington
                 b. 12 June 1954 - Hinds Co., Miss.
              2. Bruce Lamar Hennington
                 b. 8 October 1958 - Hinds Co., Miss.

          (c) Allen Berryhill
              b. 4 November 1926 - Hinds Co., Miss.
              m. Kathleen Barrett
                 b. 6 August 1927

              1. James Allen Berryhill
                 b. 26 August 1952

          (d) Herbert Berryhill
              b. 1 September 1928 - Hinds Co., Miss.
              m. Velma Louise McDonald - 25 November 1949 - Rankin Co.
                 b. 25 October 1926

              1. Herbert Lowery Berryhill
                 b. 16 November 1950
              2. Clifford Lamont Berryhill
                 b. 27 July 1954 - Hinds Co., Miss.

        3. Tiney Angela Berryhill
           b. and d. 19 August 1958 - Hinds Co., Miss.
           bur. Terry Cemetery - Hinds Co., Miss.
        4. James Melvin Berryhill
           b. 4 July 1961
           d. 27 July 1966 - Hinds Co., Miss.
           bur. Terry Cemetery - Hinds Co., Miss.

    (e) Dorothy Pearline Berryhill
        b. 12 January 1935 - Hinds Co., Miss.
        m. Edward S. Sheffield - 6 May 1964 - Hinds Co., Miss.
           b. 1 May 1919 - Brooks Co., Ga.

        1. Gregory Earl (Griffin) Sheffield
           b. 31 December 1956

    (f) Walter Berryhill
        b. 28 December 1938 - Hinds Co., Miss.
        m. Elsie Louise Moss - 10 November 1962 - Hinds Co., MS
           b. 28 May 1942

        1. Tina Angela Berryhill
           b. 6 July 1965

(14) Betty Elizabeth Berryhill
     b. 10 July 1896 - Hinds Co., Miss.
     m. Roy Graham - 5 December 1923
        b. 30 September 1893 - Jasper Co., Miss.
        d. 24 March 1963 -
        bur. Lebanon Cemetery - Hinds Co., Miss.

    (a) Anne Elizabeth Graham
        b. 16 April 1927 - Warren Co., Miss.
        m. Earl A. Allen - 26 November 1947

        1. Beverly Anne Allen
           b. 6 February 1949 - Hinds Co., Miss.
        2. Susan Elizabeth Allen
           b. 3 February 1951 - Warren Co., Miss.
        3. Earl Graham
           b. 13 September 1952 - Warren Co., Miss.

    (b) Betty Louise Berryhill
        b. 13 March 1932 - Bastrop, La.
        m. Marvin G. Bolding - 2 June 1948 - Warren Co., Miss.
           d. 8 June 1965
           bur. Bolding Cemetery - near Strong, Ark.

        1. Marvin C. Bolding, Jr.
           b. 7 October 1949 - Warren Co., Miss.
        2. Daniel Mark Bolding
           b. 8 October 1952 - Bastrop, La.
        3. Martha Gail Bolding
           b. 26 October 1955 - Bastrop, La.
        4. Marshall Lyn Bolding
           b. 18 January 1957 - Bastrop, La.

(15) Daniel T. Berryhill   SEE ADDENDA FOR MORE INFORMATION.
     b. 15 October 1897
     d. 28 June 1952 - Hinds Co., Miss.
     bur. Morrison Cemetery - Learned, Miss.
     m. Josie Bush - 22 December 1945 - Hinds Co., Miss.
        b. 11 November 1911 - Hinds Co., Miss.

    (a) Mary Jo Berryhill
        b. 20 September 1946
        m. Robert Donald Nail - 20 August 1965
           b. 20 April 1941

(16) Clara Berryhill
     b. 16 November 1899 - Hinds Co., Miss.
     m. Joseph Mattis - 4 November 1928 - Hinds Co., Miss.
        b. 3 April 1885 - Hinds Co., Miss.
        d. 17 October 1936
        bur. Utica Cemetery - Utica, Miss.

(a) Christine Mattis
    b. 12 August 1929 - Hinds Co., Miss.
    m. William H. Brown
       b. 31 July 1922 - Hinds Co., Miss.

    1. Judy Catherine Brown
       b. 14 October 1958
    2. Richard Brown
       b. 4 April 1951
    3. William Bradley Brown
       b. 16 April 1961

(b) Thomas Mattis
    b. 16 June 1931 - Hinds Co., Miss.
    m. Mary E. Garner - 12 August 1951 - Hinds Co., Miss.
       b. 5 January 1932 - Scott Co., Miss.

    1. Brenda Sue Robertson (niece of Mary)
       b. 21 August 1954 - Hinds Co., Miss.
    2. Cheryl Lyn Mattis
       b. 19 March 1954 - Hinds Co., Miss.
    3. Thomas Vance Mattis, Jr.
       b. 12 September 1966 - Mobile, Ala.

(c) JoAnne Mattis
    b. 6 July 1933 - Hinds Co., Miss.
    m. Charles H. Weems - 18 April 1954

    1. Charles H. Weems, Jr.
       b. 8 August 1956 - Rankin Co., Miss.
    2. Mark Daniel Weems
       b. 15 May 1960 - Rankin Co., Miss.

    Jo Anne Mattis m. 2nd. Charlie Serpass

(d) Jewel Mattis
    b. 12 September 1935 - Hinds Co., Miss.
    m. James L. Eady
       b. 6 November 1931 - Smith Co., Miss.

    1. James Oliver Eady
       b. 7 May 1954
    2. Joseph Michael Eady
       b. 4 January 1957
    3. Robert Jeffrey Eady
       b. 12 July 1961

(e) Joseph Mattis, Jr.
    b. 12 September 1936 - Hinds Co., Miss.
    m. Barbara Rinehart

    1. Jennese Mattis
       b. 14 September 1958
    2. Michael Vance Mattis
       b. 16 September 1963

(17) Hughie Dennis Berryhill   *SEE ADDENDA FOR MORE INFORMATION.*
     b. 31 August 1902
     d. 17 October 1933 - Hinds Co., Miss.
     bur. Utica Cemetery - Hinds Co., Miss.
     m. Ruby Mae Newsome - 24 October 1924 - Hinds Co., Miss.
        b. 21 June 1905 - Hinds Co., Miss.

    (a) Hughie Dennis Berryhill, Jr.
        b. 10 September 1926 - Hinds Co., Miss.
        m. Betty Clara Boyd
           b. 8 July 1933 - Hinds Co., Miss.

        1. Sherry Claire Berryhill
           b. 10 February 1953
        2. Hughie Dennis Berryhill, III
           b. 15 September 1954
        3. Tol Edward Berryhill
           b. 5 March 1961

        (b) Lanelle Berryhill
            b. 6 January 1929 - Warren Co., Miss.
            m. James Edward Hudson
                b. 12 March 1926 - Grant Parish, La

            1. Linda Lanelle Hudson
                b. 6 September 1949 - Warren Co., Miss.
            2. Jamie Nell Hudson
                b. 9 October 1951 - Warren Co., Miss.
            3. Vivian Ann Hudson
                b. 7 June 1955 - Warren Co., Miss.

        (c) Fay Berryhill
            b. 3 October 1932 - Hinds Co., Miss.
            m. Thomas Eugene Griffin
                b. 24 November 1928 - Hinds Co., Miss.

            1. Thomas Eugene Griffin, Jr.
                b. 24 November 1953
            2. Paula Elaine Griffin
                b. 12 May 1957
            3. Craig Franklin Griffin
                b. 24 June 1961

C. Margaret Emeline Berryhill
    b. 9 May 1842 - Marion Co., Ala.
    d. 11 June 1889 - Hinds Co., Miss.
    bur. Weeks Cemetery - Hinds Co., Miss.
    m. Joshua T. (or John T.) Adkins - 21 February 1867 - Hinds Co.
        b. 8 March 1838 - Ala.
        d. 25 January 1883 - Hinds Co., Miss.
        bur. Weeks Cemetery

    (1) Robert E. Adkins - "Bobby"
        b. 1869
        d. 1890 - Hinds Co., Miss.
        bur. Weeks Cemetery
    (2) Lucian Adkins
        b. 1868 - Hinds CO., Mis.
        Shows age as 11 years on 1880 census
    (3) Della Adkins
        b. 1870 - Hinds Co., Miss.
        m. -?- Brock and moved to Texas - no further information
    (4) Bashi Adkins
        b. 1872 - Hinds Co., Miss.
        Shows age as 8 years on 1880 census

D. Rebecca Jane Berryhill - "Becky"
    b. 1844/1845 - Marion Co., Ala.
    m. Francis Marion Wade

    (1) Mattie Wade
    (2) Illa Wade
        m. -?- Freeman
    (3) John Thomas Wade
        marker says "age 6 mo., 8 September 1876"
        bur. Weeks Cemetery - Hinds Co., Miss.

    It has been said this family moved to Texas and raised a large
    family of children. All contacts are now lost to us.

E. Alexander C. Berryhill (Spelled Elaxandia on his marker)
    b. 7 March 1846 - Marion Co., Ala.
    d. 11 November 1885 - Hinds Co., Miss.
    bur. Weeks Cemetery - 3½ miles east of Utica, Hinds Co., Miss.
    m. Georgia Salmons - 17 January 1881 - Hinds Co., Miss.

    (1) Pervie Berryhill
        b. 1882 approx. - Hinds Co., Miss.
        Is said to have married and moved to the Miss. Delta and all
        contacts are lost with him.

(2) Lizzie Berryhill
   b. 1884 approx. - Hinds Co., Miss.
   d. 1939 approx. - Raymond, Miss. area
   bur. Salem Cemetery - Raymond, Miss. area
   m. Norman Cam Flanagan

   Lost several infants
   (a) George Flanagan
      b. 1907 approx. - Hinds Co., Miss.
      d. 1935 approx. - Hinds Co., Miss.
      He cranked up a tractor while under it and was killed.
      m. Annie -?-
         She has since re-married and works at the University
         hospital in Jackson, Miss. as of 1968.

      1. Son

   This information came from Patrick Flanagan of Louisville,
   Miss. His mother died when he was about 5 years old, and
   his Uncle Cam and Aunt Lizzie (Berryhill) Flanagan kept
   him several years.
   (3) Robert Berryhill - "Bob"
      b. 1885 approx. - Hinds Co., Miss.
      d. approx. age of 13 years, he was killed by a Negro youth.
      bur. Dry Grove, Miss. Cemetery

   Did Alexander C. Berryhill first marry Mrs. T. J. Shirg -
   29 June 1871 in Hinds Co., Miss?

F. William Berryhill
   b. 1848 - Marion Co., Ala.
   d. November 1850 - Marion Co., Ala.
   bur. Berryhill Family Cemetery
   Mortality list of 1850 Marion Co., Ala. shows he died of
   Jaundice after being sick for seven months.

HINDS COUNTY, MISSISSIPPI MARRIAGES

Martha E. Berryhill & G. W. Adkins	21 January 1877
Margaret E. Berryhill & Josh T. Adkins	21 February 1867
A. C. Berryhill & Lizzie Fulgham	2 December 1870
A. C. Berryhill & Mrs. T. J. Shirg	29 June 1871
A. C. Berryhill & Georgia Salmons	27 January 1881
A. E. Berryhill & Mrs. Hattie Laura Stringer	22 September 1919
A. E. Berryhill & Miss A. L. Goodrum	28 September 1890
A. L. Berryhill & Mrs. E. J. Brock	5 January 1881
B. D. Berryhill & Miss V. G. Hartwig	8 June 1919
Charles M. Berryhill & Juanita Inabnet	27 November 1889
E. L. Berryhill & Nettie E. Cain	27 July 1904
Hugh Berryhill & Ruby Mae Newsom	24 October 1924
J. A. Berryhill & Sussie Goodrum	23 January 1895
John Martin Berryhill & Sallie Beasley	1 July 1888
John T. Berryhill & Caroline Weeks	15 April 1877
R. A. Berryhill & Mary Emma Anding	22 February 1894
Samuel N. Berryhill & Miss Emma F. Beasley	2 May 1886
W. H. Berryhill & Frances E. Davis	23 January 1896
Mrs. Minnie Berryhill & R. B. Dickson	28 December 1919

Please excuse any errors we find in these marriages as they were taken
from microfilm rolls not indexed, and cards from Jackson, Miss. had been
placed out on tables and film shot, and some are very dull. I am
sure there were others, but time did not permit chekcing out each of the
200 rolls of Miss. marriages.

But how I wish Clerks had not been so prone to use initials when they
recorded names, and even the license was often not recorded sometimes
for years.

5. Alexander Berryhill
   b. 1818
   d.
   bur.
   Living in 1870 census, but gone by 1880
   m. Celia Weeks - 1836-1837 approx. - Marion Co., Ala.
      b. 1816-1817 - Tenn.
      d. 1 January 1897 - Marion Co., Ala.
      bur. Harmony Grove Cemetery - Fayette Co., Ala.
      dau. of Benjamin Weeks & -?-
               b. 1789 - N. C.
               d. dead by 1850 census

   A. Nancy M. Berryhill
      b. 1838 - Marion Co., Ala.
   B. James M. Berryhill
      b. 1842 - Marion Co., Ala.
   C. John Jackson Berryhill
      b. 1843 - Marion Co., Ala.
   D. Charles W. Berryhill
      b. 1845 - Marion Co., Ala.
   E. Sarah Jane Berryhill
      b. 1847 - Marion Co., Ala.
   F. Susan C. Berryhill
      b. 1848 - Marion Co., Ala.
   G. Thomas Berryhill
      b. 1849 - Marion Co., Ala.
   H. Martha F. Berryhill
      b. 1851 - Marion Co., Ala.
   I. Mary E. Berryhill
      b. 1853 - Marion Co., Ala.

1850 Marion Co., Ala. Federal Census #2/#2 Beat #11

Alexander Berryhill		33	M.	Tenn.	b.	1817
Celia	"	34	F.	Tenn.		1816
Nancy M.	"	12	F.	Ala.		1838
James	"	8	M	Ala.		1842
John	"	7	M	Ala.		1843
Charles	"	5	M	Ala.		1845
Sarah Jane	"	3	F	Ala.		1847
Susan	"	2	F	Ala.		1848
Thomas	" 6/12	M	Ala.			1850

1860 Marion CO., Ala. Federal Census 183/191

Alexander Berryhill		48	M	Tenn.	1812
Celia	"	48	F	Tenn.	1812
James M.	"	19	M	Ala.	1841
Jackson	"	18	M	Ala.	1842
Charles W.	"	14	M	Ala.	1846
Sarah J.	"	13	F	Ala.	1847
Susan C.	"	11	F	Ala.	1849
Martha F.	"	9	F	Ala.	1851
Mary E.	"	7	F	Ala.	1853

1870 Fayette Co., Ala Federal Census 70/70 Western Div. P. O. Pikesville

Alexander Berryhill		57	M	Tenn.	1813
Celia	"	57	F.	Tenn.	1813
Mary E.	"	17	F	Ala.	1853
Angeline Weeks		16	F	Ala.	1854

5. Alexander Berryhill
   b. 1818 - Franklin Co., Tenn.
   d. Living in 1870 census, but gone by 1880
   bur.
   m. Celia Weeks 1836/1837 - Marion Co., Ala.
      b. 1816/1817 Tenn
      d. 1 January 1897 - Marion Co., Ala.
      bur. Harmony Grove Cemetery - Fayette Co., Ala.
      dau. of Benjamin Weeks & -?-

   A. Nancy M. Berryhill
      b. 1838 - Marion Co., Ala.
      d. After 1880 - living in 1880 with her second husband,
         Elisha Vickery
      m. Alfred L. Webster - by 1860 census
         b. 1835 - Tenn.
         d. Living in 1870 census, but apparently died soon after.

      (1) America A. Webster
          b. 1861 - Marion Co., Ala.
             Living in 1880, age 19 years old, in home of step-father
      (2) John W. Webster (his mother was a Dodson)
          b. 9 September 1862 - Marion Co., Ala.
          d. 10 April 1932
          bur. Musgrove Chapel Methodist Cemetery - Fayette Co., Ala.
          m. Sudie F. Musgrove
             b. 16 April 1867
             d. 24 December 1912
             bur. Musgrove Chapel Methodist Cemetery

          (a) Thoms M. Webster
              b. 29 May 1903
              d. 4 January 1957
              bur. Musgrove Chapel Methodist Cemetery
              m. Helen B. Riley
                 b. 13 August 1907

      (3) Newton S. Webster - said to be a Whitehead.
          b. 1868 - Marion Co., Ala.
          d. Living 1880 census, age 12 years old, in home of step-
             father, Elisha Vickery
      (4) Joannah Webster - also a Whitehead
          b. 1871 - Marion Co., Ala.
          d. Living 1880 census, age 9 years old, in home of step-
             father, Elisha Vickery

      Nancy M. Berryhill m. 2nd. Elisha Vickery - 1875 approx.
                            b. 5 January 1833 - Tenn.
                            d. 19 June 1905
                            bur. Harmony Grove Cemetery
                            Pvt., Co. F, 43rd Reg. Ala. Inf.
                            son of Parton Vickery and -?- Atkins
                                  b. 1805 - S. C.   (first wife)

      (5) George W. Vickery
          b. 1876 - Marion Co., Ala.

1860 Marion Co., Ala.   187/195
Alfred Webster		25	M	Tenn.	b. 1835	
Nancy M.	"	22	F	Ala.	1838	(Nancy M. Berryhill)
Mary J.	"	13	F	Miss.	1847	(Sister of Alfred)
Caroline G.	"	11	F	Miss.	1849	(Sister of Alfred)

1870 Marion Co., Ala.   68/68
A. L. Webster		35	M	Tenn.	b. 1835
Nancy	"	33	F	Ala.	1837
Jane	"	24	F	Miss.	1846
Gracy C.	"	23	F	Miss.	1847
America A.	"	9	F	Ala.	1861
John W.	"	8	M	Ala.	1862
Newton S.	"	2	M	Ala.	1868

```
1880 Marion Co., Ala.        Beat #12
Elisha Vickery        46 M Tenn. b. 1834
Nancy        "        38 F Ala.     1842
James W.     "        22 M Ala.     1858 Son by his first wife, Mary E.
Mary E.      "        21 F Ala.     1859 Dau." "    "    "    "
America A. Webster    19 F Ala.     1861 Step-dau.
John W.         "     18 M Ala.     1862 Step-son
Jesse B. Vickery     13 M Ala.     1867 Son of his first wife, Mary E.
Rebecca     "        12 F Ala.     1868 Dau. of his first wife, Mary E.
Newton S. Webster    12 M Ala.     1868 Step-son
Marian C. Vickery    10 F Ala.     1870 Dau. of his first wife, Mary E.
Joannah Webster       9 F Ala.     1871 Step-dau.
George W. Vickery     4 M Ala.     1876 Son of Elisha & Nancy
```

   B. James M. Berryhill
      b. 1841/1842 - Marion Co., Ala.
      1860 census shows in father's home, age 19 years. No other
      information is available on him.

   C. John Jackson Berryhill
      b. 1842/1843 - Marion Co., Ala.
      1860 census shows in father's home, age 18 years. No other
      information is available on him. One John J. Berryhill served
      in Co. L., 16 Ala Inf. Reg. as a Pvt. Age 20 years, enlisted
      in Courtland, Ala. on 19 August 1861.

   D. Charles William Berryhill - "Cap"
      b. 15 June 1846 - Marion Co., Ala.
      d. 15 September 1907 - Fayette Co., Ala.
      bur. Harmony Grove Cemetery - Fayette Co., Ala.
      Cap moved to Fayette Co. from Marion Co. in January 1899. He
      worked for the railroad Co. and always wore a cap, hence the
      nickname, and he served in Co. D., 19th Ala. Reg.
      m. Mrs. Caroline (Perry) Dickinson - 1865 approx. - Marion Co.
         b. 18 April 1840 - Fayette Co., Ala.
         d. 2 March 1920 - Anderson Co., Texas near Palestine
         bur. Pleasant Springs Cemetery - Palestine, Texas
         dau. of Auguston Perry & Allie T. -?-
                  b. 1 July 1825   b. 15 November 1836
                  d. 4 January 1915d. 4 December 1906
                  both bur. Harmony Grove Cemetery - Fayette Co., Ala.
         gr.dau. of Wiley Perry & Martha L. -?- (Wiley's 2nd wife)
                  b. 16 Feb. 1794   b. 16 Feb. 1819
                  d. 1 Aug. 1883   d. 14 Oct. 1895
                  both bur. Harmony Grove Cemetery
      The Perry family came from Ga. to Ala. in a covered wagon.

         Caroline Perry has 1st. m. George Dickinson - "Yankee"
                            b. 10 April 1836 - Cherokee Co,GA
                            d. 15 October 1863 - Marion Co.
                            bur. Harmony Grove

                            (1) Washington Dickinson - "Washie"
                                b. 1863 - Fayette Co., Ala.
                                m. Tude Weeks
      Mrs. Caroline Berryhill drew Pension #32587 in Fayette Co.
      Ala. on "Cap's" Confederate record.

   (1) Margaret M. Berryhill
       b. 1866 - Marion Co., Ala.
       d. April 1952 - Davis, Okla.
       m. Thomas T. Platt - 2 May 1886 - Fayette Co., Ala.

       (a) Washington Platt - "Washie"
           b. 1887/1888 - Fayette Co., Ala.
           d. 1900 approx. - Anderson Co., Texas
           bur. Pleasant Springs Cemetery - Anderson Co., Texas
       Margaret M. Berryhill m. 2nd. Matthew Berryhill - "Math"
       16 July 1893 - Fayette Co., Ala.

Margaret M. Berryhill   2nd.
m. Matthew Berryhill
        b. 1868 - Marion Co., Ala.
        d. November 1952 - Davis, Okla.
        son of Wm. R. A. Berryhill & Margaret -?-
                b. 1834 - Ala.   b. 1838 - Ala.

    (b) Frances Berryhill
            b. 1895 approx. Fayette Co., Ala.
            d. 1936 - Davis, Okla.
            bur. Davis, Okla.
            m. Elmer Jefcoat m. 2nd. Nila Emerson

            1. Oscar Jefcoat
            2. Irvin Jefcoat
            3. Evie Jefcoat   All of these are children of
            4. Vernon Jefcoat   Frances.
            5. Harvey Jefcoat
            6. Dorothy Jefcoat

    (c) "Babe" Berryhill (male)
            b. 1897/1898 - Fayette Co., Ala.
            d. when 18 or 19 years of age in Anderson Co., Texas
            bur. Pleasant Springs Cemetery - Anderson Co., Texas

(2) Mary Jane Berryhill
    b. 1868 - Marion Co., Ala.
    d. 1892 - Fayette Co., Ala.
    bur. Harmony Grove Cemetery - Fayette Co., Ala.
    m. Alexander Weeks - 31 January 1886 - Fayette Co., Ala.
        d. in Tenn.
        bur. in Tenn.

    (a) Dallas Weeks
            b. 1888 approx. - Fayette Co., Ala.
            never married and died in Texas
    (b) Texanna Weeks
            b. 1890 approx. - Fayette Co., Ala.
    (c) Julie Weeks
            b. 1891 - Fayette Co., Texas
            d. has deceased
    (d) Lena Weeks
            b. 1892 approx.
            d. as a child of about 12 years
    (e) Bertha Dell Weeks
            b. 1894 approx. - Fayette Co., Ala.
            m. -?- Cowart

            1. Jack Cowart

(3) John Walter Berryhill - "Johnny Doodle"
    b. 1870/1871 - Marion Co., Ala.
    d. 19 September 1957 - Buffalo, Texas
    bur. Pleasant Springs Cemetery - 2 mi. S. of Palestine, Texas
    m. Mariah M. Weeks - 22 March 1891 - Fayette Co., Ala.
        b. 9 January 1868 - Marion Co., Ala.
        d. 3 April 1907 - Marion Co., Ala.
        bur. Harmony Grove Cemetery - Fayette Co., Ala.
        dau. of John W. Weeks & Prudence -?-
                b. 1825 - Tenn b. 1824 - Ala.

    (a) Jennie Lee Berryhill
            b. 1862 - Marion Co., Ala.
            m. Monroe Ed Head - 13 September 1910 - Fayette Co., Ala.

            1. Walter Cayce Head
                b. 1919 - Palestine, Texas
                m. Ethel (Pinford) Harrison

                A. Eloise Head (twin)
                B. Louise Head (twin) - deceased
                C. Son, still born
                D. Eddie Michael Head
                    b. 1947

2. Odie Oril Head
   m. Eck Burleson

   A. Drexel Burleson
   B. Joyce Burleson
      m. Frank -?-
   C. Jerry Burleson
   D. John Hill Burleson

3. Willie Dee Head
   m. Needa -?-

   A. Alice Marie Head

4. Flora Mae Head
   m. Asberry McClellen
   2nd. m. Andrew Gan
   3rd. m. F. G. Hutchinson
5. Katherine Head
   m. Wallace Baker

   A. Frances Maritha Baker

6. Leo Head
   d. deceased
   m. Coal Garrison

   A. Edith Garrison
      m. Forest New
   B. Beatrice Garrison
      m. Paul Williams

      (1) Terry Williams
          deceased
      (2) Jerry Williams
      (3) Chelia Williams

      Beatrice Garrison m. 2nd. Charles Hamby

      (4) Jerry Wayne Hamby

   C. John Garrison
      m. July -?-
   D. Carolyn Garrison
      m. Parnell Louis
   E. Betty Garrison
   F. Linwell Garrison
   G. Girl (twin still born)
   H. Girl (twin still born)

7. Linda Head
   deceased
8. Bubby Boy Head
   deceased
9. Frances Head
   m. Cecil Cooper

   A. Gene Allen Cooper

   Frances Head m. 2nd. Charles Barnett

   B. Charles Barnett, Jr.

   Frances H. B. m. 3rd. John Harold Wates

(b) Andrew Berryhill
    b. 1893 approx. - Marion Co., Ala.
    m. Lula Cornwell

    1. Allie Berryhill
    2. A. B. Berryhill
    3. Willie Bell Berryhill
    4. Willis Berryhill
    5. Clyde Berryhill

(c) Martha Berryhill
    b. 1894 approx. - Marion Co., Ala.
    d. 1898 approx.
    bur. Harmony Grove Cemetery - Fayette Co., Ala.
(d) Susie Jane Berryhill
    died at nine days old - Marion Co., Ala.
    bur. Harmony Grove Cemetery - Fayette Co., Ala.
(e) Infant Daughter Berryhill
    d. & d. 1898 approx. - Marion Co., Ala.
    bur. Harmony Grove Cemetery - Fayette Co., Ala.
(f) George Washington Berryhill - "Washie"
    b. 1899 approx. - Marion Co., Ala.
    d. 1965 - Anderson Co., Texas
    bur. Pleasant Springs Cemetery - Anderson Co., Texas
    m. Ida Brown

    1. Della Berryhill
    2. C. A. Berryhill
    3. Daniel Berryhill
    4. Betty Berryhill
    5. Ray Berryhill
    6. Phillip Berryhill
    7. Georgia Berryhill
       m. -?- Brock

(g) Willie Benny Berryhill
    b. 22 June 1906 - Marion Co., Ala.
    m. Frankie Mae Brown - 8 December 1934
       b. 30 November 1919 - Fairfield, Freestone Co., Texas
       dau. of John Brown & Nora Connie -?-

    1. Willie Jaunitta Berryhill
       b. 28 July 1936 - Anderson Co., Texas
       m. Robby Jack Billups
          b. 14 March 1931 - Rocket, Texas
          son of W. H. Billups & Hazel Huddleston

       A. Janet Lynn Billups
          b. 13 January 1953 - Harris Co., Texas
       B. Robby Jack Billups, Jr.
          b. 8 November 1954 - Anderson Co., Texas
       C. Lisha Kandes Billups
          b. 24 July 1963 - Hunt Co., Texas

       Willie Berryhill m. 2nd. Walter Otto

       D. Paula Rene Otto
          b. 5 March 1968 - Harris Co., Texas

    2. Ruth Evelyn Berryhill
       b. 12 December 1937 - Anderson Co., Texas
       m. G. A. Walding

       A. Frida Jean Walding
          b. 13 January 1954
       B. Reta Marilyn Walding
       C. Sandra June Walding
       D. James Kevin Walding

    3. Retha Eugene Berryhill
       b. 8 May 1940 - Anderson Co., Texas
       m. A. C. Smith

       A. Jerry Dwain Smith
       B. Michael Anthony Smith
       C. Vena LaVon Smith
       D. Terry Lyn Smith

    4. Billie Frances Berryhill
       b. 19 January 1942 - Anderson Co., Texas
       m. Thomas Blackwell

       A. Danny Thomas Blackwell
       B. Tammy Lynn Blackwell

    5. James Harold Berryhill
       b. 15 May 1943 - Anderson Co., Texas
       m. Andra Gean Higginbotham

       A. James Harold Berryhill, Jr.

    6. Connie Eliece Berryhill
       b. 10 August 1946 - Anderson Co., Texas
       m. Gleen Reed

       A. David Morris Reed
       B. Derrial Green Reed
       C. Donnie Lee Reed

    7. Sandra June Berryhill
       deceased
    8. Sharon Kay Berryhill
       b. 31 January 1950 - Anderson Co., Texas
       m. Kenneth Walston

       A. Kenneth Homer Walston, Jr.

    9. Benny Norman Berryhill
       b. 11 March 1951 - Anderson Co., Texas

    10. Shelia Merrie Berryhill
        b. 28 August 1954 - Anderson Co., Texas

John Walter Berryhill m. 2nd - 24 December 1908 - Fayette Co.
m. Rose Whitley
    b. 29 September 1889 - Marion Co., Ala.
    d. 31 August 1932 - Anderson Co., Texas
    bur. Pleasant Springs Cemetery - Anderson Co., Texas

  (h) Grace Berryhill
      b. 1910 approx. - Marion Co., Ala.
      m. Lewis Lummus

      1. Rozell Lummus
      2. David Lummus
      3. George Lummus
      4. Mary Lummus

  (i) Troy Berryhill
      b. 1912 approx. - Marion Co., Ala.
      d. 1916 approx. - Marion Co., Ala.
      bur. Harmony Grove Cemetery - Fayette Co., Ala.
      Was playing in some cotton and it caved in and he
      smothered.
  (j) Elbert Lee Berryhill
      b. 1914 approx. - Anderson Co., Texas
      d. 28 December 1967 - Nacogdoches, Texas
      m. Eula Bell Lummus

      1. Dottie Berryhill
      2. Barbara Berryhill
      3. Linda Berryhill
      4. Mike Berryhill

  (k) Mary Ann Berryhill
      b. 1915 approx. - Anderson Co., Texas
      m. Alton Jefcoat

      1. Johnny Jefcoat
      2. Raymon Jefcoat
      3. Marrie Jefcoat
      4. Mary Jefcoat

  (1) Lina Berryhill
      b. 1917 approx. - Anderson Co., Texas
      m. -?- Hamlett

(4) Celia E. Berryhill
    b. 1876 - Marion Co., Ala.
    m. Columbus G. Weeks - 16 July 1893 - Fayette Co., Ala.

    (a) Charlie Weeks
    (b) Jess Weeks

```
        (c) Lon Weeks
        (d) Will Weeks
        (e) Dewey Weeks
        (f) Carrie Weeks
        (g) Retha Weeks
        (h) Belton Weeks
        (i) Robert Weeks
        (j) Berryhill Weeks

(5) William Berryhill - "Clay"
    b. 1878 - Marion Co., Ala.
    d.
    bur. Olive Branch Cemetery - new Frankston, Texas
    m. Martha Yancy Virginia Berryhill - 29 June 1896 - Fayette Co.
       b. 1882 approx. - Fayette Co., Ala.
       d. 2 June 1965 - Anderson Co., Texas
       bur. Olive Branch Cemetery - near Frankston, Texas
       dau. of John Thomas Berryhill & Rachel Caroline Weeks

    (a) Charlie Berryhill
        b. 1897 approx. - Fayette Co., Ala.
        m. Luie Bell Gatlin - Fayette Co., Ala.
    (b) Nolan Berryhill
        b. 1898 approx. - Fayette Co., Ala.
        m. Ruby Hilton
    (c) William Berryhill
        b. 17 January 1899
        d. 16 October 1899 - Fayette Co., Ala.
        bur. Harmony Grove Cemetery - Fayette Co., Ala.
    (d) Maggie Berryhill
        b. 1901 - Fayette Co., Ala.
        m. Charlie Gatlin
    (e) Eckford Berryhill
        b. 1903 approx. - Fayette Co., Ala.
    (f) Croman Berryhill
        b. 1904 approx. - Fayette Co., Ala.
    (g) Ora Berryhill
        b. 1905 approx. - Fayette Co., Ala.
        m. Rilee Robinson
        m. 2nd. Wilbur Davis
    (h) Eudean Berryhill
        b. 1907 approx. - Fayette Co., Ala.
    (i) Rollie Berryhill
        b. 1908 approx. - Fayette Co., Ala.
    (j) Cecil Berryhill
        b. 1910 approx. - Fayette Co., Ala.
    (k) Douglas Berryhill
        b. 1911 approx. - Fayette Co., Ala.
    (l) Ivory Berryhill
        b. 1912 approx. - Fayette Co., Ala.

(6) Dee William Berryhill
    b. 20 March 1880 - Marion Co., Ala.
    m. Dora Lee Richardson - 16 January 1904 - Marion Co., Ala.
       b. 7 October 1883 - Ala.
       b. 16 February 1914 - Fayette Co., Ala.
       bur. Harmony Grove Cemetery - Fayette Co., Ala.

    (a) Infant Son Berryhill
        b. 14 May 1906   d. 17 May 1906 - Fayette Co., Ala.
        bur. Harmony Grove Cemetery - Fayette Co., Ala.
    (b) Infant Daughter Berryhill
        b. & d. 7 February 1914 - Fayette Co., Ala.
        bur. Harmony Grove Cemetery - Fayette Co., Ala.

    Dee W. Berryhill m. 2nd. Elizabeth Jones -"Bet" - 1915
                               b. 1887
                               d. 1949 - Fayette Co., Ala.
                               bur. Winfield Cemetery - Marion Co.
                               dau. of Dint Jones
```

(c) Lillie Mayfield
    foster child
    m. A. N. Martin
(d) Harley Higginbotham
    foster child

Dee. W. Berryhill m. 3rd. Velma Homer - 1951
                              d. 1959
                              bur. Guin Cemetery - Guin, Ala.
Dee W. Berryhill m. 4th. Mrs. Lena (Ingram) Hobson
5 July 1962   b. 7 November 1939

(e) Phillip Hobson
    Step-son
    b. 24 October 1955
(f) Sheila Hobson
    Step-daughter
    b. 29 September 1958

E. Sarah Jane Berryhill - "Sallie"
   b. 29 June 1844 - Marion Co., Ala.
   d. 12 October 1932 - Marion Co., Ala.
   bur. Harmony Grove Cemetery - Fayette Co., Ala.
   m. Benjamin Henderson - "Ben"
      b. 12 May 1839 - Ga.
      d. 30 October 1928 - Marion Co., Ala.
      bur. Harmony Grove Cemetery
      son of Samuel B. Henderson & Josephine -?-
              b. 1813 - Ga.   b. 1818 - S. C.
              living in 1880

(1) Mary A. Henderson - "Pollie"
    b. 1862 - Marion Co., Ala.
    m. -?- Tucker

    (a) Jim Tucker

    Mary A. Henderson m. 2nd. Jule Doss

    (b) Anderson Doss
    (c) Dora Doss
    (d) Corlenius Doss
    (e) Columbus Doss

(2) Angeline Jane Henderson
    b. 1864 - Marion Co., Ala.
    m. Richard Henderson
    m. 2nd. George Freeman
    No issue by either marriage
(3) William Henderson
    b. 1867 - Marion Co., Ala.
(4) Martha E. Henderson - "Mattie"
    b. 1869 - Marion Co., Ala.
    m. Sam Henderson
       son of Richard Henderson

    (a) Holly Henderson
    (b) Richard Henderson
    (c) Benjamin Henderson
    (d) Felix Henderson
    (e) Monroe Henderson
    (f) Bessie Henderson
    (g) Lee Henderson

(5) Allie T. Henderson
    b. 20 November 1881 - Fayette Co., Ala.
    m. William Silas Berryhill - 29 December 1897 - Fayette Co.
       family recorded in preceeding pages
(6) Susie Henderson
    b. 1882 approx.
    m. Coleman Smith

    (a) Florence Smith
    (b) May Smith
    (c) Henry Smith

        (d) son who died young

    (7) Rose Henderson
        b. 1885 approx.
        m. "Pet" Watkins

        (a) Mertie Watkins
        (b) Bessie Watkins
        (c) Maggie Watkins
        (d) Jim Watkins
            m. Pheba -?-
            No issues

    (8) Louise Henderson
        b. 1886 approx.
        m. Judge Smith
        Had issues but names unknown

F. Susan C. Berryhill - "Bash"
   b. 1847/1850 - Marion Co., Ala.
   d. 26 November 1922 - Marion Co., Ala.
   bur. Harmony Grove Cemetery
   m. Meredith Jacob Couch -"Jake" - approx. 1865/1866 - Marion Co.
      b. 1846 - Ala.
      d. 1908 - Marion Co., Ala.
      bur. Harmony Grove Cemetery
      son of -?- Couch & Malindey -?-
      father died in   b. 19 September 1810 - Ala.
      Tenn. River.   d. 5 October 1876 - Marion Co., Ala.
                             bur. Harmony Grove Cemetery

    (1) John W. Couch
        b. 1867 - Fayette Co., Ala.
        d. 1946 - Wayne, Okla.
        bur. Purcell, Okla.
        m. Margaret Vickery
           b. 15 May 1865 - Marion Co., Ala.
           d. 15 October 1893 - Fayette Co., Ala.
           bur. Harmony Grove Cemetery

        (a) Martha Susan Couch
            b. 1888 approx.
            m. Boss Hawkins

            1. Dau. Hawkins
            2. Dau. Hawkins
            3. Dau. Hawkins
            4. Dau. Hawkins

        (b) Alec Andrew Couch - "Buddy"
            b. 1890 approx.
            m. Ruby Scruggs
            1. Robert Couch
            2. Alex Andrew Couch, Jr.

            "Buddy" Couch 2nd. m. Ruth -?-

            3. Son
            4. Son
            5. Son
            6. Son

        John W. Couch m. 2nd. Gattie I. Kirkland - "Gat"
                           b. 9 August 1874
                           d. 2 October 1912
                           bur. Harmony Grove Cemetery

        (c) Jessie Couch (twin)
        (d) Bessie Couch (Twin)
            both twins died young
            bur. both Harmony Grove Cemetery
        (e) Orlena Couch
            m. -?- Buchanan
        (f) Ernest Couch
        (g) Clarence Couch (twin)
        (h) Clara Couch (twin)

John W. Couch m. 3rd. Lula Bussey

(i) Johnie Lou Couch
    m. Bill Burns
(j) Myrtle Couch
(k) Anita Couch
    never married, teaches school
(l) Dawson Couch
(m) Betty Jo Couch

(2) Alexander Thomas Couch - "Alec"
    b. 6 March 1868 - Fayette Co., Ala.
    d. 12 February 1955 - Marion Co., Ala.
    bur. Winfield City Cemetery - Marion Co., Ala.
    m. Julia Ann Estes
        b. 13 March 1878 - Marion Co., Ala.
        d. 26 January 1918 - Marion Co., Ala.
        bur. Winfield City Cemetery
        dau. of James H. Estes & Drucilla C. Berryhill
            b. 1848 - Ga.   b. 1853 - Ala.

    (a) Raymond Carl Couch
        b. 1903 approx. - Marion Co., Ala.
        m. Ruby Wates

        1. Billy Couch
        2. Frances Couch
           m. -?- Pridmore
        3. Johnnie Couch
        4. David Couch

    (b) Ada Merle Couch
        b. 15 January 1905 - Marion Co., Ala.
        m. Charlie Yates
    (c) Jesse Delmas Couch
        b. 3 February 1907 - Marion Co., Ala.
        d. August 1972
        m. Frances Beck

        1. J. D. Couch, Jr.
           d. October 1947
        2. Evelyn Couch
           b. 24 September 1935 -
           m. Woodrow J. Granis
        3. Jane Ellen Couch
           b. 21 September 1949

    (d) Mack Lauren Couch
        m. Hazel Miller

        1. Barbara Couch
           m. -?- Kennard
        2. Tommy Couch
        3. Betty Ann Couch

    (e) Helen Tenelle Couch
        b. 17 May 1913
        d. 23 January 1926
    (f) Erin Couch
        b. 8 September 1914 - Gatmen, Jackson Co., Miss.
        m. James D. Burleson

        1. Jimmy Burleson

    (g) Lillian V. Couch
        b. 17 July 1916 - Marion Co., Ala.
        m. Clyde Langston

        1. Judy Langston
         . -?- Goodsey

"Alec" Couch m. 2nd. Jeffie Lee

    (h) Robert Lee Couch
        m. Dorothy Westbrook
           dau. of -?- Westbrook & Hester Ward

        1. Robert Lee Couch, Jr.
        2. Mike Couch
        3. Ken Couch

   (i) Ola Sue Couch
       m. Charles Nail, Jr.

        1. Karla Nail
        2. Lisa Nail
        3. Gena Nail
        4. Charles J. Nail, III

   (j) Jean Couch
       m. Everett E. Moore

        1. Danny Moore
        2. Larry Moore

   (k) John Thomas Couch
       m. Ruby Hollingsworth

        1. Jeff Couch
        2. Kathy Couch
        3. John Meredith Couch

   (l) Naomi Couch
       m. Kelly Waldrop

        1. Myra Waldrop
        2. Keith Waldrop

   (m) Dorothy Couch
       m. Billy R. Smith

        1. Diann Smith
        2. Karen Smith
        3. Kanda Smith

   (n) Alexander Thomas Couch, Jr.
       m. Nanna Couch

        1. Laura Couch
        2. Linda Couch

   (o) Martha Couch
       m. Earl Mims

        1. Jan Mims
        2. Mark Mims
        3. Daughter Mims

(3) Robert Andrew Couch
    b. 26 August 1871 - Fayette Co., Ala.
    d. 28 January 1920 - Wayne, Okla.
    bur. Winfield City Cemetery - Winfield, Ala.
    m. Martha Ann Ward - 17 February 1897 - Fayette Co., Ala.
       b. 16 August 1873 - Fayette Co., Ala.
       d. 22 July 1931 - Winfield, Ala.
       bur. Winfield City Cemetery
       dau. of Willis Monroe Ward, Jr. & Margaret Cordelia Kirk-
                 b. 1846   b. 1851   land
                 d. 1921   d. 1936

   (a) Carlos Belton Couch
       b. 7 March 1898 - Fayette Co., Ala.
       d. 30 March 1943 -
       bur. Winfield City Cemetery - Winfield, Ala.
       m. Savannah Viola Berryhill
          b. 23 May 1906 - Fayette Co., Ala.
          dau. of Henry David Berryhill & Tennessee Roberts
       No issue

   (b) Harvey Walton Couch
       b. 5 June 1899 - Fayette Co., Ala.
       d. 24 August 1937 -
       bur. City Cemetery - Winfield, Ala.
       m. Hazel Harris
       No issue

(c) Willis Esker Couch
   b. 16 October 1900 - Fayette Co., Ala.
   d. 19 January 1901 - Fayette Co., Ala.
   bur. Siloam Baptist Cemetery - Marion Co., Ala.
(d) Alma Couch
   b. 26 November 1901 - Fayette Co., Ala.
   d. 28 May 1922
   bur. City Cemetery - Winfield, Ala.
   Never married
(e) Beatrice Couch
   b. 23 May 1903 - Fayette Co., Ala.
   m. Clifton Vernon - 21 November 1951
      b. 23 February 1904
      son of William Arthur Vernon
   No issue
(f) Lourine Couch
   b. 19 May 1905 - Fayette Co., Ala.
   d. 2 September 1959
   bur. City Cemetery - Winfield, Ala.
   m. J. Luten Earnest

   1. Martha Ann Earnest
      m. Dudley Trollinger

      A. Christy Trollinger
         b. 1 May 1962

(g) Robert Cecil Couch
   b. 18 May 1907 - Fayette Co., Ala.
   d. 23 June 1908 - Fayette Co., Ala.
   bur. Siloam Baptist Cemetery - Fayette Co., Ala.
(h) Merdith Preston Couch
   b. 6 February 1909 - Fayette Co., Ala.
   d. 9 June 1961
   bur. City Cemetery - Winfield, Ala.
   m. Della Franks

   1. Richard A. Couch
      m. Ann Lyons

      A. Candy Couch
         b. 13 October 1963

   2. Margaret Alice Couch
      m. Bobby Chaffin

      A. Ronald Lee Chaffin
         b. 13 April 1958

(i) Ferman Hill Couch
   b. 24 July 1911 - Fayette Co., Ala.
   d. 6 January 1944
   bur. City Cemetery - Winfield, Ala.
   m. Bertha Milner

   1. Robert Hill Couch
      m. Gibbs Daniels

      A. James W. Scott Couch
         b. 16 August 1963

   2. Frances Annette Couch
      m. Jerry Elrod

      A. Jerry Lee Elroy
         b. 26 March 1963
      B. Casey Lynn Elrod

(j) Ila Mae Couch
   b. 23 May 1913 - Fayette Co., Ala.
   d. 11 August 1941
   bur. Winfield City Cemetery
   m. Rufus E. Perry

   1. Harvey Joe Perry
      b. 19 January 1940
      m. Suzanne Marcus

        A. Kimberly Ann Perry

(4) Jesse H. Couch
    b. 1873
    d. 1947
    bur. City Cemetery - Winfield, Ala.
    m. Belle Bostick
        b. 1882
        d. 1965 bur. City Cemetery

    (a) Edwin W. Couch (Physician)
        b. 1913
        d. 1 November 1967
        bur. City Cemetery - Winfield, Ala.
    (b) Amelia Couch
    (c) Maurice Couch
        d. 1965
    (d) Sam Couch
    (e) James Couch
    (f) Mary Frances Couch
    (g) Robert Earl Couch

(5) Alcie Woodville Couch
    b. 17 April 1876 - Fayette Co., Ala.
    d. 16 June 1956 - Purcell, McClain Co., Okla.
    bur. Hillside Cemetery - Purcell, Okla.
    m. Luranie Elizabeth Ward - 28 December 1899 - Fayette Co.
        b. 4 March 1882 - Fayette Co., Ala.
        d. 31 July 1964 - Purcell, Okla.
        bur. Hillside Cemetery - Purcell, Okla.
        dau. of John Ward & Emith (Hamm) McGaha m. 3 September 1877

    (a) Walter Alvis Couch
        b. December 1900 - Marion Co., Ala.
        d. March 1962 - Salinas, Calif.
        m. Mae Alcorn - Pauls Valley, Okla

        1. Walter Donald Couch

    (b) Raymond Couch
        b. 1902
        d. 1904 - Gainsville, Texas.
        bur. Gainsville, Texas
    (c) Eulalia Virginia Couch
        b. 1904 - Marion Co., Ala.
        m. Harlham H. Owen
           deceased
        m. 2nd. Leonard Benson
        No issue by either marriage
    (d) Thelma Emily Couch
        b. 23 August 1906 - Marion Co., Ala.
        m. Howard Vetter - 21 March 1951
           b. 26 May 1907 - Haldredge, Neb.
           son of Arthur W. Vetter & Lula A. Stafford
        No issue
    (e) Robert Edward Lee Couch
        b. 26 October 1908 - Marion Co., Ala.
        m. Vera Mae Burgess - 1935 - Okla.
           b. 27 July 1915 - Loco, Comanche Co., Okla.

        1. Carol Cowen Couch
           b. 30 January 1937 - Wayne, Okla.
           m. Ronald D. Baker - 23 June 1956 - Tulsa, Okla.

           A. Forrest Colenn Baker
              b. 21 April 1957 - Denver, Colo.
           B. Jamil Annette Baker
              b. 14 August 1960 - Vandalia, Ill.
           C. Stephanie Jeanne Baker
              b. 7 October 1961 - Vandalia, Ill.

        2. Sharon Sue Couch
           b. 16 June 1938 - Drumwright, Okla.
           m. -?- Easley - 23 April 1957 - Tulsa, Okla.

        A. Jeffrey Allen Easley
           b. 9 November 1958 - Austin, Texas
        B. Kelley Sue Easley
           b. 19 December 1959 - Tulsa, Okla.
        C. Amy Ann Easley
           b. 24 April 1962 - Fort Smith, Ark.
        D. Jill Ellen Easley
           b. 24 September 1964 - Fort Smith, Ark.

    3. Doris Kay Couch
       b. 8 September 1940 - Drumwright, Okla.
       m. William Morris McBride - 28 December 1955

        A. Debra Kay McBride
           b. 27 September 1956 - Tulsa, Okla.
        B. Teresa Lynn McBride
           b. 27 September 1957 - Denver, Colo.
        C. Leary Donovan McBride
           b. 18 February 1959 - Denver, Colo.
        D. Robert Morris McBride
           b. 25 August 1964 - Denver, Colo.

    4. Robert Edward Lee Couch, Jr.
       b. 13 November 1941 - Anadarko, Caddo Co, Okla.
       d. 4 March 1942 - Anadarko, Caddo Co., Okla.
       bur. Purcell Cemetery - Purcell, Okla.
    5. James Steven Couch
       b. 23 January 1948 - Tulsa, Okla.
    6. Cynthia Jane Couch
       b. 29 November 1951 - Tulsa, Okla.

(f) Lounell Couch
    b. 2 May 1910
    d. 11 September 1911 - Marion Co., Ala.
(g) Merida Rayburn Couch
    b. 17 April 1912 - Marion Co., Ala.
    m. -?-

    1. Larry Couch
    2. Merida Couch

    m. -?-

    3. Gary Ray Couch
    4. Sherri Couch
(h) Woodville Ward Couch
    b. May 1914 - Marion Co., Ala.
    m. Linn Mae McBay - 4 July 1936

    1. Myrna Couch
       b. 1937 approx.
    2. Melba Couch
       b. 1939
    3. W. W. Couch Jr.
       b. 1941 approx.
    4. Jimmy Couch
       b. 1943 approx.

(i) Floye Mae Couch
    b. 27 October 1916 - Marion Co., Ala.
    m. Lester Herr - 20 July 1936 - Lawton, Okla.

    1. Gary Gene Herr
       b. 23 July 1938 - Lawton, Okla.
       m. Ruth Robinson - 17 March 1957 - Pampa, Texas

        A. Gary Stephen Herr
           b. 22 October 1957 - Pampa, Texas
        B. Lance Allen Herr
           b. 28 April 1962 - Pampa, Texas
        C. Patrick Lee Herr
           b. 27 July 1964 - Pampa, Texas

    2. Donna Kay Herr
       b. 5 October 1941 - Lawton, Okla.
       m. Craig Verick Winborn - 29 May 1964 - Pampa, Texas

       A. Rebecca Kay Winborn
          b. 28 September 1066 - Oklahoma City, Okla.

(j) Willetta Couch
    b. 24 December 1918 - Marion Co., Ala.
    m. Samuel A. Miller

    1. Elizabeth Faye Miller
       b. 7 November 1941 - Lawton, Okla.
       m. C. J. Crawford

(k) Harold Leon Couch
    b. 1923
    d. 9 February 1925
    bur. Hoppins Cemetery near Wayne, Okla.

(6) Cora I. Couch
    b. 1878 - Fayette Co., Ala.
    d. 1964
    bur. City Cemetery - Winfield, Ala.
    m. Benjamin Salvador Ward - "Vader"
       b. 1872
       d. 1935
       bur. City Cemetery - Winfield, Ala.
       son of. Willis Monroe Ward, Jr. & Margaret C. Kirkland
                    b. 1846   b. 1851
                    d. 1921   d. 1936

    (a) Infant
        b.   and d. 15 May 1917
        bur. Harmony Grove Cemetery - Fayette Co., Ala.
    (b) Velma Ward
    (c) Sallie Ward
    (d) Willie May Ward
    (e) Willis Ward
    (f) Jesse Ward

(7) Houston Couch
    b. 1880
    d. 1955
    bur. City Cemetery - Hamilton, Ala.
    m. Stella Ward
    dau. of Ralston Ward & Molly Musbrove
    No issue
(8) George W. Couch
    b. 6 July 1881 - Fayette Co., Ala.
    d. 20 October 1952
    bur. City Cemetery - Fayette Co., Ala.
    m. Lucy Reese (twin to Lovey Reese)
       b. 3 August 1883
       d. 13 February 1913
       bur. Old Union Primitive Baptist Cemetery

    (a) Roy Couch
    (b) Jobe Couch
    (c) Mabrey Lee Couch
    (d) Malcom Couch

    G. W. Couch m. 2nd. Carrie Smith

    (e) Mollie Couch
        b. and d. 29 October 1914
    (f) George Couch
        b. and d. 24 January 1915
    (g) Louis Couch
    (h) Bobbie Couch
    (i) Bettie Couch

(9) Martha Ellen Couch
    b. 1884
    d. 1962 - Fayette Co., Ala.
    bur. Siloam Baptist Cemetery - Fayette Co., Ala.
    m. Early M. Earnest
       b. 1884

    (a) Alton Earnest
        b. and d. 1907
        bur. Siloam Baptist Cemetery
    (b) Mable Earnest
        m. Ernest Black

        1. William Black

    (c) Byron Earnest (twin)
    (d) Bythel Earnest (twin)
        m. Bernice Reed

        1. Jim Reed

    (e) Rubye Earnest
        b. 1912
        d. 1913
        bur. Siloam Baptist Cemetery
    (f) Annie Earn Earnest
        m. Riley Randolph

        1. Gary Randolph

    (g) John Meridith Earnest
        m. -?- Smith

        1. Johnny Earnest

    (h) James Edward Earnest
        d. World War II
    (i) Miriam Sue Earnest
        m. Fred Ivy

        1. Ronald Ivy

    (j) Robert K. Earnest - "Bob"

(10) Grover Cleveland Couch - "Cleve"
     b. 1892 - Fayette Co., Ala.
     m. Ruth Earnest
        b. 1895 - Fayette Co., Ala.
(11) Christopher Columbus Couch
     b. 13 September 1887 - Fayette Co., Ala.
     d. 10 February 1950 - Marion Co., Ala.
     bur. Winfield City Cemetery - Winfield, Ala.
     m. Nancy Adeline Dodson - "Nannie"
        b. 15 November 1890
        dau. of John William Dodson & Josie Cornelia Thompson

     (a) Mildred Couch
         b. 29 August 1911
     (b) Josie Willene Couch
         b. 21 November 1912
         d. 12 April 1914
         bur. Siloam Baptist Cemetery
     (c) Lanetta Couch
         b. 2 April 1916
         m. -?- White
     (d) John M. Couch
         b. 21 November 1919
         d. 19 August 1920
         bur. Siloam Baptist Cemetery
     (e) Dodson Christopher Couch
         b. 4 April 1922
         m. -?- Smith

(12) Florence Couch
     died in infancy
(13) Infant Daughter
     died in infancy

G. Thomas Berryhill
   b. 1849 - Marion Co., Ala.
   d. assumed by 1860 because he was not on the 1860 census

H. Martha F. Berryhill
   b. 1851 - Marion Co., Ala.
   d. living at time of 1860 census, age 9 years, but no other
      information available on her.

I. Mary E. Berryhill
   b. 1853 - Marion Co., Ala.
   d. Living on 1870 Fayette Co., census, age 17. No other
      information available on her.

6. Nancy E. Berryhill
   b. 1819 - Franklin Co., Tenn. near Winchester
   d. 21 January 1899 - Fayette Co., Ala.
   bur. Berryhill Family Cemetery - Fayette Co., Ala.
   m. Edward Berryhill - "Edd" - approx. 1839 - Marion Co., Ala.
      b. 4 April 1813 - Winchester, Franklin Co., Tenn.
      d. 6 October 1875 - Fayette Co., Ala.
      bur. Berryhill Family Cemetery - Fayette Co., Ala.
      son of Alexander Berryhill & Rebecca Webster (2nd. wife)
              b. 1760 N. C.   b. 1785 - N. C.
              d. 3 February 1839   d. Living 1850 census, gone by 1860

A. Thomas J. Berryhill
   b. 27 January 1840 - Marion Co., Ala.
B. Sarah J. Berryhill
   b. 1841/1842 - Marion Co., Ala.
C. George Washington Berryhill
   b. 1843/1844 - Marion Co., Ala.
D. Rufus Alsa Berryhill
   b. 1846 - Marion Co., Ala.
E. James H. Berryhill
   b. 16 February 1849 - Marion Co., ALa.
F. Robert W. Berryhill
   b. 16 November 1850 - Marion Co., Ala.
G. Mary Ann Berryhill
   b. 1851/1852 - Marion Co., Ala.
H. Benjamin F. Berryhill
   b. 21 March 1854 - Marion Co., Ala.
I. Rebecca Berryhill
   b. 1856/1857 - Marion Co., Ala.
J. Nancy Margaret Berryhill
   b. 1858 approx. - Marion Co., Ala.
K. John Edward Berryhill
   b. 21 August 1860 - Marion Co., Ala.

1850 Marion Co., Ala. Federal Census   15/15 Beat #11

Edward Berryhill		37 M	Tenn.	b. 1813	
Nancy	"	35 F	Tenn.	1815	
Thomas J.	"	10 M	Miss.	1840	
Sarah J.	"	7 F	Ala.	1843	
George W.	"	6 M	Ala.	1844	
Rufus A.	"	4 M	Ala.	1846	
James H.	"	2 M	Ala.	1848	
son, no name		1/12 M	Ala.	1850	(1860 census says Robert)

17/17
Rebecca Berryhill   65 F   N. C.   1785
living alone, in a house between her two sons, Edward and Thomas.
Widow of Alexander Berryhill b. 1760.

```
1860 Marion Co., Ala. Census
Edward Berryhill     46 M.  Tenn.   b. 1814
Nancy          "     44 F   Tenn.      1816
Thomas J.      "     19 M.  Miss.      1841
Sarah J.       "     16 F.  Ala.       1844
George W.      "     14 M   Ala.       1846
Rufus A.       "     13 M   Ala.       1847
James H.       "     12 M   Ala.       1848
Robert W.      "      9 M   Ala.       1851
Mary A.        "      7 F   Ala.       1853
Benjamin       "      5 M   Ala.       1855
Rebecca        "      3 F   Ala.       1857
Nancy M.       "      1 F   Ala.       1859

1870 Fayette Co., Ala.  13/13 p. 3.  TS13 R13 Palo, Ala.  27 August 1980
Edward Berryhill     60 M   Tenn.      1810
Nancy          "     54 F   Tenn.      1816
Robert         "     20 M.  Ala.       1850
Mary Ann       "     18 F   Ala.       1852
Benjamin       "     16 M   Ala.       1854
Margaret       "     12 F   Ala.       1858(from 1860 census Nancy Margaret)
John           "     10 M   Miss.      1860
Apparently Rebecca died young, or the census taker missed her.

1880 Fayette Co., Ala.  120/120 p 15 TS13  R13 5 June 1880
Nancy Berryhill      70 F   Tenn.  Tenn.  Tenn.  b. 1810 (Edward died)
Benjamin       "     34 M   Ala.   Tenn.  Tenn.     1846
Polly A.       "     26 F   Ala.   Tenn.  Tenn.     1854 (Mary Ann)
Margaret       "     18 F   Ala.   Tenn.  Tenn.     1862
John           "     16 M.  Miss.  Tenn.  Tenn.     1864

154/155 page 19
Robert Berryhill     30 M   Ala.   Tenn.  Tenn.  b. 1850
Mary           "     26 F   Miss.  Tenn.  Tenn.  .  1854 (Mary Justice)
John W.        "      4 M   Ala.   Ala.   Miss.     1876
Rufus          "      3 M   Ala.   Ala.   Miss.     1877
Alonzo         "      1 M   Ala.   Ala.   Miss.     1879

1880 Fayette Co., Ala. Federal Census  163/163 p 20
Thomas J. Berryhill  35 M   Ala.   Tenn.  Tenn.  b. 1845
Mary E. Bowling  "   32 F.  Ala.   S. C.  S. C.     1848
Henry D.       "      9 M   Ala.   Ala.   Ala.      1871
James R.       "      7 M.  Ala.   Ala.   Ala.      1873
William H.     "      5 M.  Ala.   Ala.   Ala.      1875

1880 Marion Co., Ala. Federal Census   147/147 p 18
Rufus Berryhill      33 M.  Ala.   Tenn.  Tenn.     1847
Nancy Justice  "     25 F   Miss.  Miss.  Miss.     1855
James          "      7 M   Ala.   Ala.   Miss.     1873
Robert A.      "                                 (died in 1875)
Laura          "      3 F   Ala.   Ala.   Miss.     1877
Mary           "      1 F   Ala.   Ala.   Miss.     1879
```

   6. Nancy E. Berryhill
      b. 1819 - Tenn (age varies from 1810 to 1916 on census)
      d. 21 January 1889 - Fayette Co., Ala.
      bur. Berryhill Family Cemetery - Marion Co., Ala.
      m. Edward Berryhill - "Edd" approx. 1839 - Marion Co., Ala.
         b. 4 April 1813 - Winchester, Franklin Co., Tenn.
         d. 6 October 1875 - Fayette Co., Ala.
         bur. Berryhill Family Cemetery
         son of Alexander Berryhill & Rebecca Wester (2nd wife)
               b. 1760 - N. C.   b. 1785 - N. C.
               d. 3 February 1839, Ala. living in 1850 gone by 1860
         A free Revolutionary marker has been placed on the grave of one
         Alexander Berryhill, as a memorial to this one, even if perhaps
         we don't have the correct Alexander Berryhill's grave.

A. Thomas Jefferson Berryhill (served in the Confederate Army)
   b. 27 January 1840 - Marion Co., Ala.
   d. 24 December 1928 - Guin, Marion Co., Ala.
   bur. Zion Baptist Cemetery - Marion Co., Ala.
   m. Mary Elizabeth Bowlin (Bowling) - 8 September 1869 - Marion Co
      b. 27 July 1846 - Marion Co., Ala.
      d. 6 January 1907 - Marion Co., Ala.
      bur. Zion Baptist Cemetery

   (1) Henry David Berryhill
       b. 22 January 1871
       d. 1 January 1957 - Marion Co., Ala.
       bur. Guin Cemetery
       m. Tennessee Roberty - "Tenny" - 18 August 1891 - Marion Co.
          b. 10 May 1876 - Fayette Co., Ala.
          d. 2 October 1956 - Winfield, Ala.
          bur. Guin Cemetery
          dau. of James Andrew Roberts & Fleeta Ida Gorham

       (a) Eli Curtis Berryhill
           b. 18 March 1892 - Guin, Ala.
           d. 26 February 1970 - Guin, Ala.
           bur. Marion Co. Memorial Gardens - Marion Co.
           m. Susie Perry - 31 August 1911 - Marion Co., Ala.
              b. 12 November 1892 - Fayette Co., Ala.
              d. 8 September 1972
              bur. Marion Co. Memorial Gardens
              dau. of Abner Perry & Martha Couch

           1. Murl Berryhill
              b. 12 November 1912 - Marion Co., Ala.
              m. Lass Hawkins - 12 May 1928
                 b. 12 February 1908
                 dau. of Bud Hawkins & Mary Jane Mills

              A. Mary Katherine Hawkins
                 b. 14 May 1929 - Marion Co., Ala.
                 m. Elige W. Reed - 15 September 1946
                    b. 1 March 1924
                    son of Wm. Andy Reed & Martha Tucker

                 (1) Williard U. Reed
                     b. 16 May 1948 - Marion Co., Ala.
                     d. 13 February 1972 -
                 (2) Brenda Gail Reed
                     b. 10 April 1950 - Marion Co., Ala.
                     m. Charles David Franks - 21 November 1964
                        b. 21 March 1948
                        son of Dock Franks, Jr. & Kathleen Reese

                     (a) Kathy Darlene Franks
                         b. 17 June 1965
                     (b) Charles David Franks, Jr.
                         b. 21 February 1967
                     (c) Judy Dianne Franks
                         b. 15 September 1968
                         d. 22 September 1968
                     (d) Cynthia Denise Franks
                         b. 12 August 1969

                 (3) Patricia "Tiny" Reed
                     b. 28 October 1953 - Marion Co., Ala.

              B. Robert Earl Hawkins
                 b. 19 April 1932 - Marion Co., Ala.
                 m. Lois Mae Wilson - 30 August 1949

                 (1) James Randal Hawkins
                     b. 28 July 1952
                 (2) Benny Jerald Hawkins
                     b. 14 November 1954
                 (3) Vanda Kay Hawkins
                     b. 5 April 1955
                 (4) Vickie Jan Hawkins
                     b. 21 July 1958

        (5) Sammy Earl Hawkins
            b. 4 October 1960
        (6) Regina Lane Hawkins
            b. 4 January 1961

C. Billy Ray Hawkins
   b. 13 November 1935 - Marion Co., Ala.
   m. Girlene Birchfield - 20 November 1954 - Columbus, MS
      b. 22 January 1939
      dau. of Gerdley Birchfield & Belma Brezzy Willcutt

   (1) Linda Rae Hawkins
       b. 26 January 1955 - Marion Co., Ala.
   (2) Cynthia Ann Hawkins
       b. 28 August 1961 - Marion Co., Ala.

D. Roy Gene Hawkins
   b. 20 May 1938
   d. 2 July 1951 - Marion Co., Ala.
   bur. Guin Cemetery - Marion Co., Ala.
E. Betty Ann Hawkins
   b. 9 December 1940 - Marion Co., Ala.
   m. Roy Lewis Youngblood - 15 June 1957 - Fulton, MS
      b. 6 May 1936
      son of Lewis Henry Youngblood & Mary Lee McKay

   (1) Benita June Youngblood
       b. 1 September 1958
   (2) Roy Mark Youngblood
       b. 5 October 1962

F. Carolyn Sue Hawkins
   b. 26 February 1943 - Marion Co., Ala.
   m. William Eddison Youngblood - 16 January 1961
      b. 26 July 1933

   (1) Wm. Gregory Youngblood
       b. 9 August 1962
   (2) Michael Wade Youngblood
       b. 5 February 1966

G. Peggy Joyce Hawkins
   b. 23 March 1944 - Marion Co., Ala.
   m. Billie Meherg - 22 December 1960
   son of Randall Meherg & Mary Bass

   (1) Rodney Gene Meherg
       b. 22 December 1961
   (2) Tammy Rena Meherg
       b. 18 August 1963

H. Doris Lynn Hawkins
   b. 23 October 1947 - Marion Co., Ala.
   m. James Norris

   (1) Melissia Anne Norris
       b. 12 December 1964

   Doris Hawkins m. 2nd. James Arthur Hardy -
   23 December 1968   b. 13 February 1946
                         son of Arthur Hardy & Inez
                         Castle

   (2) Jimmy Dale Hardy
       b. 24 February 1969
   (3) Tonia Lynn Hardy
       b. 28 December 1970

I. Larry Wayne Hawkins
   b. 26 February 1950 - Marion Co., Ala.
   m. Shelia Karen Haney - 28 June 1968
      b. 4 October 1950

   (1) Robert Dewayne Hawkins
       b. 31 December 1968

J. Deborah Jean Hawkins
   b. 25 November 1952 - Marion Co., Ala.
   m. Richard Berryhill - 26 December 1969
      b. 29 October 1948
      son of Olin Berryhill & Hattie Mae Tidwell

   (1) Angela Michele Berryhill
       b. 21 March 1971

2. Middleton Sizemore Berryhill - "Mid"
   b. 16 October 1915 - Marion Co., Ala.
   m. Norma Lee Franks - 23 October 1937
      b. 14 May 1922 - Marion Co., Ala.
      dau. of Hosie Edward Franks & Beatrice Pollard

   A. Jimmy Bryan Berryhill
      b. 30 August 1943 - Marion Co., Ala.
      m. Rachel Naomi Childers - 31 October 1963
      dau. of Hobert O. Childers & Quilla Williams
      b. 15 May 1947
      (1) Phillip Bryan Berryhill
          b. 27 October 1964 - Marion Co., Ala.
      (2) Tracie Rachelle Berryhill
          b. 8 November 1968

   B. Beverly Kay Berryhill
      b. 10 December 1952 - Marion Co., Ala.
      m. Orbie Dell Burleson, Jr.- 9 July 1971 - Marion Co.
         b. 10 September 1952
         son of O. D. Burleson & Velma Barton

3. Virginia Pearl Berryhill
   b. 10 August 1920 - Marion Co., Ala.
   m. Olen Roden, Jr. - 19 July 1947 - Marion Co., Ala.
      b. 6 August 1922
      son of Olen Roden & Frances Stevenson

4. Clifford Perry Berryhill - "Cliff"
   b. 11 March 1924 - Marion Co., Ala.
   m. Patsy Ruth Hayes - 2 February 1950 - Birmingham, Ala.
   dau. of Marion Hayes & Edna May Pinkston

   A. Donna Lynne Berryhill
      b. 8 November 1951 - Birmingham, Ala.
      m. Carl M. Evans - 17 March 1972 - Atlanta, Ga.
         b. 16 February 1952 - New Roads, La.
         son of Maxie Doyal Evans & Edna Belle Gilbert
   B. Keri Tay Berryhill
      b. 31 August 1959 - Birmingham, Ala.

5. Martha Elizabeth Berryhill
   b. 26 February 1927 - Marion Co., Ala.
   m. Golia Clay Lindsey - 8 September 1959 - Chatsworth,
      b. 1924   Calif.

   A. Stanley Lynn Lindsey
      b. 25 June 1960 - Van Nuys, Calif.

   Martha Berryhill m. 2nd. 10 July 1965 - Walker Co.Ala.
   m. Macky Barnes
      b. 10 July 1932 - Lamar Co., Ala.

6. Letuis David Berryhill
   b. 22 May 1934 - Marion Co., Ala.
   m. Betty Sue Bryant - 2 May 1953
      b. 8 October 1937
      dau. of Jack Bryant & Mary Eardeal Vickery

   A. Janet Fay Berryhill
      b. 8 August 1954 - Marion Co., Ala.
      m. Ronald B. Weaver - 18 March 1871 - Marion Co.
         b. 17 July 1953
         son of James Weaver & Penny Christine Harris

      (1) Michael Shane Weaver
          b. 18 August 1973 - Marion Co., Ala.

B. Anita Carol Berryhill
b. 27 September 1957 - Marion Co., Ala.
C. Kenneth David Berryhill
b. 16 June 1964 - Marion Co., Ala.

Letuis Berryhill m. 2nd. 22 January 1966 - Marion Co.
m. Andra Sue Stone
b. 11 March 1945 - Rosedale, Tenn.
dau. of John Samuel Stone & Maxine Seiber

D. Suzanne Rehane Berryhill
b. 17 October 1969 - Marion Co., Ala.
E. Steven Curtis Berryhill
b. 15 June 1973 - Marion Co., Ala.

(b) Olin Jefferson Berryhill
b. 27 September 1893 - Marion Co., Ala.
d. 1971
bur. Guin City Cemetery - Guin, Ala.
m. Vera Alton Westbrook - 7 October 1911 - Okolona, MS
b. 30 January 1894 - Guin, Ala.
d. 13 March 1869 - Winfield, Ala.
bur. Guin City Cemetery
dau. of John DeWitt Westbrook & Henrietta Jane Alford

1. Cornelia Henrietta Berryhill
b. 20 October 1913
d. 19 September 1957 - Guin, Ala.
bur. Guin Cemetery
m. Thayer Ingle - 10 June 1933 - Gatman, Miss.

A. Pete F. Ingle
b. 3 May 1934 - Guin, Ala.
m. Ruth Franks - 23 October 1954
b. 10 October 1935 - Guin, Ala.

(1) Judy Nelia Ingle
b. 13 January 1957 - Indianapolis, Ind.
(2) Brian Pete Ingle
b. 29 May 1959 - Indianapolis, Ind.

2. Dorothy June Berryhill
b. 26 June 1925 - Guin, Ala.
m. Jesse Willard Shirley - 8 June 1941 - Gatman, MS
b. 20 May 1923 - Tuscaloosa Co., Ala.

A. Carol Ann Shirley
b. 1 December 1944 - Jasper, Walker Co., Ala.
m. Joel Dale Pugh - 20 March 1964 - Marion Co.
b. 12 April 1943 - Marion Co., Ala.
B. Elizabeth Jane Shirley
b. 22 May 1946 - Pensacola, Fla.
C. William Alan Shirley
b. 4 May 1947 - Fayette Co., Ala.
D. Patricia June Shirley
b. 18 June 1948 - Marion Co., Ala.
m. Johnny William May - 19 November 1966
E. Larry Stephens Shirley
b. 18 February 1952 - Marion Co., Ala.

(c) James Emmit Berryhill
b. 30 October 1896 - Marion Co., Ala.
d. 28 September 1956
bur. Guin Cemetery
m. Willie Dee Wesley - November 1915
b. 9 January 1894
d. 11 November 1961
bur. Guin Cemetery

1. Johnny Edward Berryhill
b. 10 July 1916
d. 30 November 1918 - Marion Co., Ala.
bur. Guin Cemetery

2. James Wesley Berryhill
   b. 30 March 1919 - Marion Co., Ala.
   m. Jean Lockhart

   A. Roger Dale Berryhill
   B. Edward Wesley Berryhill (twin)
   C. Tony Edwin Berryhill (twin)

3. Billy Garvis Berryhill
   b. 28 December 1916 - Marion Co., Ala.
4. Jackie David Berryhill
   b. 12 December 1930 - Marion Co., Ala.
   m. Ellen A. Johnson - 22 December 1962
      b. 28 December 1943

   A. Jackie David Berryhill, II
      b. 8 April 1964
   B. Bryan Edward Berryhill
      b. 21 June 1966
   C. Marc Wayne Berryhill
      b. 22 August 1967

5. Joan Berryhill
   b. 6 September 1933 - Marion Co., Ala.
   m. George Oliver Pierce - 22 December 1952
      b. 4 May 1931

   A. Debra Ann Pierce
      b. 16 September 1953
   B. Pamela Dee Pierce
      b. 10 December 1954

   Joan Berryhill m. 2nd. James Ralph Dodson - 28 June 1964
                              b. 7 October 1929

(d) Annie Bell Berryhill
    b. 23 December 1899 - Marion Co., Ala.
    m. Alvin Eura Wesley - 23 January 1921
       b. 29 July 1897 - Clay Co., Chandler Springs, Ala.

    1. Roy Everette Wesley
       b. 9 October 1921 - Clay Co., Ala.
       m. Ruby Etta Creel - 21 September 1940 - Birmingham
          b. 1 July 1921 - Jefferson Co., Ala.

       A. David Terry Wesley
          b. 1 November 1943 - Fairfield, Ala.
          m. Donna Sullivan - 28 December 1963 - Birmingham

          (1) David Terry Wesley, Jr.
              b. 23 July 1964

          David T. Wesley m. 2nd. 10 October 1967 - Birmingham
          m. Sandra Brooks

       B. Steven L. Wesley
          b. 5 September 1948 - Fairfield, Ala.
       C. Dale A. Wesley
          b. 29 September 1952 - Fairfield, Ala.
       D. Roy E. Wesley, Jr.
          b. 31 December 1956 - Birmingham, Ala.

    2. Geraldine W. Wesley - "Jerry"
       b. 21 December 1922 - Marion Co., Ala.
       m. Harold E. Hartwig - 13 July 1945 - Miami, Fla.
          b. 4 June 1924 - Thornton, Iowa

       A. Jerry Ann Hartwig
          b. 22 July 1948 - Jefferson Co., Ala.
       B. Vickie Lynn Hartwig
          b. 13 May 1951 - Jefferson Co., Ala.

    3. Kenneth Forest Wesley
       b. 12 February 1925 - Marion Co., Ala.
       m. Margaret Ann Jackson - 13 April 1949 - Columbus, MS
          b. 12 August 1929 - Fairfield, Ala.

                    A. Kenneth F. Wesley, Jr.
                       b. 1 April 1954 - Jefferson Co., Ala.
                    B. Leigh Ann Wesley
                       b. 13 November 1967 - Jefferson Co., Ala.
          (e) Leah Mae Berryhill
              b. 22 December 1901 - Marion Co., Ala.
              m. Walter Stanley Jackson - 10 June 1933 - Lamar Co., Ala.
                 b. 18 May 1890 -
                 d. 14 August 1960 - Sulligent, Ala.
                 bur. Sulligent Cemetery
              No issue
          (f) William Leaster Berryhill - "Bill"
              b. 6 April 1904 - Marion Co., Ala.
              m. Jewel Cerell Kolb - 17 March 1927 - Marion Co., Ala.
                 b. 11 August 1905 - Sturgis, Miss.
                 dau. of James Kolb & Lula Jane Graham

              1. Ramona Jane Berryhill
                 b. 4 May 1928 - Hamilton, Ala.
                 m. James Billy Hartsfield - 5 September 1954
                                               Columbus, Miss.

                    A. Kathy Janice Hartsfield - "Jan"
                       b. 9 May 1956 - Jefferson Co., Ala.
                    B. Terri Suzanne Hartsfield
                       b. 4 November 1959 - Jefferson Co., Ala.

              2. William Kolb Berryhill
                 b. 18 May 1932 - Marion Co., Ala.
                 m. Mary Sue Weathers - 18 February 1951 - Columbus, MS

                    A. Judith Lynn Berryhill
                       b. 22 December 1951 - Jefferson Co., Ala.
                    B. Andrew Kolb Berryhill
                       b. 8 December 1956 - Jefferson Co., Ala.

                    W. K. Berryhill m. 2nd. - 25 February 1961
                    m. Sarah Ellen Sewell

                    C. Joel Porter Berryhill
                       b. 31 January 1962 - Alabaster, Ala.

              3. Rita Gay Berryhill
                 b. 27 January 1936 - Marion Co., Ala.
                 m. Gene Jerome Ballard - 21 December 1951

                    A. Maria Fay Ballard
                       b. 24 February 1954 - Sacramento, Calif.
                    B. Lisa Gay Ballard
                       b. 4 October 1956 - Jefferson Co., Ala.
                    C. Mary Kay Ballard
                       b. 28 December 1962 - Mobile, Ala.
                    D. Gene J. Ballard, Jr.
                       b. 29 April 1966 - Mobile, Ala.

              4. Sandra Fay Berryhill
                 b. 3 February 1938 - Brilliant, Ala.
                 m. Roger Clark Homer - 24 August 1960

                    A. Shawn Wyn Homer
                       b. 3 March 1962 - Jefferson Co., Ala.
                    B. Kelly Jarita Homer
                       b. 4 June 1967 - Jefferson Co., Ala.

              5. Thomas Edward Berryhill
                 b. 17 August 1943 - Jefferson Co., Ala.

```
            6. Jimmy Doyle Berryhill
               b. 14 October 1945 - Jefferson Co., Ala.

    (f) Savannah Viola Berryhill
        b. 23 May 1906 - Guin, Marion Co., Ala.
        m. Carlos Belton Couch - 23 May 1926
           b. 7 March 1898
           d. 30 March 1943 - Marion Co., Ala.
           bur. Winfield Cemetery - Winfield, Ala.
           son of Robert M. Couch & Ann Ward
        Savannah Berryhill m. 2nd. 30 December 1946 - Bainbridge,
        m. James Leslie Whiddon                          Ga.
           b. 26 May 1905 - Chattahoochee, Fla.
           d. 1 May 1950 - Ft. Lauderdale, Fla.
           bur. City Cemetery - Chattahoochee, Fla.
           son of Richard L. Whiddon & Mary Elma Williams
        Savannah Berryhill m. 3rd. 14 March 1953 - Columbus, MS
        m. William Floyd Bunnell, Sr.
           b. 6 April 1895 - Franklin Co., Ala.
           son of Joe Bunnell & Sarah Ann Swinney
        No issue

    (g) Malcum Otis Berryhill
        b. 18 November 1909 -
        m. Lula Bell Markham - 26 May 1928 - Marion Co., Ala.
           b. October 1909
        Malcum Berryhill m. 2nd.- 1 June 1940
        m. Jeanette L. Johnson
           b. 29 December 1908
           d. 13 January 1956 - Rogersville, Tenn.
           bur. Winfield Cemetery - Winfield, Ala.
        Malcum Berryhill m. 3rd. 29 June 1957 - Marion Co., Ala.
        m. Berdie Lee La Duke
           b. 21 December 1905
        No issue

(2) James Rufus Berryhill - "Jim"
    b. 1872 - Marion Co., Ala.
    d. 2 February 1934
    bur. Center Cemetery - Marion Co., Ala.
    m. Mary Savannah Wates - 24 November 1895 - Marion Co., Ala.
       b. 1877
       d. 9 February 1968
       bur. Center Cemetery - Marion Co., Ala.

    (a) Linzie Jefferson Berryhill
        b. 2 April 1897 - Marion Co., Ala.
        d. 1 September 1962 - Tuscaloosa, Ala.
        bur. Memorial Park Cemetery - Tuscaloosa, Ala.
        m. Hattie Mae Estes - 25 December 1923 - Marion Co., Ala.
           b. 26 July 1906

        1. Coleman Estes Berryhill
           b. 2 March 1926
           m. Alice Beverly Mayes - 6 September 1947 - Tuscaloosa

           A. Elizabeth Anne Berryhill
              b. 6 September 1949
              m. Robert Wallace Cleere, Jr. - 30 May 1970 - "

              (1) Alice Lee Cleere
                  b. 17 June 1972 - Tuscaloosa, Ala.
              (2) Robert Coleman Cleere
                  b. 24 October 1975 - Tuscaloosa, Ala.

           B. Alice Deborah Berryhill
              b. 2 April 1954
              m. Barry Joe Turpin - 13 February 1977 - Tuscaloosa

              (1) Keri Leigh Turpin
                  b. 7 December 1977 - Opelika, Ala.
              (2) Joseph Gaines Turpin
                  b. 2 May 1980 - Tuscaloosa, Ala.
```

       2. James Bryan Berryhill
          b. 4 October 1932
          m. Elizabeth Ann Holmes - 19 December 1954

          A. Alesia Ann Berryhill
             b. 26 October 1955
          B. Angelia Kay Berryhill
             b. 14 December 1957
             m. Johnny Rogers Edwards

             (1) Rachel Marie Edwards
                 b. 18 August 1976
             (2) Johnny Rogers Edwards, Jr. - "Shawn"
                 b. 31 July 1978
          James Bryan Berryhill m. 2nd. 20 September 1974
          m. Carol Johnson

          C. Kimberly Leigh Berryhill
             b. 1 September 1981

    (b) William Luther Berryhill
        b. 11 December 1898
        m. Ice Banks Guin
        No issue
    (c) Limmie Washington Berryhill
        b. 9 May 1901
        m. Lealer Wesley

        1. Doyle Berryhill
           m. Joyce Ann Atkinson

           A. Douglas Berryhill
           B. Cynthia Ann Berryhill
           C. Gregory Berryhill

    (d) Lonnie Haskel Berryhill
        b. 9 October 1903
        m. Bertha Flippo

        1. Carolyn Berryhill
           m. Thomas A. Nelson - "Bob"

    (e) Alferd Lawrence Berryhill
        b. 28 August 1905
        m. Annie Lee Vickery

        1. Dan Vickery
           m. Connie Downing

           A. Vickery Berryhill
           B. Darrell Berryhill

        2. Bob Berryhill

    (f) Ernest Woodrow Berryhill
        b. 2 September 1908
        m. Lourene Guin

        1. Tommie Lou Berryhill
           m. Gaston Davis

           A. Debbie Davis
              m. Ronnie Weeks
           B. Benny Davis

        2. Dorothy Ann Berryhill
           m. Charlie D. Keaton

           A. Lesia Keaton

    (g) Orville Berryhill
        b. 19 June 1911
        m. Arella Logan

        1. Rex Ray Berryhill

        Orville Berryhill m. 2nd. Grace Gilmore

        2. Gary Berryhill
        3. Kathy Berryhill

(h) Iva Lee Berryhill
   b. 2 December 1915
   m. Cliff Beauchamp - 26 September 1936

   1. Johnnie Lou Beauchamp
      b. 6 December 1938
      m. Charles Robert Powers - "Bob" - 13 June 1965

      A. William Cliff (Bill) Powers
         b. 1 October 1968
      B. Anissa Lee Powers
         b. 23 May 1970
      C. Thomas Charles Powers - "Tom"
         b. 22 August 1972
   2. James Don Beauchamp
      b. 17 October 1940
      m. Deliske Markham - 12 February 1967

      A. Chad Beauchamp
         b. 30 November 1970

   3. Annell Beauchamp
      b. 26 July 1943
      m. R. Clifton Holler, Jr. - 29 April 1972

      A. Krista Shea Holler
         b. 24 January 1974

(i) Hilton Berryhill (twin)
   b. 16 April 1917
   m. Mary May

   1. James Arthur Berryhill
      b. 6 April 1944
      m. Elizabeth Hinen
   2. Brenda Jo Berryhill
      b. 18 February 1947
      m. Donald Richardson - 4 June 1971

(j) Hilburn Berryhill (twin)
   b. 16 April 1917
   d. as a child
   bur. Zion Cemetery - Marion Co., Ala.

(3) William Houston Berryhill
   b. 9 July 1874 - Marion Co., Ala.
   d. 13 October 1948 - Beaverton, Ala.
   bur. Zion Baptist Cemetery
   m. Missouri Vianna Kuykendall - 23 February 1893 - Marion Co.
      b. 3 March 1875 - Guin, Marion Co., Ala.
      d. 17 May 19-?- Tuscaloosa, Ala.
      bur. Zion Baptist Cemetery
      dau. of Jessie Joseph Kuykendall & Sally Ann Gage
            m. 29 December 1870 - Fayette Co., Ala.

(a) Jessie Nelson Berryhill
   b. 9 May 1895
   d. 4 January 1926 - Marion Co., Ala.
   bur. Guin, Ala.
   m. Beulah Pearl May - 20 October 1912 - Marion Co., Ala.
      b. 14 September 1895
      d. 26 October 1945 - Marion Co., Ala.
      bur. Guin, Ala.
      dau. of John Jessie May & Alice Bell Kirkland

   1. Hewitt Garland Berryhill
      b. 7 September 1913 - Marion Co., Ala.
      m. Edith Earline Martine - 23 December -?- Marion Co.

      A. Harold Glynn Berryhill
         m. Lucretia Gains
      B. Patsy Sue Berryhill
         m. Stanley Norris Merrill
      C. Lisa Renee' Berryhill
      D. Edith Lynn Berryhill

139

2. Johnnie May Berryhill
   m. Carl William Edwards

   A. Donna Kay Edwards
   B. Jerry Wayne Edwards

3. Jessie Paul Berryhill
4. Robbie Lee Berryhill
   m. Melvin Herschel Gann

   A. Debra Ann Gann
   B. Keith Bann
   C. Greg Gann

B. Sarah Jane Berryhill
   b. 1843 - Marion Co., Ala.
   d. 1899 - Millport, Lamar Co., Ala.
   bur. Pleasant Ridge Cemetery - Lamar Co., Ala.
   m. Henry Wilson Miller - "Wilse" - 1867 approx. - Marion Co., Ala.
      b. 1851 - N. C.
      d. 1916 - Lamar Co., Ala.
      bur. Pleasant Ridge Cemetery
      son of C. N. Miller & Martha -?-
               b. 1819 - NC   b. 1826 - NC
               living 1870   living 1870
   Wilse Miller served in the Civil War, but his Co. is unknown.

   (1) Martha Jane Miller - "Mat"
       b. 30 October 1869
       d. 6 November 1916 - Lamar Co., Ala.
       bur. Pleasant Ridge Cemetery
       m. Alford Robert Cash
          b. 30 October 1863
          d. 7 February 1934
          bur. Pleasant Ridge Cemetery

       (a) Edward Cash
           b. 6 December 1887
           d. 13 December 1887
       (b) William Curtis Cash
           b. 11 October 1889
           d. 15 June 1950
           m. Ozie Bell Atkins - 25 November 1916
       (c) Idus Clifford Cash
           b. 3 December 1892
           m. Mellie Brassell
       (d) Herburt Lee Cash
           b. 31 August 1895
           m. Pearl Chandler
       (e) Henry Chester Cash
           b. 22 August 1898
           d. 20 May 1940
           m. Hattie Youngblood
       (f) Axie Janie Cash
           b. 28 December 1901
           m. Luther Gustafson
       (g) George Morris Cash
           b. 8 February 1905
           d. 6 January 1936
           m. Erdeal Field
       (h) Lois Mabel Cash
           b. 10 August 1907
           d. 9 November 1915 - Lamar Co., Ala.
           bur. Pleasant Ridge Cemetery
       (i) Edith Edrea Cash
           b. 22 April 1910
           m. Fletcher Dobbs
       (j) Neva Cash
           b. 29 January 1913 - Lamar Co., Ala.
           d. 21 September 1916- Lamar Co., Ala.
           bur. Pleasant Ridge Cemetery - Lamar Co., Ala.

(2) George Early Miller
    b. 10 May 1871 - Fayette Co., Ala.
    d. 23 October 1906 - Lamar Co., Ala.
    bur. Pleasant Ridge Cemetery - Lamar Co., Ala.
    m. Levanda Johnson - 8 March 1890 - Lamar Co., Ala.
        b. 2 November 1874
        d. 12 April 1961 - Lamar Co., Ala.
        bur. Millport Cemetery - Lamar Co.
        dau. of C. Gustus Johnson & Susan Cline

    (a) Floyd Miller
        b. 20 March 1892 - Lamar Co., Ala.
        d. 20 May 1953 - Ardmore, Okla.
        m. Sally Waldrop

        1. Floyd Miller, Jr.
          m. Willene -?-

          A. Eric Miller

        2. Elizabeth Gail Miller
          m. Gene Read

          A. Susan Read
          B. Mark Read

    (b) Lovie Miller
        b. 20 November 1894
        d. 25 November 1894 - Lamar Co., Ala.
        bur. Pleasant Ridge Cemetery - Lamar Co., Ala.
    (c) Lucile Miller
        b. 29 November 1895 - Lamar Co., Ala.
        m. Arthur Andrew Dobbs

        1. Arthur Miller Dobbs
          b. 23 April 1918 - Coal Valley, Ala.
          m. Christine Ratcliff
            b. 2 April 1918 - Auburn, Miss.

          A. Robert Wayne Dobbs
            b. 5 February 1945 - Yokama, Wash.

    (d) Lester Miller - "Nick"
        b. 19 December 1897 - Lamar Co, Ala.
        d. 3 January 1955
        m. Ruth -?-

        1. Nancy Ruth Miller
          b. 25 November 1932 - Barnes, Pa.
          m. David Swanson

          A. Nels Swanson
          B. Eric Swanson
          C. Kirsten Swanson
          D. Karen Swanson
          E. Karl Miller Swanson

    (e) Sarah Jane Miller - "Janie"
        b. 28 December 1899 - Lamar Co., Ala.
        d. 6 November 1955 - Lamar Co., Ala.
        bur. Millport Cemetery - Millport, Ala.
        m. Cluffie Stripling

        1. Sybil Stripling
          m. J. W. Estes

          A. Donald Estes
          B. Earl Estes
          C. Glan Estes

        2. George Stripling
          m. Virginia -?-

          A. Elizabeth Ann Stripling
          B. Charles Stripling
          C. Martha Stripling

3. Robbie Lee Stripling
   m. Durell Fant

   A. Diane Fant
   B. Kenneth Fant
   C. David Fant

4. Rudolph Stripling
   m. Betsy -?-

   A. Jimmy Stripling

5. James Lester Stripling
   m. Hazel Cannon

   A. Judy Stripling
   B.
   C.

6. Peggy Stripling
   m. J. C. Herring

   A. Charles Rodney Herring
   B. Mark Herring

7. Richard Stripling
   m. Carla -?-

(f) Grace Miller
    b. 27 September 1905 - Lamar Co., Ala.
    M. Olen Cox

    1. Eugenia Faye Cox
       b. 12 April 1944 - Birmingham, Ala.
       m. George Roberts
(3) Infant Miller

C. George Washington Berryhill
   b. 1844 - Marion Co., Ala.
   d. said to have died in the Civil War

D. Rufus Alsa Berryhill - "Rufe"
   b. 1846 - Marion Co., Ala.
   d. 30 August 1921 - Fayette Co., Ala.
   bur. Berryhill Family Cemetery - Fayette Co., Ala.
   m. Nancy Angeline Justice - possibly in Hinds Co., Miss.
      b. 29 January 1855 - Miss.
      d. 11 December 1935 - Fayette Co., Ala.
      bur. Berryhill Family Cemetery
      dau. of -?- Justice & Caroline Markham

   (1) James William Berryhill
       b. 1873 - Marion Co., Ala.
       d. 1953
       m. Rosa E. Lee
          b. 1882
          d. 1957
          bur. Berryhill Family Cemetery (both Rosa & James)

       (a) Mittie Berryhill
           b. 2 August 1900
           m. Frank Price

           1. Rena Mae Price
              b. 10 March 1919
           2. Ruby Dean Price
              b. 15 July 1922
              d. 22 March 1953
              m. Garvie J. Black
                 b. 27 February 1912
                 d. 22 February 1965

           Mittie Berryhill m. 2nd. Earvin Earl Gillain
                                  b. 29 August 1900
                                  d. 12 May 1961

142

3. Alvin David Gillain
   b. 27 August 1926
   m. Carolyn Frances Merck
      b. 14 September 1926

   A. Alvin D. Gillain, Jr.
      b. 16 November 1950
   B. Jerome Timothy Gillain
      b. 22 February 1954

4. James Doyle Gillain
   b. 1 May 1928
5. Jerry William Gillain
   b. 30 January 1930
   m. Leotha Modez Vowels
      b. 4 August 1931

   A. Earvin Earl Gillain
      b. 22 October 1956
   B. Eva Leotha Gillain
      b. 16 December 1961
   C. Robert Donald Gillain
      b. 3 August 1964

6. Bobby Farrell Gillain
   b. 2 September 1933
   m. Barbra Jean Favors

   A. Jo Alice Gillain
      b. 9 September 1954

   Bobby Farrell Gillain m. 2nd. Carol Sue Knight -
   8 June 1942

7. Linda Lee Gillain
   b. 9 October 1940
   d. 1 January 1941
8. Lee Earl Gillain
   b. 15 April 1941
9. Reba Jo Gillain
   b. 5 May 1943
   m. Daniel Charles Byrne

   A. Lydia Ann Byrne
      b. 16 March 1968

(b) Lillie Berryhill
    b. 8 November 1903
    m. Roy F. Aldridge
       b. 21 October 1896

    1. Mavis Jean Aldridge
       b. 31 July 1921
       m. Arlen Eugene Jacks
          b. 11 December 1920

       A. Billy Eugene Jacks
          b. 29 April 1942
          m. Joan Sandlin
             b. 11 October 1942
       B. Danny Joe Jacks
          b. 19 March 1947
          m. Gloria Jean Sutherland
             b. 27 July 1947
       C. Dwight Keith Jacks
          b. 11 October 1955

    2. Leroy Aldridge
       b. 27 November 1927
       m. Dorothy Mae Kilgore
          b. 31 March 1927

       A. David Wayne Aldridge
          b. 16 April 1966

        (c) Luther Alton Berryhill
            b. 27 September 1907 -
            d. 25 April 1967
            m. Carlie Jennings

            1. Joy Berryhill
               b. 1954

        (d) Lona B. Berryhill
            b. July 1909
            m. -?- Wright
        (e) Romie Lee Berryhill
            b. 30 September 1914
            m. Robert Arlon Benton
               b. 2 December 1921

(2) Robert A. Berryhill
    b. 11 December 1874
    d. 26 November 1875 - Marion Co., Ala.
    bur. Berryhill Family Cemetery
(3) Laura Ann Berryhill
    b. 1876
    d. 1943 - Marion Co., Ala.
    bur. Berryhill Family Cemetery
    m. -?- Berryhill

        (a) Nealy Arlington Berryhill
            d. and bur. near Ashford, Ala.
            m. Gertie Flippo

            1. Delmas Berryhill
               m. 1921 approx.
            2. girl   but
            3. girl   name
            4. girl   unknown

    Laura A. Berryhill m. 2nd. J. Thomas Lee - 17 September 1903
                                     b. 1857
                                     d. 1920
                                     bur. Mt. William Cemetery - Fayette

        (b) Addie Lee
            m. John Blakney

            1. James Blakney
            2. Charles Blakney

        (c) Essie Lee
            m. Walter Collins
        (d) Ira Lee
            m. Irene Reece

            1. Daughter

            Ira Lee m. 2nd. Beatrice Trantham

            2. Son who was killed in World War II
            Ira Lee m. 3rd. -?- in Miss.

            3. Kenneth Lee

            Ira lee m. 4th -?- in Miss.

            4. Hulon Lee
            5. Son

        (e) Kelsey Lee
            m. Ada McMillon
        (f) Gerlie Lee
            m. Mamie Bishop

            1. Billy Lee
               m. Jean Williams
            2. Jimmy Ann Lee
            3. Carolyn Lee

        (g) Effie Lee
        (h) Clavis Lee m. Pete -?-

(4) Mary Frances Berryhill
    b. 1 December 1878 - Marion Co., Ala.
    d. 31 October 1963
    bur. Berryhill Family Cemetery
    m. James William Taylor - 12 December 1901
       b. 4 September 1880
       d. 18 August 1960
       son of Wiley Alexander Taylor & Safronia Maddox

    (a) Lloyd Alexander Taylor
        b. 2 June 1903
        m. Icy Blakney - 11 October 1922
           b. 31 October 1902
        1. Icy Banks Taylor
           b. 15 January 1924
           m. Clifford Eugene England - 19 June 1954
              b. 5 March 1929

           A. Michael Eugene England
              b. 21 March 1955
           B. Kay Michelle England
              b. 22 October 1956
           C. Kim Renee England
              b. 5 October 1965

    (b) William Byron Taylor
        b. 18 September 1905
        m. Alma DeEtte Akers - 18 September 1937 - Marion Co., Ala.
           b. 7 September 1914
           dau. of Albert Roy Akers & Brazzie May

        1. Willie Irene Taylor
           b. 29 June 1938
           m. Stanley Vernon McDonald - 6 July 1963
              b. 5 June 1937

           A. Laura Ann McDonald
              b. 3 August 1964
           B. Roger Allen McDonald
              b. 19 April 1966

        2. Tommy Hugh Taylor
           b. 24 August 1939
           m. Marylin Sue Fowlks - 8 February 1959 - Monroe Co, MS
              b. 29 April 1939

           A. William Mikeal Taylor
              b. 2 November 1960
           B. David Eugene Taylor
              b. 7 June 1963
           C. Marylin Alesa Taylor
              b. 13 December 1966

    (c) Leland Hill Taylor
        b. 4 March 1908
        d. 25 February 1968
        bur. Siloam Baptist Cemetery
        m. Effie Arizona Fowler - 30 July 1949
           b. 9 August 1909
        1. Frances Marie Taylor
           b. 20 September 1950

    (d) Robert Lee Taylor
        b. 4 December 1910
        m. Letha Mae Walls - 29 June 1939 - Ft. Lauderdale, Fla.
           b. 14 August 1921

        1. James Robert Taylor
           b. 5 January 1941 - Belle Glade, Fla.
           m. Beverly Ann Himes - 30 May 1964 - Orland, Fla.
              b. 12 July 1942 - Biloxi, Miss.

           A. Holly Ann Taylor
              b. 18 April 1967 - Little Rock, Ark.

(c) Luther Alton Berryhill
    b. 27 September 1907 -
    d. 25 April 1967
    m. Carlie Jennings

    1. Joy Berryhill
       b. 1954

(d) Lona B. Berryhill
    b. July 1909
    m. -?- Wright
(e) Romie Lee Berryhill
    b. 30 September 1914
    m. Robert Arlon Benton
       b. 2 December 1921

(2) Robert A. Berryhill
    b. 11 December 1874
    d. 26 November 1875 - Marion Co., Ala.
    bur. Berryhill Family Cemetery
(3) Laura Ann Berryhill
    b. 1876
    d. 1943 - Marion Co., Ala.
    bur. Berryhill Family Cemetery
    m. -?- Berryhill

    (a) Nealy Arlington Berryhill
        d. and bur. near Ashford, Ala.
        m. Gertie Flippo

        1. Delmas Berryhill
           m. 1921 approx.
        2. girl   but
        3. girl   name
        4. girl   unknown

    Laura A. Berryhill m. 2nd. J. Thomas Lee - 17 September 1903
                                           b. 1857
                                           d. 1920
                                           bur. Mt. William Cemetery - Fayette

    (b) Addie Lee
        m. John Blakney

        1. James Blakney
        2. Charles Blakney

    (c) Essie Lee
        m. Walter Collins
    (d) Ira Lee
        m. Irene Reece

        1. Daughter

        Ira Lee m. 2nd. Beatrice Trantham

        2. Son who was killed in World War II
        Ira Lee m. 3rd. -?- in Miss.

        3. Kenneth Lee

        Ira lee m. 4th -?- in Miss.

        4. Hulon Lee
        5. Son

    (e) Kelsey Lee
        m. Ada McMillon
    (f) Gerlie Lee
        m. Mamie Bishop

        1. Billy Lee
           m. Jean Williams
        2. Jimmy Ann Lee
        3. Carolyn Lee

    (g) Effie Lee
    (h) Clavis Lee m. Pete -?-

(e) Irene Warren
    b. 13 July 1917 - Fayette Co., Ala.
    m. Berlie Aucie Taylor - 25 December 1935
       b. 4 May 1915 - Fayette Co., Ala.

    1. Faylene Taylor
       b. 20 August 1946 - Fayette Co., Ala.
    2. Kathy Sue Taylor
       b. 4 January 1954 - Fayette Co., Ala.

(f) Maudine Vivian Warren
    b. 21 November 1919 - Fayette Co., Ala.
    m. John Dee Hamilton - 23 May 1937
       b. 1 June 1917 - Fayette Co., Ala.

    1. James Dee Hamilton
       b. 6 April 1946 - Walker Co., Ala.

    Maudine Warren m. 2nd. George Washington Estes, Jr.
    14 July 1950   b. 24 June 1920 - Walker Co., Ala.

    2. Joel Knox Estes
       b. 7 June 1954 - Walker Co., Ala.

(g) William Garvous Warren
    b. 28 February 1923 - Fayette Co., Ala.
    m. Imogene Spann - 24 December 1946
       b. 13 August 1929 - Fayette Co., Ala.

    1. Virginia Ann Warren
       b. 11 September 1947 - Jefferson Co., Ala.
       m. Aurthor Clifford Smith - 5 June 1965
          b. 20 January 1945 - Mobile Co., Ala.
    2. Dwight David Warren
       b. 23 July 1948 - Marion Co., Ala.
    3. Mary Nell Warren
       b. 13 October 1950 - Marion Co., Ala.

(h) Hildon Brice Warren
    b. 30 August 1927 - Fayette Co., Ala.
    m. Geraldine Tucker - 22 June 1947
       b. 11 April 1932 - Marion Co., Ala.

    1. James Brice Warren
       b. 23 November 1948 - Marion Co., Ala.
    2. Billy Ray Warren
       b. 29 July 1950 - Marion Co., Ala.
    3. Mark Warren
       b. 6 January 1956 - Marion Co., Ala.

(6) Edward Berryhill - "Edd"
    b. 1885 approx. - Marion Co., Ala.
    m. Cora Crews

    (a) Claude Herman Berryhill
        m. Elsie -?-

        1. Claude Edward Berryhill

    (b) Thomas E. Berryhill
    (c) Noland Berryhill
    (d) Roland Berryhill
        b. December 1914
    (e) Beatrice Berryhill
        m. Phillip Byars

        3 sons and 2 daughters - names unknown

    (f) Arnold Berryhill

(7) George Shafer Berryhill
    b. 24 June 1891
    d. 12 October 1954
    bur. Berryhill Family Cemetery
    m. Ludie Whisenante
    No issue

(8) Nancy Jane Berryhill
    b. 23 January 1880
    d. 9 March 1966
    bur. Berryhill Family Cemetery
    m. William A. Shaw
       b. 5 August 1879
       d. 2 November 1950
       bur. Berryhill Family Cemetery
    No issue
(9) Bailey Franklin Berryhill
    m. Laura Lee

    (a) Infant Daughter
         b. & d. 29 April 1919 & bur. Berryhill Family Cemetery
    (b) Lillian Berryhill
    (c) Bailey F. Berryhill, Jr.
    (d) William Berryhill
         m. Anna Belle Shelnut

(10) Margaret Josephine Berryhill - "Jo"
     b. 2 May 1888 - Marion Co., Ala.
     d. 28 February 1963
     bur. Bluff Springs Cemetery - Ashford, Ala.
     m. Vincie Andrew Roberts - 3 August 1903
        b. 24 December 1885
        d. 5 December 1962
        bur. Bluff Springs Cemetery - Ashford

     (a) Elmer Vitleatus Roberts
         b. 9 January 1905 - Marion Co., Ala.
         m. Nettie Bell Fellows - 23 December 1930 - Dothan, Ala.
            b. 10 October 1910 - Houston Co., Ala.
            dau. of Burl Mobley Fellows & Lodie Odena Shelton
     (b) Levie Beatrice Roberts
         b. 24 October 1909 - Fayette Co., Ala.
         m. Joseph Henry Clower - 3 October 1926 - Ashford, Ala.
            b. 25 February 1899 - Dickie, Calhoun Co, Ga.
            son of Joseph Clower & Hattie Palmer

         1. Hattie Jo Clower
            b. 8 November 1937 - Houston Co., Ala.
            m. Russell Ivan Ball - 8 November 1958 - Houston Co.
               b. 29 April 1936 - Washington Co., Va.
               son of Sherman William Ball & Delta Luemma Thompson

            A. Vickie Beatrice Ball
               b. 25 August 1959 - Panama City, Bay Co., Fla.
            B. Jason Loren Ball
               b. 8 July 1963 - Denver, Colo.
            C. Jeffrey Alan Ball
               b. 31 December 1966 - Denver, Colo.

     (c) William Carson Roberts
         b. 27 May 1912 - Marion Co., Ala.
         d. 8 December 1965 - Houston Co., Ala.
         bur. Bluff Springs Cemetery - Ashford, Ala.
         m. Myrtle Rommell Jackson - 27 August 1932 - Houston Co.
            b. 3 September 1903 - Houston Co., Ala.
            dau. of Rufus Martin Jackson & Annie Agnes Addison

         1. William Manley Roberts
            b. 28 February 1935 - Houston Co., Ala.
            m. Mavis Cherry - 10 April 1953 - Donaldsonville, Ga.
               b. 25 January 1937 - Houston Co., Texas

            A. Rhonda Patricia Roberts
               b. 13 March 1954 - Houston Co., Ala.
            B. Debra Ann Roberts
               b. 5 December 1955 - Houston Co., Ala.
            C. Latricia Dawn Roberts
               b. 8 November 1961 - Houston Co., Ala.

(d) Ida Mae Roberts
   b. 12 August 1916 - Marion Co., Ala.
   m. Fred Jackson - 22 December 1938 - Houston Co., Ala.
      b. 3 November 1914 - Houston Co., Ala.
      son of Oscar Jackson & Donie -?-

   1. Katie Jackson
      b. 25 April 1955 - Houston Co., Ala.

(e) Evie Angeline Roberts
   b. 30 June 1922 - Houston Co., Ala.
   m. Willie Otho Rabon - 25 December 1958 - Houston Co.
      b. 8 February 1918
      son of Wright Coxel Rabon, Sr. & Bera Johnson

(f) Vincie Andrew Roberts, Jr.
   b. 1924 approx.

E. James Henry Berryhill - "Jim" or "Jimmy"
   b. 16 February 1849 - Marion Co., Ala.
   d. 30 January 1923 - Lafayette Co., Miss.
   bur. Dallas Cemetery - Dallas, Miss.
   m. Sarah Elizabeth Berryhill - "Betty" - 22 February 1883 -
      Lafayette Co., Miss.
      bur. Dallas Cemetery near Pontotoc, Miss.

(1) Burie Henderson Berryhill
   b. 15 November 1885 - Lafayette Co., Miss.
   d. 25 March 1935 - Lafayette Co., Miss.
   bur. Springhill Cemetery - Lafayette Co., Miss.
   m. Erma Eula Franklin - 11 January 1905 - Lafayette Co., MS
      d. before 1914/1915 - Lafayette Co., Miss.

   (a) Mosie Berryhill
      b. 1 June 1908 - Lafayette Co., Miss.
      d. 1955 approx.
      bur. Dallas Cemetery
      m. Loyce Lewellen

      1. Hazel Lewellen
      2. Hobert Lewellen

      Mosie Berryhill m. 2nd. Dock Starnes

      3. Curle Dennis Starnes - dau.
      4. Oqullie Starnes - dau.
      5. Bobby Gean Starnes

      Mosie Berryhill m. 3rd. Clealand Starnes

      6. Son
      7. Son

   (b) Eunice Berryhill
      b. 3 May 1912 - Lafayette Co., Miss.
      m. Newt Henry

      1. Mary Lillian Henry
         b. 23 July 1927 - Coahoma Co., Miss.
         m. Wm. Curtis Jenkins - December 1949

         A. Wm. Curtis Jenkins, Jr.
            b. September 1950 - Sunflower Co., Miss.
         B. Billy Joe Jenkins
            b. 5 January 1952 - Sunflower Co., Miss.
         C. James Newton Jenkins
            b. 1955
         D. Vera Elizabeth Jenkins
            b. February 1961
            d. June 1961
         E. John Henry Jenkins
            b. 28 December 1962

      2. James Alfred Henry
         b. 27 June 1931 - Sunflower Co., Miss.
         m. Roma Jean Burgess - 1952

A. Deborah Jean Henry
   b. 1954
B. Barbara Henry
   b. October 1956
C. James Alfred Henry, Jr.
   b. 1958

3. Martha Elizabeth Henry
   b. 25 September 1933 - Sunflower Co., Miss.
   m. Albert Lacy Clark - 1952

   A. James Albert Clark
      b. February 1954

4. Harry Lee Henry
   b. 11 October 1935 - Panola Co., Miss.
   m. Patricia Stanton - February 1955

   A. Bobby Joe Henry
      b. 1958
   B. Edward Henry

5. Sally Mae Henry
   b. 2 November 1937 - Sunflower Co., Miss.
   m. Luther Leigh Crook - 11 April 1957

   A. Lola Sue Crook
      b. 1 January 1958
   B. Wm. Luther Crook
      b. 18 August 1959
   C. Linda Gayle Crook
      b. 31 August 1961
   D. Carrie Lynn Crook
      b. 1 March 1963
   E. Michael Leigh Crook
      b. 21 February 1965

6. Annie Ruth Henry
   b. 17 October 1940 - Sunflower Co., Miss.
   m. Andrew John Rexroth - 23 September 1967

   A. Andrew John Rexroth, Jr.
      b. 20 April 1968

7. Billy Wayne Henry
   b. 28 October 1942 - Sunflower Co., Miss.
   m. Dorothy Lee Stanton - October 1966

   A. Michelle Rene' Henry
      b. 4 November 1967

8. Ellen Louise Henry
   b. 1 February 1944 - Sunflower Co., Miss.
   d. 31 July 1957
9. Velma Henry (twin)
   b. 28 April 1945 - Sunflower Co., Miss.
   m. John Neal Baline - 7 April 1966

   A. Lisa Dynette Blaine
      b. 6 April 1967

10. Thelma Henry (twin)
    b. 28 April 1945 - Sunflower Co., Miss.
    m. Hugh Tarvin Reed - 14 October 1964

    A. Hugh Tarvin Reed, Jr.
       b. 30 July 1966
    B. Darrell Henry Reed
       b. 28 May 1968

11. Marvin Henry
    b. 23 June 1946 - Sunflower Co., Miss.
    m. Gloria Prewitt - 9 June 1968

12. Robert Lamar Henry
    b. 2 August 1954 - Bolivar Co., Miss.

Burie Berryhill m. 2nd. - 16 May 1915 - Lafayette Co., Miss.
m. Mandy Elizabeth Henry
   b. 23 August 1895 - Lafayette Co., Miss.
   dau. of Wm. Monroe Henry & Mary Susan Turney

(c) William Woodrow Berryhill
   b. 22 April 1917 - Lafayette Co., Miss.
   m. Genette Oswalt
     b. 7 May 1930 - Quitman Co., Miss.

   1. Sue Jean Berryhill
     b. 5 May 1948 - Sunflower Co., Miss.
     m. Raymond McNeer - March 1967

     A. Mary Kathleen McNeer
       b. 12 February 1968

   2. Donnie Glenn Berryhill
     b. 15 May 1950 - Sunflower Co., Miss.
   3. Rickey Joe Berryhill
     b. 23 March 1958 - Bolivar Co., Miss.

(d) Walter A. Berryhill
   b. 8 May 1920 - Sledge, Quitman Co., Miss.
   m. Dorothy L. Stafford - 21 December 1940 - Panola Co. MS
     b. 18 December 1924 - Quitman Co., Miss.

   1. James A. Berryhill
     b. 28 March 1942 - Panola Co.
     m. Judy Henderson - 6 April 1963 - Vicksburg, Miss.
       b. 26 December 1943 - Crowley, La.

     A. Barbara A. Berryhill
       b. 7 December 1964
     B. Wanda F. Berryhill
       b. 30 October 1967

   2. Elizabeth Ann Berryhill
     b. 6 February 1947 - Quitman Co.
     m. Lee Johnson - 2 October 1964 - Panola Co.

     A. Rida G. Johnson

   3. Betty L. Berryhill
     b. 7 November 1948 - Panola Co.
     m. Gene Johnson - 4 December 1964
   4. Shirley G. Berryhill
     b. 3 February 1955
   5. Jimmy D. Berryhill
     b. 5 July 1957

(e) Lena Berryhill
   b. 18 February 1919 - Lafayette Co., Miss.
   d. 17 August 1921 - Lafayette Co., Miss.
(f) Claude Harvey Berryhill
   b. 18 February 1926
   d. 25 October 1926 - Lafayette Co., Miss.
(g) Henry Terrell Berryhill
   b. 2 April 1923 - Lafayette Co.
   m. Charlene Redd
     b. 23 June 1925 - Washington Co., Miss.

   1. Ruby Elizabeth Berryhill
     b. 25 July 1945
     m. Charles Blunt

     A. Child

   2. Henry Terrell Berryhill, Jr.
     b. 17 August 1949
   3. Charles Michael berryhill
     b. 15 August 1953
   4. Shelia Ann Berryhill
     b. 3 November 1950
     d. 6 February 1951
     bur. Greenville, Miss.

(h) Carl Dee Berryhill
    b. 11 August 1928 - Lula, Cahoma Co., Miss.
    d. 1967/1968 - Clarksdale, Miss.
    m. Clarise Modess Davis

    1. Carol Lynn Berryhill
       b. 1 May 1949
    2. Leslie Freeda Berryhill
       b. 30 April 1952
    3. Richard Dee Berryhill
       b. 19 May 1953
    4. Carl Benton Berryhill
       b. 8 January 1955
    5. Burie Randall Berryhill
       b. 15 April 1960
    6. Carl Dee Berryhill, Jr.
       b. 11 December 1967

(i) Idera Berryhill
    b. 26 July 1918 - Lafayette Co., Miss.
    m. William Henry

    1. Pauline Henry
       b. 7 October 1934
       d. 20 June 1968
    2. William Henry, Jr.

(2) Tommy Berryhill
    b. 1886 approx. - Lafayette Co., Miss.
    m. Cora Berryhill
(3) Ruthie Berryhill
    b. 1888 approx. - Lafayette Co., Miss.
    m. Albert Woods

    (a) Jimmie Lou Woods
    (b) Sherrel Woods
    (c) Marie Woods

(4) Mary Lavada Edna Berryhill
    b. 13 February 1893 - Lafayette Co., Miss.
    d. 18 May 1967 - Pontotoc, Miss.
    bur. Quin Cemetery - Pontotoc, Miss.
    m. Zollie Lewellen

LAFAYETTE COUNTY MISSISSIPPI MARRIAGES

Burie Berryhill & Eula Franklin	11 January	1905
Burie Berryhill & Mandy Henry	16 May	1915
Charles Berryhill & Verna Stewart	8 January	1914
James H. Berryhill & Sarah E. Berryhill	22 February	1883
John H. Berryhill & Clary Welch	7 August	1905
John T. Berryhill & Atlanta Dodge	20 September	1903
N. A. Berryhill & Miss A. J. Bryant	28 April	1886
W. H. Berryhill & Miss M. C. Garner	20 June	1886

F. Robert W. Berryhill - "Bob'
    b. 16 November 1850 - Marion Co., Ala.
    d. 19 October 1894 - Fayette Co., Ala.
    bur. Berryhill Cemetery - Marion Co., Ala.
    m. Mary M. Justice
       b. 26 January 1855 - Miss.
       d. 25 December 1945 - Marion Co., Ala.
       bur. Mt. Olive Cemetery - near Guin, Ala.
       dau. of -?- Justice & Caroline Markham
       she m. 2nd. Ames K. Gamm - 29 July 1904 - Fayette Co., Ala.

(1) Nancy E. Berryhill
    b. 13 September 1873 - Fayette Co., Ala.
    d. 16 November 1873 - Marion Co., Ala.
    bur. Berryhill Cemetery - Marion Co., Ala.

(2) John William Berryhill
    b. 22 September 1875 - Fayette Co., Ala.
    Never married - In 1946 was in Chicago & worked for railroad.
(3) James Rufus Berryhill
    b. 1 February 1877 - Fayette Co., Ala.
(4) Thomas Alonzo Berryhill
    b. 1 January 1879 - Fayette Co., Ala.
    Worked for the Railroad around Jacksonville, Texas
(5) Henry Wilse Berryhill
    b. 12 September 1884 - Fayette Co., Ala.
    m. Dovie Ann Burleson - 8 August 1907
       b. 15 February 1893 - Marion Co., Ala.

    (a) John Elmon Berryhill
        b. 31 July 1909 - Marion Co., Ala.
        m. Lillie Bell Franks

        1. Lola Gay Berryhill
           b. 4 July 1930 - Marion Co., Ala.
           d. 29 November 1970
        2. Jo Ann Berryhill
           b. 4 January 1934 - Marion Co., Ala.
           m. Donald Clark

           A. Jana Clark
              b. 18 March 1955
           B. Bill Clark
              b. 9 February 1959
           C. Lili Ann Clark
              b. 8 August 1966

        3. Jerry Elmon Berryhill
           b. 29 December 1940 - Marion Co., Ala.
           m. Mary Ann Clark

           A. Angie Berryhill
              b. 12 August 1971

    (b) Jesse Lou Berryhill - "Jet"
        b. 13 June 1911 - Marion Co., Ala.
        m. Doyle Cutts

        1. Billy Dale Berryhill
           b. 18 January 1932
           m. Martha Weeks

           A. Billy Dale Berryhill, Jr.

    (c) Noah Berryhill - "Bud"
        b. 5 February 1913 - Marion Co., Ala.
        d. 30 August 1971 - Wylam, Ala.
        bur. Elmwood Cemetery - Birmingham, Ala.
        m. Louise Sandlin - 15 January 1935
           b. 29 March 1916

        1. Joe Franks Berryhill
           b. 14 March 1938 - Marion Co., Ala.
           m. Martha Frances Gray - 20 August 1961

           A. Timothy Joe Berryhill
              b. 3 November 1962 - Jefferson Co., Ala.

        2. John Henry Berryhill
           b. 7 December 1940 - Marion Co., Ala.
           m. Sally Marlyn Lewis - 9 November 1963 - Jefferson Co.
              b. 16 September 1940 - Jefferson Co., Ala.

           A. Jonathan Lewis Berryhill
              b. 18 May 1970 - Jefferson Co., Ala.

    (d) Nancy Christine Berryhill
        b. 30 November 1928 - Marion Co., Ala.
        m. Kermit Treadgill
        m. 2nd. Garlan Barrett, Jr.

(e) Bobby Jean Berryhill
    b. 19 July 1932 - Marion Co., Ala.
    m. Bill Godsey
    m. 2nd. Bobby Colburn

    1. Sherri Godsey
       b. 7 March 1954 - Marion Co., Ala.
    2. Linda Dianne Colburn
       b. 5 January 1959 - Jefferson Co., Ala.
    3. Barry Christopher Colburn - "Chris"
       b. 5 January 1968 - Zion, I..

    These three children were not identified by family
    name, so I did not put one as I did not know what
    was correct.

G. Mary Ann Berryhill - "Polly"
   b. 1852 - Marion Co., Ala.
   bur. Millport Cemetery - Lamar Co., Ala.
   m. Buck Couch (his 2nd. marriage)
   No issue
   Polly (Berryhill) Couch lived with "Wilse" Miller and her
   sister, Margaret, for many years after Buck Couch died.

H. Benjamin Franklin Berryhill - "Ben"
   b. 21 March 1854 - Marion Co., Ala.
   d. 8 April 1902 - Fayette Co., Ala.
   bur. Berryhill Family Cemetery - Fayette Co., Ala.
   m Laura A. Justice - 19 January 1884 - Fayette Co., Ala.
     b. 31 July 1860 - Miss.
     d. 5 April 1926 - Fayette Co., Ala. (or d. 24 January 1910?)
     bur. Berryhill Family Cemetery
     dau. of -?- Justice & Caroline Markham

   (1) Pervy Edward Berryhill
       b. 1885 approx.
       d. 1888/1889 approx. - Fayette Co., Ala.
       bur. Berryhill Family Cemetery
   (2) Willis Alexander Berryhill
       b. 21 May 1886 - Fayette Co., Ala.
       d. 12 December 1929
       bur. Berryhill Family Cemetery
       m. Martha Collins - 23 May 1907 - Marion CO., Ala.
         m. 2nd -?- Burnett
       (a) Robert Berryhill
           b. 17 March 1908 - Marion Co., Ala.
           bur. Berryhill Family Cemetery
   (3) John Thomas Berryhill
       b. 9 December 1887/1888 approx. - Fayette Co., Ala.
       d. 9 December 1903/1904 approx. - Fayette Co., Ala. - 16 years
       bur. Berryhill Family Cemetery
   (4) Susie Ann Berryhill
       b. 4 June 1889 - Fayette Co., Ala.
       m. Henry Walter Taylor - 2 November 1906 - Marion Co., Ala.
         b. 4 June 1887
         d. 24 January 1968 - Fayette Co., Ala.
         bur. Siloam Cemetery - Fayette Co., Ala.
         son of Wiley Taylor & Safronia Maddox

       (a) Rufus Sylvester Taylor
           b. 3 October 1907 - Fayette Co., Ala.
           m. Susie Atkinson
           m. 2nd. Eula Fowler
       (b) Lester Arlington Taylor
           b. 9 January 1909 - Fayette Co., Ala.
           m. Ella Fowler
       (c) Louvadie Taylor
           b. 24 July 1912 - Fayette Co., Ala.
           m. Vardell Markham

(d) Berlie Ansel Taylor
    b. 4 May 1915 - Fayette Co., Ala.
    m. Arlene Warren
(e) Rommie Cornelius Taylor
    b. 26 June 1916 - Fayette Co., Ala.
    m. Dorris Flynn
(f) John Basol Taylor
    b. 26 April 1926 - Marion Co., Ala.
    m. Mary Mayfield

(5) William Sylvester Berryhill
    b. 11 November 1891/1892 - Fayette Co., Ala.
    d. 11 November 1903/1904 - Fayette Co., Ala - 12 years
    bur. Berryhill Family Cemetery
(6) Murry Berryhill
    b. 1893/1894 - Fayette Co., Ala.
    d. as a small child
    bur. Berryhill Family Cemetery
(7) Connie Ellon Berryhill
    b. 13 April 1900 - Marion Co., Ala.
    m. Emmitt Mills
        b. 26 April 1896 - Fayette Co., Ala.
        son of Jim Mills & Frances E. Bozeman

    (a) Zelma Mills
        b. 17 August 1917 - Walker Co., Ala.
        d. 19 August 1921 - Lamar Co., Ala.
        bur. Rag Cemetery - Gatman, Miss.
    (b) Mavis Mills
        b. 18 June 1920 - Fayette Co., Ala.
        m. Harry Bodo
        No issue
    (c) Ozie Mills
        b. 4 December 1921 - Walker Co., Ala.
        m. W. D. Owens

        1. Terry Owens
           m. Owzell Wheat
        2. Sherry Diane Owens
           b. 1949
        3. San Jean Owens
           b. 1955
        4. James Randy Owens
           b. 1957

    (d) Beulah Mills
        b. 15 August 1927
        m. W. C. Henderson

        1. W. C. Henderson, Jr.
           b. 1954
        2. Gina Carole Henderson
           b. 1958

    (e) James Arlie Mills
        b. 22 March 1925
        m. -?- Dean

        1. Darlene Mills
           b. 1947
        2. Larry Mills
           b. 1949

    (f) Joe Stewart Mills
        b. 17 January 1932
        m. Bobbie Snow

        1. Joe Douglas Mills
           b. 1953
        2. James Kenneth Mills
           b. 1955
        3. Gary Wess Mills
           b. 1961

          4. Anthony DeWayne Mills
             b. 1965

    (g) Billy Mills
        b. 22 July 1930
        m. Gertrude -?-

        1. John Mills
           b. 1967

    (h) Mattie F. Mills
        b. 9 August 1934
        m. Jack W. Swafford

        1. Brenda Joyce Swafford
           b. 1952
        2. Debra Darlene Swafford
           b. 1957

    (i) Margaret Ann Mills
        b. 12 May 1937
        m. Joseph Arnold Kimbrell

        1. David Arnild Kimbrell
           b. 1956
        2. Ricky Lee Kimbrell
           b. 1958

    (j) Emmit Mills, Jr.
        b. 1939
        m. Helen Morgan

        1. Barry Scott Mills
           b. 1965

    (k) Patricia Ellen Mills
        b. 13 December 1942
        m. Joe Niel Sargent
    (l) Constance Kay Mills
        b. 28 April 1945
        m. David Ronnie Knight

        1. David R. Knight, Jr.
           b. 1964
        2. Richard Brian Knight
           b. 1965
        3. Anglia E. Knight
           b. 15 March 1968

(8) Cleve Hanan Berryhill
    b. 7 March 1896 - Fayette Co., Ala.
    m. Sibbie L. McCluskey
       b. 4 September 1897 - Fayette Co., Ala.

    (a) Infant Daughter
        d. and d. 5 April 1918 - Fayette Co., Ala.
        bur. Mt. William Cemetery - Fayette Co.
    (b) Wilma Maurene Berryhill
        b. 23 October 1919 - Fayette Co., Ala.
    (c) Ami Louise Berryhill
        b. 19 October 1921 - Fayette Co., Ala.
        m. Henry Lawson Collier

        1. Miquleon Collier

    (d) Willie Mae Berryhill
        b. 6 March 1926 - Fayette Co., Ala.
        m. James Curtis May

        1. Linda May
        2. Ricky May

    (e) Ura Linddell Berryhill
        b. 8 January 1928 - Fayette Co., Ala.
        m. Grady Barnett

        1. Mark Barnett

(f) Stanley Wayne Berryhill
    b. 31 December 1930 - Fayette Co., Ala.
    m. Jenette Stewart

    1. Kimalee Ann Berryhill

(g) Kenneth Ray Berryhill
    b. 13 March 1937 - Fayette Co., Ala.
    m. Carolyn Brown
(h) Patricia Ann Berryhill - "Pat"
    b. 18 August 1938 - Fayette Co., Ala.

I. Rebecca Berryhill
   b. 1857 - Marion Co., Ala.
   Age 3 years on 1860 census, but gone by 1870 census, and no
   other information is available on her, so we can assume she
   died rather young.

J. Nancy Margaret Berryhill - "Marg"
   b. 1858 - Marion Co., Ala.
   bur. Millport Cemetery - Millport, Ala.
   m. Henry Wilson Miller - "Wilse" -15 October 1899 - Marion Co.
      b. 1851 - N. C.
      d. 1916 - Millport, Ala.
      bur. Pleasant Ridge Cemetery - Millport, Ala.
      son of C. N. Miller & Martha -?-
              b. 1819 - NC   b. 1826 - NC
              both living during 1870 census
   No issue
   Some say "Wilse" Miller served in the Civil War, but he was
   certainly very young!

K. John Edward Berryhill - "Johnny"
   b. 21 August 1860 - Monroe or Hinds Co., Miss.
   d. 2 February 1933 - Fayette Co., Ala.
   bur. Berryhill Family Cemetery - Marion Co., Ala.
   m. Alpha Etta Lucas Gosa
      b. 4 May 1867
      d. July 1938
      bur. Berryhill Family Cemetery

(1) Wilford Franklin Berryhill
    b. 11 December 1883 - Fayette Co., Ala.
    m. Susan Elizabeth Head - 10 March 1907 - Fayette Co., Ala.
       b. 9 May 1890 - Marion Co., Ala.
       d. 26 January 1955 - Clay Co., Miss.
       bur. -?- Cemetery - Lee Co., Miss.

    (a) William Ottis Berryhill
        b. 22 March 1910 - Marion Co., Ala.
        m. Avis Hester
           b. 23 October 1909 - Monroe Co., Miss.

        1. Mary Sue Berryhill
           b. 16 April 1936 - Monroe Co., Miss.
           m. Oren Eugene Buskirk - 29 November 1957

           A. Montie Devan Buskirk (adopted by James C. Brown)
              b. 15 July 1959 - Shelby Co., Tenn.

           Mary Berryhill m. 2nd. James Coy Brown - 4 September1962
                                    b. 2 August 1925

           B. Markus Coy Brown
              b. 26 September 1965 - Albuquerque, NM
           C. Marla June Brown
              b. 5 March 1967 - Tupelo, Miss.

    (b) Orvill Oneil Berryhill
        b. 24 April 1912 - Marion Co., Ala.
        m. Ollie Mae Vaughn - 21 June 1031 - Evergreen, Miss.
           b. 21 August 1915 - Marion Co., Ala.

1. Vernon Washington Berryhill
   b. 29 April 1932
   m. Dora Holmes - 17 July 1958 - Chicago, Ill.
      b. 17 June 1938

   A. Debbie Lynn Berryhill
      b. 6 November 1959
   B. Jimmy Berryhill
      b. 6 January 1961
   C. William Arvill Berryhill
      b. 21 February 1962
   D. Mary Jane Berryhill
      b. 6 December 1964

2. J. D. Berryhill
   b. 4 September 1936
   m. Delores Taylor - 29 December 1956 - Beecher, Ill.
      b. 18 September 1938

   1. Michal Alan Berryhill
      b. 5 February 1958
   2. Jay Danial Berryhill
      b. 2 December 1960
   3. Donna Christine Berryhill
      b. 18 November 1961
   4. Brian David Berryhill
      b. 24 January 1963

3. Ruble Franklin Berryhill
   b. 15 April 1938
   m. Betty Poole - 14 July 1956 - Chicago, Ill.
      b. 26 March 1937

   A. Linda Sue Berryhill
      b. 24 April 1957
   B. William Franklin Berryhill
      b. 31 December 1959
   C. Mary Darlene Berryhill
      b. 30 January 1961
   D. -?- Berryhill
      b. December 1968

4. Dorothy Faye Berryhill
   b. 14 April 1940
   m. Bobby Kindall Church - 26 April 1958 - Chicago, Ill
      b. 5 September 1936

   A. Susan Lynn Church
      b. 4 January 1962
   B. Bobby Darrell Church
      b. 28 February 1963
   C. Karen Kay Church
      b. 11 January 1965
   D. Steven Scott Church
      b. 1 March 1967

5. Geraldine Berryhill
   b. 12 November 1947
   m. James Peacock - 9 January 1965 - Chicago, Ill.
      b. 2 January 1947

(c) Murry Hollis Berryhill
    b. 27 November 1915 - Marion Co., Ala.
    d. 26 January 1944 - killed in World War II
(d) Roy Mayfield Berryhill
    b. 21 April 1918 - Monroe Co., Miss.
(e) James Bernice Berryhill
    b. 24 January 1920 - Monroe Co., Miss.
    m. Frances Caradine - 23 March 1946
       b. 9 September 1925 - Clay Co., Miss.

   1. Gloria Jean Berryhill
      b. 12 April 1947 - Lowndes Co., Miss.
      m. Samuel Thomas Criddle - 3 June 1967
         b. 19 April 1945 - Chickasaw Co., Miss.

(f) Grady Berryhill
   b. 16 August 1923 - Monroe Co., Miss.
   m. Jimmie Dell Caradine - 28 May 1946
      b. 26 March 1928 - Clay Co., Miss.

   1. Linda Carolyn Berryhill
      b. 10 March 1948 - Clay Co., Miss.
   2. Judy Marolyn Berryhill
      b. 23 March 1949 - Clay Co., Miss.
      m. Melvin Roger Smith - 24 August 1968

(g) Hershel Reed Berryhill
   b. 26 August 1926 - Monroe Co., Miss.
   d. 17 December 1961 - Chicago, Ill.
   bur. Lee Co., Miss.
   m. Ava -?-

   1. Linda Sue Berryhill
      b. 11 December 1953 - Chicago, Ill.

(h) Eva Mae Berryhill
   b. 23 August 1930 - Monroe Co., Miss.
   m. Kenneth Ray Williams - 26 May 1947
      b. 16 November 1929 - Lamar Co., Ala.

   1. Brenda Delores Williams
      b. 30 March 1948 - Lowndes Co., Miss.
   2. Margaret Ann Williams
      b. 20 March 1950 - Lowndes Co., Miss.
      d. 2 April 1950 - Lowndes Co., Miss.
   3. Kenneth Wayne Williams
      b. 7 July 1952 - Lowndes Co., Miss.
   4. Peggy Sue Williams
      b. 23 January 1956 - Shelby Co., Ala.

(i) Lillie Ann Berryhill - Should have been (a), but this
   is late information.
   b. 17 September 1907 - Fayette Co., Ala.
   m. Sidney Houston Kennedy - 31 March 1923 - Monroe Co.
      b. 21 November 1905 - Ittawamba Co, Miss.
   1. Jennie Mae Kennedy
      b. 30 December 1924 - Ittawamba Co., Miss.
      m. Elbert Freeman - 3 August 1945 - George Co.
         b. 9 October 1923 - Cullman Co., Ala.
   2. Charles A. Lindberg Kennedy
      b. 30 January 1930 - Lee Co., Miss.
      d. 4 March 1956
      m. Christine Dodson - 12 June 1949 - Ittawamba Co.

      A. Larry Charles Kennedy
         b. 6 May 1950 - Monroe Co., Miss.
         d. 6 January 1951 - Ittawamba Co., Miss.

   Lillie Berryhill m. 2nd. Calvin Bunch - 18 April 1967

(2) Findora Ellen Berryhill
   b. 2 May 1886
   d. 7 January 1913 - Fayette Co., Ala.
   bur. Berryhill Family Cemetery
(3) Nancy Virginia Berryhill - "Jennie"
   b. 7 January 1888 - Fayette Co., Ala.
   d. 4 November 1965 - Norman, Okla.
   bur. I. O. O. F. Cemetery - Norman, Okla.
   m. William L. Brombloe - 6 June 1909 - Fayette Co., Ala.
   m. 2nd. John Daniel Markham - 1912
   No issue

(4) Harvey Houston Berryhill (twin)
    b. 10 August 1889 - Fayette Co., Ala.
    d. 15 June 1968 - Huntsville, Ala.
    bur. Maple Hill Cemetery - Huntsville, Ala.
    m. Addie Lee Norris - 27 November 1919 - Huntsville, Ala.
       b. 4 January 1887 - Dora, Minn.
       d. 17 November 1945 - Huntsville, Ala.
       bur. Maple Hill Cemetery
       dau. of Jacob L Norris & Rosa Dalton

    (a) Rosa Belle Berryhill
        b. 30 October 1920 - McMinnville, Tenn.
        m. Richard P. Van Valkenburgh - 15 August 1938
           b. 20 March 1916 - Huntsville, Ala.
           son of Joseph Bradley Van Valkenbury & Margaret Powell

        1. Charlotte Ann Van Valkenburg
           b. 27 August 1939 - Huntsville, Ala.
           m. Gary Max Byrd - 27 December 1959 - Birmingham, Ala.
              b. 25 June 1939 - Hartford, Ala.

           A. Susan Elizabeth Byrd
              b. 3 July 1963
           B. Katherine Ann Byrd
              b. 15 March 1966

        2. Richard Powell Van Valkenburg, Jr.
           b. 15 June 1942 - Huntsville, Ala.
           m. Nancy Ann Wilkerson - 15 September 1963 - Claxton,GA
              b. 8 February 194-?-

           A. Victoria Lea Van Valkenburg
              b. 16 May 1966

        3. Robert Forrest Van Valkenburg
           b. 19 May 1947 - Huntsville, Ala.
           m. Susan Carol Smith - 17 June 1967 - Hunstville, Ala.

    (b) Doris Marie Berryhill
        b. 30 March 1922 - Huntsville, Ala.
        m. Francis Winfred Gold - 18 July 1941 - Huntsville, Ala.
           b. 27 March 1922 - Huntsville, Ala.
           son of Roy Gold & Selma Wakefield

        1. Francis Winfred Gold, Jr. - "Frankie"
           b. 28 November 1942 - Huntsville, Ala.
           m. Katha D. Miley - August 1963 - Ozark, Ark.
              b. 1 November 1946
              dau. of Don Miley & Ruth -?-

           A. Shelia Dawn Gold
              b. 9 April 1964 - Auburn, Ala.

    (c) Harvey Houston Berryhill, Jr.
        b. 4 January 1928 - Huntsville, Ala.
        m. Virginia Jackson

        1. Virginia Dianne Berryhill
           b. 9 February 1950 - Dallas, Texas
        2. James Allen Berryhill
           b. 14 August 1952 - Key West, Fla.
        3. John Phillip Berryhill
           b. 8 July 1953 - Key West, Fla.

        Harvey Berryhill, Jr. m. 2nd. Betty Lou Benham

        4. Craig Lee Berryhill
           b. 11 February 1961 - Oxnard, Calif.
        5. Lisa Berryhill
           b. and d. November 1962 - Santa Monica, Calif.

        Harvey Berryhill, Jr. m. 3rd. - 2 December 1967 - Oxnard
        m. Marilyn Marie (Weiss) Iversen
           b. 15 July 1932
           dau. of Paul L. Weiss & Esther Ann Volkert

            6. Linda Esther Iverson (step-dau.)
               b. 7 May 1958 - Norway
               dau. of Ole Iversen & Marilyn Marie Weiss

      (d) Glendon Elaine Berryhill
          b. 22 August 1931 - Huntsville, Ala.
          m. Earl Stephenson Daniel - 28 December 1952 - Huntsville
             b. 11 November 1928 - Florence, Ala.
             son of Emmett S. Daniel & Martha Caroline Box

          1. Cynthia Elaine Daniel
             b. 19 November 1956 - Fairfield, Texas
          2. Emily Carol Daniel
             b. 22 January 1958 - Huntsville, Ala.

   Harvey H. Berryhill m. 2nd. 17 November 1959 - Huntsville, Ala.
   m. Bennie Jean Fears
      b. 13 July 1934

      (e) Rickey Lee (Fears) Berryhill
          b. 23 February 1955
      (f) Mary Jo Berryhill
          b. 18 December 1963 - Huntsville, Ala.
      (g) Connie Lynn Berryhill
          b. 8 October 1966 - Huntsville, Ala.

(5) Infant Daughter Berryhill (twin)
    b. and d. 10 August 1889 - Fayette Co., Ala.
    bur. Berryhill Family Cemetery
(6) Mary Florence Berryhill
    b. 2 May 1891 - Fayette Co., Ala.
    m. William Franklin Short - 23 March 1917
       b. 14 April 1890 - Fayetteville, Tenn.

      (a) William Franklin Short, Jr.
          b. 27 October 1919 - Huntsville, Ala.
          m. Kathryn Louise Theresa Harkins - 18 February 1946
             Lebanon, Pa.
             b. 9 March 1921 - Lebanon, Pa.

          1. Larry Frederick John Short
             b. 5 February 1947 - Lebanon, Pa.

      (b) Alice Floy Short
          b. 16 April 1922 - Huntsville, Ala.
          m. Lawrence Kenneth Carrigan - 14 July 1956
             b. 4 May 1923 - Indianapolis, Ind.

          1. Kenney Lee Carrigan
             b. 28 July 1957 - Zionsville, Ill.
          2. Becky Lyn Carrigan
             b. 20 March 1959 - Zionsville, Ill.
          3. Cindy Lou Carrigan
             b. 9 September 1960 - Zionsville, Ill.

      (c) Lucy Florence Short
          b. 29 December 1923 - Huntsville, Ala.
          m. LeRoy John Sandberg - 12 July 1942
             b. 7 June 1917 - Chicago, Ill

          1. Michael Swen Sandberg - "Mike"
             b. 2 March 1946 - Lyons, Ill.
          2. Sheron Anne Sandberg
             b. 1 August 1948 - Lyons, Ill.

(7) Troy Cleveland Berryhill
    b. 14 April 1893 - Fayette Co., Ala.
    m. Sallie Luella Estes - 3 January 1920
       b. 19 April 1896 - Walker Co., Ala.

      (a) Joseph Troy Berryhill
          b. 10 January 1923 - Winfield, Ala.
          m. Jean Lewis - July 1946
             b. 22 March 1931

        1. Joyce Berryhill
           b. 6 May 1951 - Birmingham, Ala.
        2. David Berryhill
           b. 29 April 1955 - Birmingham, Ala.
        3. James Nathan Berryhill
           b. 29 June 1960 - Birmingham, Ala.

    (b) Milton Douglas Berryhill
        b. 31 July 1924
        m. Audrey Martin
        m. 2nd. Addie Belle (Madison) Atkinson
    (c) Amaryllis Berryhill
        b. 25 August 1927
        m. Travis Duckworth - December 1946
           b. 15 September 1921

        1. Cheryl Darlene Duckworth
           b. 21 September 1950 - Birmingham, Ala.
        2. Cynthia Denise Duckworth
           b. 4 May 1955 - Birmingham, Ala.

(8) Mervyn Clarnce Berryhill
    b. 31 October 1895 - Marion Co., Ala.
    m. Pearl M. Fowler - 3 January 1920
       b. 27 January 1902 - near Tupelo, Miss.
       dau. of Mecenia Parham Fowler & Frances K. Martin

    (a) Mervyn Carroll Berryhill
        b. 30 August 1921 - Wannetta, Okla.
        m. Leona -?-

        1. Allen Berryhill
           b. 1953

    (b) Velma Roena Berryhill
        b. 13 August 1923 - near Stratford, Okla.
        m. Bick Mayo - 27 November 1043
        No issue
    (c) Clifford Berryhill
        b. 12 September 1925 - Shawnee, Okla.
        m. Joan McClade

        1. Norman Berryhill
           b. 1950
        2. Marsha Berryhill
           b. 1952
        3. Dorinda Berryhill
           b. 1954

    Mervyn Berryhill m. 2nd. - 21 December 1945
    m. Fern Frances Geno
       b. 19 September 1907 - Lexington, Okla.

(9) Addie Berryhill
    b. 24 October 1897 - Fayette Co., Ala.
    m. Carlie Haskel Weeks - 31 January 1918
       b. 4 April 1891 - Marion Co., Ala.

    (a) Scott Oden Weeks
        b. 31 March 1938 - Marion Co., Ala.
        m. Mary Ann Mays

        1. Debra Kaye Weeks
           b. 19 October 1959
        2. Donna Faye Weeks
           b. 9 November 1961
        3. William Carlie Weeks
           b. 16 August 1964

(10) Fred Edward Berryhill
b. 14 July 1899 - Fayette Co., Ala.
d. 12 October 1966 - Huntsville, Ala.
bur. Maple Hill Cemetery - Huntsville, Ala.
m. Jimmie Lee King - 12 November 1924 - Fayettesville, Tenn.
b. 30 October 1901
d. 10 March 1955
bur. Maple Hill Cemetery

(a) Alton Edward Berryhill
b. 14 December 1925
m. Margaret Vesta Rousseau - 26 August 1947 - Huntsville
b. 26 January 1926

1. Darryl Eddie Berryhill
b. 2 June 1949 - Huntsville, Ala.
2. Rhonda Cheryl Berryhill
b. 2 March 1952 - Huntsville, Ala.

Fred Berryhill m. 2nd. Edna Potts Foster - 22 September 1959

(11) Margaret Essie Berryhill
b. 22 December 1901 - Fayette Co., Ala.
m. Walter Perry Dodson - 16 December 1928
b. 25 April 1902
son of James Hamilton Dodson & Ethel Hubbard
they were married on 7 February 1895
b. 22 September 1863   b. 6 May 1874
d. 20 December 1933   d. 29 July 1945

(a) Flora Maye Dodson (twin)
b. 2 October 1929 - Fayette Co., Ala.
m. William Daniel Helton - 11 June 1954
b. 5 September 1929 - Fayette Co., Ala.

1. Janice Lynn Helton
b. 22 October 1956 - Birmingham, Ala.
2. Stephen Daniel Helton
b. 15 June 1959 - Birmingham, Ala.
3. Carol Ann Helton
b. 26 May 1961 - Birmingham, Ala.

(b) Lora Faye Dodson (twin)
b. 2 October 1929 - Fayette Co., Ala.
(c) Elreta Dodson - "Boots"
b. 21 March 1931 - Fayette Co., Ala.

(12) Naomi Louise Berryhill
b. 3 January 1904
d. 7 August 1904 - Fayette Co., Ala.
bur. Berryhill Family Cemetery
(13) Arley Weldon Berryhill
b. 27 April 1905 - Fayette Co., Ala.
d. 11 March 1966 - Glendale, Calif.
bur. Forest Lawn Memorial Park - Glendale, Calif.
m. Eunice Leona Kay
b. 24 October 1907 - Stillwell, Okla.
dau. of J. P. Kay & Bonnie -?-

(a) James Ralph Berryhill - "Jim"
b. 25 June 1928 - Huntsville, Ala.
m. Irma Lee Fligelman
b. 1 May 1930 - Chicago, Ill.
dau. of Morris Fligelman & Minnie Bernstein

1. Debra Kay Berryhill
b. 14 March 1962 - Harris Co., Texas
2. James Carroll Berryhill
b. 22 January 1963 - Glendale, Calif.
3. Wendy Arleen Berryhill
b. 17 April 1967 - Harris Co., Texas

(b) William Weldon Berryhill - "Bill"
b. 1 July 1930 - Dalhart, Texas
m. Joan Marie Reina

163

            1. Debra Sue Berryhill
               b. 8 March 1956 - Glendale, Calif
            2. Rebecca Ann Berryhill
               b. 27 May 1957 - Glendale, Calif.
            3. James Arley Berryhill
               b. 10 April 1959 - Glendale, Calif.
            4. David Wayne Berryhill
               b. 26 May 1960 - Glendale, Calif.

        (c) John Walter Berryhill
           b. 10 December 1944- Glendale, Calif.
           m. Shirley Smith

           1. Justina Louise Berryhill
               b. 23 April 1964 - Glendale, Calif.
           2. Michael John Berryhill
               b. 28 March 1965 - Glendale, Calif.

  (14) Annie Jane Berryhill
      b. 17 December 1907
      d. 2 July 1908 - Fayette Co., Ala.
      bur. Berryhill Family Cemetery
  (15) John Murl Berryhill
      b. 12 June 1910 - Fayette Co., Ala.
      m. Christine Mullins - 28 January 1948
      No issue

7. Thomas Berryhill
  b. 1820 - Franklin Co., Tenn. near Winchester
  d. 1855/1860 - Marion Co., Ala.
  m. Rachel Gage
    b. December 1821 - Ala.
    d. 3 July 1897 - Fayette Co., Ala.
    bur. Goodwater Baptist Cemetery - Fayette Co., Ala.
    She was called "Granny Rachel", and was a mid-wife, and in her
    last years, she was blind.

  A. Margaret Ann Berryhill - "Mother Harris"
    b. 22 May 1842 - Marion Co., Ala.
    d. 30 October 1907 - Marion Co., Ala.
    bur. Goodwater Baptist Cemetery
    m. George Shafer Harris
      b. 23 July 1837 - Ala.
      d. 10 August 1913 - Marion Co., Ala.
      bur. Goodwater Baptist Cemetery
      son of Moses Harris   and   Drucilla Walker
            b. 18 November 1799 - SC   b. 12 May 1803 - SC
            d. 27 March 1871 - Ala   d. 5 April 1876 - Marion
                                     Co., Ala.
        both bur. Goodwater Baptist Cemetery - Fayette Co., Ala.

    (1) John Harris
        b. 28 October 1858 - Marion Co., Ala.
        d. 22 February 1932 - Mineola, Texas
        bur. Sand Springs Cemetery - Mineola, Texas
        m. Mary Jane Bishop - October 1878
          b. 10 February 1862 - Marion Co., Ala.
          d. 25 May 1934 - Mineola, Texas
          bur. Sand Springs Cemetery
          dau. of Calvin Bishop & Katherine Whitehead

        (a) William Erastus Harris
           b. 8 September 1879 - Marion Co., Ala.
           d. March 1935 - Athens, Texas
           m. Cora Gillian

           1. Lloyd A. Harris
              b. 28 September 1899 - Mineola, Texas
              m. Addie May
              No issue

           William Harris m. 2nd. Keeley Hoyket

2. Margie Harris
   m. Grady Holt
3. Earline Harris
   m. Roy McGlohn
4. E. J. Harris
   m. Ruth Boggs
5. Infant Harris
   d. in infancy
6. Tommy Harris
   m. Mary -?-
7. Dorothy Harris
   m. Ray -?-
8. Infant Harris
   d. in infancy
9. Cecil Harris
10. "Shorty" Harris

(b) Virginia Pearl Harris
    b. 27 September 1882 - Marion Co., Ala.
    d. 17 September 1899 - Mineola, Texas
    bur. Sand Springs Cemetery - Mineola, Texas
(c) Georgia Verona Harris
    b. 20 February 1886 - Marion Co., Ala.
    m. William Alvin Smiley - 9 December 1906 - Wood Co., TX
       b. 20 August 1885 - Love Dale, Tenn. (now Kingsport)
       d. 25 April 1956 - Mineola, Texas
       bur. Sand Springs Cemetery - Mineola, Texas
    son of Madison Monroe Smiley & Mattie Johnson

    1. Bernice Odell Smiley
       b. 4 March 1908 - Mineola, Texas
       m. C. D. Dixon - 27 February 1923 - Smith Co., Texas
          b. 9 February 1900 - Emery, Rains Co., Texas
          d. 15 June 1963 - Mineola, Texas
          son of James Dixon & Lizzie Copeland

       A. Gaston Paul Dixon
          b. 16 October 1925 - Wood Co., Texas
          d. 10 January 1941 - Mineola, Texas
          bur. Sand Springs Cemetery - Mineola, Texas
       B. Bonnie Louise Dixon
          b. 25 November 1927 - Mineola, Texas
          m. Wallace Mize - 25 May 1946 - Wood Co., Texas
             b. 29 November 1922 - Mineola, Texas
             son of Bert Mize & Cecil Wyburn

          (1) Wanda Ann Mize
              b. 5 February 1947 - Mineola, Texas
              m. Wayne Blackburn - 20 August 1962 - Harris Co.
                 b. May 1942

              (a) Karen Denise Blackburn
                  b. 20 April 1963 - Harris Co., Texas
              (b) Mark Wayne Blackburn
                  b. 30 June 1964 - Harris Co., Texas

          (2) Jimmie J. Mize
              b. 11 January 1948 - Harris Co., Texas
          (3) Gary Wallace Mize
              b. 21 July 1955 - Harris Co., Texas

       C. Charles Ray Dixon
          b. 25 June 1930 - Mineola, Texas
          m. Elinor Glenn Clark - 21 July 1961 - Wood Co., TX
             b. 17 September 1932 - Mineola, Texas
             dau. of Glenn Clark & Eloise Patrick

          (1) Michael Ray Dixon
              b. 30 January 1955 - Harris Co., Texas

D. Emmett Roger Dixon
   b. 11 October 1932 - Mineola, Texas
   m. Claudett Milburn - 18 February 1956 - Harris Co.
      b. 17 November 1937 - Harris Co., Texas
      dau. of Claude Milburn & Mildred Jurgen

   (1) Jerry Wayne Dixon
       b. 31 July 1956 - Harris Co., Texas
   (2) Roger Emmett Dixon
       b. 17 December 1958 - Harris Co., Texas
   (3) Tommy Dixon
       b. 12 November 1961 - Harris Co., Texas

2. William Archibald Smiley
   b. 14 October 1916 - Mineola, Texas
   d. 17 March 1958 - Mineola, Texas
   bur. Sand Springs Cemetery - Mineola, Texas
   m. Dorothy Boggs - 9 February 1935 - Wood Co., Texas
      b. July 1917 - Mineola, Texas
      dau. of Jeff Boggs & Ann Pitchers

   A. Thomas Alvin Smiley
      b. 28 October 1942 - Mineola, Texas
      m. Lou Ella -?-

      (1) Mary Michael Smiley
          b. May 1962 - Grand Saline, Texas
      (2) John William Smiley
          b. April 1967 - San Antonio, Texas

(d) Lela Claude Harris
    b. 27 February 1889 - Marion Co., Ala.
    d. 27 December 1915 - Mineola, Texas
    bur. Sand Springs Cemetery - Mineola, Texas
    m. Roxie Hallbrooks

    1. Mary Evelyn Harris
       b. 12 November 1915 - Mineola, Texas
       m. Seab Martin

       A. Patricia Martin

(e) Calvin Clyde Harris
    b. 3 December 1891 - Mineola, Texas
    d. 15 May 1902 - Leuders, Texas
(f) Lillie B. Harris
    b. 7 July 1897 - Mineola, Wood Co., Texas
    m. Frank Mize

    1. J. T. Mize
       b. 19 August 1916 - Mineola, Texas
       d. 10 May 1962 - Palm Beach, Fla.
       bur. Lakeworth Military Cemetery - Lakeworth, Fla.
       m. Effie Mae Smith

       A. Franklin Tyrone Mize
          b. 29 September 1940 - Lake Worth, Fla.
          m. Nelda Dawn Lee

          (1) Franklin Tyrone Mize, Jr.
              b. 13 June 1959 - Dallas, Texas
          (2) Wendy Lanett Mize
              b. 15 January 1961 - Lakeworth, Fla.
          (3) Donna Jane Mize
              b. 21 August 1962 - Lakeworth, Fla.
          (4) John Troy Mize
              b. 22 May 1967 - Garland, Texas

Lillie B. Harris m. 2nd 10 September 1952 - Dallas Co., TX
m. Crowell Foard Stovall
   b. 30 January 1893 -
   d. 6 December 1963 - Terrell, Kaufman Co, Texas
   bur. Oakland Memorial Park Cemetery, Terrell, Texas

(g) Rutha Lee Harris
    b. 6 April 1901 - Mineola, Texas
    d. 6 January 1906 - Marion Co., Ala (while on a visit)
    bur. Goodwater Baptist Cemetery - Marion Co., Ala.

(2) Rachel Drucilla Harris - "Sis"
    b. 16 November 1859 - Fayette Co., Ala.
    d. 4 February 1909 - Wood Co., Texas - near Mineola
    bur. Sand Springs Cemetery - Wood Co., Texas
    m. Silas Patton Curl - 18 November 1875 - Fayette Co., Ala.
       b. 10 September 1856 - Fayette Co., Ala.
       d. 3 March 1912 - Wood Co., Texas
       bur. Sand Springs Cemetery
       son of Wm. Henry Curl & Martha Jane Crawford
               b. 11 March 1813 - Pa. b. in Virginia

    (a) William Thomas Curl - "Will"
        b. 19 July 1876 - Fayette Co., Ala.
        d. 27 January 1928 - Wood Co., Texas
        bur. Sand Springs Cemetery
        m. Rosa Rupel

        1. Valdon Curl
        2. Vera Curl
        3. Verna Curl
        4. Vada Curl
        5. Villard Curl
        6. Violet Curl
        7. Velma Curl
        8. Victor Curl

    (b) George Washington Curl
        b. 24 October 1878 - Fayette Co., Ala.
        d. 21 January 1932 - Wood Co., Texas
        bur. Sand Springs Cemetery
    (c) Infant Boy Curl
        b. and d. 1880 approx.
        bur. Fayette Co., Ala.
    (d) Ella Virginia Curl
        b. 13 February 1883 - Fayette Co., Ala.
        m. George Pinkney Null - 5 October 1902 - Wood Co., Texas
           b. 24 October 1879 - Smith Co., Texas
           son of Jessie Null & Leoria -?-

        1. Jessie Herman Null
           b. 3 July 1903 - Wood Co., Texas
           m. Bessie Massey - 4 July 1924

           A. Virginia Catherine Null
              b. 29 January 1926
              m. Gaston Land

              (1) Monty Land
                  m. Michael Hess - 4 July 1966
              (2) Billy Reed Land
                  m. Boneito Leitch
              (3) Donna Jean Land
                  m. Harold Goodman

        2. George William Null
           b. 16 August 1905 - Wood Co., Texas
           m. Janice Melvin

           A. Vickie Lynn Null
              m. Robert Brown
           B. Avie Nell Null
              d. in infancy

        3. Silas Byron Null
           b. 1906 approx. - Wood Co., Texas
           m. Sybil Scott - 26 November 1932

           A. Lynette Null
              m. Bill Logan

          B. Lloyd Null
             m. Ann McClenney
          C. Imogene Null
             m. Christopher Bell
          D. George Curtis Null
             b. 1947

       4. Virgil Theodore Null
          b. 18 July 1908 - Wood Co., Texas
          m. Margie Abrams - 15 October 1931

          A. Virgil Avon Null
             m. Barbara Shires
          B. Mary Ruth Null
             m. Chester Hickenbotham
          C. Caroline Sue Null
             m. Don Griffin

       5. Oran York Null
          b. 1910 approx. - Wood Co., Texas
          m. Bertie Sellers - 26 November 1932

          A. Jerry York Null
             m. Catheryne Stricklin

(e) Mary Ludella Curl - "Lula"
    b. 8 October 1886 - Fayette Co., Ala.
    m. Tom Scott

    1. Annette Scott
    2. Tyrus Scott
    3. Baudie Scott
    4. Luie Thomas Scott

(f) Ethel Irene Curl
    b. 27 July 1889 - Fayette Co., Ala.
    m. James Willingham

    1. Rachel Louise Willingham
    2. Catheryne Willingham
    3. James Willingham

(g) John Franklin Curl
    b. 4 April 1892 - Fayette Co., Ala.
    m. Grace Yates

    1. Daughter Curl
       d. in infancy
    2. Maurine Curl
    3. Mary Virginia Curl
    4. Grace Curl
    5. LaVerne Curl
    6. Dorothy Curl
    7. Sylvia Curl
    8. John Truman Curl
    9. Bobbie Charles Curl

(h) Henry Earl Curl
    b. 15 December 1895 - Wood Co., Texas
    m. Della Love

    1. Frances Curl
    2. DeVeral Curl
    3. Loretta Curl
    4. Janice Curl

(i) Olin Lee Curl
    b. 28 July 1897 - Wood Co., Texas
    d. 7 November 1918 - Wood Co., Texas
    bur. Sand Springs Cemetery - Wood Co., Texas near Mineola

(j) Infant Daughter Curl
    b. and d. 1905 - Wood Co., Texas
    bur. Sand Springs Cemetery

(3) Nancy E. Harris
    b. 2 December 1861 - Marion Co., Ala.
    d. 16 December 1883 - Fayette Co., Ala.
    bur. Goodwater Baptist Cemetery - Fayette Co., Ala.
    m. James Adron Northcutt - "Jim" - 5 January 1882 - Fayette Co.
       b. 10 July 1859 - Marion Co., Ala.
       d. July 1920 - Washington, Okla.
       bur. Lexington Cemetery - Lexington, Okla.
       son of A. Benson Northcutt & Nancy Dodson
              b. 1837 - Tenn   b. 1837 - Ala.

    (a) James Walter Northcutt
        b. 5 June 1883 - Marion Co., Ala.
        d. 1957/1958 - near Birmingham, Ala. around Warrior, Ala.
        bur. Warrior, Ala.
        m. Lulla Berryhill - 2 January 1910 - Marion CO., Ala.

        1. Murray Northcutt
        2. Dorothy Northcutt

(4) Georgia Ann Harris
    b. 1 September 1864 - Fayette Co., Ala.
    d. August 1943 - Marion Co., Ala.
    bur. Goodwater Baptist Cemetery - Fayette Co., Ala.
    m. Dr. James William Collins, Sr. of Berry, Ala.
       b. 17 December 1850
       d. 26 December 1913
       bur. Berry City Cemetery - Berry, Ala.
    m. 2nd. William Thomas - "Bill" - of Walker, Ala.
    Georgia Ann was quite an individual, and was called "Aunt
    McMinn" by her father, George S. Harris. He was evidentially
    referring to Nancy Ellen Harris, who married Berry Hicks Mc-
    Minn, and by 1860 they had moved to Choctaw Co., Miss, where
    she died.

(5) Mary Melissa Harris
    b. 22 November 1866 - Fayette Co., Ala.
    d. 16 June 1949 - Baytown, Texas
    bur. Lexington Cemetery - Lexington, Okla.
    m. James Adron Northcutt - "Jim" - 18 January 1893 - Fayette
       b. 10 July 1859 - Marion Co., Ala.
       d. July 1920 - Washington, Okla.
       bur. Lexington Cemetery
       son of Adrain Benson Northcutt - "Tade" and Nancy C. Dodson
              b. 1837 - Tenn.   b. 7 February
                                                    1836 - Ala.
    Jim had first married Nancy E. Harris, sister of Mary M.

    (a) Guy Belton Northcutt
        b. 11 January 1894 - Marion Co., Ala.
        m. Beatrice Greer - 2 May 1920 - Davis, Okla.
           b. Davis, Okla.
           d. April 1921 - Oklahoma City, Okla.
           bur. Lexington Cemetery
           dau. of J. R. Greer & -?-

        1. Wee Boy Northcutt
           b. and d. April 1921 - Oklahoma City, Okla.
           bur. Lexington Cemetery - Lexington, Okla.

        Guy Northcutt m. 2nd. Mary Mercedes Fleming - 2 May 1923
                            b. 16 June 1904 - Maxwell, Okla.
                            dau. of McMahan Fleming & Sadie
                                                        Stalcup

        2. Mack Adron Northcutt
           b. 9 September 1924 - Washington, Okla.
        3. Guy Belton Northcutt, Jr.
           b. 27 November 1926 - Washington, Okla.
           m. Mrs. Jean Pollock - 17 February 1959 - Washington Co.

           A. John Victor Northcutt
              b. 7 October 1959 - Oklahoma City, Okla.

4. Lucy Jane Northcutt
   b. 26 April 1937 - Washington, Okla.
   m. Robert G. Wilson - 17 February 1956
   son of Roy G. Wilson & -?-
   A. Marshall Grant Wilson
      b. 17 February 1957 - Purcell, Okla.

   Lucy Northcutt m. 2nd. William Terrance Fitzgerald
   B. William T. Fitzgerald, Jr.
   C. Jay Patrick Fitzgerald
   D. Nick Yates Fitzgerald
5. Sara Ione Northcutt
   b. 18 March 1939 - Purcell, Okla.
   m. Don Welcher - 1962 - Farmington, N. Mex.
   A. Rance Welcher
      b. 18 January 1964 - Plainview, Texas
   B. Candice Welcher
      b. 4 November 1967 - Santa Anna, Calif.

(b) Lena Northcutt
    b. 23 August 1896 - Hamilton, Ala.
    m. Roy Edward Burnett - 21 August 1916 - Pauls Valley, OK
    b. 15 January 1893 - Hico, Texas
    son of Henry A. Burnett & Martha A. Woods

    1. Roy Edward Burnett, Jr.
       b. 7 August 1921 - Lindsay, Okla.
       m. Doree Beavers - 21 September 1941
       A. Pamela Gae Burnett
          b. 25 December 1944 - Baytown, Texas
          m. Freddie Harrelson - 19 October 1963 - League City
          (1) Kenneth Alan Harrelson
              b. 19 October 1966 - Harris Co., Texas
       B. Roy Edward Burnett, III
          b. 1 February 1949 - Bryan, Texas
       C. Patricia Dae Burnett
          b. 11 December 1950 - Bryan, Texas
       D. Martha Jane Burnett
          b. 17 March 1955 - Houston, Texas

(c) Bessie Lee Northcutt
    b. 21 October 1897 - Marion Co., Ala.
    d. 13 February 1899 - Marion Co., Ala.
    bur. Goodwater Baptist Cemetery - Fayette Co., Ala.
(d) Ruth Irene Northcutt
    b. 26 February 1900 - Marion Co., Ala.
    m. Erby Richard Burnett
    1. Thelma Lorene Burnett
       b. 17 July 1918 - Maysville, Okla.
       m. J. W. Ainsworth
       A. Richard Blake Ainsworth
       B. Craig Ainsworth

    2. Erby Richard Burnett, Jr.
       b. 29 June 1920 - Maysville, Okla.
       m. Olga Carter
       A. Gary Michael Burnett
       B. Sharon Lynn Burnett m. -?- Masters

    3. Jo Ann Burnett
       b. 14 April 1922 - Pauls Valley, Okla.
       m. Walter Lehde
(e) Vera Northcutt
    b. 23 October 1902 - Marion Co., Ala.
    m. Roscoe H. Turner - 13 April 1925
    1. Carolyn Sue Turner
       b. 1929 - Washington, Okla.
       m. Stanley Irons
    2. Sally Daisy Turner
       m. Virgil Tague

A. Mark William Tague

(f) Carrie Northcutt
    b. 22 May 1905 - Marion Co., Ala.
    m. Brown Lowe Magness - 8 August 1926 - Harris Co., Texas
        b. 3 August 1902 - Bastrop, Texas
        d. 19 May 1967 - Harris Co., Texas
        bur. Cedar Crest Cemetery
        son of Thomas Henry Magness & Nettie Lawrence

    1. Barbara Jane Magness
        b. 20 August 1929 - Goose Creek, Texas
        m. Chares R. Head - 26 August 1949 - Harris Co., Texas
            b. 26 October 1927

        A. Janie Lane Head
            b. 15 June 1952 - Harris Co., Texas
        B. Charles Head
            b. 9 January 1954 - Harris Co., Texas

(g) Mable Northcutt
    b. 18 January 1907 - Lexington, Okla.
    m. Bert Howard Black - 2 May 1926 - Liberty Co., Texas
        b. 14 January 1907 - McCullar Co., Texas
        d. 12 April 1963 - Harris Co., Texas
        bur. Forest Park Cemetery - Houston, Texas

    1. Mary Ann Black
        b. 22 September 1929 - Goose Creek, Texas
        m. James Savell
            b. 20 August 1928

        A. James Savell, Jr.
            b. 26 December 1948 - Harris Co., Texas
        B. Danny Wayne Savell
            b. 15 September 1950 - Harris Co., Texas
        C. Melissa Ann Savell
            b. 25 February 1952 - Harris Co., Texas
        D. Melinda Sue Savell
            b. 9 January 1957 - Harris Co., Texas

(h) Victor Cruce Northcutt
    b. 28 July 1910 - Lexington, Okla.
    m. Anita Lee Sloan

    1. Zona Paul Northcutt
        b. 21 February 1936 - Goose Creek, Texas

(6) Virginia A. Harris
    b. 8 July 1869 - Fayette Co., Ala.
    d. 22 July 1872 - Fayette Co., Ala.
    bur. Goodwater Baptist Cemetery
(7) Moses Walker Harris
    b. 11 December 1871 - Fayette Co., Ala.
    d. 28 April 1958 - Marion Co., Ala.
    bur. Goodwater Baptist Cemetery - Fayette Co., Ala.
    m. Joanna Smith Whitehead - 9 January 1895
        b. 12 August 1873 - Fayette Co., Ala.
        d. 10 March 1961 - Marion Co., Ala.
        bur. Goodwater Baptist Cemetery - Fayette Co., Ala.
        dau. of William Smith Whitehead & Nancy Caroline Harris Moss
            bur. Between his two   dau. of Thomas Harris
                wives at Harmony   d. 1884
                Grove Cemetery   bur. Harmony Grove

(a) Ruby Kathleen Harris
    b. 1 November 1895 - Fayette Co., Ala.
(b) Lilliam Margaret Harris
    b. 13 January 1897 - Fayette Co., Ala.
    m. Pervy W. Matthew - 13 November 1917 - Fayette Co.
        b. 21 April 1891 - Fayette Co., Ala.
        d. 28 February 1941 - Birmingham, Ala.
        bur. Elmwood Cemetery - Birmingham
        son of Lee Matthews & Ella Dodson

1. Ella Jo Matthews
   b. 20 August 1920 - Jefferson Co., Al.
   m. David Avery Boyd - 1 June 1946 - Jefferson Co., Ala.
      b. 11 July 1920 - Jefferson Co., Ala.
      son of Felix Daughtery Boyd & Bessie Lee Whims

   A. David Ross Boyd
      b. 1 June 1947 - Jefferson Co., Ala.
   B. Joanne Elizabeth Boyd
      b. 23 June 1955 - Jefferson Co., Ala.

2. Pervy Walker Matthews
   b. 21 August 1924 - Jefferson Co., Ala.
   m. Lora Frances Brown - 18 August 1949
      b. 15 October 1927 - Jefferson Co., Ala.
      dau. of James Pink Brown & Artie Zannah King

   A. Larry Walker Matthews
      b. 10 August 1952 - Jefferson Co., Ala.
   B. Lora Kay Matthews
      b. 23 January 1960 - Jefferson Co., Ala.

(c) Virginia Lee Harris - "Virgie"
    b. 27 July 1899 - Fayette Co., Ala.
    m. William Larkin Stewart - 5 April 1917 - Fayette Co.
       b. 28 September 1896 - Fayette Co., Ala.
       son of Charles Jefferson Stewart & Winfield Thompson -
       "Winnie"

1. Quinton Wayne Stewart
   b. 28 January 1920 - Fayette Co., Ala.
   m. Evelyn Williams - 30 June 1943 - Fayette Co., Ala.
      b. 13 May 1927 - Madison Co., Ala.
      dau. of Claude Pettus Williams & Laura Brinn
2. William Earl Stewart
   b. 11 September 1925 - Fayette Co., Ala.
3. Winnie Jo Stewart
   b. 15 March 1930 - Fayette Co., Ala.
   m. Cecil Howton - 17 September 1950
      b. 22 February 1927 - Fayette Co., Ala.
      son of George Matthew Howton & Geneva Patterson

   A. Virginia Dianne Howton
      b. 25 January 1960 - Tuscaloosa Co., Ala.
   B. Lisa Renee Howton
      b. 12 November 1965 - Tuscaloosa Co., Ala.

(d) George Benton Harris
    b. 23 October 1901 - Fayette Co., Ala.
    d. 8 March 1963 - Birmingham, Ala.
    bur. Elmwood Cemetery
    m. Bernice Smith - 12 March 1926
       dau. of William Franklin Smith & Mittie Belle Ward
(e) Hudson Raymond Harris
    b. 14 November 1903 - Fayette Co., Ala.
    m. Annie Florence (Morton) Walsh - 8 February 1941
       b. 29 October 1917 - Jefferson Co., Ala.
       d. 27 January 1946 - Birmingham, Ala.
       bur. Forest Hill Cemetery - Birmingham, Ala.
       dau. of Robert Morton & Ethel York

1. Hudson Walker Harris
   b. 15 October 1941 - Jefferson Co., Ala.
   m. Gladys Henry - 1 July 1961
      b. 4 April 1924 - Blount Co., Ala.
      dau. of Wm. Arthur Henry & Mattie Jane Kimbrell

   A. Suzanne Marie Harris
      b. 27 April 1963 - Tuscaloosa, Ala.
   B. Hudson Raymond Harris, II
      b. 9 May 1968 - Birmingham, Ala.

172

Seated L. to R.
Juanita (Inabnet) Berryhill, Minna (baby),
Ruby and Charles Monroe Berryhill
Standing: Prentice Berryhill

James Carl Berryhill

Martha Ann (Berryhill) White

Fola Berryhill

Lt. James T. Berryhill

Nora (Berryhill) Couch, Mertie Bell Berryhill, John Thomas Berryhill,
Rachel C. (Weeks) Berryhill & baby Deen Couch
Back Row: Marion Thomas Couch & Rastus Floyd Berryhill

John Thomas Berryhill

&

Maud Virginia White

John Ellis White

Seated L. to R.: Mary Isabell (Berryhill) Lee, Anthony Fee White, Martha Ann (Berryhill) White & Jim White

Standing L. to R.: Forest White, Olive (White) Harris, Dessie Webb, Hight (White) Berryhill, Emmie (White) Smith, Maud Virginia (White) Berryhill

Nathan A. Berryhill

Willis Robin Berryhill &
Margaret Elizabeth
(Gorner) Berryhill

Nathan Basil & Nora Ludy Berryhill

Front: Martha Jane Hight White
Back L. to R.; Emmie, Maud Virginia
& Olive White

John Thomas Berryhill

Monroe Jasper Berryhill - "Tony"

Polk Dallas Berryhill

Nancy Elizabeth (Glover) Harper
& William Jefferson Harper

Nancy Jane (Berryhill) Harper
James K. Polk Berryhill
Mollie (Lindsey) Berryhill

Seated: James Van Buren Mills &
Sarah Elizabeth (Berryhill) Mills
Standing: George Olanger &
Belle (Mills) Olanger

L. to R. front: Wm Andrew Henderson, Myrtle, Rachel Louise (Berryhill) Henderson

L. to R. back: Frances, Passie & Julie Henderson

The James Rufus Berryhill Family

L. to R.: Wennie, Alla beatrice (Rowe) holding Jessie
James Rufus holding Norman, Emmet,
Standing in back: Vivian Ollie

L. to R. 1st Row: George S. Harris, Walter Northcut, Margaret (Berryhill) Harris, Mary (Harris) Northcut, Velma Northcut, Clyde Northcut, Jim Harris. Back row L. to R: T. V. Trull, Emma Jane (Harris) Trull, Georgeann Harris, Rena Harris, Nora Lee Harris, David S. Harris, Moses Walker Harris.

Seated L. to R.: Benjamin, Henry Alexander, Newman,
                  & Clara Ann (Ballard) Berryhill
Standing L. to R.: Clifton S., Thomas Winifred,
                    Rhodellen & Mulvenie Berryhill

Becky Jane White
(Harper)

Nora Berryhill
& Flora Berryhill

William Robert Alexander Berryhill - "Bill"
Born 25 February 1831. Died 1899 approx.

Josh Robert and Anna Pearl (Easley) Berryhill

Josh Robert and Anna Pearl Berryhill Family

Seated. Anna Pearl and Josh Robert Berryill

First Row, Left to Right; Lugene Dobrava, Lorene Bailey, Edith Price, Ola Howard, Eula DeShazo, Josephine Gottman. Second Row, Left to Right: Faye Day, Helen Lanier, Robert Berryhill, Betty Kingsbury, Laveda Kelly.

Josephine "Jo" Berryhill, m. Vincie Roberts
Two Roberts children

William Howard Berryhill

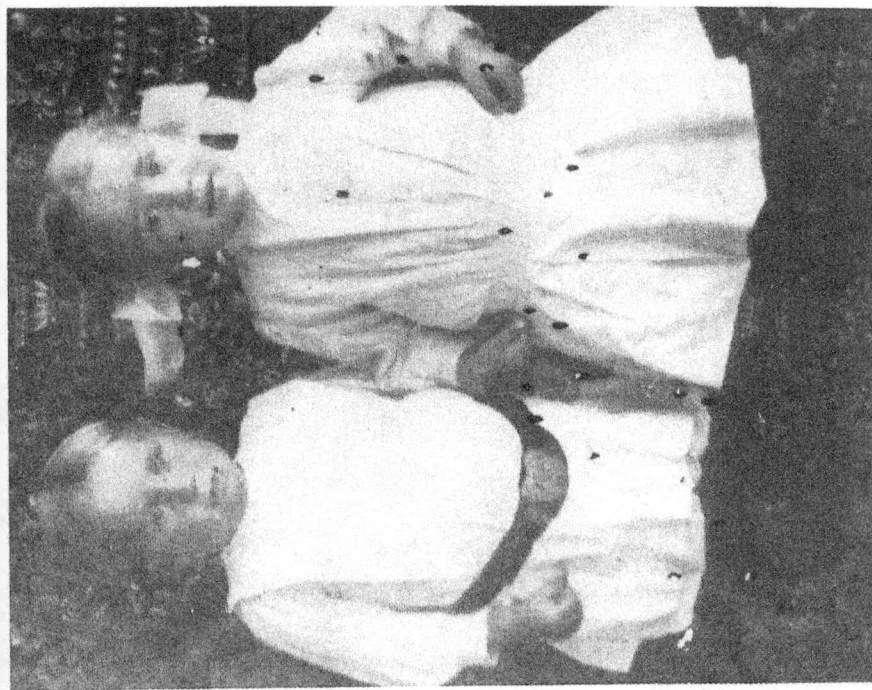

Ira William Berryhill (left)
Harvie Lillian Berryhill (right)

Standing L. to R.: Josh Berryhill,
   Allie Langston Berryhill, Margaret
   C. Roberts Berryhill
Babies L. to R.: Ira William and
   Harvie Lillian Berryhill

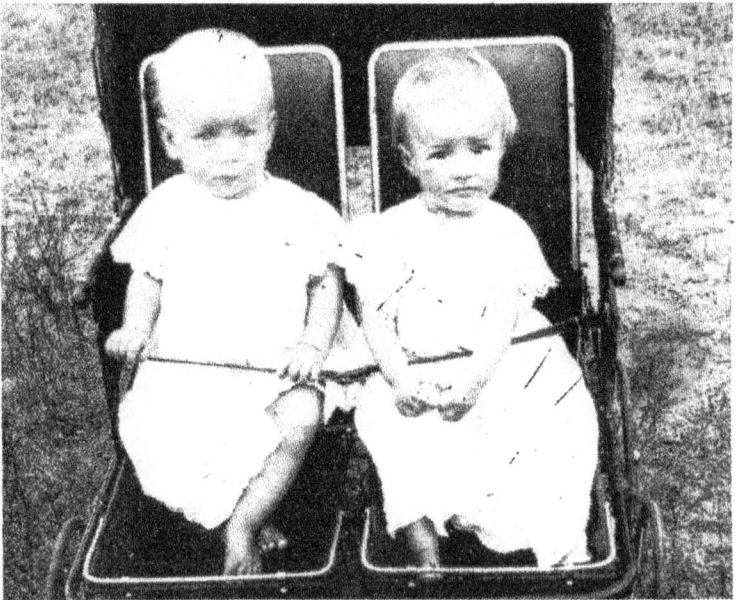

Left: Ira William Berryhill
Right: Harvie Lillian Berryhill
(Picture taken around June 1910)

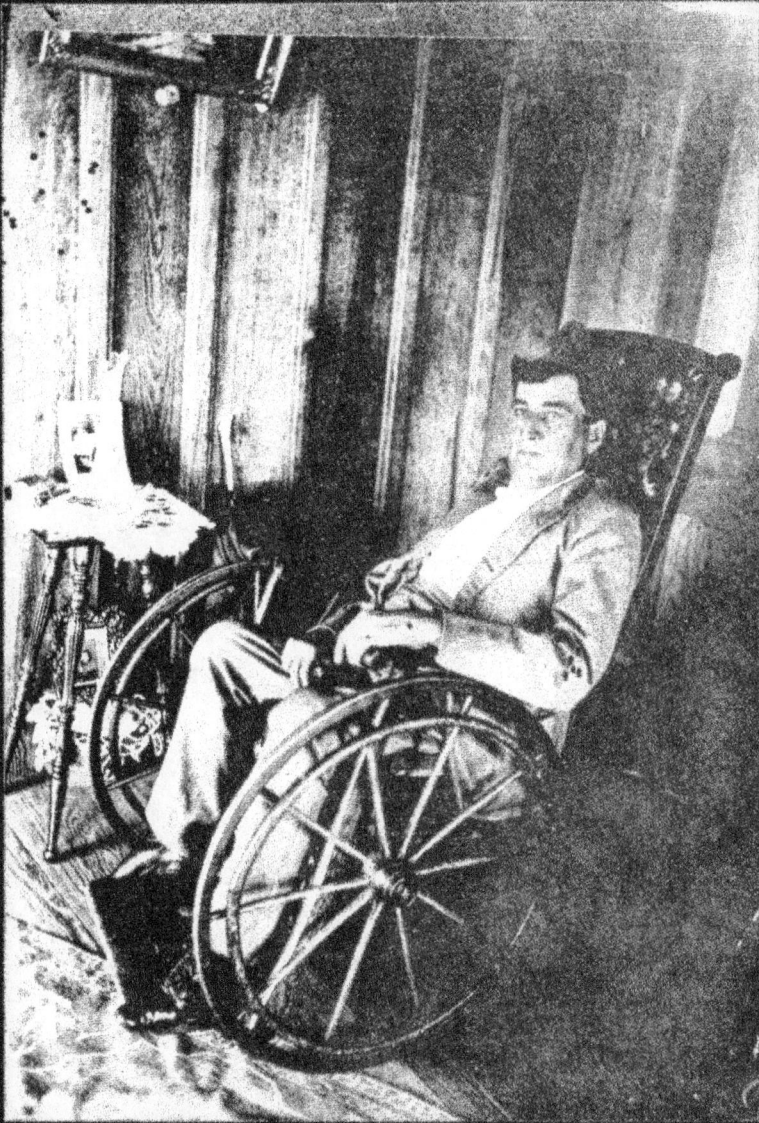

James Elisha Berryhill

William A. Dunn
&
Mulvenie (Berryhill) Dunn

Rose Berryhill, dau. of:
  Rufus Berryhill & Angie Justice
m. Knox Warren
    Two Warren children

James Rufus Berryhill and Alla Beatrice (Rowe) Berryhill
Child: Vivan Ollie Berryhill

```
            Hudson Harris m. 2nd. - 9 February 1952
            m. Dillie Amanda (Creel) Trawick
                 b. 30 October 1908 - Bibb Co., Ala.
                 dau. of Jeremiah Festus Creel & Usiba Josephine Emily
                                                                 Akins

      (f) Mary Etta Harris
           b. 23 April 1906
           d. 16 March 1909 - Fayette Co., Ala.
           bur. Goodwater Baptist Cemetery - Fayette Co., Ala.
      (g) Joseph Quinton Harris
           b. 19 February 1909 - Fayette Co., Ala.
           d. 28 December 1972 - Fayette Co., Ala.
           bur. City Cemetery - Fayette
           m. Susie (South) Logan - 9 November 1945
                 b. 11 October 1908 - Fayette Co., Ala.
                 dau. of Martin Dickenson South & Nina Louise Hyde
      (h) William Smith Harris
           b. and d. 16 November 1911 - Fayette Co., Ala.
           bur. Goodwater Baptist Cemetery - Fayette Co., Ala.

(8) Emma Jane Harris
     b. 20 July 1874 - Fayette Co., Ala.
     d. 9 November 1940 - Fayette Co., Ala.
     bur. Goodwater Baptist Cemetery
           m. Thomas Virgil Trull - 4 February 1894 - Fayette Co.
                 b. 17 January 1868 - Lamar Co., Ala.
                 d. 20 April 1955 - Fayette Co., Ala.
                 bur. Goodwater Baptist Cemetery
                 son of Wm. Jasper Trull & Lorina Virginia Kirkland

      (a) Alma Trull
           b. 19 December 1894
           d. 7 March 1895 - Fayette Co., Ala.
           bur. Goodwater Baptist Cemetery
      (b) Katherine Trull
           b. 15 May 1898 - Marion Co., Ala.
           m. Edd Lee Caddell - 17 December 1922
                 b. 28 December 1891 - Gattmon, Miss.
                 son of L. G. Caddell & Ella Musgrove

           1. Margaret Inez Caddell
                 b. 30 June 1925 - Fayette Co., Ala.
                 m. William Douglas Wright - 25 October 1952
           2. Mary Eloise Caddell
                 b. 2 November 1929 - Fayette Co., Ala.
                 m. Jerry Donald Mills - 28 August 1948

                 A. Jan Mills
                      b. 26 August 1951
                 B. Jerry Mills
                      b. 19 May 1964

      (c) Mamie Lee Trull
           b. 8 June 1904
           d. 15 February 1905 - Fayette Co., Ala.
           bur. Goodwater Baptist Cemetery
      (d) George Barton Trull
           b. 16 November 1905
           d. 18 November 1905 - Fayette Co., Ala.
           bur. Goodwater Baptist Cemetery
      (e) Eula May Trull
           m. William Newton Mills

           1. Eugene Mills
           2. George Mills
           3. Emma Mills
           4. Thomas Mills
           5. Quinton Mills
           6. Frank Ruedolph Mills
           7. Va. Faye Mills
           8. Mary Berta Mills
           9. Wm. Newton Mills
```

          10. Martha Lou Mills

     (f) Thomas Hill Trull
         m. Edna Louise Reece
     (g) Mattie Lou Trull
         m. Hubert Tucker
     (h) John Cullen Trull
     (i) Mary Montine Trull
         m. Lowell Aubry Howell

         1. Bettye Jean Howell
            m. John William Brod
         2. Thomas Aubry Howell
         3. Mary Ellen Howell

     (j) William Jasper Trull
         m. Virginia Patchen

         1. William Dene Trull

(9) David Smith Harris - "Dave"
    b. 11 April 1876 - Fayette Co., Ala
    d. 9 December 1944
    bur. Winfield Cemetery - Winfield, Ala.
    m. Susan Florence Ward
       b. 19 May 1880
       d. 27 December 1958 - Carbon Hill, Ala.
       bur. Winfield Cemetery
       dau. of Willis Monroe Ward, Jr. & Margaret C. Kirkland

    (a) Homer Chappell Harris
        b. 15 February 1902 - Marion Co., Ala.
        m. Erdeal Jones - 3 August 1930 - Garvin Co., Ala.
           b. 27 September 1909 - Fayette Co., Ala.
    (b) David Ralph Harris
        b. 25 April 1903 - Fayette Co., Ala.
        m. Mary Louise Kelley - 20 January 1928
           b. 13 February 1907
           d. 27 March 1965
           bur. Eldridge Cemetery - Walker Co., Ala.

        1. Ralph Rogers Harris
           b. 9 March 1929 - Fayette Co., Ala.
           m. Eleanor Armbrester - 2 July 1928 - Talladego Co.
              b. 27 July 1928 - Talladego Co., Ala.

           A. Mary Ellen Harris
              b. 23 August 1952 - Auburn, Ala.
           B. Ralph R. Harris, II
              b. 21 August 1954 - Auburn, Ala.
           C. Joseph Charles Harris
              b. 15 July 1960 - College Station, Texas

        2. Marilyn Virginia Harris
           b. 20 September 1930 - Fayette Co., Ala.
           m. James Edward Byars - 26 June 1960 - Marion Co., Ala.
              b. 4 January 1924 - Pickens Co., Ala.

           A. Janice Marie Byars
              b. 4 April 1962 - Tuscaloosa, Ala.

    (c) Annie Lucille Harris
        b. 7 November 1905
        d. 23 June 1950
        m. William Mode McCrary - 9 December 1924
           b. 25 December 1885 - Fayette Co., Ala.
           son of Wm. Jefferson McCrary & Mary Elizabeth Dodson
                   b. 1853   b. 1960

        1. Betty Sue McCrary
           b. 17 April 1926 - Marion Co., Ala.
           m. Charles Durward Blackwell - 24 December 1949 -
              Caledonia, Miss.

           A. Charla Sue Blackwell
              b. 25 March 1952 - Birmingham, Ala.

2. Margaret Ann McCrary
   b. 14 January 1928 - Marion Co., Ala.
   m. Edwin Webster Reed - 29 December 1946
      b. 29 March 1924

   A. Margaret Edwinia Reed
      b. 25 November 1948 - Fayette Co., Ala.
      m. Wm. Marion Corbett - 23 September 1967
         b. 26 March 1947 - Marion Co., Ala.
   B. Annie Lou Reed
      b. 16 October 1950 - Marion Co., Ala.
   C. Joyce Fay Reed
      b. 30 November 1951 - Marion Co., Ala.
   D. Homer Steve Reed
      b. 6 August 1955 - Marion Co., Ala.

3. Mary Bell McCrary
   b. 20 October 1929 - Marion Co., Ala.
   m. Slater Bunch Page - 12 October 1950 - Marion Co.
      b. 15 October 1919 - Mobile Co., Ala.

   A. Robert Gregory Page
      b. 5 November 1951 - Birmingham, Ala.
   B. Donald Slater Page
      b. June 1954 - Birmingham, Ala.

4. William Dave McCrary
   b. 15 April 1939 - Fayette Co., Ala.
   m. Faye West
      b. 13 October 1942 - Birmingham, Ala.

   A. Amanda Leigh McCrary
      b. 23 November 1966 - Bluefield, W. Va.

(d) Harold Monroe Harris
    b. 31 May 1906 - Fayette Co., Ala.
    m. Lillian Boyd Haden - 11 August 1934 - Lee Co., Ala.
       b. 9 July 1910 - Shorter, Ala.

    1. Harold M. Harris, Jr.
       b. 2 November 1939 - Montgomery Co., Ala.
       m. Claudia Ann Hall - 24 February 1962 - Lee Co., Ala.
          b. 17 May 1940 - Walker Co., Ala.

       A. Robert Shepherd Harris
          b. 28 January 1963 - Lee Co., Ala.
       B. Stephanie Ann Harris
          b. 19 January 1965 - Lee Co., Ala.

    2. Lillian Haden Harris
       b. 27 April 1942
       m. James Rees Pickle - 25 July 1964 - Montgomery Co.
          b. 7 April 1942 - Nashville, Tenn.

       A. James Rees Pickle, III
          b. 20 December 1967 - Nashville, Tenn.

    3. James Boyd Harris
       b. 13 February 1948 - Montgomery Co., Ala.

(e) Margaret Harris - "Margie"
    b. 8 September 1909 - Marion Co., Ala.
    m. Baxter Rose - 25 November 1932
       b. 24 February 1906
       son of Wm. Reuben Rose & Belle Lambert

    1. Flo Isabelle Rose
       b. 17 September 1933
       m. Olon Bradford Cunningham - 19 December 1954
          b. 15 January 1931 - Walker Co., Ala.

       A. Margaret Rose Cunningham
          b. 8 September 1957 - Marion Co., Ala.
       B. Sherry Elaine Cunningham
          b. 5 May 1959 - Marion Co., Ala.

                    C. Mary Susan Cunningham
                       b. 11 November 1960 - Marion Co., Ala.
                    D. Olon B. Cunningham, Jr.
                       b. 2 September 1965 - Marion Co., Ala.
                    E. Tina Marie Cunningham
                       b. 29 March 1967 - Marion Co., Ala.

               2. Mary Angeline Rose
                  b. 9 April 1937 - DeKalb Co., Ala.
                  m. William Denver Vickery - 12 July 1953
                     b. 12 October 1932 - Marion Co., Ala.

                    A. Wm. Baxter Vickery
                       b. 20 March 1955 - Columbus, Ga.
                    B. Vickie Angeline Vickery
                       b. 10 October 1961 - Colbert Co., Ala.

               3. William Harris Rose
                  b. 19 March 1940 - Fayette Co., Ala.
                  m. Kathleen Ann Smith - 24 August 1964 - Orange Co.,
                     b. 29 May 1944 - Detroit, Mich.   Calif.

          (f) John Raye Harris
              b. 24 January 1913 - Fayette Co., Ala.
              m. Larine Elrod
                 b. 4 December 1917 - Fayette Co., Ala.

               1. Martha Raye Harris
                  b. 10 September 1939 - Fayette Co., Ala.
                  m. Gerald Glen McDonald
                     b. 29 August 1937 - Henderson, Texas

                    A. Sharon Leigh McDonald
                       b. 10 September 1964 - Madison Co., Ala.

               2. Sylvia Jean Harris
                  b. 3 April 1943 - Jefferson Co., Ala.
                  m. Howard Ray Shoults
                     b. 15 May 1937 - Jefferson Co., Ala.

                    A. Michael Allan Shoults
                       b. 22 April 1962 - Madison Co., Ala.
                    B. Jeffrey Howard Shoults
                       b. 13 May 1964 - Madison Co., Ala.

               3. John Davis Harris
                  b. 11 April 1946 - Jefferson Co., Ala.
               4. Richard Terrell Harris
                  b. 9 August 1955 - Jefferson Co., Ala.

     (10) Lorena Savannah Harris - "Rena"
          b. 25 February 1879 - Fayette Co., Ala.
          d. 21 June 1966 - Marion Co., Ala.
          bur. Goodwater Baptist Cemetery - Fayette Co., Ala.
          m. John Perry - 20 October 1910
             b. 22 November 1885 - Cullman Co., Ala.
          No issue

     (11) Nora Lee Harris - "Node"
          b. 20 July 1881
          d. 14 February 1930 - Fayette Co., Ala.
          bur. Goodwater Baptist Cemetery - Fayette Co., Ala.
          m. Leonard Parks Hosch
             b. 12 August 1884 - Dalton Co., Ga.
             d. 5 April 1932 - Fayette Co., Ala.
             bur. Goodwater Baptist Cemetery
             son of Sammy Matthew Hosch & Mary Frances Donahue

          (a) Grady Earnest Hosch
              b. 22 September 1907 - Fayette Co., Ala.
              m. Lillian Bell Jones
                 b. 11 August 1906 - Fayette Co., Ala.
                 dau. of Felix Lee Jones & Alice Gertrude McAuther

1. Dorothy Genell Hosch
   b. 23 July 1928 - Fayette Co., Ala.
   m. James Wilburn Tune
      son of Wm. Franklin Tune & Emma Audelia Johnson

   A. James Payton Tune
      b. 11 February 1954 - Walker Co., Ala.
   B. William Earnest Tune
      b. and d. 15 August 1962
   C. John Parks Tune
      b. 21 April 1964 - Jefferson Co., Ala.

(b) Margurite Ollie Hosch
    b. 2 June 1909 - Fayette Co., Ala.
    m. Earnest Rivero
(c) Arvel Parks Hosch
    b. 14 December 1911 - Fayette Co., Ala.
    m. Vereta Mae Bowling
       b. 5 June 1916 - Fayette Co., Ala.
       dau. of William Bowling & Alma Bussey
(d) Mary Frances Hosch
    b. 24 November 1915 - Fayette Co., Ala.
    m. Edward Ray Caddell
       b. 23 March 1914 - Fayette Co., Ala.
       son of Alonzo D. Caddell & Lula Pearl Tucker
(e) Sammie Lee Hosch
    b. 19 May 1918
    d. 2 June 1932 - Fayette Co., Ala.
    bur. Goodwater Baptist Cemetery
    Caught his foot in the harness of a run-away mule and
    was accidentally dragged to death.
(f) Georgia Kate Hosch
    b. 10 January 1922 - Fayette Co., Ala.
    m. Nelson Clark
       b. 20 January 1923 - Walker Co., Ala.
       son of Robert Clark & Sadie Bell Barton

    1. Patricia Ann Clark
       b. 31 March 1942 - Fayette Co., Ala.
       m. Charles E. Martin
          son of Lonnie Martin & Willedean Love

       A. Charles E. Martin, Jr.
          b. 2 January 1960 - Walker Co., Ala.
       B. Melinda Kay Martin
          b. 29 September 1965

1850 Marion Co., Ala. Federal Census 82/83

Thomas Berryhill		30 M	Tenn.	b. 1820
Rachel	"	28 F	Ala.	1822
Margaret	"	8 F	Ala.	1842
Mary E.	"	6 F	Ala.	1844
Nancy J.	"	4 F	Ala.	1846

1860 Marion Co., Ala. 76/79

Rachel Berryhill		36 F	Tenn.	b. 1824 (widow of Thomas)
Elizabeth	"	17 F	Ala.	1843
Nancy	"	13 F	Ala.	1847
Silla	"	8 F	Ala.	1852
Susan J.	"	6 F	Ala.	1854

1870 Marion Co., Ala. 21/21 p 3. PO Palo, Ala. Township #13, Range #12

Rachel Berryhill		47 F	Tenn.	b. 1823
Nancy Jane	"	22 F.	Ala.	1848
Drucilla C.	"	19 F	Ala.	1851
Susan J.	"	16 F	Ala.	1856

```
1880 Marion Co., Ala.   6/6 p 13 TS13, R12   7 June 1880
James H. Estes         b. 1848      Ala.
Drucilla C.   "           1853      Ala.
Mary E.       "           1875      Ala.
Ida J.        "           1876      Ala.
Julia A.      "           1879      Ala.
Rachel Berryhill          1826      Tenn.   Mother-in-law
Nancy Berryhill           1848      Ala.    Sister-in-law

1860 Marion Co., Ala.
George S. Harris      21 M        Ala.    b. 1839
Margaret       "      18 F        Ala.       1842 (Margaret Berryhill)
John           "       1 M        Ala.       1859
Rachel         "     6/12 F       Ala.       1860
```

B. Mary Elizabeth Berryhill - "Betty"
   b. 14 November 1844 - Marion Co., Ala.
   d. 4 August 1896 - Fayette Co., Ala.
   bur. Goodwater Baptist Cemetery - Fayette Co., Ala.
   m. J. Mack Spann 1866/1867 - Marion Co., Ala.
     b. 3 February 1840
     d. 12 April 1900 - Fayette Co., Ala.
     bur. Goodwater Baptist Cemetery

  (1) Bell Spann
     b. 28 March 1868
     d. 25 December 1955
     bur. Musgrove Chapel Methodist Cemetery - Fayette Co., Ala.
     m. William A. Roberts
       b. 17 July 1867
       d. 15 March 1934
       bur. Musgrove Chapel Methodist Cemetery
       son of J. C. Roberts & E. A. Musgrove - 12 April 1855
          b. 1 March 1833 - S.C.   b. 15 May 1830 - S. C.
          d. 24 October 1910   d. 22 February 1900 - Ala.
          bur. Musgrove Chapel Methodist Cemetery (both)

    (a) Hollie Roberts
       m. Willie Aston
    (b) Walter Roberts
       m. Sally Smith
    (c) Elsie Roberts
       m. Houston Smith
    (d) Ruby Roberts
       m. Eldridge Crenshaw

       1. E. B. Crenshaw

    (e) Dewey Roberts
       m. Lossie Wheeler
    (f) Alta Roberts
       m. Clyde Stewart

       1. Gwendolyn Stewart
         m. Sam Sanders
    (g) Gordon Roberts
       m. Sammye Lee Earnest
    (h) Moody Roberts
       m. Mildred Couch
         dau. ·of C. C. Couch & Nannie Dodson
    (i) Joe Roberts
       m. Sallye McConnell
    (j) Ruth Roberts
       m. Velta Hassell
    (k) Carrie Nell Roberts
       m. Fred Webster

  (2) Missouria Spann - "Zoo"
     b. 19 October 1869
     d. 20 September 1949
     bur. Musgrove Chapel Methodist Cemetery

(3) John Benjamin Spann - "Ben"
    b. 17 March 1874
    d. 19 January 1914
    bur. Harmony Grove Cemetery
    m. Sarah F. Couch
        b. 8 October 1878
        d. 15 October 1906
        bur. Harmony Grove Cemetery
        dau. of Wm. Couch "Bill" & Eliza J. Perry

    (a) William Roston Spann
        b. 22 February 1897
        m. Mertie Bell Webster

        1. Glenn Spann
           b. 7 May 1921
           d. 5 December 1927
           bur. Goodwater Baptist Cemetery

    (b) Flora Jane Spann
        b. 21 November 1903
        d. March 1967

    John Spann m. 2nd. Lucy Bell Webster

    (c) Chlo Spann
        b. 17 March 1910
        m. Buster South

(4) Ann Spann
    b. 22 December 1876
    bur. Musgrove Methodist Chapel Cemetery
    m. Willie E. Hodge
        b. 6 July 1876
        d. 12 October 1950
        bur. Musgrove Methodist Chapel Cemetery
        son of Joseph Stevens Hodge & Josephine Harris
            b. 29 July 1844   b. 28 April 1850
            d. 27 April 1920   d. 18 December 1924
            bur. Hodge Family Cemetery - Fayette Co. (both)

    (a) Charlie Hodge
        b. 21 September 1899
        d. 22 March 1924
        bur. Musgrove Methodist Chapel Cemetery
        m. Florence Belk
    (b) Lucy Hodge
        m. Raymond Riley
    (c) Daisy Hodge
        m. Marvin Smith

(5) Mandy Spann
    m. Mart Mills

    (a) Elena Mills
        m. John Burra Weeks
           b. 1899
           d. 11 January 1972
           bur. White Springs Methodist Cemetery

        1. Paula Beth Weeks
           m. -?- Mayfield
        2. Jimmy C. Weeks

    (b) Leburn Mills
        m. Mary Jane Tremin
    (c) Lecil Mills
        m. Geuarty Porter
    (d) Alice Mills
        m. Sherman Sebster
    (e) Luther Mills
        m. Mary Jones

    (6) Alice Spann
        m. Andren Philleps Estes
    (7) Anna Spann
        m. Wm. Bowling - "Bill"

C. Nancy Jane Berryhill
   b. 25 July 1846 - Marion Co., Ala.
   d. 24 January 1910 - Fayette Co., Ala.
   bur. Goodwater Baptist Cemetery
   Nancy and her mother, Rachel (Gage) Berryhill raised the Estes'
   children after their parents died.

D. Drucilla C. Berryhill
   b. 1853 - Marion Co., Ala.
   d. April 1894 - Fayette Co., Ala.
   bur. Goodwater Baptist Cemetery
   m. James Henley Estes - 1 December 1870 - Fayette Co., Ala.
        b. 1848 - Ga.
        d. 26 February 1890 - Fayette Co., Ala.
        bur. Goodwater Baptist Cemetery
        son of C. Bealey Estes & Elizabeth B. -?-
                b. 1814 - S.C.   b. 13 October 1822 - Ga.
                d. Ala.   d. 21 April 1880 - Fayette Co.
                                    bur. Antioch Freewill Baptist Cemetery

    (1) Mary E. Estes - "Mollie"
        b. 1875 - Fayette Co., Ala.
        d. January 1968 - Dallas, Texas
        bur. Dallas, Texas
        m. Lace Atkins

        (a) Leslie Atkins
        (b) Roy Atkins
        (c) Venola Atkins
        (d) Mattie Atkins
        (e) Loucille Atkins
            m. -?- Fitzgerald

    (2) Ida J. Estes
        b. 1876 - Fayette Co., Ala.
        m. William Couch - "Bill"
            b. 14 February 1865
            d. 18 January 1909
            bur. Goodwater Baptist Cemetery

        (a) Edith Couch
            m. -?- Tidwell
        (b) Infant Couch
            b. and d. 22 February 1907
            bur. Goodwater Baptist Cemetery
        (c) Dixie Couch
            m. -?- Gann

        Ida J. Estes m. 2nd. B. Frank Green

        (d) Lorene Green
            m. -?- Otts
        (e) Infant Green
            b. and d. 12 September 1917
            bur. Goodwater Baptist Cemetery

    (3) Julia Ann Estes
        b. 13 March 1878
        d. 26 January 1918 - Marion Co., Ala.
        bur. Winfield City Cemetery - Winfield, Ala.
        m. Alexander Thomas Couch - "Alec"
            b. 6 March 1868 - Fayette Co., Ala.
            d. 12 February 1955 - Marion Co., Ala.
            bur. Winfield City Cemetery - Winfield, Ala.
            son of Meredith Couch & Susan Berryhill

(a) Raymond Carl Couch
    b. 1903 approx. - Marion Co., Ala.
    m. Ruby Wates

    1. Billy Couch
    2. Frances Couch
       m. -?- Pridmore
    3. Johnnie Couch
    4. David Couch

(b) Ada Merle Couch
    b. 15 January 1905 - Marion Co., Ala.
(c) Jesse Delmas Couch
    b. 3 February 1907 - Marion Co., Ala.
    m. Frances Beck

    1. J. D. Couch, Jr.
       d. October 1947
    2. Evelyn Couch
       b. 24 September 1935
    3. Jane Ellen Couch
       b. 21 September 1949

(d) Mack Lauren Couch
    m. Hazel Miller

    1. Barbara Couch
       m. -?- Kennard
    2. Tommy Couch
    3. Betty Ann Couch

(e) Helen Tenelle Couch
    b. 17 May 1913
    d. 23 January 1926
(f) Erin Couch
    b. 8 September 1914 - Gatman, Jackson Co., Miss.
    m. James D. Burleson

    1. Jimmy Burleson

(g) Lillian V. Couch
    b. 17 July 1916 - Marion Co., Ala.
    m. Clyde Langston

    1. Judy Langston
       m. -?- Goodsey

(4) Rachel E. Estes
    b. 1880 approx. - Fayette Co., Ala.
    d. 1907 approx. - Winfield, Ala. (age 27 years)
    bur. Goodwater Baptist Cemetery - Marion Co., Ala.
    m. James "Jim" Raines - 8 December 1904 - Marion Co., Ala.
       b. 1880 approx.

    (a) Alfred Raines
        b. 26 June 1906 - Marion Co., Ala.
        d. 1935 - Marion Co., Ala. (age 29 years)
        bur. Goodwater Baptist Cemetery
    (b) John Valton Raines
        d. in infancy
        bur. Goodwater Baptist Cemetery

(5) George Lafayette Estes
    b. 11 August 1888 - Fayette Co., Ala.
    m. Dorabelle Dodson
       b. 27 January 1893
       dau. of John William Dodson & Cornelia Josephine Thompson

    (a) George Lafayette Estes, Jr.
        b. 2 June 1924 - Amory, Miss.
        m. Demple McKinney

        1. Thomas Ray Estes
        2. Charlotte Ann Estes

(b) Dorothy Bell Estes
    b. 21 October 1926 - Amory, Miss.
    m. Eldon Ashley Selman

    1. James A. Selman
    2. Bobby Selman
    3. Sarah Selman

(c) John Dodson Estes
    b. 16 January 1930 - Amory, Miss.
    m. Evelyn Beard

    1. Janice Marie Estes
    2. John Thomas Estes

(6) James A. Estes - "Jim"
    b. 24 December 1889 - Marion Co., Ala.
    d. 30 September 1927 - Denver, Colo.
    bur. Goodwater Baptist Cemetery - Fayette Co., Ala.
(7) Julius Estes
    b. 1890 approx. - Marion Co., Ala.
    m. Jane Smith - 3 November 1904

    (a) Vertus Estes
        m. Harold Roberts

(8) Ada Jane Estes
    b. 4 January 1882 - Marion Co., Ala.
    d. 12 February 1956 - Birmingham, Ala.
    bur. City Cemetery - Winfield, Ala.
    m. Eckford Smith
        b. 23 November 1879 - Marion Co., Ala.
        bur. City Cemetery - Winfield, Ala.
        son of Daniel Frank Smith & Drucilla -?-

    (a) James Floyd Smith
        b. 12 September 1900 - Marion Co., Ala.
        m. Mary Thompson

        1. Floyd Ervin Smith
        2. Mary Ketherin Smith
        3. Bob Smith
        4. Jimmie Smith
        5. Paul Smith

    (b) Tela Agnes Smith
        b. 4 June 1902 - Marion Co., Ala.
        m. William Curtis Weeks

        1. James Edward Weeks
           b. 22 November 1922
           m. Helen Louise Cook

           A. Charlotte Ann Weeks
           B. James Edward Weeks, Jr.

    (c) Luey Franklin Smith
        b. 24 August 1904 - Marion Co., Ala.
        m. Inez Byrd

        1. Harold Smith
        2. Joy Smith
        3. Dru Ellen Smith
        4. Frankie Jean Smith

    (d) Clarence Lethon Smith
        b. 24 September 1906 - Marion Co., Ala.
        m. Marie May

        1. Tommy Smith
        2. Robert Smith
        3. Michael Smith
        4. Patricia Smith
        5. Rebecca Smith

    (e) Johnny Leon Smith
        b. 30 November 1908 - Marion Co., Ala.
        m. Ora Taylor

182

       1. Jane Smith
       2. Jeanette Smith
       3. Wyte Smith
       4. Bettye Smith

    (f) George Hill Smith
        b. 6 September 1910 - Marion Co., Ala.
        m. Inez Linzy

       1. Diane Smith

    (g) Ada Beatrice Smith
        b. 8 April 1913 - Marion Co., Ala.
        m. Dewel McClain

       1. Louis McClain

    (h) Rachel Pauline Smith
        b. 19 April 1915 - Marion Co., Ala.
        m. Elmer Byrd

       1. Carolyn Sue Byrd
       2. Glenda Faye Byrd

    (i) Ralph Bernice Smith
        b. 30 July 1917 - Marion Co., Ala.
        m. Johnie Mae Stidum

       1. James Ralph Smith
       2. Rayburn Smith
       3. Kenneth Smith
       4. Glennon Smith

E. Susan Jane Berryhill
   b. 11 January 1855 -
   d. 8 March 1932 - Marion Co., Ala.
   bur. Goodwater Baptist Cemetery - Fayette Co., Ala.
   m. Julius Tarpley Spann - 9 November 1871 - Fayette Co., Ala.
      b. 28 May 1850
      d. 9 October 1933 Marion Co., Ala.
      bur. Goodwater Baptist Cemetery

   (1) Pinkney Rice Spann
       b. 17 September 1872 - Fayette Co., Ala.
       d. 15 September 1957 - Oklahoma City, Okla.
       bur. Sunny Lane Cemetery - Oklahoma City, Okla.
       m. Carrie Jane Logan·- August 1895 - Ala.
          b. 27 October 1878 - Ala.
          d. 6 September 1962 - Oklahoma City, Okla.
          bur. Sunny Lane Cemetery
          dau. of Robert Barnie Logan & Victory Bowling
          gr. dau. of Martin Caston Bowling & Kizzia Jane Bridges

       (a) Gradie Lee Spann
           b. 10 October 1896 - Marion Co., Ala.
           m. Charles Oscar Keys

          1. Sally Inez Keys
             b. 12 May 1912
             m. Pete Sumner

             A. Nancy Lee Sumner
                b. 1934
                m. Fred Jones

                (1) Kathy Lynn Jones
                (2)·Pamanalea Kimberly Jones
                (3) Kent Jones

          2. Nancy Irene Keys
             b. 13 December 1916
             d. 1921

(b) Georgia Irene Spann
    b. 16 January 1899 - Wood Co., Texas
    m. Alex Edwin Carson - 11 December 1915
       b. 22 January 1896 - Springer, Okla.
       son of Thomas Carson & Elizabeth Knight

    1. Reita Murrell Carson
       b. 23 December 1916 - Wayne, Okla.
       m. William Stein Thomas - December 1942

       A. Richard Edwin Thomas
          b. 6 November 1943 - Breckenridge, Texas

    2. Robert Burnie Carson
       b. 13 September 1920 - Wayne, Okla.
       m. Allyne Maynard - 1946

       A. Camera Lynn Carson
          b. 4 December 1947 - San Antonio, Texas
       B. Elizabeth Ann Carson
          b. 30 December 1950 - San Antonio, Texas
       C. James Edward Carson
          b. 17 January 1953 - San Antonio, Texas
       D. Bobby Sue Carson
          b. 5 January 1955 - San Antonio, Texas
       E. Patrick Curtis Carson
          b. 2 September 1966 - San Antonio, Texas

    3. Betty Jane Carson
       b. 22 August 1923 - Wayne, Okla.
       m. Samuel Vernon Hudman
          b. 28 June 1920

       A. Samuel Vernon Hudman, III
          b. 7 November 1947 - Corpus Christi, Texas
          m. Donna Green - October 1965

          (1) Scott Carson Hudman
              b. 1966 - Corpus Christi, Texas

       B. Edwin Carson Hudman
          b. 21 December 1953 - Corpus Christi, Texas

(c) Fredie Victoria Spann
    b. 3 March 1902 - Wood Co., Texas
    m. Charles Z. Huddleston

    1. Charles Pinkney Huddleston
       b. 31 August 1923 - Purcell, Okla.
       m. Freda -?-

       A. Milton Howard Huddleston
          b. 1967

    2. Ralph Spann Huddleston
       b. August 1925 - Purcell, Okla.
       m. Margie Graham

       A. Vicki Lou Huddleston
       B. Stephen Huddleston
       C. Susan Jane Huddleston

(d) Burnie Bascom Spann
    b. 15 October 1904 - Wood Co., Texas
(e) Foy Jane Spann
    b. 17 May 1907 - Coke Co., Texas
    m. Clifford McGhee
       b. 25 November 1904 - Blossom, Texas
(f) Julius Tarply Spann
    b. 4 January 1910 - Coke Co., Texas
    m. Lillian Morse
(g) Ray Brandsom Spann
    b. 10 March 1912 - McClain Co, Okla.
    m. Margaret -?-
(h) Daisy Lou Spann
    b. 24 September 1916 - Wayne, Okla.
    m. Clyde Lynn

184

(i) Pinkney Rice Spann, Jr.
    b. 23 September 1916 - Wayne, Okla.
    m. Rena Lovely

    1. Gary Don Spann
       b. 1941
(2) William Franklin Spann
    b. 17 April 1874 - Marion Co., Ala.
    d. 1939 - Oklahoma City, Okla.
    married, and had a family, but no contacts were made.
(3) James Wesley Spann - "Jim"
    b. 3 March 1876 - Marion Co., Ala.
    m. -?-

    (a) Julius Spann
    (b) Willie Gray Spann
    (c) S. T. Spann
    (d) Leon Spann
    (e) Richard Spann
    (f) W. T. Spann
    (g) Johnny Spann
    (h) Mae Spann
        m. -?- May
    (i) Virgie Dell Spann

    James Spann m. 2nd. -?-

(4) Columbia Francis Spann
    b. 29 December 1877 - Marion Co., Ala.
    m. Jim Weeks

    (a) Arlene Weeks
        m. Largus Bostick
    (b) Lurline Weeks
        single
    (c) Luther Weeks
        m. Ila Ballard
    (d) Lehman Weeks
        m. Fanny Estes
    (e) Joe Weeks
        m. Dipalea (Gladden) Ballar
    (f) Eline Weeks
        m. Lore Sandlin
    (g) Audry Weeks
        m. Alore Ward

(5) Robert Silvester Spann
    b. 27 September 1879
    d. 11 February 1890 - Marion Co., Ala.
    bur. Goodwater Baptist Cemetery
(6) Harvey Bell Spann
    b. 7 October 1883 - Marion Co., Ala.
(7) Ivy Lena Chatherine Spann
    b. 3 May 1888 - Marion Co., Ala.
(8) Burnie Lee Spann
    b. 12 March 1891 - Marion Co., Ala.
    m. Lema Marshall
    b. 1886
    d. 1930
    bur. Sand Springs Cemetery - Fayette Co., Ala.

    (a) Marshall Spann
    (b) Annie Lee Spann

(9) Jonas Young Spann
    b. 15 August 1893 - Fayette Co., Ala.
(10) Joseph Leaster Spann
    b. 8 December 1881
    d. 1953 - Marion Co., Ala.
    bur. Goodwater Baptist Cemetery
    m. Sarah Smith
       b. 1882

```
            (a) Joseph L. Spann, Jr.
                b. 17 June 1925
                d. 7 February 1940
                bur. Goodwater Baptist Cemetery

      (11) Infant Spann
           b. and d. 1883 approx.
           bur. Goodwater Baptist Cemetery
      (12) Raston Spann
           b. 1885 approx.
           m. Myrtie Bell Webster

8. Sarah Ann Berryhill
   b. 1882 - St. Clair CO., Ala. or Marion Co., Ala.
   d. 1851 approx. - Marion Co., Ala.
   bur. Wheeler's Chapel Cemetery - it is thought.
   m. Silas L. Webb - "Sie" - 1837/1838 approx. - Marion Co., Ala.
      b. 15 September 1817 - Tenn.
      d. 2 January 1898 - Hinds Co., Miss.
      bur. Weeks Cemetery - Hinds Co. by his 2nd. wife Nancy E. (Berry-
                                                      hill) Harris

   A. Joab Silas Webb
      b. 1838 - Marion Co., Ala.
      m. Prudence Roberts - by 1860 Marion Co., Ala. Federal Census
         b. 1836 - Ala.

   B. William Thomas Webb
      b. 1839 - Marion Co., Ala.
      d. living at time of 1870 census
      m. Margaret -?-
         b. 1840 - Ala.
         d. living at 1870 census

      (1) Sarah Ann Webb
          b. 1859/1860 - Marion Co., Ala.
      (2) Martha Webb
          b. 1862 - Marion Co., Ala.
      (3) Joab Webb
          b. 1865 - Marion Co., Ala.
      (4) Rosana Webb
          b. 1867 - Marion Co., Ala.
      (5) William Webb
          b. 1868 - Marion Co., Ala.
      (6) Mary Webb
          b. February 1870 - Marion Co., Ala.

   C. Thadius W. Webb
      b. 1840 - Marion Co., Ala.

   D. Hannah Webb
      b. 1846 - Marion Co., Ala.
      m. Phillip Beasley

      (1) Sallie Anne Beasley
          b. 1871
          d. 1934
          m. John Martin Berryhill
      (2) Billy Beasley
          m. Emma Stubbs
      (3) Emma F. Beasley
          m. Samuel Newton Berryhill
      (4) Alice Beasley
          m. -?- Reed
      (5) Viola Beasley
          m. -?- Reed
      (6) Lucy Ann Beasley
          m. Allison B. Bayless
```

9. Benjamin Franklin Berryhill
   b. 17 December 1833 - Marion Co., Ala.
   d. 14 October 1903 - Covington, Texas
   bur. Detroit, Ala.
   m. Rebecca Vickery - "Becky" - 1857/1858 approx. Marion Co., Ala.
      b. 1831 - Tenn. (some census records say 1828)
      d. before 1903
      bur. Detroit, Ala.
      dau. of Parten Vickery & 1st wife, -?-
              b. 1805 - S.C.   d. before 1850 census
              d. 1859 approx.

A. Henry Alexander Berryhill - "Alec"
   b. 13 December 1858 - Marion Co., Ala.
   d. 22 January 1946 - Brownwood, Texas
   bur. Cottonwood Cemetery - Hill Co., Texas
   m. Clara Ann Ballard - 31 January 1881
      b. 31 May 1865 - Lamar Co., Ala.
      d. 4 December 1908 - Abilene, Texas
      bur. Cottonwood Cemetery

   (1) Newman Veldon Berryhill
          b. 3 December 1881 - Marion Co., Ala.
          d. 16 July 1904 - Malone, Texas
          bur. Cottonwood Cemetery - Hill Co., Texas
   (2) Mulvenie Berryhill
          b. 28 March 1883 - Marion Co., Ala.
          m. William A. Dunn - 21 April 1901
             b. 1 December 1879
             d. 1 December 1956
             bur. Mt. Olivet Cemetery - Fort Worth, Texas

          (a) E. L. Dunn
          (b) Jewel Dunn
          (c) Opal Dunn
          (d) Ruby Dunn
          (e) Orean Dunn

   (3) Benjamin Monroe Berryhill - "Boss"
          b. 28 July 1885 - Marion Co., Ala.
          m. Annie Yoe Leggett

          (a) B. M. Berryhill
          (b) Veldon Berryhill
          (c) Geneve Berryhill
          (d) Robert Berryhill

   (4) Rhodellen Berryhill
          b. 26 February 1887 - Marion Co., Ala.
          d. 4 July 1905 - Malone, Texas
          bur. Cottonwood Cemetery - Hill Co., Texas

   (5) Clifton Shakespear Berryhill
          b. 12 July 1889 - Marion Co., Ala.
          d. 11 July 1961 - Big Spring, Texas
          bur. City Cemetery - Big Spring, Texas
          m. Allie Mae Smith - 10 October 1910 - Dallas, Texas
             b. 6 April 1893 - Marshall, Texas

          (a) Annie Lee Berryhill
                 b. 2 January 1912 - Dallas, Texas
                 m. Clarence Stanton Bennett - 27 May 1932 - Brownsville
                    b. 17 June 1911 - Olmito, Texas
                    d. 10 April 1965 - Brownsville, Texas
                    bur. Buena Vista Burial Park - Borwnsville, Texas

                 1. Clara Ann Bennett
                       b. 11 March 1949 - Brownsville, Texas
                 2. Betty Lee Bennett
                       b. 23 May 1952 - Brownsville, Texas

          Clifton S. Berryhill m. 2nd. 16 October 1921 - Taylor Co., TX
          m. Ethyl Dea Cross
             b. 28 April 1901 - Buffalo Gap, Texas

(b) Clara Elizabeth Berryhill - "Beth"
   b. 28 September 19-?- Brownwood, Texas
   m. James L. Bradley

   1. Joyce Emily Bradley
      b. 16 January 1950 - Big Spring, Texas
      m. -?- Nelson

   Clara E. Berryhill m. 2nd. Cleo William Nelson
                            b. Tulsa, Okla.

   2. Stephen William Nelson
      b. 5 October 1954 - Big Spring, Texas

(c) Joyce Adelle Berryhill
   b. 4 April 1928 - Brownwood, Texas
   d. 24 April 1946 - Brownwood, Texas
   bur. City Cemetery - Brownwood, Texas

(6) Thomas Winifred Berryhill
   b. 4 February 1891 - Marion Co., Ala.
   d. 1965 - Brownwood, Texas
   bur. Brownwood, Texas
   m. Mary Moore
      bur. Mt. Olivet Cemetery - Fort Worth, Texas

   (a) T. W. Berryhill, Jr.

(7) Infant Berryhill
   b. and d. 11 March 1895
   bur. Hubbard City, Texas

B. Jessie Burton (or Birl) Berryhill
   b. 7 April 1861 - Marion Co., Ala.
   d. 15 July 1941 - Azle, Texas
   bur. Ash Creek Cemetery - Azle, Texas
   m. Vilantia Cantrell - 6 March 1883 - Marion Co., Ala. - Rev.Tomlin
      b. 13 August 1867 - Marion Co., Ala.
      d. 21 August 1947 - Azle, Texas
      bur. Ash Creek Cemetery

   (1) Marshall Henry Berryhill
      b. 12 December 1884 - Marion Co., Ala.
      d. 7 May 1942 - Hillsboro, Texas
      bur. Cottonwood Cemetery - Hill Co., Texas
      m. Elsie Zinn - 7 October 1905
         b. 19 February 1889

      (a) Jack Berryhill
      (b) Warren Berryhill
      (c) Travis Berryhill
      (d) William Thomas Berryhill
      (e) Lois Berryhill
      (f) Mozell Berryhill
      (g) Robert Berryhill
      (h) Billie Joe Berryhill
      (i) Infant Berryhill
         d. in infancy
      (j) Infant Berryhill
         d. in infancy

   (2) Ben David Berryhill
      b. 23 February 1887 - Marion Co., Ala.
      d. 1954 - Gladewater, Texas
      bur. Friendship Cemetery - Gladewater, Texas
      m. Ora Blanche Moore
         d. 1955 - Gladewater, Texas
         bur. Friendship Cemetery

      (a) Doris Berryhill
      (b) Earl Berryhill
      (c) Estelle Berryhill
      (d) Nelda Berryhill

(3) Geater Woodson Berryhill - "Wood"
    b. 21 May 1890 - Marion Co., Ala.
    d. 1 January 1953 - Dallas, Texas
    bur. Ridgepark Cemetery - Hillsboro, Texas
    m. Martha Jane Hight White - 22 December 1912 - McLennan Co.,
       b. 10 March 1891 - Winfield, Marion Co., Ala.   Texas
       dau. of John Ellis White & Martha Ann Berryhill

    (a) James Terrance Berryhill
        b. 18 July 1918 - Penelope, Hill Co., Texas
        d. 30 July 1943 - Kessel, Germany (in World War II action)
        bur. Fort Sam Houston National Cemetery - San Antonio, TX
        m. Thelma Mann
        No issue
    (b) Reba Jean Berryhill
        b. 9 January 1921 - Penelope, Hill Co., Texas
        m. Harold P. Angel - 3 December 1940
           b. 29 September 1918

        1. Beverly Jean Angel
           b. 6 November 1942 - Waco, Texas
           m. Douglas Averitt - 30 June 1062
              b. 28 April 1939

           A. Michael Averitt
              b. 9 September 1963
           B. Steven Averitt
              b. 18 October 1966
           C. Richard Averitt
              b. 7 May 1968

        2. James Terrance Angel
           b. 6 June 1945 - Waco, Texas
           m. Bettie Wulff - 13 December 1961
        3. Harvey Woodson Angel
           b. 6 April 1952 - Dallas, Texas
        4. Kyp Randolph Angel
           b. 22 October 1959 - Garland, Texas

    (c) Ruby Olive Berryhill
        b. 22 August 1923 - Penelope, Hill Co., Texas
        m. Chauncey Roebuck, Jr. - 18 August 1943
           b. 18 July 1922

        1. Chauncey Roebuck, III
           b. 18 August 1951 - Dallas, Texas

(4) Susie Rebecca Berryhill
    b. 17 January 1892 - Chickasha, Okla.
    m. Elton Zinn

    (a) Hilda Zinn
    (b) May Zinn
    (c) Vance Zinn
    (d) Barbara Zinn
    (e) Oleta Zinn

(5) Myrtle Daisy Berryhill
    b. 6 March 1895 - Penelope, Hill Co., Texas
    d. 7 May 1933 - Fort Worth, Texas
    bur. Dido Cemetery - Fort Worth, Texas
    m. Charles H. Nelson - 1913
       d. 1940 approx.
       bur. Albany, Texas

    (a) Kelsey Nelson
    (b) Wm. Joseph Nelson
    (c) W. L. Nelson
    (d) "Buddy" Nelson

(6) Rudolph Dan Berryhill
    b. 3 August 1897 - Penelope, Hill Co., Texas
    d. April 1958 - Mathis, Texas
    bur. Mathis Cemetery - Mathis, Texas
    m. Ida Meador
        d. 1928

    (a) Marjorie Berryhill
    (b) Wayne Berryhill

(7) Jettie May Berryhill
    b. 7 January 1900 - Penelope, Hill Co., Texas
    m. Walter Meador - 1923 - Alze, Texas
        d. 1954

    (a) Paul Meador
    (b) W. D. Meador
    (c) Sue Meador
    (d) Waymond Meador
    (e) Infant Meador
        d. in infancy

(8) Jess Burton Berryhill - "J. B."
    b. 17 October 1901 - Penelope, Hill Co., Texas
    m. Cleta Strickland - 1925 - Fort Worth, Texas
        b. 20 December 1906
(9) Jessie Elliott Berryhill
    b. 27 November 1903 - Penelope, Hill Co., Texas
    m. Jess Holden - 1926

    (a) O'Neal Holden

(10) William E. Berryhill - "Bill"
    b. 1 May 1906 - Penelope, Hill Co., Texas
    m. Cleo A. Harris - 11 January 1931 - Marietta, Okla.
(11) Geneva Gertrude Berryhill
    b. 29 November 1908 - Stanford, Texas
    m. Melvin Wiley - December 1929
        b. 1903
        (a) Norma Jean Wiley
(12) Carl Clide Berryhill
    b. 11 July 1911 - Stanford, Texas

C. Margaret Ellen Berryhill
   b.1862 - Marion Co., Ala.
   d. Abilene, Texas
   m. -?- Barton

   (1) Adalie Barton
   (2) Shirlie Barton
   (3) Grover Barton
   (4) Ora Barton
   (5) Wilmer Barton
   (6) Daughter Barton

D. Mary Alabama Berryhill - "Bama"
   b. 1864 - Marion Co., Ala.
   d. 1941 - Itasca, Texas
   bur. Itasca Cemetery - Itasca, Texas
   m. R. J. Young

   (1) Johnnie Young
       female
   (2) May Young
   (3) Vestal Young
   (4) Jessie Young
   (5) Ben Young
   (6) Belton Young
   (7) Lena Young
   (8) Revis Young
   (9) Talmadge Young

E. John Thomas Berryhill
   b. 13 January 1868 - Marion Co., Ala.
   d. 21 October 1915 - Highbank, Falls Co., Texas
   bur. Cottonwood Cemetery - Hill Co., Texas
   m. Maud Virginia White - 18 November 1900 - Blanchard, La.
      b. 12 February 1875 - Marion Co., Ala.
      d. 29 November 1962 - Dallas, Texas
      bur. Cottonwood Cemetery - Hill Co., Texas
      dau. of John Ellis White & Martha Ann Berryhill

   (1) Fola Berryhill
       b. 29 November 1901 - Marion Co., Ala.
       d. 11 February 1907 - Penelope, Hill Co., Texas
       bur. Cottonwood Cemetery
   (2) Thomas Raymond Berryhill - "Tom"
       b. 19 April 1914 - Highbank, Falls Co., Texas

F. James Elisha Berryhill - "Lish"
   b. 1869 - Marion Co., Ala.
   d. April 1914 - Penelope, Hill Co., Texas
   bur. Cottonwood Cemetery
   Was crippled and confined to a wheel chair.

1860 Marion Co., Ala. Federal Census   162/168
Benjamin F. Berryhill   32 M   Ala.   b. 1828
Rebecca Vickery   "   32 F   Tenn.   1828
Henry   "   1 M   Ala.   1859
Jesse B.   " 3/12 M   Ala.   1860

I was unable to find them on 1870 census

1880 Lamar Co., Ala. Federal Census 23/24 p3 Beat #6, Township #2
Range 15
Benjamin Berryhill   52 M   Ala. Ga.   Ga. b. 1828
Rebecca Vickery   "   52 F   Tenn. Tenn. Tenn.   1828
Alexander   "   21 M   Ala. Ala. Tenn.   1859
Jesse B.   "   20 M   Ala. Ala. Tenn.   1860
Margaret C.   "   18 F   Ala. Ala. Tenn.   1862
Mary A.   "   14 F   Ala. Ala. Tenn.   1864
John T.   "   13 M   Ala. Ala. Tenn.   1867
James E.   "   11 M   Ala. Ala. Tenn.   1869

10. Margaret Ann Berryhill
    b. 6 June 1829 - Marion Co., Ala.
    d. 26 November 1910 - Fayette Co., Ala.
    bur. Harmony Grove Cemetery
    m. Francis Marion Couch - "Frank" - 6 June 1856 - Marion Co., Ala.
       b. 11 June 1835 - Ala.
       d. 29 October 1890 - Fayette Co., Ala.
       bur. Harmony Grove Cemetery
       son of -?- Couch & Matilda -?-
                        b. 19 September 1810
                        d. 5 October 1876
                        bur. Harmony Grove Cemetery

A. William B. Couch - "Bill"
   b. 1857/1858 - Marion Co., Ala.
   m. Eliza J. Perry - 31 December 1873 - Fayette Co., Ala.
      b. 1858 - Ala.

   (1) Leolar M. Couch
       b. 1876 - Fayette Co., Ala.
   (2) Sarah F. Couch
       b. 8 October 1878
       d. 15 October 1906
       bur. Harmony Grove Cemetery
       m. John Benjamin Spann - "Ben"
          b. 17 March 1874
          d. 19 January 1914
          bur. Harmony Grove Cemetery

191

```
        (a) William Roston Spann
            b. 22 February 1897
            m. Bertie Bell Webster

            1. Glen Spann
               b. 7 May 1921
               d. 5 December 1927
               bur. Goodwater Baptist Cemetery

        (b) Flora Jane Spann
            b. 21 November 1903
            d. March 1967

   (3) Marvin G. Couch
       b. January 1880 - Fayette Co., Ala.
       m. -?-

       (a) Graham Couch
           b. and d. 7 November 1934 - Fayette Co., Ala.
           bur. Old Union Primitive Baptist Cemetery

   (4) Tom Couch
   (5) Margaret Couch
       m. Tom M. Henderson - 16 December 1907 - Marion Co., Ala.


B. Mary Frances Couch
   b. 3 April 1857
   d. 28 August 1876 - Fayette Co., Ala.
   bur. Harmony Grove Cemetery
   m. Andy J. Weeks
      b. 10 August 1850 - Ala.
      d. 3 December 1917 - Fayette Co., Ala.
      bur. Harmony Grove Cemetery
      Andy Weeks 2nd. m. Martha Vickery, after Frances died)

   (1) William Weeks
       b. 1874 - Fayette Co., Ala.
       m. Sarah Vickery
   (2) Alse F. Weeks
       b. 1875 - Fayette Co., Ala.
       m. Nan Henderson

       (a) Edna Weeks
           m. -?- McDonald
       (b) Bash Weeks


C. John Thomas Couch
   b. 21 September 1858
   d. 17 March 1889 - Fayette Co., Ala.
   bur. Harmony Grove Cemetery
   m. Rebecca Virginia Vickery
      b. 1856 - Ala.
      dau. of Elisha Vickery & Tebitha -?-
              b. 1815 - Tenn    b. 1828 - Tenn.

   (1) James D. Couch
       b. 1877 - Fayette Co., Ala.
       m. Louise Weeks
          dau. of Terrell Weeks
   (2) Thomas Marion Couch - "Tom"
       b. 25 January 1875 - Fayette Co., Ala.
       d. 7 October 1951 - Bristow, Okla.
       bur. Magnolia Cemetery - Bristow, Okla.
       m. Nora Drewrilla Berryhill - 10 January 1904 - Fayette Co.
          b. 2 December 1886 - Fayette Co., Ala.
          dau. of John Thomas Berryhill & Rachel Caroline Weeks
   (3) Melverde Couch
       b. 1880 approx. - Fayette Co., Ala.
       d. 1924 - Jasper, Ala.
       m. Glen Henderson

       (a) Rosa Henderson
           m. Jessie Vaughn
       (b) Lucie Henderson
```

        (c) Jessie Henderson

    (4) Annie Couch
        b. 1882 approx. - Fayette Co., Ala.
        d. May 1936 - Tupelo, Miss.
        m. Joe Berryhill
           son of John Silas Berryhill & Elizabeth Tucker

        (a) Margaret Berryhill
        (b) Trilla Berryhill
        (c) Rilla Berryhill
        (d) Bessie Berryhill
        (e) Raymond Berryhill
        (f) Luella Berryhill
        (g) John Hubert Berryhill
        (h) Thomas Berryhill

  D. Bashie E. Couch
     b. 1860 - Fayette Co., Ala.

  E. James M. Couch
     b. 17 April 1862
     d. 23 August 1879 - Fayette Co., Ala.
     bur. Harmony Grove Cemetery

  F. Martha Couch
     b. 1868 - Fayette Co., Ala.

11. Susan Berryhill - "Suzie"
    b. 1830 - Marion Co., Ala.
    d. living 1880 census, age 55 years
    m. Partain Vickery
       b. 1805 - S. C.
       d. 1859 approx. - living 1858, when issue born, gone by 1860)
    He had first married -?- Atkins and had children before 2nd. m.)

  A. James P. Vickery - "Jim"
     b. 20 August 1844
     d. 12 September 1917 - Marion Co., Ala.
     bur. Harmony Grove Cemetery
     m. Charlotte -?-
        b. 1845 - Ala.

     (1) Susan Vickery
         b. 1867 - Marion Co., Ala.

  B. Sarah M. Vickery
     b. 1847 - Marion Co., Ala.

  C. Charles Thomas Vickery
     b. 1849 - Marion Co., Ala.
     m. Peggy Ann Moss

     (1) Willie B. Vickery
         b. 1872 - Marion CO., Ala.
     (2) Sarah Elizabeth Vickery - "Sabe"
         b. 1873 - Marion Co., Ala.
         m. John Townley

         (a) Mary Jane Townley
             m. Berry Clardy
         (b) Charlie Franklin Townley
         (c) Ida Mae Townley
         (d) Minnie Belle Townley
         (e) Susie Malinda Townley
             m. Frank "Shorty" Vickery
         (f) Nellie Lee

     (3) George Vickery

     Charles Thomas Vickery m. 2nd. Mary M. Reed
                                 b. 1850 - Ala.

(4) Suzann Vickery
   m. James L. Brown - 7 December 1899 - Marion Co., Ala.
(5) Nancy Vickery
(6) Jesse Vickery
   b. 24 December 1883
   m. Effie Mills
      b. 1 December 1886
      dau. of "Bob" Mills & Martha Frances Berryhill

   (a) Belton Vickery
      m. Lillie Casken
   (b) Mennie Vickery
      m. Tompie Anderson
   (c) Martha Vickery
      m. Clebbon Goodwin
   (d) Lander Vickery
      m. Lucille Willcutt
   (e) Carrie Vickery
      m. Clyde Burks
   (f) Troy Vickery
      m. Earline Homby
   (g) Bertie Vickery
      m. J. C. Davis

(7) James "Bud" Vickery
(8) G. V. Vickery
(9) John Vickery

D. Nancy E. Vickery
   b. 1853 - Marion Co., Ala.

E. William Vickery - "Bill"
   b. 1855
   d. 1895 - Marion Co., Ala.
   bur. Harmony Grove Cemetery
   m. Leah Hawkins
      b. 1859
      d. 1947
      bur. Harmony Grove Cemetery

(1) John Daniel Vickery - "Dan"
   d. 1947 - Winfield, Ala.
   bur. City Cemetery - Winfield, Ala.
   m. Missouri Weeks - 8 March 1904 - Marion Co., Ala.
      bur. City Cemetery - Winfield, Ala.
      dau. of Henry W. Weeks & Martha E. Couch
            b. 1847   b. 1841 - Ala.
            d. 1927   d. 1921

   (a) Annie Lee Vickery
      m. Lawrence Berryhill
         son of James R. Berryhill & Mary Savannah Wates
   (b) Lillian Vickery
      m. Wally Bartholomew
   (c) Ed Vickery
   (d) Robert Vickery
   (e) Rubye Vickery

(2) Bert Vickery
   m. Bell Markham
(3) Jess Vickery
   m. Eddie Weeks
(4) Connie Vickery
   m. Ike Perry
(5) Edie Vickery
   m. Perry Weeks
(6) Grady Vickery

F. John Boy Vickery (Not Partain Vickery's child. Illegitimate)
   b. 16 March 1861
   d. 8 February 1942 - Marion Co., Ala.
   bur. Harmony Grove Cemetery
   m. Lular E. Guin
      b. 30 May 1868
      d. 6 March 1940
      bur. Harmony Grove Cemetery

   (1) Rheubin C. Vickery
       b. 27 March 1896
       d. 18 October 1897
       bur. Harmony Grove Cemetery
   (2) Clarence Vickery
   (3) Walter Vickery
   (4) Samantha Vickery

1850 Marion Co., Ala. 106/107
Parton Vickery		45 M	S. C.	b. 1805	
Susan	"	24 F	Ala.	1826	(Susan Berryhill, 2nd. wife)
Jesse	"	18 M	Tenn.	1832	(son by first wife)
Rebecca	"	19 F	Tenn.	1831	(dau. by first wife)
Elisha	"	17 M	Tenn.	1833	(son by first wife)
William D.	"	15 M	Ala.	1835	
Henry W.	"	12 M	Ala.	1838	(twin)
John A.	"	12 M	Ala.	1838	(twin)
Noah	"	10 M	Ala.	1840	(Last issue by first wife?)
James	"	6 M	Ala.	1844	
Sarah	"	3 F	Ala.	1847	
Charles T.	"	1 M	Ala.	1849	

1860 Marion Co., Ala.   159/165
Susan Vickery		30 F	Ala.	b. 1830	(Parten is dead)
James P.	"	14 M	Ala.	1846	
Sarah M.	"	11 F	Ala.	1849	
Thomas	"	10 M	Ala.	1850	
Nancy E.	"	7 F	Ala.	1853	
William	"	2 M	Ala.	1858	

1880 Marion Co., Ala.   95/95 P. 11 Beat #12
William Vickery		20 M	Ala.	b. 1860	
Luisia	"	20 F	Ala.	1860	(wife)
John	"	16 M	Ala.	1864	(brother)
Susan	"	55 F	Ala.	1825	(mother)

12 Edward Berryhill - "Edd"
   b. 1830/1835 - Marion Co., Ala.
   d. during Civil War
   m. Susan Flurry - 1860/1861 - Marion Co., Ala.
      b. 1842 - Ala.
      d. living 1880 census, 38 years)
   Susan m. 2nd. Charles Weeks
           b. 1840 - Ala.

   A. Jefferson Davis Berryhill - "Jeff"
      b. 8 December 1862 - Marion Co., Ala.
      d. 20 January 1914 - Monroe Co., Miss.
      bur. Liberty Cemetery - on line of Monroe & Itawamba Cos., Miss.
      m. Nancy Chaffin - 23 January 1884 - Fayette Co., Ala.
         b. 22 November 1868
         d. 28 November 1914
         bur. Liberty Cemetery
         dau. of Calvin Chaffin & -?-

      (1) Charlie Calvin Berryhill
          b. 18 October 1884
          m. Virgie Rollins
          m. 2nd. Clara Fortner
      (2) James Andrew Berryhill
          b. 27 November 1887
          m. Mable Duncan - 6 February 1916 - Lee Co., Miss.

(3) Martha Jane Berryhill
    b. 1887/1888
    d. 1912
    m. Alvie Brown
(4) Susie Berryhill
    b. 12 January 1888
    m. Alvie Brown
(5) Minnie Berryhill
    b. 1 February 1889
    d. 10 February 1948
    bur. Liberty Cemetery
    m. W. A. Bates
      b. 1881
      d. 27 November 1967
(6) Winnie Berryhill
    b. 7 August 1891
    m. J. U. Hester
      b. 1890
      d. 1941
(7) Nora E. Berryhill
    b. 15 November 1894
    d. 6 October 1918
    m. Ben Rayborn
(8) Joseph Isaac Berryhill
    b. 9 April 1896
    d. 12 September 1962
    m. Evelyn Farris - 6 June 1923 - Lee Co., Miss.
(9) Adolph Berryhill
    b. 6 October 1897
    d. 26 January 1914
(10) Millie Berryhill
    b. 28 January 1899
    m. Edgar H. Tackett
(11) Cola B. Berryhill
    b. 25 March 1901
    m. -?- Jones
(12) Hattie Mae Berryhill
    b. 21 April 1902
    m. Jess Payne
(13) Robert Grady Berryhill
    b. 15 March 1904
    m. Tempie McCormich - 24 December 1924 - Lee Co., Miss.
      b. 26 August 1904

    (a) Roy Grady Berryhill
        b. 4 February 1926 - Lee Co., Miss.
        d. 1 July 1945 - killed in plance crash in U. S. Army
    (b) Robert Grady Berryhill, Jr.
        b. 14 May 1929 - Lee Co., Miss.
        m. Elizabeth Jane Hussey - 9 July 1949 - Lee Co., Miss.
          b. 10 December 1931 - Lee Co., Miss.
        Robert - Indian Welfare Director at Philadelphia, Miss.

        1. Robert Michael Berryhill
          b. 2 March 1956 - Lowndes Co., Miss.
        2. Janet Lynn Berryhill
          b. 16 July 1958 - Lauderdale Co., Miss.

    (c) Ralph Dale Berryhill
        b. 24 April 1931 - Lee Co., Miss.
        m. Joe Nell Carlile - 24 December 1951 - Lee Co., Miss.
          b. Monroe Co., Miss.

        1. Robert Carlton Berryhill
          b. 24 May 1951 - Lee Co., Miss.
        2. Brenda Sue Berryhill
          b. 21 November 1959 - Lee Co., Miss.

    (d) William David Berryhill
        b. 8 September 1933 - Lee Co., Miss.
        m. Mae Carol (Brown) Mays - 22 November 1959 - Prentiss Co.
          b. 2 September 1935 - Prentiss Co., Miss.

                    1. James Emmitt Mays, III
                       b. 26 June 1954 - Prentiss Co., Miss.
                    2. John Carroll Mays
                       b. 14 August 1955 - Prentiss Co., Miss.
                    3. Jeff David Berryhill
                       b. 6 January 1961 - Lee Co., Miss.
                    4. William Joseph Berryhill
                       b. 12 January 1964 - Hinds Co., Miss.

               (e) Donnie Wayne Berryhill
                   b. 11 October 1940
                   m. Judy Baine - 12 September 1963 - Huntsville, Ala.
                   b. 8 August 1941

                    1. Phillip Clayton Berryhill
                       b. 28 June 1965
                    2. Ginger Elizabeth Berryhill
                       b. 9 November 1966

               (f) James Gwin Berryhill
                   b. 13 August 1950

        (14) Lillian Lucille Berryhill
             b. 9 July 1905
             m. William Pruitt
        (15) Effie Berryhill
             b. 27 March 1907
             d. 3 March 1914
        (16) Ivy Lee Berryhill
             b. 14 May 1908
             m. Bernie Payne
        (17) Gussie Berryhill
             b. 11 February 1910
             d. 15 January 1913
        (18) Jeff Davis Berryhill
             b. 15 June 1914
             m. Earlene Franks

   B. Andrew Jackson Berryhill
      b. 1864 - Marion Co., Ala.
      m. -?-

      (1) Nola Berryhill
          m. Bill Bozeman
      (2) Charlie Berryhill
          Lived around Tuscumba, Ala. His grandmother, Grandma Susan
          (Flurry) Berryhill Weeks lived with him at one time near
          Guin, Ala.
          No contacts could be made with this family.

13. Infant Male Berryhill
    b. 1830/1835 - according to census
    d. probably young

14. Francis Berryhill
    b. 1836 - Marion Co., Ala.
    living on 1850 census, age 14 years, but no more information on him.

15. Rachel Catherine Berryhill
    b. 1838 - Marion Co., Ala.
    living 1870 DeSoto Co., Miss. Census.
    m. -?- Scott
       d. by 1870 census

    A. Robert L. Scott
       b. 1867 - DeSoto Co., Miss.

    The 1870 census shows Rachel C. and her son, Robert L. Scott,
    in her mother's household.

William Berryhill, Sr. m. 2nd. around this point, but we do not know exactly what issues are by his second wife.

William Berryhill, Sr.
m. Elizabeth Webster
    b. 1820 Tenn. or Ala. - census shows both states
    d. after 1880 DeSoto Co., Miss census was taken
    bur. DeSoto Co., Miss.

16. Isabella Berryhill
    b. 1841 - Marion CO., Ala.
    d. living 1880 DeSoto Co., Miss. Census
    m. -?- Gilchrist
        d. by 1880 census time

17. John Booker Silas Berryhill (Confederate Pension #12672 - Co. H, 26th
    b. 1841/1842 - Marion Co., Ala.   Ala. Reg.
    d. 17 June 1918 - 4 miles east of Tupelo, Miss.
    bur. Gilvo Cemetery near Tupelo, Miss.
    m. Phebe Elizabeth Tucker - 4 February 1872 - Fayette Co., Ala.
        b. 1850 - Ala.
        d. 1923 - Winston Co., Ala.
        bur. Winston Co., Ala.

    A. Elizabeth Berryhill
        b. 1877 - Fayette Co., Ala.
        d. was 3 years old on 1880 census, but said to have died young.

    B. William Silas Berryhill
        b. 10 September 1875 - Fayette Co., Ala.
        d. 2 November 1955 - near Tupelo, Miss.
        bur. Oakhill Cemetery - near Tupelo, Miss.
        m. Allie Tom Henderson - 19 December 1897 - Fayette Co., Ala.
            b. 20 November 1881 - Fayette Co., Ala.
            dau. of Benjamin Henderson & Sarah Jane Berryhill
                    b. 12 May 1839   b. 29 June 1844
                    d. 30 October 1928   d. 12 October 1932

        (1) Charles Edmon Berryhill - "Charlie"
            b. 16 September 1898 - Marion Co., Ala.
            m. Delia Williams - 14 December 1920 - Lee Co., Miss.
                dau. of James Robert Williams & Molly Savannah Conway

            (a) Albert Stonewall Berryhill
                m. -?- Jamison
            (b) Christine Berryhill
                m. -?- Wilson
            (c) Lurene Berryhill
                m. -?- Hester
            (d) Charles Edward Berryhill
                m. -?- Payne
            (e) Bettie Jean Berryhill
                m. -?- Bright

        (2) Exie Berryhill
            b. 28 September 1900 - Fayette Co., Ala.
            m. Jess S. Strickland - 23 May 1923 - Fayette Co., Ala.

            (a) Ida Strickland
                b. Bart Blackwell
            (b) Lillie May Strickland
                m. Johnnie Reeves
            (c) Mary Strickland
                m. Albert Morris
            (d) Lois Strickland
                d. Deceased
                m. Albert Morris
            (e) Jerry Strickland

(3) Mattie Berryhill
    b. 26 January 1903 - Fayette Co., Ala.
    m. Robert Strickland - "Bob"

    (a) Jean Strickland
        m. -?- Stovall
    (b) Bobby Strickland

(4) Essie Berryhill
    b. 11 February 1906 - Fayette Co., Ala.
(5) Ollie Berryhill
    b. 18 November 1908 - Fayette Co., Ala.
    m. Jim Miller

    (a) James Miller
    (b) Buddy Miller
    (c) Billy Miller

(6) Annie Lee Berryhill
    b. 11 June 1913 - Fayette Co., Ala.
    m. Herman Tackett

    (a) Joanna Tackett
        m. -?- Reynolds
    (b) Larry Thomas
    (c) Gene Thomas
    (d) Ronnie Thomas
    (e) Rickey Thomas

(7) James William Berryhill
    b. 13 March 1915 - Fayette Co., Ala.
    m. Ruth Stephens

    (a) Delithie Berryhill
        m. Roy Norris
    (b) Glendale Berryhill

(8) Telsa Berryhill
    b. 9 September 1918 - Lee Co., Miss.
    m. Bodie Tackett

    (a) Darlene Tackett
    (b) James Henry Tackett
    (c) Clyde Tackett
    (d) Donnie Tackett

(9) Joseph Vardaman Berryhill
    b. 1 April 1921 - Lee Co., Miss.
(10) Lurie Marie Berryhill
    b. 1 November 1926 - Lee Co., Miss.
    m. -?- Hand

    (a) Kennet Hand
    (b) Shela Hand
    (c) Jerrel Wayne Hand
    (d) Mike Hand

C. Joseph Berryhill - "Joe"
    b. 1878 approx. - Fayette Co., Ala.
    d. 1953 approx.
    m. Annie Couch
        b. 1882 approx. - Fayette Co., Ala.
        d. 6 April 1936 - near Tupelo, Miss in a tornado
        dau. of John Thomas Couch & Rebecca Virginia Vickery

    Issues listed in preceding pages.

D. Viola Berryhill
    b. 1880 approx. - Fayette Co., Ala.
    m. John A. Bozeman - 3 December 1908 - Marion Co., Ala.

    (1) Charlie Bozeman
    (2) Elmer Bozeman

Family history tells that William Berryhill died after the Civil War started, and while John Booker Silas Berryhill was in the war, his step-mother, Elizabeth (Webster) Berryhill, with her children, moved from Ala. to DeSoto Co., Miss., where she was still living in 1880.

John Booker Silas Berryhill served in Co. H, 26th Regt. as a Private, enlisted July 1861 at Wright's Store in Marion Co., Ala., was discharged in 1865, and was wounded at Richmond, Va. He drew Pension #12672 in Fayette Co., Ala. with witnesses: John F. Kelly & James V. Mills signing he did serve in the war.

18. Charles Robert Berryhill - "Bob"
    b. 1846 - Marion Co., Ala.
    d. living 1880 DeSoto Co., Miss. census
    bur. Harmony Grove Cemetery - Fayette Co., Ala. the following dates
        are given, but there is no verification that this is the same
        Charles Berryhill.
        b. 15 June 1846
        d. 15 September 1907
        bur. Harmony Grove Cemetery - Fayette Co., Ala.
    m. Susan -?-
        b. 1853 - Miss.
        d. living at time of 1880 DeSoto Co., Miss. census

    A. John Berryhill
        b. 1865 - Tenn.

    B. Martha Berryhill
        b. 1875 - Tenn.

    C. Joseph Berryhill
        b. January 1880 - DeSoto Co., Miss.

19. Richard Perry Berryhill - "Dick"
    b. 1848 - Marion Co., Ala.
    Was born crippled, never walked, and is said to have died about the
    time he was grown. No other information is available on him.

William Berryhill, Sr. m. 3rd. Elizabeth Webster - Marion Co., Ala.
                            b. 1810/1814 - Tenn.
                            d. living at 1880 census for DeSoto Co.

Here again, we do not know where her children began, but we feel it is safe to say that those who went to Miss. with her were apparently her own children.

20. Joseph J. N. C. Berryhill - "Joe"
    b. 1849 - Marion Co., Ala.
    m. Mary Imes - 29 January 1869 - DeSoto Co., Miss.
    No futher information is available on this couple.

21. Andrew Berryhill - "Andy"
    b. 1852/1855 - Marion Co., Ala.
    d. living at time of 1880 DeSoto Co., Miss. census.
    m. Ada Bouldwin - 2 October 1888 - DeSoto Co., Miss.
    No further information is available on this couple.

22. George Washington Berryhill
    b. 1853/1854 - Marion Co., Ala.
    d. living at time of 1880 DeSoto Co., Miss. census
    m. Elizabeth Gellispie
        b. 1860 - Miss.
        dau. of -?- and Mrs. Frances (-?-) Gellispie
                            b. 1826 - Ala.
    No further information is available on this couple.

1870 DeSoto Co., Miss. Federal Census   Township #2, Range #6
Olive Branch, Miss.   5 September 1870

Elizabeth Berryhill	60	F	Ala.	b.	1810	
Catherine Scott	30	F	Ala.		1840	(daughter)
Robert Berryhill	22	M	Ala.		1848	(son)
Andrew Berryhill	16	M	Ala.		1854	(son)
Robert L. Scott	3	M	Miss.		1867	(grandson, surely Catherine's)

1880 DeSoto Co., Miss. 109/121 p. 12. Pleasant Hiss Dist. 12 June 1880

Charles Berryhill	34	M	Ala.	b.	1846	
Susan	"	27	F	Miss.	1853	
John	"	15	M	Tenn.	1865	
Martha	"	5	F	Tenn.	1875	
Joseph	"	5/12	M	Miss.	1880	(January)

From two of his children it is learned that he did live in Tenn. before
coming back into Miss., where his family lived.

Plumb Point, Miss. 21 June 1880 101/102 - p. 12

John P. Hobbs	65	M	Va.	b.	1815	
Julia A. "	57	F	Ala.		1823	
Elizabeth "	35	F	Ala.		1845	(daughter)
Isabell Gilchrist	34	F	Ala.		1846	(daughter-in-law)

Surely this is Isabell Berryhill, who evidentially has married a son.
Perhaps of Mrs. Julia A. (Gilchrist) Hobbs!

Note the closeness of the "house-hold" numbers on census of these
families.

103/103 p. 12

Andrew Berryhill	25	M	Ala.	b.	1855	(still single on 1880 census)
Elizabeth "	66	F	Tenn.		1814	(mother)
William Lane	10	M	Tenn.		1870	(Andrew's nephew)
John Lane	7	M	Tenn.		1873	(Andrew's nephew)

Evidentially one Berryhill sister of Andrew married -?- Lane and lived
in Tenn. and has these two sons, and apparently she died young.

104/104 p. 12

George Berryhill	27	M	Ala.	b.	1853	
Elizabeth "	20	F	Miss.		1860	(surely Elizabeth Gellispie)
Frances Gellispie	54	F	Ala.		1826	(mother-in-law)
Fannie Cotton	50	F	Mass.		1830	

Many rumors are circulated around with the relationship of William
Berryhill, Sr., born 1781 in Georgia and Alexander Berryhill, born 1760
in North Carolina.

True, Alexander Berryhill did come from Tennessee into Marion County, Ala.
about 1826, where he applied for a Rev. Pension.

But William Berryhill, Sr. was in St. Clair County, Alabama as early as
the 1819/1820 tax list. By 1830 he showed in Marion County, Alabama.

I have found NO PROOF anywhere to prove either version of the rumors:
one person said Alexander and William were brothers. Others say
William was a son of Alexander by his first marriage.

But it seems to be an accepted fact that two sons of Alexander by his
second wife, Rebecca Webster married two daughters of William.

If William was a son of Alexander, this would be making William's two
daughters marry their "half-uncles". I find this hard to accept that
two father's would let their children marry such close kin.

In none of the old Wills and estate settlements I've bought, and copied,
do I find anyone family who lists sons named both William and Alexander.

But, due to the fact evidentially there was some relationship, we are also including the family of Alexander as a separate chapter.

1830 Franklin Co., Tenn. Federal Census   #109
James J. Berryhill
1 male 20/30 (James J.)
1 female under 5 years of age
1 female 20/30

#112
Lensfield Berryhill
1 male under 5 years of age
1 male 20/30 (Lensfield)
1 female under 5 years of age
1 female 15/20

#112
Alexander Berryhill
2 males 10/15 (Edward and Thomas)
1 male 60/70 (Alexander)
1 female 50/60 (Rebecca Webster, 2nd wife)

It seems reasonable to assume that James J. and Lensfield are sons of Alexander and in fact, family history knows Alexander did have a son, Lensfield, but Lensfield and his family remained in Franklin Co., Tenn. when the others came to Alabama. Berryhills were still marrying in that county as late as 1874.

I feel the fact James J. and his family did come on to Alabama with old Alexander, that he is a son of Alexander.

Alexander Berryhill, Rev. Pensioner No. 16639

Brief in the case of Alexander Berryhill, county of Franklin, in the
State of Tennessee Act 7th June 1832. He stated he was 69 years old,
thus making him be born in 1763 (approximately.) He stated he served
for 10 months as a Private in 1781 under Captain Martin and Colonel Polk.
That he was engaged in battles at Eutan Springs and Dorchester. That
he entered from Mecklenburg County, North Carolina.

ORIGINAL CLAIM Declaration of ALEXANDER BERRYHILL in order to be placed
on the pension list and obtain the benefit of the Act of Congress passed
June 7th, 1832.

State of Tennessee (
Franklin County   (

On the 3rd of September 1832 personally appeared in open Court before the
Justice of the Peace of pleas and quarter session of said county, now
setting, the same being a correct record of ALEXANDER BERRYHILL, a
resident of Franklin County in Tennessee aged about sixty-nine (69)
years, who first being duly sworn to obtain the benefit of the Act of
Congress passed June 7, 1832. That he entered the service of the United
States and served under the following officers and served as herein
stated:

"In the year 1781 he enlisted in the State of North Carolina in the town
of Charlotte and Mecklenburg County for the term of ten months; he
believing as well as recollection serves him he entered the service of
the U.S. in the month of June, 1781, but does not remember the day -
that he enlisted under Captain James N. Martin and belonged to the third
regiment commended by Colonel William Polk, in which Regiment he served
until his term of service expired on the 17th day of April, 1782, on
which day he received from Colonel Polk the discharge council filed and
left the service."

"Here I would like to break into the record to say this: Alexander
Berryhill tells us plainly he entered from North Carolina and returned
there. Now IF William was his son, he would have always showed on
census he was born in North Carolina, but every year he showed he was
born in Georgia. One reason it is hard for me to accept that William
can be Alexander's son." Virginia T. Brittain

"February Term of court, 1821 Alexander Berryhill presented to the Court
an additional declaration and schedule of his property which is in the
words and figures following, viz: This day appeared in open court being
a Circuit Court of accord for the county of Franklin in the state of
Tennessee, ALEXANDER BERRYHILL, aged sixty years, by occupation a
farmer who being first duly sworn according to a law on his oath makes
the following declaration in order to obtain the provisions made by an
Act of Congress of the 18th of March, 1818 the first of May, 1820 entitle
an Act to provide for certain previous engaged in the land and naval
service of the United States in the revolution war and the said ALEXANDER
BERRYHILL who is now an inhabitant of Franklin County in the state of
Tennessee in the year 1781 he enlisted in the State of North Carolina
for the term of ten months in the Continental establishment under
Captain James N. Martin and William Polk was the Colonel under whom he
served in the 2nd Regiment of the line of the state of North Carolina
that he continued the service of the United States until he served out
his term of entestment, when at Orangeburg he received a permit from
General Thomas Sumpter to return home and that he received and was
directed by General Sumpter to attend at New Market to receive pay that
he did attend at the time and place according to his instructions and
never received any pay for the same and he states that he never received
any other kind of discharge that during his term of enlistment he was in
the battle of Eutaw Springs and in the battle at Biggans Church and at
the battle of the -?- in South Carolina (unable to read record for name -
V.T.B.) and that he has no other evidence in his power of said facts but
his own oath and the deposition of James Evans which accompanies this
declaration and his has to answered and states further that he is a very

infirm and frail man and has lost the sight of one of his eyes that he
has a wife named REBECCA about forty-six years (46) old much afflicted
with rheumatic pains, that he has one daughter named POLLY, aged sixteen
(16) years, and one son named LENSFIELD about fourteen years (14) old,
and one son named EDWARD about six years (6) old, and one son named
THOMAS age four years (4) old, that he has forty-two acres of extremely
poor land on which is a small log cabin in which he now lives with a
little personal property in the schedule hereto answered. And in
accordance of the Act of Congress the first day of May, 1820, I do
solemnly swear that I was a resident citizen of the United States on the
18th day of March, 1818 and that I have not since that time by gift,
sale or in any other manner disposed of any property or any part thereof
with the interest thereby so to diminish it as to bring myself with the
provisions of an Act of Congress entitled an act to provise for certain
previous engaged in the land and naval service of the United States in
the Rev. War passed on the 18th day of March, 1818, and that I have not
nor has any person in trust any property or securities contract or debts
due to me nor have I any income other than is contained in the schedule
hereto assigned and by me subscribed. Sworn to and subscribed in open
Court 15th of February, 1821"

J. H. Robertson, Clerk

Schedule
42 acres of land ....$ 52.50
3 head of horses 40.00
4 cows and calves 32.00
2 steers and 40 head of hogs 16.00

4 sheep, 1 cart 11.00
4 hoes, 1 axe 1.75
3 plows and gears 4.00
3 dishes and 3 baskets 25.00
6 pots and ovens 6.00
1 frying pan 1.00
                                                             $166.75

                                              his
                             ALEXANDER   X BERRYHILL
                                             mark

The State of Alabama
Fayette County
On this the first day of March, 1838, before me the subscribed a Justice
of the Peace for the said county of Fayette, state of Alabama personally
appeared ALEXANDER BERRYHILL of the county of MARION aforesaid state who
on his oath declares that he is the same person who formerly belonged to
the company commanded by Captain James N. Martin in the Regiment commanded by Colonel William Polk in the service of the United States and
that his name was placed on the roll of the state of Tennessee (on the
26th day of April, 1833) from where he has removed about two years ago.
That he now resides in the state of Alabama in Marion County where he
intends to remain. And wishes his pension to be then payable to wit:
AT DECATUR, MORGAN COUNTY, ALABAMA. The following are his reasons for
removing from Tennessee to Alabama, Marion County. That he might enjoy
the society and be with his relative and to advantage of praticable his
interest. And the reason for making the proof in Fayette County and not
in Marion County is that the Fayette there is a seal for the County
Court Clerks Office and now in Marion County and the Justice of the
Peace in said County is near me before whom he has to be carried in a
carriage he living near the County Line.

Sworn to and subscribed before me, William Ham
an acting Justice of the Peace for Fayette County, Alabama his
this the first of March, 1838   ALEXANDER X BERRYHILL
                                                        mark

I, William Ham, an acting Justice of the Peace of the County of Fayette, Alabama do certify that the Willis Ward and William Berryhill are good and worthy citizens of said County of Marion and are men of veracity and entitled to full faith and credit. Given under my hand and seal at office this 1st day of March, 1838."

Surely there can be no doubt from the above depositions that the following are issues of old Alexander: Polly, Lensfield, Thomas and Edward.

But as to WHAT RELATIONSHIP William, born 1781 - Georgia and James J. are to old Alexander is still a question mark. Certainly it seems acceptable that James J. can be his son since he continued to live around him in Tennessee and came on to Alabama with him. But naturally Alexander named only his children who still lived in his home when he applied for his pension.

A free Rev. marker has been applied for from the Government for the grave of Alexander Berryhill, and also one for William Berryhill for his War of 1812 service. They should be on the graves before the end of the summer.

The General Accounting Office in Washington, D. C. has a record showing the Alexander Berryhill, Pensioner Certificate No. 7542, Alabama Agency, left a surviving widow. Rebecca Berryhill, who was paid his arrears due the deceased for a period of September 4, 1838 to February 3, 1839, were paid to her September 30, 1939, at the Pension Agency in Huntsville, Alabama.

I have a lot of research from Amite County, Mississippi, Choctaw County, Mississippi, and some notes from the book of Poems by Samuel Newton Berryhill, who was called the Backwoods Poet.

One War of 1812 record from one Alexander Berryhill states he entered from Amite County, Mississippi and drew his travel pay in Natchez, Mississippi to return to Amite County, Mississippi, his residence.

This record has been taken by others thinking it was the Alexander Berryhill who served in the Rev. War, but I ordered it from Washington, D. C. to find it is the Alexander Berryhill of Amite County, Mississippi.

Anyone who is interested in the families of Robert and John Berryhill, who from all accounts seem to be sons of Samuel Berryhill who died by 12 August 1795 in Richmond County Georgia, I would be happy to see what I have that might help you.

CHAPTER II

THE

ALEXANDER

BERRYHILL

FAMILY

II. Alexander Berryhill
   b. 1760 approx. - Mecklenburg Co., N. C.
   d. 3 February 1839 - Marion Co., Ala.
   bur. Berryhill Family Cemetery - Fayette Co., Ala.
   m. -?-. His first wife's name is unknown, and apparently she died
           around 1810.

   1. James J. Berryhill
      b. 1800/1803 - Ga., possibly near Augusta

   2. Mary Berryhill - "Polly"
      b. 1805 - Ga., possibly near Augusta

   3. Lensfield Berryhill
      b. 1807 - Ga., possibly near Augusta

      Alexander Berryhill m. 2nd. 1811/1812 approx. - perhaps in Tenn.
      m. Rebecca Webster
         b. 1785 - N. C.
         d. after 1850. She was 65 years old at the time of the 1850
            census, but was gone by the 1860 census.

   4. Edward Berryhill
      b. 4 April 1813 - Franklin Co., Tenn - near Winchester

   5. Thomas Berryhill
      b. 9 May 1815 - Franklin Co., Tenn. - near Winchester

   1. James Joseph Berryhill
      b. 1800/1803 - Ga., possibly near Augusta
      m. Esther -?-
         Some say she was his second wife. He did marry the second time
         around 1874, but he has not been located on 1880 census.
         b. 1806 - Tenn.
         d. living during 1860 census, but dead by 1870 census in Miss.

      A. Julia Berryhill
         b. 1829 - Franklin Co., Tenn.
         No futher information is available on her, except she was 21
         years of age on the 1850 Marion Co., Ala. census and she was
         living in her parents home.

      B. Mary E. Berryhill
         b. 1830 - Franklin Co., Tenn.
         No further information is available on her, except she was 20
         years of age on the 1850 Marion Co., Ala. census and she was
         living in her parents home.

      C. William Robert Alexander Berryhill - "Bill"
         b. 25 February 1831 - Marion Co., Ala.
         d. 1899 approx. - living 1880 Marion Co., Ala. census
         m. Margaret C. Roberts - dau. of S. C. Roberts & M. -?-
            b. 10 June 1838 - Ala.   b. 1811 d. 1879 b. 1801 d. 1887
            d. living during 1880 census at Marion Co., Ala.
            bur. Sulphur Springs Cemetery - near Palestine, Texas
         (1) Thadious M. Berryhill - "Thaddie"
             b. 26 October 1860
             m. Ophelia Hall

             (a) Della Berryhill   SEE ADDENDA FOR MORE INFORMATION.
                 m. Ben Ward - 14 November 1901 - Fayette Co., Ala.
             (b) Lovella Berryhill
             (c) "Boss" Berryhill
                 m. Louise -?-

                 1. Mary Ann Berryhill

             (d) Grover Berryhill
             (e) Tishie Berryhill
                 m. -?- Lang

     (f) Eugie Berryhill
         m. -?- Parr
     (g) Eardeal Berryhill
     (h) Emma Jane Berryhill
         m. Dallas Haden May

(2) Samuel Berryhill- "Sammie"
    b. 4 August 1862 - Marion Co., Ala.
(3) Mathew J. Berryhill- "Math"
    b. 23 February 1867
    m. Margaret M. (Berryhill) Platt - 16 July 1893 - Fayette Co.
(4) Mary Frances Berryhill - "Mollie"
    b. 11 May 1869 - Marion Co., Ala.
    d. 2 August 1903 - Fayette Co., Ala.
    bur. Harmony Grove Cemetery - Fayette Co., Ala.
    m. Archie William Perry - 1 September 1888 - Fayette Co., Ala.
       b. 3 November 1869 - Fayette Co., Ala.
       d. 9 September 1964 - Winfield, Ala.
       bur. Harmony Grove Cemetery

     (a) Martha Ann Perry - "Annie"
         b. 30 April 1890 - Fayette Co., Ala.
         m. George Augustus Sullivan
            b. 6 May 1883
            d. 16 April 1949

         1. Jimmie Lou Sullivan
            b. 24 June 1925 - Fayette Co., Ala.
            m. Ray Clinton

            A. Elizabeth Clinton
               b. 17 December 1945
               m. Bunk Beasley

               (1) Doug Beasley

            B. Bobby Ray Clinton
               b. 1 August 1947 - Fayette Co., Ala.
            C. Eddie Clinton
               b. 22 January 1959 - Fayette Co., Ala.
            D. Laura Clinton
               b. 26 October 1961 - Fayette Co., Ala.

         2. Troy Sullivan
            b. 16 August 1927 - Fayette Co., Ala.
            m. Jo Hayes

            A. Ann Sullivan
               b. 30 July 1948
               m. James Watson

               (1) Donna Watson
               (2) Michael Watson

            B. Barbara Sullivan
               b. 18 November 1951 - Fayette Co., Ala.
            C. Roger Dale Sullivan
               b. 23 September 1953 - Fayette Co., Ala.
            D. Wanda Jo Sullivan
               b. 21 September 1959 - Fayette Co., Ala.
            E. Sandra Sullivan
               b. 4 November 1961 - Marion Co., Ala.

         3. .Bonnie May Sullivan
            b. 4 August 1929 - Fayette Co., Ala.
            m. George E. Trimble

            A. Marcia Lynne Trimble
               b. 14 November 1955
            B. Sue Ellen Trimble
               b. and d. 27 April 1963
               bur. Old Bethel Cemetery - Nauvoo, Ala.

         4. Mary Annis Sullivan
            b. 31 July 1931 - Fayette Co., Ala.
            m. Lewis N. Fleetwood

A. Juanita Fleetwood
   b. 6 March 1962
B. Dexter Fleetwood
   b. 30 April 1955
C. Melanie Louise Fleetwood
   b. 1 February 1962

(b) William I. Perry
   b. 5 March 1893 - Fayette Co., Ala.
   d. 5 May 1941
   bur. Harmony Grove Cemetery - Fayette Co., Ala.
   m. Hettie I. Weeks - 4 February 1914
      b. 18 November 1895

   1. Clyde Atwell Perry
      b. 18 September 1915 - Fayette Co., Ala.
      d. 18 March 1916
      bur. Harmony Grove Cemetery - Fayette Co., Ala.
   2. Reedus Perry
      b. 13 July 1917 - Fayette Co., Ala.
      m. Willie Tucker
   3. Earlene Perry
      b. 5 March 1922 - Fayette Co., Ala.
      m. Boss Tucker
   4. Blanche Perry
      b. 12 October 1927 - Fayette Co., Ala.
      m. Milford Baker
   5. Billy Joe Perry
      b. 29 November 1932 - Fayette Co., Ala.
      m. Melva Lee Phillips

(c) Columbus Joshua Perry
   b. 9 August 1895 - Fayette Co., Ala.
   m. Lena A. Webster - 13 February 1916
      b. 17 April 1897

   1. Seburn Perry
      b. 28 December 1919
      d. 3 June 1945
   2. Vergie Lee Perry
      b. 1922
      m. Augustine Baccus
   3. Christine Perry
      b. 3 April 1925
      m. Andrew Smith
   4. Amogene Perry
      b. 26 March 1927
      m. Elwood Waldrop
   5. Hollis Ray Perry
      b. 26 July 1928
      m. Nita Ozella
   6. Kudell Perry
      b. 30 May 1930
      m. Virginia -?-
   7. Maurice Perry
      b. 29 March 1932
      m. Dorothy Perry
   8. Jessie Perry (twin)
      b. 6 October 1936
   9. Jimmie Perry (twin)
      b. 6 October 1936

(d) Lynwood Thomas Perry
   b. 7 July 1900 - Fayette Co., Ala.
   m. Dora Mills

   1. Rubye Perry
   2. Ezell Perry
   3. D. L. Perry

(5) Martha Elizabeth Berryhill - "Lizzie"
   b. 3 November 1870 - Marion Co., Ala.
   m. Will Henderson

SEE ADDENDA SECTION FOR
ADDITIONAL DATA CON-
CERNING ISSUE OF MARTHA
ELIZABETH BERRYHILL.

(a) Annie Bell Henderson
    m. Steve Flynn
(b) Ruffus Henderson
(c) -?-   (d) -?-   (e) -?-   (f) -?-

(6) William Howard Berryhill
    b. 16 September 1872 - Marion Co., Ala.
    m. -?- , and has 3 issues, but names are unknown.
(7) M. C. Berryhill
    b. 28 March 1874
    d. 5 April 1875 - Marion Co., Ala.
    bur. Berryhill Family Cemetery
(8) Evline Berryhill
    b. 25 November 1875
    d. 26 November 1875 - Marion Col., Ala.
    bur. Berryhill Family Cemetery
(9) John C. Berryhill
    b. 16 November 1876
    d. 18 February 1888 - Marion Co., Ala.
    bur. Berryhill Family Cemetery
(10) Vergle E. Berryhill
    b. 29 June 1879
    d. 5 July 1879 - Marion Co., Ala.
    bur. Berryhill Family Cemetery
(11) Josh Robert Berryhill
    b. 16 October 1884 - Marion Co., Ala.
    d. 29 April 1961
    bur.
    m. Anna Pearl Easley - 17 July 1911 - Palestine, Texas
      b. 29 November 1894 - Van Zandt Co., Texas

(a) Eula Mae Berryhill
    b. 12 August 1912 - Palestine Texas
    d. 25 June 1973
    m. D. L. DeShazo - 4 August 1932 - Maysville, Okla.
      b. 9 November 1910 - Mill Creek, Okla.

    1. Winnie Mae DeShazo
       b. 8 September 1933 - Maysville, Okla.
       m. Jack C. Fenimore - 11 July 1952 - Blanchard, Okla
        b. 31 May 1933 - Little Field, Texas

       A. Vivian Sue Fenimore
         b. 28 September 1954 - Edmond, Okla.
       B. Jack Curtis Fenimore
         b. 25 September 1956 - Claremore, Okla.
       C. Vareeda Gale Fenimore
         b. 12 November 1957 - Claremore, Okla.

    2. Paul Gene DeShazo
       b. 26 July 1939 - Maysville, Okla.
       m. Mary Ann McCord - 24 June 1965 - Oklahoma City, OK
        b. 27 February 1943 - Sentinal, Okla.
    3. Alice Ann DeShazo
       b. 24 November 1940 - Maysville, Okla.
       m. A. Lee Frederick - 1 November 1961 - Miami, Okla.
        b. 15 April 1933 - Harrison, Ark.

       A. Cheryl Ann Frederick
         b. 23 August 1962 - Springdale, Ark.
       B. Lisa Machelle Frederick
         b. 5 May 1970 - Claremore, Okla.

    4. Jessie Stephen DeShazo
       b. 10 September 1947 - Blanchard, Okla.
       m. Glenda Haught - 31 December 1965 - Marlow, Okla.
        b. 1 December 1946 - Marlow, Okla.

       A. Mark Alan DeShazo
         b. 13 May 1968 - Marlow, Okla.
       B. Chris Wayne DeShazo
         b. 17 May 1970 - Marlow, Okla.

        C. Brian Scott DeShazo
           b. 4 January 1973 - Marlow, Okla.

     5. Ellen Ruth DeShazo
        b. 8 July 1957 - Claremore, Okla.
        d. 25 June 1973

(b) Ola Marie Berryhill
    b. 3 August 1914 - Palestine, Texas
    m. Joseph Carl Howard - 19 July 1931 - Maysville, Okla.
       b. 8 January 1910 - Council Hill, Okla.

     1. Anna Marie Howard
        b. 19 January 1935 - Morris, Okla.
        m. Jim Luroy Davis - 7 August 1954 - Morris, Okla.
           b. 22 November 1934 - Sulphur, Okla.

        A. Sherry Ann Davis
           b. 18 May 1955 - Muskogee, Okla.
        B. Jimmy Lee Davis
           b. 19 October 1956 - Muskogee, Okla.
        C. Janet Lynn Davis
           b. 19 October 1956 - Muskogee, Okla.
        D. Jerry Howard Davis
           b. 22 January 1960 - Okmulgee, Okla.

     2. Caroline Sue Howard
        b. 28 September 1937 - Morris, Okla.
        m. Richard Tinley Walters - 5 June 1953 - Morris, OK
           b. 1 May 1936 - Morris, Okla.

        A. Cynthia Sue Walters
           b. 26 December 1953 - Okmulgee, Okla.
           m. Larry LaVerne Thompson - 18 August 1972 - Okla-
              homa City, Okla.
              b. 27 September 1951 - Oklahoma City, Okla.
        B. Karen Marthetta Walters
           b. 1 May 1957 - Okmulgee, Okla.

     3. Patricia Elaine Howard
        b. 17 November 1943 - Okmulgee, Okla.
        m. Richard Wayne Carpenter - 1 June 1962 - Morris, OK
           b. 13 February 1940 - Morris, Okla.

(c) Edith Margaret Berryhill
    b. 31 March 1917 - Palestine, Texas
    m. Joseph Wendell Price - 18 December 1935 - Maysville
       b. 19 March 1917 - Walters, Okla.

     1. Ginger Margaret Price
        b. 12 September 1938 - Maysville, Okla.
        m. Vernon Eugene McCarty - 27 January 1957 - Ada, OK
           b. 11 November 1937 - Jessie, Okla.

        A. Tonya Elaine McCarty
           b. 10 November 1959 - Ada, Okla.
        B. Gary Wayne McCarty
           b. 19 July 1962 - Okmulgee, Okla.
        C. Russel Wade McCarty
           b. 2 February 1966 - McAlester, Okla.

     2. Sandra Jo Price
        b. 8 June 1947 - Oklahoma City, Okla.
        m. Larry Wayne Jackson - 26 November 1963 - Stone-
           wall, Okla.
           b. 27 November 1943 - Burr Valley, Okla.

        A. Kimberly Ann Jackson
           b. 26 August 1965 - Ada, Okla.
        B. Leslie Renee Jackson
           b. 26 January 1967 - Ada, Okla.

     3. Orville Lee Price
        b. 30 June 1950 - Oklahoma City, Okla.
        m. Ruth Ann Sparks - 22 December 1970 - Stonewall, OK
           b. 4 October 1953 - Ada, Okla.

A. Kelley Ann Price
   b. stillborn - Sulphur, Okla.
   bur. Ada, Okla.

(d) Lola Lorene Berryhill
   b. 12 December 1918 - Palestine, Texas
   m. Walter Sanford Bailey - 26 June 1937 - Ada, Okla.
      b. 16 January 1915 - Van Buren, Ark.

   1. Anna Grace Bailey
      b. and d. 9 September 1938 - Ada, Okla.
   2. Robert Sanford Bailey
      b. 25 November 1939 - Ada, Okla.
      m. Dorothy Jean Peters - 28 July 1957 - Midwest City,
         Oklahoma
         b. 6 September 1940 - Oklahoma City, Okla.

      A. Robert Wayne Bailey
         b. 28 October 1961 - Dallas, Texas
      B. Rickey Glen Bailey
         b. 16 March 1963 - Dallas, Texas
      C. Michal Joe Bailey
         b. 29 August 1965 - Irving, Texas

   3. Walter Richard Bailey
      b. 27 September 1941 - Hobart, Okla.
      m. Donna Carol Dean - 30 June 1961 - Prague, Okla.
         b. 3 October 1942 - Prague, Okla.

      A. Richard Dean Bailey
         b. 9 December 1965 - Irving, Texas
      B. Angela Gail Bailey
         b. 19 December 1966 - Irving, Texas

   4. Kenneth Ray Bailey
      b. 5 April 1943 - Ada, Okla.
      m. Margaret Mee Dragg - 11 July 1966 - Ardmore, Okla.
         b. 11 August 1945 - Oklahoma City, Okla.

      A. Elenora Rene Bailey
         b. 11 July 1967 - Irving, Texas
      B. Deborah Sue Bailey
         b. 11 June 1969 - Ardmore, Okla.
      C. Kenneth Michael Bailey
         b. 5 July 1971 - Ardmore, Okla.

   5. Frances Kay Bailey
      b. 14 January 1946 - Brittion, Okla.
      m. Carl David Latham - 27 February 1965 - Ardmore, OK
         b. 30 January 1945 - Killeen, Texas

      A. De Anna Kay Latham
         b. 18 December 1966 - Ardmore, Okla.
      B. Teri Lynette Latham
         b. 19 July 1969 - Irving, Texas
      C. Shauna Carol Latham
         b. 13 March 1971 - Irving, Texas

   6. Thomas Gene Bailey
      b. 10 April 1952 - Oklahoma City, Okla.
      m. Carolyn Sue Williams - 5 June 1971 - Dallas, Texas
         b. 29 December 1951 - Dallas, Texas

      A. Brian Thomas Bailey
         b. 13 August 1972 - Dallas, Texas

(e) Lula Lugene Berryhill
   b. 12 December 1918 - Palestine, Texas
   m. Joseph C. Dobrava - 30 June 1972 - Midwest City, Okla.
      b. 9 August 1911 - Ammansville, Texas
(f) William Robert Berryhill
   b. 19 April 1921 - Altus, Okla.
   m. Opal Justina Edwards - 31 January 1941 - Shawnee, OK
      b. 12 September 1920 - Atwood, Okla.

1. Barbara Ann Berryhill
   b. 15 September 1943 - Oklahoma City, Okla.
   m. George Lewis Tracy - 15 September 1967 - Midwest,
   Okla.
   b. 29 May 1939 - Stillwater, Okla.

   A. Robert Lewis Tracy
      b. 5 May 1968 - Oklahoma City, Okla.
   B. Karis Lynn Tracy
      b. 29 December 1969 - Oklahoma City, Okla.

2. Jeaneane Berryhill
   b. 8 March 1947 - Oklahoma City, Okla.
   m. Charles Edward Johnson - 27 August 1967 - Midwest
   b. 12 December 1945 - Oklahoma City, Okla.

   A. James Jay Johnson
      b. 18 March 1966 - Oklahoma City, Okla.
   B. Richard Tobin Johnson
      b. 2 June 1968 - Oklahoma City, Okla.

3. Karen Berryhill
   b. 14 July 1948 - Oklahoma City, Okla.
   m. William Oliver Sprague, II - 1 May 1964 - Oklahoma
   City, Okla.
   b. 11 November 1945 - Oklahoma City, Okla.

   A. William Oliver Sprague, III
      b. 17 December 1964 - Oklahoma City, Okla.
   B. Eric Vaughn Sprague
      b. 20 July 1967 - Oklahoma City, Okla.

4. Robert Bruce Berryhill
   b. 20 April 1952 - Oklahoma City, Okla.

(g) Helen Lenora Berryhill
    b. 27 August 1924 - Maysville, Okla.
    m. Daniel Crockett Lanier, Jr. - 9 November 1942 - Las
    Vegas, Nev.
    b. 17 March 1919 - Ada, Okla.

   1. David Allen Lanier
      b. 17 August 1943 - Long Beach, Calif.
      m. Terrie Lee Gordon - 14 December 1968 - Long Beach
      b. 26 March 1943 - Long Beach, Calif.
   2. Phillip Thomas Lanier
      b. 19 December 1955 - Long Beach, Calif.

(h) Agnes Faye Berryhill
    b. 9 March 1926 - Maysville, Okla.
    m. Richard Earl Day, Sr. - 29 July 1945 - Midwest, Okla.
    b. 5 February 1926 - Sherman, Texas

   1. Richard Earl Day, Jr.
      b. 4 July 1946 - Oklahoma City, Okla.
      m. Barbara Jane Olson - 18 May 1968 - Omaha, Neb.
      b. 30 April 1946 - Staples, Minn.

      A. Elizabeth Marilys Day
         b. 18 March 1969 - St. Paul, Minn.
      B. Rebecca Jane Day
         b. 15 December 1970 - Philadelphia, Pa.
      C. Jonathan Richard Day
         b. 20 July 1972 - Rochester, N. Y.

   2. Lawrence Michael Day
      b. 15 July 1949 - Long Beach, Calif.
      m. Carol Ann Kochis - 12 August 1972 - Pueblo, Colo.
      b. 31 March 1952 - Pueblo, Colo.
   3. Candace Lugene Day
      b. 2 June 1952 - Waco, Texas
      m. Jesus' Guerrero, Jr. - 15 May 1971 - Colorado
      Springs, Colo.
      b. 26 January 1947 - Oak Creek, Colo.

(i) Baby Berryhill
    b. and d. 29 February 1928 - Maysville, Okla.
    bur. Maysville, Okla.
(j) Betty June Berryhill
    b. 20 June 1929 - Maysville, Okla.
    m. Bill Kingsbury - 12 November 1946 - Riverside, Calif.
    b. 12 September 1927 - Ventura, Calif.

    1. Kathryn Fayth Kingsbury
       b. 12 October 1947 - Santa Barbara, Calif.
       m. Richard Calvin Prescott, Jr. - 29 December 1966 -
       Westminister, Calif.
       b. 26 April 1945 - Queens, N. Y.

       A. Lorena Kay Prescott
          b. 15 August 1967 - Anaheim, Calif.
       B. Sandra Louise Prescott
          b. 4 September 1969 - Burbank, Calif.
       C. Amanda Renee Prescott
          b. 4 April 1971 - Huntington Beach, Calif.

    2. Dianna Lynn Kingsbury
       b. 19 April 1949 - Santa Barbara, Calif.
       m. Royce Richard Reese, Jr. - 5 July 1969 - Las Vegas
       b. 30 January 1947 - Detroit, Mich.

       A. Tami Lynn Reese
          b. 1 July 1970 - Newport Beach, Calif.

       Dianna Kingsbury m. 2nd. 15 November 1975 -
       m. Charles Thomas Atkinson   - Fountain Valley, Calif.
       b. 15 August 1938

       A. Tami Lynn Atkinson
          b. 1 July 1970 - Newport Beach, Ca.
          Tami was adopted by Charles T. Atkinson during
          this second marriage of Dianna Kingsbury.

    3. William Michael Kingsbury
       b. 2 March 1953 - Santa Barbara, Calif.
       d. 26 September 1953 - Santa Barbara, Calif.
       bur. Santa Barbara, Calif.
    4. Michael Lorne Kingsbury
       b. 14 May 1966 - Anaheim, Calif.

(k) Gladys Laveda Berryhill
    b. 27 May 1932 - Maysville, Okla.
    m. Harry Edward Kelly - 13 January 1951 - Oklahoma City
    b. 24 July 1929 - Oklahoma City, Okla.

    1. Deborah Marie Kelly
       b. 6 April 1952 - Oceanside, Calif.
    2. Belinda Carol Kelly
       b. 30 January 1954 - Midwest City, Okla.
    3. Brad Edward Kelly
       b. 10 April 1956 - Oklahoma City, Okla.

(1) Katherine Josephine Berryhill
    b. 11 November 1938 - Maysville, Okla.
    m. John Ray Gottman - 20 June 1958 - Midwest City, Okla.
    b. 25 July 1937 - Shawnee, Okla.

    1. John William Gottman
       b. 21 November 1959 - Shawnee, Okla.
    2. James Alan Gottman
       b. 29 October 1961 - Shawnee, Okla.
    3. Janna Leigh Gottman
       b. 19 November 1967 - Duncan, Okla.

D. Sarah C. Berryhill
  b. 1835 - Marion Co., Ala.
  m. James S. Porter
    b. 1832 - Ala.

     (1) Nancy Porter
        b. 1858 - Marion Co., Ala.
     (2) James Porter
        b. 1860 Marion Co., Ala.

E. Abigail Berryhill
   b. 1836 - Marion Co., Ala.
   No further information on her, except she was living, age 14
   years, in her parents home on 1850 Marion Co., Ala. Census.

F. Thomas J. C. Berryhill
   b. 1839 - Marion Co., Ala.
   d. 1917 - Okanulgee, Okla
      living in Hinds Co., Miss. at time of 1870 census.
   m. Nancy Jane Heideron by 1860 Marion Co., Ala. census
      b. 9 March 1843
      d. 1 September 1924 - Corbet, Texas
      living in Hinds Co., Miss at time of 1870 census

     (1) Benjamin Berryhill
        b. 1861 - Marion Co., Ala.
     (2) James Berryhill - "Bud"
        b. 1863 - Marion Co., Ala.
     (3) William Berryhill
        b. 1865 - Hinds Co., Miss.
     (4) Easter C. Berryhill
        b. 1869 - Hinds Co., Miss.
     (5) Alley Berryhill
        b. 1873
        d. about age 13
     (6) Andrew Berryhill
        b. 1876
        d.
        bur. Navarro County, Texas
     (7) John Thomas Berryhill
        b. 7 August 1878
        d. 2 December 1959
     (8) Kate Berryhill
        m. -?- Huggins

        (a) Will Huggins

     (9) Frank Berryhill
        b. 27 July 1883 - Texas
        d. 7 April 1937 - Corsicana, Texas
        bur. Dresden Cemetery - Navarro County, Texas
        m. Gertha Morrison
          b. 19 April 1890 - Ellis Co., Texas
          d. 3 October 1967 - Ennis, Ellis Co., Texas
          bur. Dresden Cemetery - Navarro County, Texas

        (a) Ruby Jane Corilla Berryhill
           b. 31 March 1906
           d. 30 May 1931
           m. Elbert Stovall

           1. Frank Newton Stovall
           2. Nathan Stovall

        (b) Clarence Sylvester Berryhill
           b. 6 June 1908
           d. 14 August 1972
           m. Lorrene Thompson

           1. Baby Boy Berryhill
           2. Judy Zane Berryhill
           3. Brenda Berryhill
           4. Ronald Berryhill
           5. Baby Boy Berryhill

        (c) Jessie Faye Berryhill
           b. 29 April 1910
           m. Jim C. Cagle

            1. Reba Sue Cagle
            2. Wanda Willene Cagle

        Jesse Faye Berryhill m. 2nd. Raymond Heine

            3. Raymond Ray Heine

    (d) Roy Edward Berryhill
        b. 7 May 1912
        d. 12 November 1974
        m. Vestal Eulalar Jayroe
    (e) Eugene Kelton Berryhill
        b. 12 September 1914
        m. Nora B. Price - 7 April 1936

        1. Maggie Lou Berryhill
            b. 9 August 1937
            m. Robert McQuilken

            A. Jeffery Robert McQuilken
            B. Kim Marie McQuilken

            Maggie Lou Berryhill m. 2nd. Jack U. Gibbs

            C. Tammy Lunn Gibbs

        2. Deleata Ann Berryhill
            b. 15 November 1939
            m. C. D. Gideon

            A. Debra Ann Gideon
            B. David Lee Gideon

            Deleata Ann Berryhill m. 2nd M. L. Stewart

        3. Theresa Youvonne Berryhill
            b. 27 January 1942
            m. W. D. Eddleman

            A. Shirley Ann Eddleman
            B. Lisa Lynette Eddleman
            C. George Dewayne Eddleman
            D. Patricia Kaye Eddleman
            E. James Curtis Eddleman
            f. Travis McCoy Eddleman

        4. Kenneth Brian Berryhill
            b. 18 July 1944
            m. Meda Sue Quick

            A. Gwendolyn Annett Berryhill
            B. Mary Sue Berryhill
            C. Brian Keith Berryhill

        5. Shirley Marie Berryhill
            b. 17 October 1948
            m. F. L. Oliver

            A. F. L. Oliver, Jr.
            B. Shaunda Maire Oliver

        6. Eugene Lee Berryhill
            b. and d. 10 May 1952

    (f) Ira Lee Berryhill
        b. 27 November 1916
        m. Dorothy Jones

        1. Darrell D. Berryhill
        2. Patricia Darnell Berryhill
        3. Waymond Lee Berryhill

    (g) Rufus Gordan Berryhill
        b. 28 July 1919
        d. 14 September 1948
        m. Maudena Scruggs

        1. Ronald H. Berryhill
        2. -?-
        3. James Berryhill

(h) Thurman Wallace Berryhill
    b. 21 September 1921
    m. Dora Jones

    1. Hazel Luella Berryhill
    2. Baby Boy Berryhill

(i) Glen Doyle Berryhill
    b. 20 October 1923
    m. Elroy Jackson

    1. Donnie Dale Berryhill
    2. Deborah Kay Berryhill
    3. Baby Boy Berryhill

(j) Travis Grady Berryhill
    b. 27 April 1926
    m. Joyce Ruth McCluney

    1. Roger Dale Berryhill
    2. Jerry Berryhill
    3. Janet Berryhill
    4. Michael Berryhill
    5. Linda Berryhill

(k) Bobbie Marie Berryhill
    b. 25 February 1930
    d. 9 December 1930
(l) Daisy Vestal Berryhill
    b. 7 February 1932
    m. R. R. Jackson

    1. Ray Edward Jackson
    2. Ricky Earl Jackson
    3. Billy Dan Jackson
    4. Beverly Luann Jackson
    5. Randy Jackson

G. Charles Berryhill
   b. 1849 - Marion Co., Ala.
   Gone from parents home on 1860 census, so we can assume he
   died young.

H. Alexander Berryhill
   b. 7 March 1848
   d. 11 November 1885
   bur. Weeks Cemetery
   The 1860 census shows him as 13 years old, so by 1870, he would
   be 23 years old and probably married. I found several marriages
   in Hinds Co., Miss. for various Alexanders, but have found no
   one who can tell he WHO he married.

I. John Riley Berryhill
   b. 7 March 1846 - Marion Co., Ala.
   Living in parents' home, age 15 years, at time of 1860 census,
   but no further information is available on him.

   John Riley Berryhill served in Co. A, 4th Ala. Reg't. Says he
   was both 7th March 1846 in Marion Co., Ala. Enlisted Fall of
   1862, at Tuscumbia and continued until paroled at Columbus, MS
   in May of 1865. Address Kino, Ala. in Lawrence County.

James J. Berryhill m. 2nd. Martha Barten - 18 June 1874 - Lee Co.
Mississippi.

217

```
1850 Marion Co., Ala. Census 101/102
James J. Berryhill    43 M    Ga.   b. 1807
Ester            "    44 F    Tenn.    1806
Julia            "    21 F    Tenn.    1829
Mary E.          "    20 F    Tenn.    1830
William R.       "    17 M    Ala.     1833
Sally C.         "    15 F    Ala.     1835
Abigail          "    14 F    Ala.     1836
Thomas J.        "    11 M    Ala.     1839
Charles          "     1 M    Ala.     1849 - some say 1st issue by Ester

1860 Marion Co., Ala.  71/74 page 11
James J. Berryhill    53 M    Ga.      1807
Esther           "    54 F    Tenn.    1806
Thomas           "    19 M    Ala.     1841
Nancy Jane       "    18 F    Ala.     1842 - wife of Thomas
Alexander T. (or L.)" 13 M    Ala.     1847
John R.          "    15 M    Ala.     1845
Mary E.          "    10 F    Ala.     1850 - cannot account for her)

1870 Hinds Co., Miss. 23 July 1870 - Bolton, Miss.  Ts #7 114/114 p. 15
James J. Berryhill    63 M.   Ga.      1807 - we know Esther is dead
Thomas J. C.     "    38 M    Ala.     1832
Jane             "    28 F    Ala.     1842
Benjamin         "     9 M    Ala.     1861
James            "     7 M    Ala.     1863
William          "     5 M    Miss.    1865
Easter C.        "     1 F    Miss.    1869

115/115 - page 15 Bolton, Miss.
James S. Porter      38 M    Ala.  b. 1832
Sarah C.        "    35 F    Ala.     1835 - dau. of J. J. Berryhill next
Nancy           "    12 F    Ala.     1858   door
James           "    10 M    Ala.     1860
Nancy J.        "     8 F    Ala.     1862
Robert Lee      "     4 M    Ala.     1866
Mary Berryhill       10 F    Ala.     1850 - dau. of James J. Berryhill
                                             next door

Lee County, Miss. Marriage
J. J. Berryhill & Martha Barten     18 June 1974
J. I. Berryhill & Eva Farris         6 June 1923
R. G. Berryhill & Tempie McCormick  24 Dec. 1924
Andrew Berryhill & Mable Duncan      6 Feb. 1916
Charley Berryhill & Della Williams  14 Dec. 1920

HOW I wish Clerks would not use initials!!
```

2. Mary Ann C. Berryhill - "Polly"
   b. 7 March 1806 - Jefferson Co., Ga.
   d. 28 June 1887 - Fayette Co., Ala.
   bur. Old Union Primitive Baptist Cemetery - Fayette Co., Ala.
   m. Willis Monroe Ward - 1826/1827 - Franklin Co., Tenn.
      b. 19 June 1802 - N. C.
      d. 15 December 1876 - Fayette Co., Ala.
      bur. Old Union Primitive Baptist Cemetery
      son of -?- Ward and Mary -?- Ward
            d. by 1830   b. 1780/1790

A. Americus Mary Melinda Ward
   b. 27 July 1828 - Franklin Co., Tenn.
   d. 22 April 1898 - Marion Co., Ala.
   bur. Zion Missionary Baptist Church Cemetery - Marion Co., Ala.
   m. Louis Fennel May
      b. 7 June 1828 - Tenn.
      d. 13 September 1883 - Marion Co., Ala.
      bur. Zion Missionary Baptist Church Cemetery
      son of George Robert May & Hannah Henderson

   (1) William Henderson May - "Buck"
       b. 28 December 1847 - Marion Co., Ala.
       d. 24 November 1921 - Fayette Co., Ala.
       bur. Siloam Baptist Cemetery - Fayette Co., Ala.
       m. -?- Adams
       m. 2nd. Emma Melton
               b. 22 August 1855
               d. 31 October 1932
               bur. Siloam Baptist Cemetery

      (a) Thomas May
          bur. Berryhill Family Cemetery - Fayette Co., Ala.
          m. Susie Weeks

          1. Morgan May
             m. -?-

             A. Arvil May
                m. and has two daughters

             Morgan May m. 2nd and has 3 daughters

          2. Raymond May
             bur. Freewill Baptist Cemetery - Marion Co., Ala.
             m. -?- Akers

             A. Eugene May
             B. Edrill May

          3. Freeman May
             bur. Center Cemetery - Marion Co., Ala.
             m. Lizzie Williams

             A. Beatrice May
                m. -?- Mayfield
             B. Hurshell May
                m. -?- Smuthers
             C. Luie Joe May
                m. June Tucker
             D. Kenneth May
             E. Edger May
                m. Elizabeth Cottney

          4. Qubell May
             m. -?- Ledlow
             m. 2nd. Nelce Burlson
             bur. Zion Missionary Baptist Cemetery
          5. Garvin May

      (b) Harve May
          bur. Zion Missionary Baptist Cemetery
          m. Sarah Ann Haney
             bur. Zion Missionary Baptist Cemetery

1. 2. 3. 4. 5. deceased infants May
6. Ruth May
   m. Lee Benton
   bur. Okla

   A. Son Benton

7. Marshall May
   m. Annie Lue Miles

   A. Dexter May
   B. Son May
   C. Angela May
      d. 5 years old, killed by a lumber truck

8. Irene May
   m. Dempsey Franks
   lives in Okla.
9. Edna May
   m. "Luke" Riley
   lives in Okla.
10. Harlon May
    m. Ruby Knight

    A. Son May
    B. Son May
    C. Daughter May

11. Minar May
    m. Buford Hawkins
    bur. Zion Missionary Baptist Cemetery

    A. Son Hawkins
    B. Daughter Hawkins

12. Kathleen May
    b. 1914

Wm. Henderson May m. 2nd. Emma Melton
                        b. 22 August 1955
                        d. 31 October 1932

(c) Villie May
    bur. Old Union Primitive Baptist Cemetery
    m. Dolpha Taylor
       bur. Berryhill Family Cemetery

1. Jessie Taylor
   m. Sammie Lee Roberts

   A. Jo Ann Taylor
   B. Jimmie Taylor

2. William Taylor
   m. Ruby Hollis

   A. Billy Hugh Donald Taylor
   B. Shirley Taylor

Villie (May) Taylor m. 2nd. "Buse" Atkinson

3. Roy Atkinson
   b. 29 August 1915
   m. Ola Mae Harper

   A. Daughter Atkinson
   B. Jimmy Atkinson

4. Troy Atkinson
   m. -?- Webster
5. Williene Atkinson
   b. 4 March 1922
   m. Paul Smith - they have three sons

(d) William May
    m. Chessie Taylor

1. Arlie May
   m. Vista Fowler - they have two sons

    2. Rubin May
    3. Jolia May
       m. Roston White

       A. David White

    4. Lomaz May
    5. Floy Banks May
    6. Vonceel May
       m. Robert Wymond Humber

       A. Twin Girl Humber
       B. Twin Girl Humber

    7. Glen May
    8. Morris May

(e) Lizzie May
    m. John Taylor
    bur. both at Mt. Willing Baptist Cemetery

    1. Artie Taylor
       bur. Mt. Willing Baptist Cemetery
       m. Granvil Haney
    2. Autie Taylor
       m. William Cook

       A. Son Cook
       B. Son Cook

    3. Onie Taylor
       b. 1 May 1910
       m. James Shafter Warren
          b. 23 January 1912
    4. Nellie Taylor
       b. 1913
       m. Howard McDonald

       A. Son McDonald

(f) Millie May
    m. Talmadge Fowler

    1. Redus Fowler
       m. Ruth Burnett
    2. William Fowler
       b. 6 October 1917
       m. Parnell Guin
          b. 6 October 1917
          dau. of Walt Guin & Myrtle Louise Henderson

       A. Patsy Loretta Fowler
       B. Jimmy Fowler

    3. Beatrice Fowler
       m. James Chester Trimm
    4. Albert Fowler
    5. Ray Fowler
    6. Novelene Fowler
    7. Son Fowler

(g) Bruse Dense May
    m. Villie Weeks
       bur. Berryhill Family Cemetery - Fayette Co., Ala.

    1. Audrie May
       m. Roy Smith
          bur. Mt. Vernon Cemetery - Fayette Co., Ala.

       A. Daughter Smith
       B. Son Smith
       C. Son Smith

    2. Alton May
       m. Adell Span
          dau. of Lester Spann
       A. Daughter May
          m. Bob Mullins

Alton May m. 2nd. Coy McCawer Tucker

3. Ina Lee Mary
   m. Hershell Trimm
      d. killed in World War II
      bur. Berryhill Family Cemetery

   A. Rex Trimm
      b. 1941
      m. -?- Sanderson

(h) Cly May
    d. 1969
    m. Annie McDonald

    1. Lucille May
       m. Lemmie Warren
    2. Clanton May
       m. -?- Chaffin
    3. Curtous May
       m. Willie Mae Berryhill
    4. Claytos May
       d. in World War II
       bur. Siloam Church Cemetery
       m. Mary Lue Markham
    5. Clara Lee May
       m. -?- Spears
    6. Avie May
       b. 4 August 1899
       d. 15 February 1918
       bur. Siloam Cemetery
    7. Roman May
       m. Mae Span
          dau. of Jim Span

       A. James William May
          b. 1927
       B. Little Fay May
          m. Wytman Humbers

          (1) Son Humbers
          (2) Son Humbers
          (3) Daughter Humbers

       C. Lex May

(2) Willis Alexander May
    b. 4 May 1850
    d. 21 May 1937
    bur. Siloam Cemetery - Fayette Co., Ala.
    m. Susan Eleanor Malcie Carnela Martha Josephine Kirkland
       b. 25 August 1855
       d. 16 January 1933
       bur. Siloam Cemetery
       dau. of Louis Jayhugh Kirkland & Parmelia Ann Chappel
                b. 4 April 1812   b. 6 February 1817
                d. 12 November 1888   d. 26 October 1903

    (a) Infant Son May
        b. and d. September 1873
        bur. Zion Baptist Cemetery
    (b) Luther May
        b. 12 December 1874
        d.   April 1878
        bur. Zion Baptist Cemetery
    (c) Nora May
        b. 15 April 1876
        d. 4 October 1958
        bur. Fayette City Cemetery
        m. Mathew Sims

(d) Riley Albert May - (twin)
   b. 6 November 1877
   d. 15 July 1955
   bur. Winfield City Cemetery
   m. Nannie Bell Aston
(e) Robert Elbert May - (twin)
   b. 6 November 1877
   d. 3 September 1954
   bur. Lexington, Okla.
   m. Ethel Lee Burrows
      b. 17 March 1886 - Correll Co., Texas

   1. Wilma Etna May
      b. 26 November 1904 - Wanette, Okla.
      m. Harvie Corm

      A. Dorothy Gale Corm
      B. Vernon Corm
      C. Quinton Corm
      D. Lotella Corm
      E. Wyman Corm
      F. Donald Corm

   2. Jewell Estell May
      b. 26 May 1907 - Box, Okla.
      m. L. D. Holsonbake

      A. Levon Holsonbake
      B. Norma Jean Holsonbake
      C. Marcill Holsonbake
      D. Rummell Holsonbake
      E. Dwight Holsonbake
      F. Joan Holsonbake
      G. Marlin Holsonbake
      H. Freddie Kay Holsonbake
      I. Sharon Holsonbake
      J. Linda Holsonbake
      K. Janis Sue Holsonbake

   3. Clovis Alexandra May
      b. 9 June 1920
      d. 22 June 1964
   4. Bernice May
      b. 23 May 1911 - Corbett, Okla.
   5. Albert Kirk May
      b. 5 April 1914
      m. Clara Crews

      A. Sue Francis May

   6. Wanda Omega May
      b. 21 August 1916 - Corbett, Okla.
      m. John Cheatwood

      A. Bryan Cheatwood
      B. Bryce Cheatwood
      C. Edwin Cheatwood
      D. Jonetta Cheatwood

   7. Gaylis Adair May
      b. 29 January 1921 - Corbett, Okla.
   8. Bryce Winston May
      b. 20 May 1918 - Corbett, Okla.
      m. Vertie Jo Elenger

      A. Wilda May
      B. Lynn May
      C. Bobby May

(f) James May
   b. 5 November 1879
   d. 9 February 1962
   bur. Winfield City Cemetery
   m. Lula Aston

(g) Louis J. Hugh May
    b. 8 June 1881 - Marion Co., Ala.
    d. 6 February 1963 - Lexington, Okla
    bur. Cleveland Co., Okla.
    m. Lillie Grace Jarboe - 18 November 1905 - Cleveland
       Co., Texas
       b. 27 December 1884 - Wise Co., Texas
       d. 11 January 1951 - Lexington, Okla.
       bur. Lexington, Okla.

1. Jewel Lee May
    b. 19 February 1907 - Cleveland Co., Okla.
    m. Henry Clay Wilmoth - 23 January 1932 - Oklahoma
      City, Okla.
      b. 28 December 1900 - Putnam Co., Tenn.
      son of Jacob Lavender Wilmoth & Martha Adelia
                                Rayburn

    A. Bette Lou Wilmoth
       b. 6 September 1932 - Oklahoma City, Okla.
       m. George Odett Brooks - 31 July 1953
         b. 24 October 1932
         son of Talmadge Brooks & Sylvia Coories Jones

       (1) Terri Lynn Brooks
          b. 3 March 1955 - Lawton, Okla.
       (2) Karen Ann Brooks
          b. 29 June 1958 - Oklahoma City, Okla.
       (3) Jeffrey David Brooks
          b. 21 August 1962 - Oklahoma City, Okla.

    B. Jewell Louise Wilmoth
       b. 2 September 1933 - McClain Co., Okla.
       m. Arthur Baker Fent, Jr. - 23 December 1953
         b. 21 February 1931 - Oklahoma City, Okla.
         son of A. B. Fent & Mary Ann Bochnke
    C. Diana Sue Wilmoth
       b. 17 September 1945 - Oklahoma City, Okla.
       m. Richard Walden Tucker - 23 June 1966
         b. 20 May 1945 - Russell, Kansas

2. Lester Raymond May
    b. 29 June 1908
    m. Gladys Mozelle Drummond - 28 April 1928 - McClain
      Co, Okla.
      b. 28 December 1909
      dau. of Jess Wm. Drummond & May Bell Oaks

    A. Jacqueline Joyce May
       b. 1 May 1929
       m. Don Cheatham
         b. 31 January 1929

       (1) Donna Elaine Cheatham
          b. 27 September 1953
       (2) Kathleen Cheatham
          b. 14 July 1956

    B. Wanda Lou May
       b. 20 November 1931
       m. Sam Asseo - 1 February 1952 - Oklahoma City, OK
         b. 21 June 1921 - Tampeco, Mexico

       (1) Roger Kendall Asseo
          b. 11 November 1952
       (2) Lourie Ann Asseo
          b. 6 July 1956

    C. Robert Darrell May
       b. 23 July 1932
       m. Coralee Fullerton
         b. 13 May 1931

```
                (1) Phillip Scotty May
                    b. 10 February 1963
                (2) Stephen Neil May
                    b. 1 May 1964

         D. Sandra Elaine May
            b. 3 September 1945
            m. Maurice Plaster

                (1) Lesa Elaine Plaster
                    b. 20 March 1967

  3. Jesse Haill May
     b. 30 October 1909
     m. Allyene Headrick
        dau. of Walter Headrick & Ozzie Powers

     A. Baby Girl stillborn
     B. Ruby Dolores May
        b. 19 January 1937
        m. Gene Latham
           b. 13 August 1931

           (1) Wonda Lou Latham
               b. 8 September 1954
           (2) John Joseph Latham
               b. 3 January 1971 (adopted)

     C. Ted Lewis May
        b. 19 April 1933
        m. Marie -?-
        m. 2nd. Janet Lee Bates
           b. 22 September 1941

           (1) Ted Anthony May
               b. 5 August 1956
           (2) Tim Allen May
               b. 10 October 1958
           (3) Maurine Lynn May
               b. 27 June 1958
           (4) Tom Albert May
               b. 25 August 1960
           (5) Steven Lewis May
               b. 28 August 1961

     D. Billie Don May
        b. 15 March 1935
        m. Lela -?-

           (1) Vicki Lynn May
               b. 12 February 1961
           (2) Diane  Louise May
               b. 29 August 1962

        Billie Don May m. 2nd. -?-

           (3) Lisa  Donnette May
               b. 12 November 1970

     E. Pat Wayne May
        b. 27 July 1943
        m. Marilyn Barker
           b. 19 October 1944
     F. Beverly Ann May
        b. 15 March 1945
        m. Eddie Smalridge
           b. 25 October 1943

           (1) Darin James Smalridge
               b. 19 October 1967
           (2) Denice Jeanine Smalridge
               b. 20 December 1970

     G. Ray Allen May
        b. 26 July 1953
```

4. Walter Willis May
   b. 3 March 1911 - Cleveland Co., Okla.
   m. Essie Pauline Woods - 27 July 1940
   b. 31 July 1931 - Izard Co, Ark.
   dau. of James Swan Woods & Nancy Elizabeth Dillard

   A. Ginny Carol May
      b. 6 October 1942 - Oklahoma City, Okla.
      m. Donald M. Fitzgerald - 2 November 1968
         son of Edward Husing Fitzgerald & Ruby Lillian
                                                    -?-

   B. Lou Ann May
      b. 1 January 1945 - Oklahoma City, Okla.
      m. Edward Harold Rahm, Jr. - 24 November 1961 -
      Oklahoma City, Okla.
         b. 13 August 1942 - Macomb Co., Mich.
         son of E. H. Rahm & Rosella -?-

      (1) Kenneth Edward Rahm
           b. 28 November 1964 - Peer Co., Mich.
      (2) Cinthia Michelle Rahm
           b. 3 October 1968 - Macomb Co., Mich.

5. Edna Irene May
   b. 16 August 1913 - Cleveland Co, Okla.
   m. Henry Lloyd Wilson - 14 August 1932
   b. 16 April 1913 - McClain Co, Okla.
   son of Thedora Arthur Wilson & Millie Ann Morehead

   A. Kenneth Leo Wilson
      b. 20 January 1934 - Wayne, Okla.
      m. Betty Kackson - 2 October 1955 - Carson City,NV
         b. Kern Co., Calif.

      (1) Brenda Ann Wilson
          b. 28 July 1956 - Pittsburg, Contra Costa Co.
          California
          m. Lonnie English - Norcross, Ga.

          (a) Karrie Elizabeth English
              b. 4 May 1973 - Atlanta, Ga.

   Kenneth Wilson m. 2nd. Ruth -?-
                        b. 1932 - St. George, Utah
   B. Marilyn Sue Wilson
      b. 16 March 1936 - McClain Co., Okla.
      d. 22 February 1952 - Calif. - car accident
      bur. Delano, Calif.
   C. LaNitta June Wilson
      b. 28 September 1938 - Tulare, Calif.
      m. Melvin Dean Sims - 2 September 1955 - Tulare,CA
         b. 21 January 1935 - Paragould, Ark.

      (1) Pamelia Ann Sims
          b. 23 June 1956
      (2) Patti Denice Sims
          b. 7 September 1957
      (3) Meilssa Diann Sims
          b. 12 April 1966
      (4) Melvin Keith Sims
          b. 2 April 1969

   D. Bobby Dean Wilson
      b. 1 January 1940 - Bakersfield, Kern Co, Calif.
      m. Mary Lou Harris - 18 February 1962 - Las Vegas
         b. 26 August 1943 - Kalamazoo Co., Mich.

      (1) Jennifer Diana Wilson
          b. 12 May 1963 - Sacramento, Calif.
      (2) Jeffrey David Wilson
          b. 15 April 1964 - Sacramento, Calif.
      (3) Paul Jason Wilson
          b. and d. 14 September 1970 - Provo, Utah

        (4) Robert Loyd Wilson
           b. 14 January 1972 - American Fork, Utah
        (5) Michael Kenneth Wilson
           b. 8 January 1973 - American Fork, Utah
        (6) Jonathan David Wilson
           b. 29 January 1974 Boise, Idaho

  E. Sharon Ann Wilson
     b. 26 August 1944 - Lindsay, Tulare Co., Calif.
     m. Michael Ray Kent - 14 September 1962 - Las
       Vegas, NV
       b. 18 September 1944 - Bakersfield, Kern Co.,
         Calif.
         son of William Fred Kent & Marie Buttle
             b. 8 April 1915 - Watertown, Tenn.

    (1) Destry Lee Kent
       b. 11 April 1964 - Kern Co., Calif.
    (2) Kevin William Kent
       b. 2 July 1966 - Kern Co., Calif.

6. Lewis Jay May
  b. 6 January 1914
  m. Dixie Lee Woods - 16 December 1939 - Oklahoma City
  b. 12 April 19-?-
  dau. of James Swan Woods & Nancy Elizabeth Dillard

  A. Beauford Lynn May
     b. 3 January 1941
     m. Rosetta Fay McCleary - 1 August 1965 - Norman,
       Oklahoma

    (1) Larla Lynn May
       b. 5 June 1968

  B. Russell Wayne May
     b. 10 December 1948
     m. Jacqueta Fay Gathers

    (1) Jeffrey Wayne May
       b. 26 January 1969

  C. Paul Allen May
     b. 16 August 1954

7. Vernon Howard May
  b. 13 September 1915
  m. Opal Gertrude Thompson - 10 November 1945
  b. 17 December 1921
  dau. of Thomas David Thompson & Vera Hester
  Christmas

  A. Ralph Lee May
     b. 7 November 1946
     m. Carol Darlene Mays
       b. 16 August 1947
  B. Howard Glen May
     b. 3 November 1949

8. Robert Albert May
  b. 25 August 1917
  m. Joyce Gravely

  A. Myra Sue May
     b. 17 March 19-?-
     m. David F. Jarrell - 27 March 1970 - Pauls
       Valley, Calif.
  B. Bobette May
     b. 27 December 19-?-
  C. Ricky May
     b. 23 October 19-?-
  D. Valrie May
     b.   July 19-?-

9. Grace Evelyn May
  b. 29 October 1919
  m. Bernard Chassot

A. Linda Chassot
   m. Dwayne Cypert

   (1) Patricia Cypert
   (2)
   (3) Timothy Cypert

B. Stephenie Chassot
   b. 20 August 1956

10. Dorothy Jo May
    b. 16 April 1925 - McClain Co., Okla.
    m. Warren George Suchy - 26 January 1942 - McClain Co.
       b. 20 November 1920
       son of John Suchy & Dessie Odom

    A. John Warren Suchy
       b. 13 August 1947 - Waco, Texas
    B. Jennifer Suchy
       b. 30 September 1950 - Oklahoma City, Okla.
    C. Janelle Suchy
       b. 11 July 1955 - Oklahoma City, Okla.

11. Edwin Dale May
    b. 22 October 1928 - McClain Co., Okla.
    m. Ester Faye Bailey - 21 January 1959 - Oklahoma City
       dau. of Joseph Earnest Bailey & Maude Clara Russell

(h) William M. May
    b. 22 April 1883
    d. 3 May 1917
(i) Brazzie May
    b. 20 November 1884
    d. 10 November 1963 - Marion Co., Ala.
    bur. Siloam Church Cemetery - Fayette Co., Ala.
    m. Albert Roy Akers - 14 February 1909 - Marion Co., Ala
       b. 15 September 1886
       d. 22 February 1959 - Marion Co., Ala.
       bur. Siloam Church Cemetery
       son of Meridith Akers & Telitha Carlina Miller
                            dau. of C. Nathaniel Miller
                            and Martha Sarah Kennedy
                               dau. of Lee Roy Kennedy,
                               Judge of Lamar Co., Ala.
       grandson of Meridith Akers, Sr. & -?- Green, who
       came from Tenn. to Ala.

    1. Infant Daughter Akers
       b. and d. 8 May 1910
       bur. Siloam Baptist Cemetery
    2. Infant Daughter Akers
       b. 11 October 1912
       d. 14 October 1912
       bur. Siloam Baptist Cemetery
    3. Alma De Ette Akers
       b. 7 December 1914
       m. William Byron Taylor
    4. Infant Daughter Akers
       b. and d. 9 April 1919
       bur. Siloam Baptist Cemetery
    5. Hubert Lee Roy Akers
       b. 3 November 1921
       m. Clairena Taylor

(j) Dallas Haden May
    b. 8 October 1886 - Marion Co., Ala.
    m. Emma Jane Berryhill
       dau. of Thadius Berryhill & Ophelia Hall
(k) John Daniel May - (twin)
    b. 8 September 1888 - Marion Co., Ala.

(1) Permelia Ann May - (twin)
    b. 8 September 1888 - Marion Co., Ala.
    d. 15 November 1955 - Marion Co., Ala.
    bur. Old Union Primitive Baptist Cemetery - Fayette Co.
    m. John McDonald
        son of George McDonald & -?- Mobley
(m) Grandville Calhoun May - "Grant"
    b. 23 June 1890 - Marion Co., Ala.
    d. 16 April - 1936
    bur. Siloam Baptist Church Cemetery - Fayette Co., Ala.
    m. Aver Mae Porter - 1914
        b. September 1893 - Fayette Co., Ala.
        dau. of Anderew Jackson Porter & Connie Emer Loftis
                b. 16 September 1865   b. 15 February 1870
                d. 16 October 1895   d. 24 October 1924
                bur. Musgrove Chapel Cemetery - both

    1. Roy May
        b. 3 September 1915 - Fayette Co., Ala.
        m. Eugenia Josephine Williams - "Jene" - 1 May 1946 -
           Colbert Co., Ala.
           b. 2 September 1923 - Colbert Co., Ala.
           dau. of Oliver Eugene Williams & Alice Rivers
                                            McMahon
                    b. 22 November 1888-Ark. b. 30 March 1896
                                                Iuka, Miss.

        A. Richard Edwin May
           b. 7 June 1950 - Florence, Ala.
        B. Warren Oliver May
           b. 4 May 1953 - Florence, Ala.

    2. Oveat Porter May
        b. 5 September 1917 - Fayette Co., Ala.
        m. Aline Smith

        A. Gary May
           b. September 1952 - Indianopolis, Ind.

    3. Joe Neal May
        b. 30 September 1922 - Fayette Co., Ala.
        m. Wilma Lee
           b. 1922
           d. October 1966
           bur. City Cemetery - Winfield, Ala.

        A. Robert Joe May
           b. 10 March 1947

    4. Ellis May
        b. 13 August 1926 - Fayette Co., Ala.

(n) Infant Son May
    b. and d. 1896 - Fayette Co., Ala.
    bur. Siloam Cemetery
(o) Washington Foy May
    b. 6 June 1894 - Fayette Co., Ala.
(p) Dona Melinda May
    b. 21 November 1898 - Fayette Co., Ala.
    m. Hosea Moss Morris - 26 November 1915 - Fayette Co.
       b. 4 August 1893 - Ga.
       d. 15 May 1966 - Purcell, Okla.
       bur. Hillside Cemetery - Purcell, Okla.

    1. Rayferd Morris
        b. 11 October 1916 - Fayette Co., Ala.
        m. Phyllis Jane Conger - 28 June 1945 - Los Angeles
           Co., Calif.
           b. 1 April 1928
           dau. of Albert R. Conger & Emily -?-

A. Sharon Rae Morris
   b. 12 February 1947
   m. Charles Davis - 21 December 1968 - Sacramento,
      California
B. Jerry Lee Morris
   b. 21 June 1948
C. Ronald Gene Morris
   b. 5 June 1949
D. Victoria Jeanette Morris
   b. 10 May 1964

2. Willis J. Morris
   b. 18 November 1918 - Fayette Co., Ala.
   m. Frieda M. Zuck - 3 May 1942 - Cabool, Mo.
      b. 3 March 1921 - Eldorado, Kan.

   A. Catherine L. Morris
      b. 24 April 1948 - Cabool, Mo.
      m. Wendell E. Dennis - 1 November 1964 - Cabool
         b. 26 April 1946 - Mt. Grove, Mo.

      (1) James Warren Dennis
          b. 27 December 1965

   B. Susan Morris
      b. 29 September 1949 - Cabool, Mo.
      m. Ronald Allen Deeds - 27 May 1967 - Cabool
         b. 7 December 1947 - Mt. Grove, Mo.
   C. David Glen Morris
      b. 19 December 1950 - Cabool, Mo.
      m. Margaret Taylor - 16 August 1968 - Mt. Grove
         b. 14 April 1052
   D. William Dean Morris
      b. 5 July 1958 - Cabool, Mo.

3. Margie Lou Morris
   b. 15 June 1920 - Fayette Co., Ala.
   m. Ural Don Carpenter - 30 January 1937
   son of Marvin R. Carpenter & Hazel -?-

   A. Laverna Mae Carpenter
      m. -?- Long

      (1) Jimmy Don Long
          b. 27 May 1958
      (2) Lisa Dian Long
          b. February 1961

      Laverna Mae Carpenter
      m. 2nd. Duel Thompson

   B. Don Morris Carpenter
      b. 16 April 1942
      m. Vicki Morris - 25 March 1967

      (1) Bryon Morris Carpenter

   C. Glenda Faye Carpenter
      m. Johnnie Paul Yancy - 28 April 1964

      (1) Johnnie Paul Yancy, Jr.

   D. Judy Ann Carpenter
      m. Dennis Scroggins - 14 August 1967
   E. Mark Anthony Carpenter
      b. and d. 19 October 1956 - Oklahoma City
      bur. Sunnyland Cemetery - Oklahome City, Okla.

4. Una Mae Morris
   b. 6 May 1922 - Cleveland Co., Okla.
   m. James Kenneth Murnan - 10 July 1942 - Norman, OK
      b. 8 September 1920 - Noble, Okla.

A. Kenneth Ray Murnan
   b. 27 May 1945 - Purcell, Okla.
   m. Sandra Kay Eller - 17 March 1965 - Stillwater
      b. 3 May 1947 - Fritch, Texas

   (1) Shawn Ray Murnan
       b. 6 February 1968 - Chickasha, Okla.
   (2) Brandi Kay Murnan
       b. 21 December 1969 - Seminole, Okla.

5. Helen Frances Morris
   b. 11 July 1924
   m. Chester LaMoine Zuck - 24 July 1946 - Wichita, KS
      b. 15 November 1919
   son of Guy Glen Zuck & Cholor Helen Morehead

   A. Chester LaMoine Zuck, Jr.
      b. 12 June 1947
      m. Marilyn Lou Barnhart - 17 September 1966 -
         Eldon, Mo.
         b. 27 May 1947

      (1) Robert Eugene Zuck
          b. 10 September 1969

6. Harold Moss Morris
   b. 16 October 1926 - Okla.
   m. Clara Va. Conger - 15 February 1947 - Eldorado, AR
      b. 8 November 1924 - Eldorado, Ark.
   dau. of Carl Samuel Conger & Birdie Eunice French

   A. Harold Glen Morris
      b. 2 December 1949 - Purcell, Okla.
      m. Anita Harrington - 12 April 1969 - Wayne, Okla
         b. 18 September 1952
         dau. of Virgil Harrington & Helen Brakefield
   B. Bobby Jack Morris
      b. 14 July 1952
      d. 16 July 1954 - Purcell, Okla.
      bur. Hillside Cemetery - Purcell, Okla.
   C. Joe Wayne Morris
      b. 13 April 1956 - Purcell, Okla.
   D. Janey Lynn Morris
      b. 30 April 1957 - Purcell, Okla.

7. Juanita Jo Morris
   b. 25 November 1929 - Okla.
   m. Kenneth A. Miller - 15 September 1951 - Wayne, OK
      b. 7 September 1924
   son of Ira A. Miller & Ossie Eliz. Fickle

   A. Kerry Joe Miller
      b. 24 July 1952
   B. Nancy Susan Miller
      b. 6 June 1954
   C. Mark Lynn Miler
      b. 6 December 1958

8. Billie Jean Morris
   b. 1 February 1932 - Purcell, Okla.
   m. Donald Lee Schmidt - 13 September 1963 - Harris
      County, Texas
      b. 16 April 1926
   son of W. C. Schmidt & Sue -?-

   A. Melinda Sue Schmidt
      b. 16 January 1967

(q) Gordy Olen May
    b. 29 July 1902 - Fayette Co., Ala.

(3) Polly Ann May
    b. 1852 - approx.
    m. Lark Akers
    This family moved to Texas, and there is no information.

(4) Rile May
    m. Jocie -?-
    m. 2nd. -?- and moved around Steans, Miss. They raised a
        family, but there is no further information available.
(5) Jim May
    b. 1855 - approx.
    m. "Bunk" Melton

    (a) Lon May
        m. Anie Owings

        1. Vennon May
        2. Lorene May
        3. Gurlene May
        4. Lennen May
        5. Odean May
        6. Bessie May
           m. John Smith

           A.   Balcas Smith   B. and C. Daughthers Smith
           D.   Thurmon Smith
    (b) Bessie May
    (c) Polly Ann May
        m. "Lumb" Burlson

        1. Girtrue Burlson
        2. Alnie Burlson
        3. Wymon Burlson
        4. Dolton Burlson
        5. Carry Lee Burlson
        6. Inilee Burlson

    (d) Moman May
        m. -?-
        has three sons
    (e) Tess May
        m. Ivas Dodson

        1. Engle Dodson
        2. Fermon Dodson
        3. Mary Lue Dodson
        4. Suetro Dodson

    (f) Cole May
        m. Lena Owings

        1. Perl May
        2. Owings May
        3. Orin May
        4. Helen May
        5. Mary May
        6. Brownie May
        7. Little May
        8. Dane May

    (g) Lessie May
        m. Curt Mobly

        1. Claudie Lee Mobly
        2. Ettma Mobly
        3. Eve Nell Mobly
        4. Daughter Mobly
        5. Edd Mobly

    Jim May m. 2nd. Bula Gibson

    (h) Larnce May
        died as a youngster
    (i) Earnest May
        m. Effie Pyron
        have four daughters and two sons
    (j) LouCella May
        died as a young lady

        (k) Florine May
            m. Lomaz Span
            have two sons and a daughter

    (6) John May
        b. 1857 - approx.
        m. Alacia Kirkland
            dau. of Will Kirkland & -?-

        (a) Mattie May
            m. Henry McDonald

            1. Alton McDonald
            2. Hattie McDonald
            3. Girtie McDonald
            4. Ben McDonald
            5. Huston McDonald

        (b) Hattie May
            m. Cleve Franks
        (c) Carrie May
            m. Frank Bowling
        (d) Walter May
            m. Malta -?-
        (e) Carlos May
            m. Cloe Stanford
        (f) Luther May
        (g) Ila May

    (7) Grant May
        b. 1859 approx.
        d. as a young man
    (8) Ment May
        b. 1860 approx.
        m. Becckie Kirk

        (a) Velma May
        (b) Luis May
        (c) Fred May
        (d) Carl May
        (e) Rayburn May
        (f) Arnal May
        (g) Marie May
        (h) Baisol May

B. Solomon A. Ward
   b. 1831 - Marion Co., Ala.
   d. -?-, but living 1860 at time of Marion Co., Ala. Census
   m. Lucy A. P. -?-
      b. 1830 - Tenn.
      d. -?- , living at time of 1860 census

   (1) Willis W. Ward
       b. 1854 - Marion Co., Ala.
   (2) Mary J. Ward
       b. 1853 - Marion Co., Ala.
       d. 1932
       bur. Old Union Primitve Baptist Cemetery
       m. Miles W. Kirkland - 5 February 1874 - Fayette Co., Ala.
          b. 1845
   (3) John H. Ward
       b. 1860 - Marion Co., Ala.

C. Robert P. Ward
   b. 1833 - Marion Co., Ala.
   m. Mariah L. Thompson
      b. 1836 - Ala.
      dau. of Charity -?- Thompson
               b. 1807 - NC - living in 1860

   (1) Mary F. Ward
       b. 1855 - Marion Co., Ala.

        (2) Martha M. Ward
            b. 1856 - Marion Co., Ala.
        (3) Nancy M. Ward
            b. 1859 - Marion Co., Ala.

    D. Benjamin Franklin Ward
        b. 30 November 1835 - Marion Co., Ala.
        d. 19 November 1906 - Fayette Co., Ala.
        bur. Siloam Baptist Cemetery - Fayette Co., Ala.
        m. Mary M. -?-
            b. 2 June 1838 - Ga.
            d. 1 September 1926
            bur. Siloam Baptist Cemetery

        (1) Rebecca A. Ward
            b. 18 March 1857 - Marion Co., Ala.
            d. 25 October 1873
            bur. Siloam Baptist Cemetery
        (2) James W. Ward
            b. 1858 - Marion Co., Ala.
            d. 1946
            bur. Harmony Grove Cemetery - Fayette Co., Ala.
            m. Julia M. -?-
                b. 1870
                d. 1 February 1958
                bur. Harmony Grove Cemetery
        (3) Benjamin LaFayette Ward
            b. 8 June 1860 - Marion Co., Ala.
            d. 13 May 1923
            bur. Siloam Baptist Cemetery
            m. Etta Roberts
                b. 10 September 1869
                d. 8 March 1939
                bur. Siloam Baptist Cemetery

            (a) T. Bailey Ward
                m. Exie Perry
                   dau. of Lee Perry

                1. Allen Ward
                   m. Audrie Weeks
                2. Thomas Thaman Ward
                   m. Sarah Grey
                3. Clara Etta Ward
                4. Frankie Nell Ward
                5. Dortha Ward
                6. Jene Ward

            (b) Clarence Ward
            (c) Mitto Ward
                m. Jerry McCombs
                   bur. Siloam Baptist Cemetery

                1. Euthel McCombs
                   b. December 1914
                   d. 1941
                   bur. Siloam Baptist Cemetery
                2. Jammie Nell McCombs
                   m. Dalton Morrison
                3. Buford McCombs
                4. Luie McCombs
                5. Morris McCombs
                6. Dan McCombs

            (d) Avis Ward
                m. John Riley

                1. Johnnie Gray Riley

            (e) Hester Ward
                m. Letha Westbrook
                have four children

        (f) Uless P. Ward
            b. 1901
            m. Bertha Dodd Agee
               b. 1910
               d. 1964

            1. Mary Ward
               b. July 1938
            2. Benjamin Lafayette Ward
               b. 6 March 1945
               d. 10 October 1946
               bur. Siloam Baptist Cemetery
            3. Daughter Ward
            4. Daughter Ward
            5. Son Ward
            6. Son Ward

E. Jane Hattie V. Ward
   b. 22 November 1836 - Marion Co., Ala.
   d. 24 November 1886 - Fayette Co., Ala.
   bur. Old Union Primitive Baptist Cemetery

F. James N. Ward
   b. 2 June 1839 - Marion Co., Ala.
   d. 26 November 1917
   bur. Old Union Primitive Baptist Cemetery
   m. Arzeley (or Onzelia) Bynum - 9 January 1879 - Fayette Co.
      b. 12 March 1855
      d. 5 May 1924
      bur. Old Union Primitive Baptist Cemetery

G. John W. Ward
   b. 17 November 1841 - Marion Co., Ala.
   d. 19 November 1906
   bur. Old Union Primitive Baptist Cemetery
   m. Emily C. McGaha - 3 September 1877 - Fayette Co., Ala.
      b. 13 January 1847
      d. 21 August 1915
      bur. Old Union Primitive Baptist Cemetery

   (1) Infant Son Ward
       b. 1890
       d. 1891
       bur. Siloam Baptist Cemetery
   (2) Elizabeth Lurania Ward
       b. 4 March 1881
       d. 31 July 1964
       bur. Hillside Cemetery - Purcell, Okla.
       m. Aucie Woodville Couch - 28 December 1899
          b. 1875
          d. June 1956 - Purcell, Okla.
          bur. Hillside Cemetery - Purcell, Okla.
   (3) Ralston Ward
       m. Molly Musgrove

       (a) Stella Ward
           m. Houston Couch

H. Willis Monroe Ward, Jr.
   b. 5 March 1846 - Marion Co., Ala.
   d. 2 November 1921 - Fayette Co., Ala.
   bur. Old Union Primitive Baptist Cemetery
   m. Margaret Cordelia Kirkland - 7 December 1869 - Fayette Co.
      b. 23 September 1851
      d. 3 December 1936
      bur. Old Union Primitive Baptist Cemetery
      dau. of J. C. Krikland & Permelia -?-
                 b. 4 April 1812 b. 6 February 1817
                 d. 12 Nov. 1888 d. 26 October 1903

(1) James Dallas Ward
    b. 10 September 1870 - Fayette Co., Ala.
    d. 26 March 1952 - Pauls Valley, Okla.
    bur. Pauls Valley Cemetery
    m. Martha Frances Couch - 5 January 1890
        b. 1872 - Marion Co., Ala.
        d. 29 April 1951 - Pauls Valley, Okla.
        bur. Pauls Valley, Okla.
        dau. of William "Buck" Couch & Katherine Y. Harris
                b. 1833 - Ala.   b. 1835 - Ala.

    (a) William Walter Ward
        b. 28 October 1890
        d. 16 June 1892 - Fayette Co., Ala.
        bur. Zion Cemetery - Winfield, Ala.
    (b) Eddie Lee Ward
        b. 3 September 1892 - Fayette Co., Ala.
        m. Curtis Whitehead - 26 August 1912 - Pauls Valley

        1. Clifton Ward Whitehead
            b. 3 November 1913 - Pauls Valley, Okla.
            m. Geneveve Tapscott

            A. Larry Whitehead
                b. 15 April 1938 - Norman, Okla.
                m. Nancy Tate - 22 August 1958
            B. Martha Lynn Whitehead
                b. 28 July 1946 - Oklahoma City, Okla.
                m. Allen Carter - 10 August 1964

                (1) Ann Dee Carter
                    b. 8 May 1965

        2. William Whitehead - "Bill"
            b. 4 February 1918 - Pauls Valley, Okla.
            m. Mary Howell

            A. Billy Whitehead
                b. 14 July 1943 - Memphis, Tenn.
            B. Stephen Dallas Whitehead
                b. 27 July 1957

    (c) Claud Ward
        b. 18 August 1894 - Fayette Co., Ala.
        d. 22 October 1956 - Pauls Valley, Okla.
        bur. Pauls Valley, Okla.
    (d) Ollie Lenora Ward
        b. 22 March 1898 - Fayette Co., Ala.
        m. Jim Webster - 2 September 1922

        1. Kathleen Webster
            b. 3 August 1923 - Whitehead, Okla.
            m. Earl Clayton Roberts - 15 August 1944 - Las Vegas
                b. 23 March 1924 - Chicopee Falls, Mass.

            A. Kathy Dean Roberts
                b. 27 June 1948 - Taft, Calif.

        2. Grace Dean Webster
            b. 22 April 1928 - Pauls Valley, Okla.
            m. Thomas Brown - 23 May 1948 - Bakersfield, Calif.

            A. Amanda Brown
                b. 11 May 1953 - Tampa, Fla.
            B. Rebecca Brown
                b. 22 October 1956 - Okinawa
            C. Tamara Brown
                b. 8 May 1958 - Victoria, Texas
            D. Matthew James Brown
                b. 6 August 1964 - Wiesbader, Germany

    (e) Mary Lena Ward
        b. 28 May 1901 - Coke Co., Texas
        d. 27 March 1909 - Coke Co., Texas
        bur. Coke Co., Texas

236

(f) Opal Ward
    b. 18 March 1905 - Coke Co., Texas
    d. 13 January 1955 - Pauls Valley, Okla.
    bur. Pauls Valley Cemetery
    m. Chester Barrett - 17 April 1926
(g) William Newman Ward
    b. 21 March 1909 - Coke Co., Texas
    m. Fay -?- - 10 June 1933

    1. James Ray Ward
       b. 22 June 1934
       m. Reba Jo Chaufty

       A. Mikkie Ward
          b. 8 June 1954 - Sulphur, Okla
       B. Jay Ward
          b. 2 October 1957 - Pauls Valley, Okla.
       C. Lisa Ward
          b. June 1963 - Wilburton, Okla.

(2) Benjamin Salvador Ward - "Vader"
    b. 12 February 1872 - Fayette Co., Ala.
    d. 4 March 1936
    bur. City Cemetery - Winfield, Ala.
    m. Cora Couch - 19 December 1907
       b. 1878
       d. 1964
       bur. City Cemetery - Winfield, Ala.
       dau. of Meredith Jacob Couch & Susan C. Berryhill
                   b.   1848   b. 1850
                   d.   1908   d. 1922

    (a) Velma Ward
        b. 4 October 1908
        m. Carl Berryhill - 27 June 1925
           b. 7 November 1905
           son of John Robert Berryhill & Zora Williams

        1. Willowdean Berryhill
           b. 13 July 1926
           m. Readus Danial Fountain - 19 July 1945

           A. James Richard Fountain
              b. 6 August 1946
              m. Judy Saunders - 31 December 1965
           B. Terry Edward Fountain
              b. 16 November 1955

        2. Mary Sue Berryhill
           b. 26 February 1928
        3. Donna Sue Berryhill
           b. 8 September 1954 (twin)
        4. Loyd David Berryhill
           b. 8 September 1954 (twin)
        5. Pamela Louise Berryhill
           b. 17 August 1955
        6. Carl Daniel Berryhill
           b. 12 April 1957
        7. Michael Wayne Berryhill
           b. 16 November 1958

    (b) Willis Monroe Ward
        b. 23 April 1910
        m. Sarah Joyce Smith - 16 July 1958

        1. Elizabeth Ann Ward
           b. 22 November 1960

    (c) Sallie Lee Ward
        b. 4 December 1912
        m. Valcus Webster - 27 October 1935

        1. Betty Jo Webster
           b. 22 November 1936
           m. Wilburn Perry - 21 May 1955

237

                    A. James Michael Perry
                       b. 29 February 1956
                    B. Richard Lee Perry
                       b. 3 December 1958
                    C. Tammy Perry
                       b. 13 October 1961

             2. James Ward Webster
                b. 24 April 1938
                m. Doris Perry - 9 March 1963

                    A. Mary Allison Webster
                       b. 17 January 1964

        (d) Willie Mae Ward
            b. 16 July 1915 - Fayette Co., Ala.
        (e) Infant Ward
            b. and d. 15 March 1917
            bur. Harmony Grove Cemetery
        (f) Jesse Cleveland Ward
            b. 2 May 1918
            m. Jean White - 16 November 1940

(3) Martha Ann Ward
    b. 16 August 1873 - Fayette Co., Ala.
    d. 22 July 1931 - Winfield, Ala.
    bur. City Cemetery - Winfield, Ala.
    m. Robert Andrew Couch - 17 February 1897 - Fayette Co., Ala.
      b. 26 August 1871 - Fayette Co., Ala.
      d. 28 January 1920 - Wayne, Okla.
      bur. City Cemetery - Winfield, Ala.
      son of Meredith Jacob Couch & Susan C. Berryhill
           b. 1846   b. 1850   See Couch
           d. 1908   d. 1922   Family

(4) Harvey Watson Ward
    b. 30 June 1875 - Fayette Co., Ala.
    d. 22 August 1959
    m. Irene Stephenson - 1906

    (a) Pauline Ward
        m. Gillard Hunt

        1. Jane Hunt
        2. Tommy Hunt
        3. John Hunt

    (b) Vera Nell Ward
        m. Whitfield T. Huson
    (c) Harvey Watson Ward, Jr.
        b. 3 February 1920
        d. 1965
        m. Carolyn Thornton

        1. Harvey Watson Ward, III

(5) Susan Florence Ward
    b. 19 May 1877 - Fayette Co., Ala.
    d. 27 December 1958
    bur. City Cemetery - Winfield, Ala.
    m. David S. Harris - 3 March 1901
      b. 11 April 1876
      d. 9 December 1944
      bur. City Cemetery - Winfield, Ala.
      son of George Shaffer Harris & Margaret Ann Berryhill
           b. 23 July 1837   b. 22 May 1842
           d. 10 August 1913   d. 30 October 1907
      See Harris family
(6) Pervey Willis Ward
    b. 8 March 1879
    d. 5 June 1947
    bur. Old Union Primitive Baptist Cemetery

(7) William Hughell Ward
    b. 24 January 1881
    d. 7 August 1944
    m. Carrie Belle Hodges

    (a) Clytee Ward
        m. James Spicer

        1. Jane Hodges Spicer
        2. Ann Spicer
        3. Jamie Spicer

    (b) William Hodges Ward
        d. Blount Co., Ala.
        bur. Oneonata Cemetery - Oneonata, Ala.
        m. Carolyn Bynum

        1. William Ward - "Bill"

(8) Mittie Bell Ward
    b. 26 January 1882
    d. 24 January 1922 - Fayette Co., Ala.
    bur. Musgrove Cemetery - Fayette Co., Ala.
    m. Willie Franklin Smith - 19 November 1905
       b. 18 April 1884

    (a) Berniece Smith
        b. 1906/1907
        m. George B. Harris
           b. 23 October 1901
           d. 8 March 1963
    (b) Clyde Franklin Smith
        b. 28 October 1908 - Fayette Co., Ala.
        m. Mary Elizabeth Wood

        1. William Franklin Smith - "Frank"
           b. 1 September 1942
           m. Cecelia Ann Mays

           A. Wm. Franklin Smith, II
              b. 2 September 1962

    (c) Bonnie Lee Smith
        b. 1910 approx - Fayette Co., Ala.
    (d) Cecil Ward Smith
        b. 19 April 1913
        m. Hazel Virginia Holliman - 21 January 1939 - Fayette CO

        1. Ted Smith

    (e) Jo Nell Smith
        b. 23 December 1916
        d. 5 June 1921 - Fayette Co., Ala.
        bur. Musgrove Chapel Cemetery - Fayette Co., Ala.

 (9) Hattie Virginia Ward
     b. 22 November 1886
     d. 24 July 1887 - Fayette Co., Ala.
(10) Emma Lee Ward
     b. 15 July 1888 - Fayette Co., Ala.
(11) Houston Monroe Ward
     b. 4 December 1891
     d. 6 February 1957
     bur. Old Union Primitive Baptist Cemetery - Fayette Co., Ala.
(12) Jesse Morgan Ward
     b. 8 November 1893 - Fayette Co., Ala.
     m. Pearlie Webster

     (a) Kenneth Ward
         b. 28 September 1923
         m. Carrie Fox

         1. Daughter Ward

(b) Marion Ward
     b. 12 January 1926
     m. John Craig

     1. Susan Craig
        b. 18 September 1948
     2. Joe Craig
        b. 6 December 1950
     3. Carol Craig
        b. 23 August 1956
     4. Mandy Craig
        b. 31 May 1965

(c) Margaret Lynn Ward
     b. 8 March 1929
     m. William H. Havens

     1. Catherine Ann Havens
        b. 3 November 1952
     2. Lynda Sue Havens
        b. 3 January 1954
     3. Jannett Lee Havens
        b. 18 June 1955

(d) Willie Hal Ward
     b. 19 May 1932
     m. Bobbie Ferguson

     1. Jess Willis Ward
        b. 5 December 1955
     2. Robin Lynn Ward
        b. 22 February 1957
     3. Henry Wayne Ward
        b.   September 1958
     4. April Deone Ward
        b.   October 1959

(e) Robert Howard Ward
     b. 15 December 1934
     m. Cynthia Fisher
        b.   January 1938

     1. Wm. Kenny Ward
        b. 23 January 1957
     2. Cindy Ward
        b.   October 1959
     3. Jerry Ward

(13) Carolyn Ward
     b. 7 January 1899 - Fayette Co., Ala.
     m. Arnold Thomas Sizemore
        son of Joel Rufus Sizemore & Virgie Flynn

     (a) Caroline Sizemore
          b. 18 December 1922 - Jefferson Co., Ala.
          m. Robert Warren Andrews

          1. Patricia Carol Andrew - "Pat"
             b. 3 November 1943 - Corpus Christi, Texas
             m. James Manley Fogle - 15 August 1964
          2. Robert Warren Andrews, Jr. - "Bob"
             b..19 October 1945 - Pa.

I. Rebecca E. Ward
     b. 1849 - Marion Co., Ala.
     d. Living in 1860, age 10 years in her parents' home. No
        further information is available on her.

1830 Franklin Co., Tenn. Federal Census   page 57
Mary Ward
1 m. 5/10
1 m.15/20
1 m.20/30 (1800-1810) Willis M. Ward who m. Mary "Polly" Berryhill
2 f. 5/10
1 f.10/15
1 f.20/30 (1800-1810) Mary "Polly" Berryhill
1 f.40/50 (1780-1790) Mary Ward, mother of Willis M. Ward, who shows as
                      head of her household.

1840 Marion Co., Ala. #51
Willis Ward
1 m. under 5 yrs.
1 m. 30/40 (1800-1810) Willis Ward
1 m. 60/70 cannot account for him.
1 f. under 5 years
1 f. 10/15
1 f. 15/20
2 f. 30/40 (1800-1810) Mary Polly Berryhill Ward is one, and we know
                       from later census, Rebecca Ward, sister of Willis
                       Ward lived with the family.

1850 Marion Co., Ala. 35/36
Willis Ward   48 M.   N.C.   b. 1802
Mary A.   "   44 F   Ga.   1806 - Mary A. Polly Berryhill
America   "   22 F   Tenn.   1828
Solomon A."   19 M   Ala.   1831 - Came to Ala before Alex
Robert P. "   17 M   Ala.   1833
Benjamin F. Ward   15 M   Ala.   1835
Jane   "   13 F   Ala.   1837
James N.   "   11 M   Ala.   1839
John W.   "   9 M   Ala.   1841
Willis M.   "   5 M   Ala.   1845
Rebecca   "   1 F   Ala.   1849
Rebecca   "   44 F   S. C.   1806 - Sister of Willis Ward'

1860 - Marion Co., Ala. 339/347 - p. 50 3 July 1860 P.O. Aston Store, Ala
Willis Ward   58 M   S.C.   1802
Mary   "   53 F   Ga.   1807
James N.   "   21 M   Ala.   1839
John W.   "   18 M   Ala.   1842
Willis M. "   14 M   Ala.   1846
Rebecca E. Ward   10 F   Ala.   1850

This tells us either Rebecca Ward, born 1806, sister of Willis Ward,
has either died, or married, or was living elsewhere.

338/346 p 50
Robert Ward   26 M   Ala.   1834
Mariah L. "   24 F   Ala.   1836 - Mariah L. Thompson
Mary F.   "   5 F   Ala.   1855
Martha M. "   4 F   Ala.   1856
Nancy M. "   10/12 F   Ala.   1859
Charity Thompson   53 F   N. C.   1807 Mother of Mariah L.

337/345 p 50
Benjamin F. Ward   24 M   Ala.   1836
Mary M.   "   22 F   Ga.   1838
Rebecca A.   "   3 F   Ala.   1857 - see note below
James W.   "   1 M   Ala.   1859
Benjamin L.   :   2/12 M   Ala.   1860

Note that all three of the above households live next door to each other.
Rebecca was b. 17 march 1857, d. 25 October 1873, bur. Siloam Baptist Ceme.

327/325 p. 48
Solomon Ward   28 M.   Ala.   1832   Mary J. Ward 2 F. Ala. 1858
Lucy A. P. "   30 F   Tenn. 1830   John H. Ward
Willis W. "   6 M   Ala.   1854   5/12 M Ala. 1860

241

3. Lensfield Berryhill
   b. 1807 - Gerogia, perhaps near Augusta
   m. -?-
      b. 1810/1815
   A. Son Berryhill
      b. 1826/1830 - Franklin Co., Tenn.
   B. Daughter Berryhill
      b/ 1826/1830 - Franklin Co., Tenn.

1830 Franklin Co., Tenn. p 112
Lensfield Berryhill
1 m. under 5 (1826-1830)
1 m. 20-30   (1800-1810) Lensfield Berryhill
1 f. under 5 (1826-1830)
1 f. 15/20   (1810-1815) Wife of Lensfield

I did not follow up on census, marriages, Wills, etc. on Lensfield Berryhill because of lack of time, and many have worked on the Berryhills. So
perhaps someone with pick up where I left off. Many still there as late
as 1874.

Franklin Co., Tenn. Marriages
Martha Berryhill & Oliver M. Posey   25 January 1848
Martha Berryhill & Henry W. Walls   22 July   1852
Lensfield Berryhill & Mary A. Wilks   17 January 1854
Lewis Berryhill & Sarah Mahafee   27 February1863
Susan Berryhill & Hiram Mahathy   10 October 1868
Jane Berryhill & R. E. Sharp   31 August 1872
Joe Berryhill & Mary Delzell   17 December1874

4. Edward Berryhill - "Edd"
   b. 4 April 1813 - near Winchester, Franklin Co., Tenn.
   d. 6 October 1875 - Fayette Co., Ala.
   bur. Berryhill Family Cemetery
   m. Nancy E. Berryhill
      b. 1819 - Tenn. possibly Franklin Co.
      d. 21 January 1889 - Fayette Co, Ala.
      bur. Berryhill Family Cemetery
      dau. of Willaim Berryhill & Margaret Weeks
            b. 1781 - Ga.   b. 1785
   See William Berryhill's Family

5. Thomas Berryhill - "Tommy"
   b. 9 May 1815 - near Winchester, Franklin Co., Tenn.
   d. 17 May 1917 - Hinds Co., Miss. near Utica
   bur. Weeks Cemetery - 3½ miles east of Utica
   m. Basheba Berryhill - "Bashey"
      b. 9 May 1817 - possibly in Franklin Co., Tenn.
      d. 6 February 1892 - Hinds Co., Miss.
      bur. Weeks Cemetery
      dau. of William Berryhill & Margaret Weeks
            b. 1781 - Ga.   b. 1785
   See William Berryhill's Family

CHAPTER III

THE

WILLIAM

BERRYHILL

FAMILY

CHAPTER III

WILLIAM BERRYHILL'S LAND PATENT

No. 199, Vol. 8
In the name of the State of Texas
To all to whom these presents shall come know ye, I George T. Wood,
Governor of the State aforesaid, by virtue of the power invested in me by
law and in accordance with the laws of said State in such case made and
provided do by these presents grant to WILLIAM BERRYHILL his heirs or
assigns forever. One league and one labor of land, situated and described
as follows:

I Harrison District, Upshur County about nine miles N by W from Gilmer
on the waters of Lillys Creek by virtue of Certificate No. 542 issued to
said WILLIAM BERRYHILL by the board of land Commissioners of Shelby County
on the 8th day of October, 1838.

Beginning at a SW corner of M. Cartwright's survey a stake on the S.
boundary of survey No. 45, from which a hickory marked J.H. bears S 55 W
16½ varas a hickory marked M C bears N 69 degrees W 4&8/10 varas;

Thence West with survey No. 45 and N Lilly and W.H. Teals surveys at 2829
varas the Cherokee Tract at five thousand and ninety nine varas a stake
from which a Black Jack marker M.L. bears S 19 degrees E 2 varas a Pine
marked "X" bears N 88 degrees E 14
varas: thence South at 1400 varas a branch at five thousand and ninety-
nine varas a stake S 82½ W 6 and 6/10 varas both marked J.H.B.; thence
East at 1850 varas a spring branch at 3370 varas same at 3690 varas said
tract at five thousand and ninety-nine varas a stake on the W boundary of
survey No. 74 from which a Red Oak bears S 18 degrees E 6 and 8/10 varas
another bears N 54 degrees W 1 varas both marked J.B.B.W.L.B.X.

Thence North at five thousand and ninety-nine varas the beginning. Hereby relinquishing to him the said WILLIAM BERRYHILL and his heirs or
assigns forever all the right and title in and to said land heretofore
held and possessed by the said State and I do hereby issue this Letter
Patent - for the same.

In Testimony whereof, I have caused the seal of the State to be affixed
as well as the seal of the General land office.

Done at the City of Austin on the eleventh day of December in the year of
our Lord one thousand eight hundred and forty - eight.

George T. Wood, Governor

Commissioner of the GL. LD. Office.
   The above land patent was filed in lffice at two o'clock on the 11th
day of April A.D., 1849.

Copy secured: Given under my hand andseal of office at Gilmer, Texas,
this the 6th day of May, A.D. 1850, James Poole, County Clerk, Upshur
County, Texas

We do not know the connection between these two men we find in Rusk Co.,
Texas, and the Berryhills in Alabama, but apparently there is some since
we note that William Berryhill born 1791 in Georgia shows in Alabama by
1836, approximately the same time those from Tenn. came into Marion Co.,
Ala. with old Alexander Berryhill, Rev. Pensioner. From the birth states
of William's children, he stayed in Ala. until after 1845, yet was in
Texas by 1850, where he joined his brother, Thomas, it would seem.

1850 Rusk Co., Texas Federal Census 100/100
William Berryhill   59 M   Ga.   b. 1791 - farmer $300.00
Georgia   "   22 F   Ga.   1828 - daughter
John   "   33 M   Ga.   1817 - son
Robert   "   24 M   Ga.   1826 - son
Andrew   "   20 M   Ga.   1830 - son
Nathaniel   "   18 M   Ga.   1832 - son
America M. S.   "   14 F   Ala.   1836 - daughter - WB now in Ala.
William   "   5 M   Ala.   1845 - son

Apparently his wife died after 1845, yet before 1850.

Nathaniel Berryhill, born 1832 in Georgia, is the one who gave some
testimony in Indian Territory in Oklahoma and Mr. Will Price now
deceased, of Utica, Miss. was very disturbed and could not understand
how "Nathan" could give it, as he felt Nathan did not know his family.
But we now know from census that indeed Nathan did know his own family
lines. He testified in 1893 in Okumlgee, Oklahoma.

1850 Rusk Co., Texas 193/193 September 28, 1850
Thomas Berryhill   45 M   Ga.   1805 - farmer 150.00
Elizabeth   "   45 F   Ga.   1805
Albin   "   16 M   Ark.   1834 - TB arrived through Ark.
Sophronia   "   15 F   Ark.   1835
Millinda   "   12 F   Ark.   1838
Alonzo   "   8 M   Texas   1842 - now in Texas
Julia A.   "   5 F   Texas   1845
John   "   4 M   Texas   1846
Jane   "   3 F   Texas   1847

Rusk Co., Texas Marriages
Georgianna Berryhill & Vardy J. Wells   23 October 1850
Clarindy Berryhill & Samuel Self   1 January 1852
America M. S. Berryhill & John C. Self   25 January 1853
Melinda A. Berryhill & John Douglas   12 April   1853
Julia A. Berryhill & Thomas Swain   19 December 1867
John Berryhill & Mrs. Mary P. Baggett   30 August 1870

Probate Records of Rusk Co., Texas
John Berryhill, deceased, case #281, filed 25 March 1853
Robert N. Berryhill, deceased, case #282, filed 9 March 1853
William Berryhill, deceased, case #364, filed 10 April 1854

I did not folow up on this Berryhill line as I did not know how they
connected to ours in Alabama.

The following material gives proof of this family.

Alexander Berryhill
m. Lady Jane Cartwright
sons
  John
  William
  Samuel
  Andrew

A letter dated 1897 from George W. Berryhill of Eupora, Miss stated:
Two of the above men mentioned as brothers, married two Creek Indian
girls. Geo. W. Berryhill stated his grandfather sprang from one of them.

John Berryhill enrolled but never came here.

Samuel, son of John Berryhill has a son "Nathan" Nathaniel Berryhill
who was the father of George W. Berryhill born in Miss and lived there
all his life, so his letter stated.

William, son of John Berryhill, lived and died in Texas. He was born in
Georgia in 1791. Was in Ala. by 1838 and in Texas by 1845. His son,
"Nathan" Nathaniel Berryhill was born in 1832 in Ga., living on 1850
Rusk Co., Texas census. Was a member of Broken Arrow. William, II, son
of William, lived and died in Alabama. (I find son William, b. 1845, Ala.
in Rusk Co., Texas on 1850 census, so I do not agree with information.
V.T.B.)

John Dallas Berryhill, son of old John Berryhill, was b. 1817, Ga.,
shows on 1850 Rusk Co., Texas census.

I cannot agree that Thomas Berryhill b. 1805 Ga, is a son of William
Berryhill b. 1791 Ga. William Would only be 14 years old, when Thomas
was born. I feel they were brothers. (V.T.B.)

We must remember we are dealing with many William, John and Thomas &
George Berryhills.

Joseph Berryhill is recorded as a member of Creek Nation. Nathan's
Great uncle lived and died in Georgia.

The letter, as I do not have a copy of it, States: George W. Berryhill
says, "Gr. father and his brother, William, served in the Rev. War.
Grandfather was born in Muskogee Nation 1762 or 3 and died in the
Territory near where Muskogee now is, in 1831. Three brothers came and
settled in Georgia. Calls his grandfather John. Referred to Pink
Hawkins, who shows on 1857 census roll."

This has to show us we are dealing with several men by the same common
name.

1840 Clark Co., Ga.
Junius Berryhill
1 male 30/40
2 females up to age 5 years.
1 female 5/10
1 female 20/30

1850 Clark Co., Ga. - Buncombe Dist.
James W. Berryhill   42 M. Ga.
Eliza   "   32 F Ga.
Emily   "   15 F Ga.
Mary   "   12 F Ga.
Martha   "   10 F Ga.
Nancy P.   "   8 F. Ga.
Susan   "   6 F Ga.
Eleanor   "   4 F Ga.
Frances   "   6/12 F Ga.

```
1860 Morgan Co., Ga. - Wellington Dist.
James W. Berryhill    50 M.    Ga.   House Carpenter
  Eliza          "     42 F    Ga.
  Emily          "     25 F    Ga.
  Mary           "     21 F    Ga.
  Nancy          "     16 F    Ga.
  Susan          "     14 F    Ga.
  Ellender       "     12 F    Ga.
  Francis        "     10 M    Ga.
  William A.     "      7 M    Ga.
  Everline       "      3 F    Ga..

1870 Morgan Co., Ga - Madison
Eliza Berryhill       52 F    Ga. Keeing House ( James W. is Dead)
  Emily          "     35 F    Ga.
  Susan          "     25 F    Ga.
  Elizda F.      "     21 F    Ga. -this is Frances
  M. Eveline     "     13 F    Ga

1880 Walton Co, Ga. - District 559
Susan Berryhill       35 F  Ga.  Ga.  Ga.
  Fanny          "     28 F  Ga.  Ga.  Ga.  - daugher working in factory
  A. E.          "     60 F  Ga.  Ga.  Ga.  - Mother

1880 Walton CO., Ga. - District 454
W. A. Craft           26 M  Ga.  NC   Ga.
  M. E.          "     23 F  Ga.  Ga.  Ga.  wife
  J. S.          "      4 M  Ga.  Ga.  Ga.  son
  R. J.          "      2 M  Ga.  Ga.  Ga.  son
  Peggy          "     65 F  Ga.  Ga.  Ga.  Mother
  Cela           "    102 F  Va.  Va.  Va.  Grandmother

1900 Walton Co., Ga. - Good Hope
William A. Craft      46 M  Ga.  b. July 1853
  Lula           "     34 F  Ga.  b. Sept 1865 (2nd wife)
  John S.        "     24 M  Ga.     Dec  1875
  Robert         "     22 M  Ga.     May  1878
  Maudie         "     18 F  Ga.     Feb  1882
  Kittie         "     16 F  Ga.     Oct  1883
  Golden         "     12 M  Ga.     Oct  1887
  Pansy          "      5 F  Ga.     May  1895
  Heater         "      3 F  Ga.     Oct  1896


James W. Berryhill
b. 1808 - Ga.
d. 1860/1870
m. A. Eliza -?-
   b. 1818 - Ga.
   d. after 1880

   1. Emily Berryhill
      b. 1835 - Ga.
   2. Mary Berryhill
      b. 1838 - Ga.
   3. Martha Jane Berryhill
      b. 14 March 1840 - Ga.
      d. 22 April 1899 - Texas
      m. William Dennington - 27 August 1857 - Morgan Co., Ga.
         b. 3 September 1836 - S.C.
         d. 24 July 1906 - Ellis Co., Texas.

      A. John Dennington
         b. 5 July 1860 - Ga.
         d. 8 August 1916 - Shawnee, Okla.
         m. Martha Warren - 5 March 1880
            b. 1865 - Ga
            d. about 1886 - Ga.
```

(1) Maude Dennington
   b. 28 September 1881 - Dunwoody, Ga.
   d. 30 September 1966 - Skokie, Ill
   m. William Pender - 1 September 1897
      b. 18 January 1871 - Brownsville, Tenn.
      d. 22 April 1922 - Shawnee, Okla.

   (a) Margaret Pender
      b. 5 January 1912 - Shawnee, Okla.
      m. Norman Munson - 4 June 1932
         b. 7 June 1913 - Necedah, Wis.

      1. Bernice Munson
         b. 16 July 1933 - Chicago, Ill.
         m. Kelly F. Jump - 1 December 1951

4. Nancy P. Berryhill
   b. 1842 - Ga.

5. Susan Berryhill
   b. 1844 - Ga.

6. Eleanor Berryhill
   b. 1846 - Ga.

7. Eliza Frances Berryhill
   b. 1849 - Ga.
   m. G. L. Smith - 16 August 1908

8. William A. Berryhill
   b. August 1852 - Ga.
   d. 13 September 1915 - Ala.
   m. Julia V. Dorsey - 12 May 1875 - Walton Co., Ga.

9. Margaret Eveline Berryhill
   b. 1857 - Ga.
   d. before 1894
   m. William A. Craft - 21 February 1875 - Walton Co., Ga.
      b. 1854 - Ga.
      d. living 1900 with 2nd wife, Lula, who was born in 1865

   A. John S. Craft
      b. December 1875 - Ga..
   B. Robert J. Craft
      b. May 1878 - Ga.
   C. Maudie Craft
      b. February 1882 - Ga.
   D. Kittie Craft
      b. October 1883 - Ga.
   E. Golden Craft
      b. October 1887 - Ga.

   William A. Craft m. 2nd. Lula -?-
                        b. 1865
   F. Pansy Craft
      b. May 1895 - Ga.
   G. Heater Craft
      b. October 1896 - Ga.

Mrs. Mernice (Munson) Jump would like contacts with anyone working on, or connected with this family.

Mrs. Bernice Jump
Star Rte. West - Box 422
Necedah, Wis. 54646

CHAPTER IV

THE

THOMAS

PRICIE

BERRYHILL

FAMILY

Abstract of testimony of Nathan Berryhill at Muskogge, Okla in reference to application of J. C. Berryhill et. al., for citizenship in the Creek Nation. Dates 1897.

Lives in Olaulgee, Okla.; born in Georgia in 1830; age 67 years (1897); citizen of Creek Nation; 5 yrs. citizen now; belonged to Broken Arrow town; came there from Rusk Co., Texas; lives there a litte over 40 yrs.; Came to Rusk Co., Texas from Randolph Co., Ala.; Very young when came from Georgia; son of William Berryhill; William Berryhill was a son of John Berryhill; William Berryhill was a brother to John Dallas Berryhill; John, father of William, enrolled bu never came here; no name besides William; William had a cousin William M. Berryhill; Nathan had a brother William; William brother to Nathan had these children:

> issue : Mary (Berryhill) Foshee
> Jurisha (Berryhill) Gibson
> Thomas Berryhill
> Silas Berryhill
> Another Daugher, name unknown

William, brother of Nathan, lived and died in Ala. and left all his children there; my grandfather, John Berryhill, had a brother named Joseph who lived and died in Georgia, and was a recognized member of the Creek Tribe of Indians; my father, William, died in Texas at the last of the Civil War; my uncle Joseph Berryhill, had a son named William, who was a 1st cousin on mine; this William had a son by the name of William, who was a grandson of Joseph Berryhill; I know of personal knowledge that Joseph Berryhill, my great uncle, was a brother of my grandfather, and had a son by the name of William Berryhill, who died near the Miss - Ala. line, but I only know from general information that he is the father of these applicants, great grandchildren of Joseph Berryhill. I know appli- cant George W. Berryhill who was born in Miss. and has lived there all his life. I know that he is the son of Samuel Berryhill, who was a son of John Berryhill and a brother to my father William Berryhill.

To comment on the testimony of Nathaniel "Nathan" Berryhill, he is making the following statements:
John Berryhill, 1st Gen.
John Dallas Berryhill, 2nd. Gen.
William Berryhill, also 2nd Gen.
> son of William Berryhill
> 1. Nathaniel "Nathan" Berryhill (gave testimony) b. 1830 in Georgia.
> 2. William Berryhill (lived and died in Ala.)
Samuel Berryhill; 2nd. Gen.
> 1. George W. Berryhill (lived and died in Choctaw Co., Miss.)
Joseph Berryhill, 1st Gen. (brother to John Berryhill, 1st Gen. above)
> (lived and died in Ga. and a recognized member of the Creek Tribe
> of Indians)
William Berryhill, 2nd. Gen. (I wonder if this is our William b. 1780 in Georgia?)
> 1. William Berryhill

1850 Randolph Co., Ala.

Name		Age	Sex	Place	b. Year	Note
Thomas N. Berryhill		45	M	Ga.	b. 1805	
Mary A.	"	45	F	Ga.	1805	
Alexander	"	20	M	Ga.	1830	
Hannah A.	"	18	F	Ga.	1832	
Frances	"	16	F	Ga.	1834	
Martin	".	14	M	Ala.	1836	- family now in Alabama
Margaret	"	10	F	Ala.	1840	
Martha	"	8	F	Ala.	1842	
John	"	4	M	Ala.	1846	
Elizabeth	"	2	F	Ala.	1848	
William Berryhill		30	M	Ga.	1820	- Older son of Thomas N.
Jane	"	20	F	Ga.	1830	
Cynthia	"	1	F	Ala.	1849	

When I received the material Mrs. Elizabeth B. Haas compiled, this was the only Alexander Berryhill whose age fit hers. I am not saying this son of Thomas N. and Mary A. Berryhill is her Alexander. But his Confederate Record also fits this Alexander born in Georgia. Further research   to be done on this.

Census of CHEROKEE AND CREEK NATIONS - 1899 - Indian Territory, Okla.
Simon Berryhill m. Martha -?-   - these are possibly the parents
                                          of John B. b. 1858

John Berryhill		41 M	b. 1858	
Hokosy	"	41 F	1858	- Her name indicates she is Indian
Houston	"	17 M	1882	
Lucinda	"	15 F	1885	
Martha	"	12 F	1888	

A. J. Berryhill m. Marie -?-
Andrew Berryhill   43 M   1856

A. J. Berryhill m. Lula -?-
Buford   "   12 M   1888
Altie   "   4 M   1895
Walter Ray   "   2 M   1897

Eli Berryhill m. Elizabeth -?-
Zacahariah T. Berryhill 48 M   1851

Eli Berryhill m. Evaline -?-
Ida Belle Berryhill   4 F   1895

Simon Berryhill m. -?-
Sam   "   37 M   1863
Sophie   "   21 F   1878
Maudie   "   6 F   1893
Louise   "   1 F   1898

John Berryhill m. America -?-
Thomas H. Berryhill   56 M   1843

John Berryhill m. 2nd. Sarah -?-
Theodore F.   "   23 M   1876
John P.   "   20 M   1879
Cora F.   "   15 F   1884
William T.   "   11 M   1888
Della I.   "   7 F   1892

The following pages contain information sent in by Mrs. Elizabeth B. Haas
                                        1203 Nelson Grove
                                        Ocean Springs
                                        Mississippi
                                        39564

Alexander E. Berryhill
b. 1825/26 - Jones Co., Ga.
d. 27 June 1863 - Vicksburg, Miss.
He was a private in Co. B, 6th Miss. Infantry of 15th Miss Inf. from
Rankin Co., Miss.
m. Mary N. Liles - 3 March 1859 - Rankin Co, Miss.
   dau. of Eli Liles and Sarah Mulhollandd

   1. William Harmon Berryhill
      b. 1860 - Brandon, Miss
      d. 1954
      m. Annie Elizabeth Berry - 1880
         b. 29 December 1860 - Gulfport, Miss.
         d. 1928
         dau. of Halbert Berry & Mary Gitella Robinson

251

A. Mary Ethel Berryhill
   b. 1881
   d. 1948
   m. Samuel Allen J. Baker - 26 December 1901
      b. 1873
      d. 193?

  (1) Samuel Allen Baker
      b. 18 September 1903
      m. Gertrude Cobb
         b. 1906

    (a) Lillian Frances Baker
        b. 12 January 1929
        m. H. R. Bond - May 1950

        1. H. Ray Bond
           b. May 1951
        2. Pat Bond
        3. Keith Bond
        4. Richard Bond
        5. Cynthia Bond
           b. 1 November 1965

    (b) Samuel Allen Baker, III
        b. 3 September 1930
        m. Vesta Eseds
           b. 31 December 1932

        1. Terry Baker
           b. 3 June 1954
           m. Donna Monroe

           A. Alssa Baker
           B. Jarrett Baker

        2. Marilyn Baker
           b. June 1958
           m. John Murray

           A. Michelle Murray

    (c) John Ware Baker
        b. 8 September 1937
        m. Laverne Hegwood

        1. John Ware Baker, Jr.
        2. Stevie Baker
        3. Julia Baker

    (d) Elizabeth Hane Baker
        b. 7 January 1939
        m. Bill Byrd

        1. Andrea Jane Byrd
        2. Denise Elizabeth Byrd

    (e) James Neil Baker
        b. 31 December 1939
        m. Linda -?-

        1. James Edgar Baker
        2. Wanda Baker

  (2) Ethel Marie Baker
      b. 14 July 1905
      m. Clifton Capers

    (a) Archie Clifton Capers
        b. 19 October 1927
        m. Marion Roberts
           b. 31 July 1927

        1. Clifton Dennis Capers
           b. 20 March 1952
           m. Jaqueline Criser
              b. 7 February 1953

```
                A. Scott Capers
                B. Michael Capers
             2  Dan Corley Capers
                m. Beth Bellman
                   b. 22 October 1953

                A. Angie  Capers
                B. Corley Capers
             3  Thomas Archie Capers
                b. 9 June 1959
             4  Robert Glen Capers    Ethel Marie Baker m. 2nd.
                b. 15 March 1962      Dan M. McKinnon, b. 17 Jan. 1902
        (b) Ethel Marie McKinnon
            b. 5 March 1936
            m. Paul Davis Yates
               b. 21 July 1928

            1. Paul Davis Yates, Jr.
               b. 1 August 1955

               A. Jennifer Yates

            2. Ethel Quinnette Yates
               b. 31 July 1958
               m. Tony Stevenson

               A. John Stevenson

            3. Dan Martin McKinnon Yates
               b. 27 December 1960
            4. Carol Marie Yates
               b. 10 September 1966

        (c) Janis Carol McKinnon
            b. 29 August 1940
            m. Ralph Thomas Rich

            1. Cynthia Michelle Rich
               b. 5 September 1968
            2. Kendall Rich
               b. 4 April 1971

        (d) Louise Rae McKinnon
            b. 31 December 1941
            m. Gerald Lynn Jones - 10 October 1964
               b. 19 August 1942
            1. Gerald Lynn Jones, Jr.
               b. 11 October 1966
            2. Glenn Martin Jones
               b. 19 October 1969

(3) Hazel Elizabeth Baker
    b. 17 January 1907
    m. Cyril Raymond Haas - 31 August 1941
       b. 1894

    (a) Sarah Baker Haas
        b. 27 February 1945
        m. Dr. Atkinson Winan Longmire
           b. 1 June 1945

        1. Lela Darcy Longmire
           b. 6 April 1973
        2. Jerusha Elizabeth Longmire
           b. 1 September 1974
        3. Atkinson Garrett Longmire
           b. 6 February 1978

    (b) Elizabeth Ray Haas
        b. 23 February 1946
        m. David Joseph Wyatt

        1. Natalie Teresa (Wyatt) Bostick
           b. 14 October 1969

        Elizabeth Ray Haas m. 2nd. Lynn Bostick

        2. Tara Teneal Bostick
           b. 19 August 1976
```

3. Katherine Lynelle Bostick
   b. 25 November 1977

Elizabeth Ray Maas m. 3rd. James Edgar Maruer
                              b. 19 September 1944

(4) William Bertram Baker
    b. 29 July 1909
    m. Ellen Medora Henderson
       b. 28 October 1910

    (a) William Bertram Baker, Jr.
        m. Nancy Shirley

        1. Steven Goodman Baker
           b. 28 August 1964
        2. Samuel Jackson Baker
           b. 17 July 1967

    (b) Virginia Ellen Baker
        b. April 1948
        m. Joe Vidovich

(5) Dorothy May Baker
    b. 12 July 1911
    m. Ezra Winford Freeman
       b. 1 September 1910

    (a) Elizabeth Ann Freeman
        b. 23 February 1939
        m. Bill Cutter
           b. 15 August 1931

    (b) James Allen Freeman
        b. 4 August 1947
        m. Mary Henderson
           b. 4 November 1945

        1. James Allen Freeman, Jr.
           b. 11 September 1970
        2. Jay Jack Freeman
           b. 21 September 1972

(6) Katherine Lucille Baker
    b. 19 October 1914
    m. Walter Lee Wood
       b. 9 June 1910

    (a) Walter Lee Wood, Jr.
        b. 18 June 1942
        m. Olivia Kemp - 2 July 1966
           b. 18 June 1942
        1. Katherine Olivia Wood
           b. 24 May 1969
        2. Sarah Elizabeth Wood
           b. 17 December 1973

B. Katherine Berryhill - "Kate"
   b. 1888 - Miss.
   d. 1963 - N.C.
   m. George Ira Horne
      d. 1958 - Jackson, Miss.

   (1) Margerite Horne
       m. -?- Babock

       (a) Phyllis Ann Babcock
           m. -?- Norton
       (b) George Phillip Babcock
       (c) Margaret Catherine Babcock
           m. Ralph M. Mims

           1. Clayton Scott Mims
           2. Leslie Ann Mims
           3. Donald Wayne Mims

C. Annie Lee Berryhill
   b. 1879 - Miss.
   d. 1950
   bur. Gulfport, Miss.
   m. William J. Alman
      b. 1879
      d. 1950

   (1) Berniece Alman
       b. 1910
       m. John Paul Gill

       (a) John Paul Gill, Jr.
           b. 1937

   (2) Urmede Alman
       m. Jessie Broadus

       (a) Sharon Broadus
           m. Bobby Pate

           1. Tonya Pate

       (b) Vicki Broadus
           m. Ronald Alan Gorham

           1. Lee Dillon Gorham

       Urmede Alman m. 2nd. John Martin

D. Lorena Mae Berryhill
   b. 1883
   d. 1957
   m. Bane Farr
      b. 1870
      d. 1959

E. Verna Berry Berryhill
   b. 15 February 1889
   d. March 1973
   m. James Leonard Galloway
      b. 1881
      d. 1925

   (1) Elizabeth Hortense Galloway
       b. 1913
       m. Rossie Lee Johnson
          b. 1911

       (a) Myrtie Lee Johnson
           b. 1937
           m. James D.Brasher
              b. 1936
       (b) Verna Frances Johnson
           b. 1938
           m. Bobby Whindam
              b. 1939

           1. Scott Whindam
              b. 1972
           2. April Elizabeth Whindam

       (c) Lorene Johnson
           b. 1940
           m. Marvin Roy Hutchens
              b. 1937

           1. Dawn Elizabeth Hutchens
              b. 1968

       (d) Rossie Lee Johnson, Jr.
           b. 1941
           m. Bobbye Ray Hutchens

           1. Barry Lee Johnson
              b. 1963

                    2. Gregg Johnson
                       b. 1966

               (e) Linda Faye Johnson
                   b. 1946
                   m. Larry Hinton
                      b. 1943

                    1. John A. Hinton
                       b. 1968

          (2) Hazel Genevieve Galloway
              b. 1917
              m. Edd Barr
                 b. 1921
                 d. 1968

F. William Roy Berryhill
   d. 1964
   m. Julia Guard

      (1) Louise Berryhill
          b. 27 November 1925
      (2) William Roy Berryhill, Jr.
          b. 8 March 1931
          m. Verleyan Berryhill

          (a) William Paul Berryhill
          (b) Edward Berryhill

      (3) Anna Caterine Berryhill
          b. 6 September 1932
          m. Henry Stafford

      William Roy Berryhill m. 2nd. Grace White

      (4) James W. Baxter Berryhill
          b. 31 July 1936
      (5) Bain B. Berryhill
          b. 24 July 1937
      (6) Guy Allen Berryhill
          b. 17 January 1939
      (7) Barbara Sue Berryhill
          b. 14 May 1941
          m. David Alan Leary
             b. September 1940

          (a) D. A. Leary, Jr.
              b. 10 February 1961
          (b) Susan Michelle Leary
              b. 15 August 1963
          (c) Mark Leary
              b. 1974

G. Zula Hortense Berryhill
   d. 1945
   m. William Smith

      (1) William Smith, Jr.
      (2) Zula Hortense Smith

H. Hazel Augusta Berryhill
   b. 1896
   m. Henry Guest

      (1) Anna Berry
          m. Richard Suko

          (a) Diana Suko
              b. February 1955
          (b) Scott Suko
              b. 1963

      (2) Ray Guest

I. Holbert Berryhill
   m. Glayds Parish

   (1) William H. Berryhill, Jr.
   (2) Peggy Berryhill
   (c) Son Berryhill

   Holbert Berryhill m. 2nd. Pat -?-

J. Guy Robinson Berryhill
   b. 18 January 1902
   m. Marjorie -?-

Thomas Jefferson Berryhill m. Nancy Sizemore
Andrew Jackson Berryhill - "Jake"   42 M. b. 1857
James Berryhill   18 M   1881
Rachel Berryhill   16 F   1883
Gertrude Berryhill   12 F   1887
Bessie Berryhill   7 F   1892
Lee Berryhill   3 M   1896

Z. T. Berryhill m. Martha -?-
William F. Berryhill 25 M.   b. 1874

L. A. Foshee m. May -?-, who apparently 1st. m. a Berryhill
Susannah Berryhill

George W. Berryhill m. Ara Ann -?-
Stanford Berryhill   43 M   1856 - called "Uncle Dump"

George W. Berryhill m. Ara Ann -?-
Joan Martin   "   29 F   1870   Lucinda -?- was mother of these
George Franklin   "   23 M   1877   John H. Berryhill 9 M b. 1890
William   "   23 M   1872   David   "   8 M   1891
Colubmus   "   33 M   1866   William   "   6 M   1893
Emma   "   32 F   1867   Albert   "   5 M   1894
                                       Daniel   "   3 M   1896
                                       Columbus D.   "   1 M   1898
                                       Ara Ann   "   1 F   1898

George W. Berryhill m. Nancy -?-
Jessie   "   14 M   1885
Bluford   "   11 M   1888
George   "   8 M   1891
Carl   "   5 M   1894
Charles L.   "   2/12 M   1899

Jefferson Berryhill m. Nancy -?-
Pleasant Luther   "   43 M   1856 - "Duke" see note below
Sarah Lee   "   30 F   1869
Sam   "   13 M   1886
Oscar   "   11 M   1888
Josephine   "   9 F   1890
Clarence   "   7 M   1892
Effie   "   5 F   1894

Pleasant Luther Berryhill was called Duke, and on the first of May 1896
he was in Okmulgee, Okla. He was selected by his good Indian friend,
Timmie Jack, to execute him. Timmie Jack was the last Indian who was
executed under Creek Law, Duke shot him.

Polk Dallas Berryhill m. Mary -?- Foshee, widow of L. A. Foshee.
Isabenda Berryhill

Jim Berryhill m. Lucy -?-
William B.   "   56 M   1843
Jennie   "   48 F   1851

```
John Berryhill m. Nicey -?-
Kansie Berryhill        19 F  1880

Thomas H. Berryhill m. Sarah -?-
Rosa Lee Berryhill       2 F  1897

Robert Berryhill m. Elsie -?-
Harrison          "      28 M  1871
Bettie            "      25 F  1874
William           "       8 M  1891
Elizabeth         "       3 F  1896
Lucy              "    8/12 F  1898/1899

Alexander Berryhill m. Annie -?-
Peggy             "       2 F  1897

George W. Berryhill m. Alice -?-    George W. Berryhill m. Ara Ana -?-
Joseph F.         "       1 M  1898  Theodore Berryhill  24 M  b. 1875
Nevada                 5/12 F  1899

George W. Berryhill m. Rilla -?-
Loney Love        "       3 F  1896
Jackson           "       2 M  1897
Ollie             " 2 wk.     1899

George F. Berryhill m. Nellie Endsley    George F. Berryhill m. Clementine
Gracie I.         "     1½F  1897         Andrew Berryhill 6/12 b. 1899

John Berryhill m. America -?-
Littleton         "      49 M  1850

Simon Berryhill m. Martha -?-
Joseph            "      36 M  1863
Sallie            ".     28 F  1871
Annie             "       6 F  1893
John              "       4 M  1895
Anderson          "       2 M  1897
Louisa            "      16 F  1883

Samuel Berryhill m. Anna Bruner
Charlie           "       4 M  1895
Susanna           "       2 F  1897

1850 Tishomingo Co., Miss. Federal Census - 9 November 1950   #893
H. W. Berryhill         24 M  N.C.  b. 1826
Artilla           "     22 F  Ga.     1828 - Artilla Wilson
Levi              "   4/12 M  Miss    1850 b. in August

#894
T. P. Berryhill         49 M  N.C.    1801
Cynthia           "     45 F  N.C.    1805
William           "     19 M  N.C.    1831
James             "     13 M  N.C.    1837
Leander           "     11 M  N.C.    1839
Thomas            "      7 M  Ga.     1843

#895
H. Partin               22 M  S.C.    1825
Mary      "             25 F  N.C.    1825 - Mary Berryhill
Joel      "              4 M  Ga.     1846
Elizabeth Partin         1 F  Ga.     1849

1860 Franklin Co., ALa. P. O. Mountain Spring, Ala.
J. H. W. Berryhill      32 M  N.C.    1828
Artilla           "     31 F  Ga.     1829
George R.         "      6 M  Miss    1854
John T.           "      5 M  Miss    1855
Minton Emaline    "      3 F  Ala.    1857
Margaret M.       "   3/12 F  Ala.    1860
```

```
27 October 1860 - P. O. Newburg, Ala.
James L. Berryhill    22 M   N.C.    B. 1838
Mary R.         "     17 F   Tenn       1843
William H. H.   "      1 M   Ala.       1859

T. P. Berryhill       59 M   N.C.       1801.
Cynthia         "     57 F   N.C.       1803
Thomas F. K.    "     16 M   Ga.        1844
William W.      "     27 M   N.C.       1833
Elizabeth       "     21 F   Ala.       1839 - Elizabeth Stackton

1870 Franklin Co., Ala.  #1
William Berryhill     34 M   N.C.       1836
Elizabeth       "     30 F   Miss       1840
Mary            "      4 F   Ala.       1866
James           "      1 M   Ala.       1869
Minair?         "     63 F   N.C.       1807 - Cynthia Mintair (Todd)
                                               Berryhill it is believed
George          "     15 M   Miss.      1855 - nephew of William

#2
Levi Berryhill        40 M   N.C.       1830
Mary            "     30 F   Ala.       1840
Lane            "      9 M   Tenn.      1861
Lucy            "      1 F   Ala.       1869

1870 Franklin Co., Ala.  Township 7 Range 11, #120 P. 18
Leander Berryhill     30 M   Ga.        1840 - see #894 on 1850 census
Julia           "     27 F   Tenn.      1843
Sarah           "      5 F   Ala.       1865
Robert          "      2 M   Ala.       1868
Nancy           "   1/12 F   Ala.  Apr.1870

#92
Mary Berryhill        26 F   Tenn.      1844
Harvey          "     11 M   Ala.       1859
Emily           "      9 F   Ala.       1861
Jennie          "      5 F   Ala.       1865

1880 Franklin CO., ALa.  #248
Alan J. Franks
Lucy B. Berryhill     11 F. Ala. Ga. Ala. b. 1869 - Step-dau. of AJF
Homer           "      6 M  Ala. Ga. Ala.    1874 - Step-son
These are children of Levi and Mary Berryhill.  Levi evidentially has
died and Mary remarried.
```

Thomas Pricie Berryhill and his wife, Cynthis M. Todd, and three sons
settled in Franklin Co., Ala. in 1855 approx. Land records show that
the father and two sons, John H. W. & William N. took up land in secs. 31
and 32; TS 7S - R 10W. The 1860 census shows the other son, Thomas,
living with his paretns. In addition, the death record of Thomas Berryhill, Jr. gave his father's name as Thomas, but not his mother's name.
Thomas & William N. moved to Bonham, Fannin Co., Texas sometime after
1870 census was taken and their families are located there yet.

John H. W. Berryhill died of wounds received in the Civil War. One of
John's two surviving children, however, claimed the children of Thomas
William as cousins and they did likewise.

There is no proof that John was a brother of the other two. But he
seems to always live next door to Thomas P. Berryhill, or near by, so we
can assume he was a son of Thomas P. & Cynthia (Todd) Berryhill. Doubt-
less there were some other children of Thomas P. & Cynthia. She is
probably the Cynthia M. Tood who married Thomas P. Berryhill 3 March 1821
in Mecklenburg Co., N.C.

From the family Bible of William N. Berryhill 282, (1833-1907), in possession of Mrs. Al Read of Honey Grove, Texas, we learn that Thomas Pricie Berryhill & Cynthia Todd were married in Mecklenburg, N.C. and the parents of ten children.

Thomas G. Berryhill
Mary L. Berryhill
John H. W. Berryhill
Levi H. Berryhill
William N. Berryhill
Martin V. B. Berryhill
James L. Berryhill
Lawrence L. Berryhill
Leroy R. Berryhill
Thomas F. K. Berryhill

In the 1st. edition of this book we stated on page 268, that there was no proof John Berryhill was a brother of the other two Berryhill shown on census. The Bible record now gives us proof. (V.T.B.)

Thomas Berryhill, Jr. served in Co. H, 16th Ala. Inf. and enlisted as a Private, age 17 years, and John H. W. Berryhill served in Co. I, 41st Roddey's Ala. Cavalry.

Thomas F. K. Berryhill indicated he lived in Ladonia, Texas, 42 years, so he must have come there about 1887.

from G. W. Berryhill

Eupora Miss

Feb 11th 1897

Mr. M J Berryhill

Dear Cousin

I rec. your very welcome letter some few days ago. and was real glad to hear from you. my health is not good this winter We have had some very hard weather here. but snow only once and then not very heavy. now in regard to the matter that you wrote about I have searched all my brothers old papers and can find no history of the family with this exception. Gr. father and his bro. Wm served in the revolution war. he was born in the Muskogee nation in year 1762 or 3 and died in the terr. near where Muskogee now is, in 1831. and his wife died in 1833. I can give you the history of the Berryhill family as I understand it. three Bros. came over to america from Ireland years before the breaking out of the war with the mother country and settled in the territory of Geo. (Ga.) they perhaps come with the first emigrants to that colony. at any rate two of them married indian women of the Muskogee tribe of indians. and gr. father John sprang from one of the other them. and that acts. for there being two separate families being akin to the indians. If you will go and see Pink Hawkins, (if alive) he is a very old man. and lives on Deep Fork 18 miles south of Okmalgee he told me at Concil that he knew all my people in the old country you could get cos Nathan Berryhill to go with you. he knows him. he may be dead now it has been two years since I saw him. give my love to Jacob and family when you see them. write often.

Yours truly

GW Berryhill B. 1822

(son of Samuel Berryhill)
Grandson of John Berryhill
B. 1852 Choctaw Co. Miss.

Thomas Pricie Berryhill   *SEE ADDENDA SECTION FOR CONSIDERABLY MORE DATA ON FAMILY*
b. 22 January 1802 - N.C.   *OF THOMAS PRICIE BERRYHILL.*
d. 9 May 1862 - Franklin Co., Ala.
m. Cythia Minair Todd - 6 March 1821 - Mecklenburg Co., N.C.
    b. 20 August 1802 - N.C.
    d. 12 December 1871 - probably in Franklin Co., Ala.

    1. Thomas Griffith Berryhill
       b. 15 June 1823 - Mecklenburg Co., N.C.
       d. 4 December 1824 - Mecklenburg Co., N.C.
       bur. Mecklenburg, Co., N.C.

    2. Mary L. Berryhill
       b. 26 May 1825 - N.C.
       d. living 1850 - Tishomingo Co., Miss.
       m. Hubert Partain - 28 July 1846 - Ga?
          b. 1825 - S.C.
          d. living 1850 census

       A. Joel Partain
          b. 1846 - Ga.

       B. Elizabeth Partain
          b. 1849 - Ga.

    3. John H. W. Berryhill
       b. 20 April 1827 - Mecklenburg Co., N.C.
       d. 27 April 1863 - in the Civil War
          he served in Co. I, 41st Roddey's Ala. Cav.
       m. Artilla Wilson - 5 September 1847
          b. 1 December 1828 - Ga.
          d. 10 July 1906 - Headrick, Okla.
          bur. Headrick, Okla.
          m. 2nd. Samuel Long
          m. 3rd. Bull -?-

       A. Levi Berryhill
          b. August 1850 - Tishomingo Co., Miss.
          d. Gone from his parents home by 1860, so we know he evidentially
             died young as he would only be 10 years old.

       B. Eugenia Adaline Berryhill
          b. and d. 28 August 1851 - Tishomingo Co., Miss.
          bur. probably in Tishomingo Co., Miss.

       C. George Right Berryhill
          b. 11 October 1853 - Tishomingo Co., Miss.
          d. 1930 - Dexter, Chavez Co., NM
          bur. Tatum (Bluewater) Cemetery - Tatum, Lea Co., N.M.
          m. Martha Sylvania Isabelle Bynum - 3 November 1880
             b. 19 September 1863 - Blount Co., Ala.
             d. 26 March 1928 - Tatum, Lea Co., N.M.
             bur. Tatum (Bluewater) Cemetery
             dau. of Daniel Bailey Alexander Bynum & Louvenia Bynum

          (1) Wallace Alexander Berryhill
              b. 21 August 1883 - Zephyr, Brown Co., Texas
              d. 27 December 1952 - Albuquerque, Bernalillo Co., N.M.
              bur. Sunset Memorial Park Cemetery - Albuquerque, N.M.
              m. Annie May Martin - 4 February 1906 - Snyder, Scurry Co.
                 b. 11 January 1883 - Comanche Co.,   Texas

              (a) Thelma May Berryhill
                  b. 2 December 1906 - Scurry Co., Texas
                  d. 4 December 1916 - Tatum, Lea Co., N.M.
                  bur. Lovington, Lea Co., N.M.
              (b) Velma Fay Berryhill
                  b. 26 October 1908 - Scurry Co., Texas.
                  d. 15 July 1964   bur. Grants, N. M.
                  m. Dalton G. Wilcoxson, 14 June 1924 - McKinley Co., N.M.

1. Garland Wilcoxson - b. 9 April 1925, d. 3 June 1972
   m. Ruby Heath   bur. Grants, NM

   A. Judy Darlene Wilcoxson
   B. Jody Diane Wilcoxson

   Garland Wilcoxson m. 2nd. - 24 August 1952
   m. Nancy Morrison
      b. 27 November 1936 - Nebraska City, Neb.

   C. Myra Lavon Wilcoxson
      b. 15 July 1953 - Gallup, N.M.
   D. Victoria Lynn Wilcoxson
      b. 14 May 1955 - Gallup, N.M.
   E. Velma Ellen Wilcoxson
      b. 18 September 1956 - Gallup, N.M.
   F. Irvin Duane Wilcoxson
      b. 20 April 1958 - Gallup, N.M.
   G. Alvin Davis Wilcoxson
      b. 31 December 1960 - Gallup, N.M.
   H. Cindy Lee Wilcoxson
      b. 20 September 1966 - Gallup, N.M.

2. Betty Lou Wilcoxson *See Addenda for more information.*
   b. 21 March 1930 - Gallup, N.M.
   m. Phillip Harris - 5 November 1945 - Apache Co., AZ
      b. 5 May 1928 - Bluewater - Valencia Co., N.M.

   A. Larry Harris
      b. 21 September 1946 - Gallup, N.M.
      m. Sherry Brannon - 3 January 1966 - Mancos, Colo.
         b. 3 April 1946
   B. Billy Wayne Harris
      b. 24 September 1948 - Gallup, N.M.
   C. Tyra Ann Harris
      b. 20 October 1949 - Grants, N.M.
      m. Mevlin Darby - 23 October 1964
         b. 24 November 1945 - Grants, N.M.

      (1) Spurlin Darby
          b. 29 July 1965 - Grants, N.M.
      (2) Ty Darby
          b. 26 June 1966 - Grants, N.M.

   D. Bucky Miles Harris
      b. 12 August 1958 - Gallup, N.M.
   E. Tonya Lee Harris
      b. 31 July 1960 - Gallup, N.M.

(c) Wallace Adrian Berryhill   *See Addenda for more information.*
    b. 16 July 1910 - Seminole, Scurry Co., Texas
    m. Gladdus Marinda Tietjen - 27 December 1939 -
       McKinley Co., N.M.
       b. 25 August 1914 - McKinley Co., N.M.

1. Linda Joyce Berryhill
   b. 15 November 1940 - Grants, N.M., d. 18 Jan. 1972, bur.
2. Ann Lee Berryhill   Grants, N.M.
   b. 27 July 1943 - Grants, N.M.
   d. 12 May 2959 - Grants, N.M.
   bur. Grants, N.M.

(d) Edna Beatrice Berryhill   *See Addenda for more information.*
    b. 23 April 1912 - Seminole, Scurry Co., Texas
    m. Thomas Jefferson Tietjen - 11 October 1930 -
       McKinley Co., N.M.
       b. 25 December 1908 - Bluewater, N.M.
       d. 29 May 1968 - Albuquerque, N.M.
       bur. Bluewater Cemetery - Bluewater, N.M.
       son of Joseph E. Tietjen & Maud Hunt

1. Larry Joe Tietjen
   b. 7 October 1931 - Bluewater, N.M.
   m. Beverly Wilhelm - 25 August 1962 - Mesa, Ariz.

   A. Tammy Tietjen
      b. 10 December 1963

2. Gary Lane Tietjen
   b. 12 October 1932 - Bluewater, N.M.
   m. Geraldine Bond - 5 September 1958 - Mesa, Arix.
   b. 7 January 1931 - Ramah, N.M.

   A. Garth Tietjen
      b. 31 August 1959 - Gallup, McKinley Co., N.M.
   B. Lauretta Tietjen
      b. 11 July 1961 - Salt Lake City, Utah
   C. Leah Tietjen
      b. 29 November 1963 - Salt Lake City, Utah

3. Thomas Jefferson Tietjen, Jr.
   b. 22 September 1934 - Bluewater, Vlaencia Co., N.M.
   m. Christine Wilkins - 20 March 1959 - Mesa, Ariz
   b. 25 December 1940 - Ramah, N.M.

   A. Allen Clay Tietjen
      b. 11 May 1960 - St. John, Ariz
   B. Jeffrey Lynn Tietjen
      b. 7 May 1962 - Homer, Alaska
   C. Bruce Randall Tietjen
      b. 8 July 1964 - Homer, Alaska
   D. Carl Douglas Tietjen
      b. 16 September 1966 - Homer, Alaska

4. Wallace Lee Tietjen
   b. 22 May 1936 - Bluewater, N.M.
   d. 4 August 1945 - Bluewater, N.M.
   bur. Bluewater Cemetery - Bluewater, N.M.
5. Jeryl Wayne Tietjen
   b. 28 March 1942 - Grants, N.M.
   m. Nelda Lambson - 9 June 1961 - Mesa, Ariz.
   b. 10 March 1943 - Ramah, N.M.
6. Sheryl Ann Tietjen
   b. 22 November 1944 - Albuquerque, N.M.
   m. Keith Clawson - 19 October 1963 - St. Johns, Ariz.
   b. 2 March 1941 - Ramah, N.M.

   A. Phyllis Clawson
      b. 2 April 1965 - Homer, Alaska
   B. Kathy Clawson
      b. 29 January 1967 - Homer, Alaska

(e) Cecil Duane Berryhill   *See addenda section for more info*
    b. 9 April 1918 - Tatum, Lea Co., N.M.
    m. Nelda Elkins - 26 May 1947 - Valencia Co., N.M.
    b. 26 May 1925 - McKinley Co., N.M.

    1. Ina May Berryhill
       b. 27 February 1949 - Albuquerque, N.M.
    2. Nelda Ray Berryhill
       b. 22 April 1950 - Albuquerque, N.M.
    3. Glenda Kay Berryhill
       b. 11 August 1952 - Albuquerque, N.M.
    4. Duana Gay Berryhill
       b. 8 March 1958 - Albuquerque, N.M.
    5. Wallace Jay Berryhill
       b. 6 October 1964 - Grants, N.M.

(2) Marvin Ollie Berryhill   *See Addenda for more information.*
    b. 4 April 1886 - Zephyr, Brown Co., Texas
    d. 27 December 1952
    m. Willie Lee Carey - 10 July 1906,   d. 6 May 1966, bur.
                                           Levelland, Texas

    (a) Ramon Berryhill
        m. Loyce Huddleston

1. Lowell Ray Berryhill
   m. Donna Wallis

   A. Patricia Rae Berryhill

2. Delphane Berryhill
   m. Bobby Gray
3. Betty Louise Berryhill
   m. John Duke

(b) I.B. Berryhill
    m. Hazel Holcomb, d. 30 January 1960

   1. Vianna Kay Berryhill
      m. Fred Spears

      A. Berry Dan Spears

(c) Garth Berryhill
    m. Helen Morrow, d. 2 February 1962, bur. Levelland, Tx.

   1. Janice Marie Berryhill

(d) Marguerite Berryhill
    d. at age two years
(e) Doris Berryhill (twin)
    died in infancy
(f) Coris Berryhill (twin)
    died in infancy
(g) Rudene Berryhill
    m. Wayne Gladson

   1. Sherene Gladson
   2. Phyllis Lynn Gladson
   3. Denise Ozella Gladson

(h) Lafon Berryhill
(i) LaNell Berryhill
    m. Jimmie Hogan

   1. Jimmie Alton Hogan
   2. Kenneth Michael Hogan

(3) Mary Katherine Berryhill
    b. 12 June 1888 - Zephyr, Brown Co., Texas, d. 18 July 1978
    m. Charles Dee Foster - 22 May 1905
       d. 1946

(a) Homer D. Foster
    m. Violet Sutton

   1. Frank D. Foster
      m. Bernice Tidwell

      A. Gayla Lynn Foster

   2. Wilma Jean Foster
      m. Clarence W. Freeman

      A. Alvin Glenn Freeman - (twin)
      B. Calvin Lynn Freeman - (twin)
      C. Carroll Worth Freeman
      D. Barbara Jeanine Freeman
      E. Darla Jeatonne Freeman
      F. Ricky Bob Freeman

   3. Wayne Foster
      m. Louise Rundell

      A. Robert DeWayne Foster
      B. Vondale Foster
      C. Jack Meredith Foster

   4. Roy Allen Foster
      m. Barbara Autrey
   5. Lynn Foster
      m. Ronald McDougall
   6. Micky Sue Foster

(b) Berta Lee Foster
    m. Ross Block

    1. Virginia Lee Block
       m. Jake Miller

       A. Donna Vee Miller
       B. David Ross Miller

(c) Durard Foster

(4) Roy M. Berryhill
    b. 1 June 1891 - Zephyr, Brown Co., Texas
    d. 30 November 1918 - Kenna, N.M.
    bur. Kenna, N.M.
    m. Minnie Belle Easley - 4 September 1913

    (a) Rosalie Berryhill
        m. -?- Wilson
        have three children
    (b) Edgar William Berryhill
        d. at age 19 years
    (c) Mozelle Berryhill
        m. Fred Murray

(5) Fred Bynum Berryhill
    b. 27 November 1893 - Comanche Co., Texas
    d. 1 July 1965 - Albuquerque, N.M.
    bur. Kenna, N.M.
    m. Vera Leslie Martin - 25 July 1919 - Albuquerque, N.M.
       b. 13 July 1900 - Sipe Springs, Texas
       d. 13 August 1955 - Albuquerque, N.M.
       bur. Kenna, Roosevelt Co., N.M.

    (a) LaVeta Berryhill   *See Addenda for more information.*
        b. 17 November 1920 - Kenna, N.M.
        m. Wayne Vaughan - 4 October 1939 - Roswell, Chavez Co.
        d. 23 February 1945 - in Germany in WW II

        1. Belva Lee Vaughan
           b. 13 October 1940 - Portales, N.M.
           m. William R. South - 15 July 1955 - Belen, N.M.

           A. Jimmy Wayne South
              b. 18 August 1957 - Albuquerque, N.M.
           B. Pamela Sue South
              b. 3 August 1960 - Portales, N.M.

           Belva Lee Vaughan m. 2nd. - 22 June 1963 -
           m. Harvey Butterfield
              b. 10 December 1931 - Bancroft, Idaho

    (b) LaVon Berryhill
        b. 9 January 1922 - Kenna, N.M.
        m. Vernon Payton - 7 June 140 - Roswell, N.M.
           b. 11 April 1917 - Mills, N.M.
    (c) Freddy Irene Berryhill
        b. 10 January 1924 - Kenna, N.M.
    (d) Frankie Jo Berryhill
        b. 3 August 1926 - Kenna, N.M.
        m. James A. Coleman - 17 December 1949 - Aubuquerque,NM
           b. 9 June 1924 - Huntington Park, Calif., d. 24 June
                                                     1981, bur.
        1. Susan Irene Coleman   Riverside,CA
           b. 28 March 1952 - Albuquerque, N.M.
        2. Roger Steven Coleman
           b. 7 March 1954 - Albuquerque, N.M.

    (e) Billie Jean Berryhill   *SEE ADDENDA FOR MORE INFORMATION.*
        b. 16 May 1930 - Kenna, N.M.
        m. Clayton D. Simmons - 13 July 1946 - Elida, N.M.
           b. 24 January 1924 - Headley, Texas

        1. Ricky Dale Simmons
           b. 4 August 1953 - Deming, N.M.

2. Debbie Renae Simmons
   b. 8 January 1955 - Portales, N.M.

   Billie Jean Berryhill m. n 2nd. - 8 June 1964 -
   m. Frank Bobb in Albuquerque, N.M.

3. David Wayne Bobb
   b. 16 March 1965

(f) Peggy Berryhill   *SEE ADDENDA FOR MORE INFORMATION.*
    b. 21 August 1934 - Kenna, N.M.
    m. Jack Anthony - 17 July 1953 - Belton, Texas
       b. 9 December 1932 - Hobbs, N.M.

    1. Vera Lynn Anthony
       b. 29 June 1956 - Albuquerque, N.M.
    2. Michael Ray Anthony
       b. 4 July 1959 - Albuquerque, N.M.

(6) Myrtle May Berryhill
    b. 25 December 1895 - Brownwood, Brown Co., Texas, d. 25 May 1979
    m. Vernon Braswell - 6 March 1913   Bakersfield, CA
       b. 20 November 1885 - DeKalb, Texas

    (a) Eva Mae Braswell
        b. 13 August 1916 - McDonald, N.M.
        m. Dennia Pollard - 8 June 1935 - Oilton, Okla.
           b. 6 October 1913 - Duncan, Okla.

        1. Gwendolyn Gayle Pollard
           b. 24 February 1936 - Oilton, Okla.
           m. Donald Goodrich - 8 June 1956

           A. Dawn Denise Goodrich
              b. 16 July 1957
           B. Lisa Gay Goodrich
              b. 8 August 1960
           C. Ken Wayne Goodrich
              b. 2 February 1964

        2. Betty Moonyeen Pollard
           b. 1 August 1939
           m. Gary Wood - 5 August 1960

           A. Becky Leigh Wood
              b. 3 August 1963
           B. Melissa Lane Wood
              b. 8 May 1965

        3. Denny Pollard
           b. 2 September 1944 - Salem, Ill.

    (b) Vernon Leon Braswell
        b. 20 January 1923 - Oilton, Okla.
        m. Bobbie Jo Jernigan - 21 October 1951
           b. 12 March 1933

        1. Carrie Denise Braswell
           b. 6 September 1955 - Bakersfield, Calif.

    c) Floyd Elroy Braswell
       b. 5 February 1925 - Oilton, Okla.
       d. 14 May 1960 - Bakerfield, Calif.
       m. Mrs. Margie White - 5 June 1953 - Bakersfield, Calif.

       1. Dianna Lynn Braswell
          b. 20 January 1954 - Bakerfield, Calif.

(7) Lillian Mellsenia Berryhill   *SEE ADDENDA FOR MORE INFORMATION.*
b. 3 March 1899 - Knapp, Scurry Co., Texas
m. Steven Lee Scott - 31 December 1915 - Plains, Texas
    b. July 1895 - Anson, Jones Co., Texas

  (a) Orville Lee Scott
     b. 1918 - McDonald, N.M.
     m. Ida May Duke - 1941

     1. Janet Faye Scott
       b. 16 May 1942
       m. Don Raymond - 1958

       A. Debbie Raymond

     2. Orville Lee Scott, Jr.
       b. 1944 ·approx.

     Orville Lee Scott m. 2nd. Mary de Mare - 3 Sept. 1946

     3. Frank Eugue Scott (twin)
     4. Frances Darlene Scott (twin)
     5. Mitchelle Lee Scott

  (b) Earlagene Scott
     b. 1928
     m. Earl L. Wilson - 1951

     1. Debra Kathleen Wilson
       b. 9 November 1960 Bakersfield, California (adopted)

  (c) Marion Dee Scott
     b. 1932
     m. Jeanne Leslie Rosske - 20 June 1952

     1. Sharon Lorraine Scott
     2. Stephen M. Scott

(8) Lee Berryhill   *SEE ADDENDA FOR MORE INFORMATION.*
b. 23 January 1901 - Gale, Borden Co., Texas
m. Ruth Hickey - 10 December 1927 - Lea Co., N.M.
    b. 2 October 1906 - near Knoxville, Tenn.

  (a) Gloria Ilene Berryhill
     b. 12 September 1928 - Tatum, Lea Co., N.M.
     m. George Hamlin
       b. 15 December 1922

     1. George Theron Hamlin
       b. 16 March 1949 - Clovis, N.M.

  (b) Gary Berryhill
     b. 23 July 1930
     m. Wanda Autry - Okla.

     1. Phillip Royce Berryhill
       b. 1 November 1955 - Hobbs, N.M.
     2. Brian Douglas Berryhill
       b. 2 November 1960
     3. Lisa Ann Berryhill

  (c) Bernarr David Berryhill
     b. 5 July 1934 - Tatum, N.M.
     m. Carol Collins
       b. 1936

     1. David Greg Berryhill
       b. 30 December 1955 - Hobbs, N.M.
     2. Stormi Lynn Berryhill
       b. 29 December 1957
     3. Sherlene Berryhill
       b. 31 December 1959

  (d) Sheril G. Berryhill
     b. 16 November 1936 - Tatum, N.M.
     m. Aletha Boykin
     m. 2nd. Marion Brown

          1. Perry Lee Berryhill
             b. 17 May 1963
          2. Samuel Darren Berryhill
             b. 16 February 1966

      (e) Patricia Ann Berryhill
          b. 28 September 1945 - Hobbs, N.M.

  (9) Lou Berryhill   *SEE ADDENDA FOR MORE INFORMATION.*
      b. 27 November 1902 - Gale, Borden Co., Texas
      m. William Horace Belcher - 20 September 1919
         b. 8 May 1897

      (a) Faye Oleta Belcher
          b. 23 May 1920
          m. Carol Payton - 17 March 1940
             b. 26 September 1914

          1. J. W. Payton
             b. 1 March 1941 - Roswell, N.M.
             m. Breena Margaret Kaso - 10 April 1966
                b. 3 April 1945

             A. Tommy Harlan Payton
                b. 8 January 1967

          2. Linda Joyce Payton
             b. 26 October 1943 - Portales, N.M.
             m. Leon Earl Kenny - 24 May 1962 - Slayton, Texas
                b. 14 September 1941

             A. Michael Douglas Kenny
                b. 26 September 1966 - Caleb, R.I.
             B. Timothy Miles Kenny
                b. 10 June 1968 - Leonard Town, Md.

      (b) Billie Evelyn Belcher
          b. 19 December 1928 - Tatum, N.M.
          m. Bruce Payton - 14 June 1946
             b. 6 June 1923

          1. Judy Sharon Payton
             b. 23 August 1947 - Roswell, N.M.
             m. Leenville Tisdale - 31 May 1968 - Bayfield, Colo.
          2. William Douglas Payton
             b. 16 August 1949 - Gentry, Ark.

D. John Thomas Berryhill
   b. 25 -?- 1855 - Miss., possibly Tishomingo Co.
   d. 1862 - Franklin Ala., living at 1860 census time

E. Minton Emaline Berryhill
   b. 1 October 1858 - Franklin Co., Ala.
   d. living at 1860 census time, but died young

F. Mary M. Berryhill
   b. 14 February 1860 - Franklin Co., Ala.
   d. 8 September 1942 - Okla.
   bur. Navajo, Okla.
   m. William H. Payne - 2 July 1876
      bur. Navajo, Okla.

   (1) Ira Payne
       b. 1878 approx.
       bur. Navajo, Okla.
   (2) Lina Payne
       b. 1880 approx.   bur. Altus, Okla.
       m. -?- Glisson
   (3) Nora Payne
       m. -?- Cantrell
   (4) Artilla Payne
       bur. Altus, Okla.
       m. -?- Ewing

        (5) Pearl Payne
            m. Frank Schultz
        (6) Altus Erby Payne
            bur. Altus, Okla.

4. Levi H. Berryhill
   b. 11 August 1829 - N.C.
   d. after 1874, but approx. 1875 - Franklin Co., Ala.
   m. Harriet A. Mize - 1 November 1849
      No further information is available on her, but apparently she
      died soon after.
   m. 2nd. Mary -?-
            b. 1840 - Ala.
            d. Living in 1880, and m. 2nd. Alan F. Franks
   Levi was a Pvt in Co. H. - 16 Ala. Inf. Reg. enlisted 16 August
   1861 at the age of 20 years.

   A. Lane Berryhill
      b. 1861 - Tenn.
      Her mother could be Harriett.

   B. Lucy B. Berryhill
      b. 1869 - Ala.
      At age 11 years, she was in her Step-father's home on 1880
      Franklin Co., Ala. Census. Her step-father was Alan J. Franks.

   C. Homer Berryhill
      b. 1874 - Ala.
      At age 6 years was in his step-father's home on 1880 census
      in Franklin Co., Ala. Step-father was Alan J. Franks.

5. William N. Berryhill
   b. 7 February 1833 - N.C.
   d. 30 January 1907 - Bonham, Fannin Co., Texas
   bur. Mt. Carmet Cemetery - Gober, Texas
   m. Elizabeth C. Stockton - 3 December 1859
      b. 11 April 1840 - Miss.

   A. Mary Lee Berryhill
      b. 14 September 1862 - Franklin Co., Ala.
      m. -?- Stoddard

      (1) Pinkney Stoddard
      (2) Robert Stoddard

   B. James Franklin Berryhill
      b. 11 October 1868 - Russellville, Franklin Co., Ala.
      d. 23 August 1942 - Fannin Co., Texas
      bur. Bonham, Fannin Co., Texas
      m. Minnie Isabel Watson - 23 May 1901 - Dodd City, Texas
         b. 22 July 1879

      (1) Eugene Pinkney Berryhill
          b. 12 February 1902 - Lannins, Texas
      (2) Allen Monroe Berryhill
          b. 21 December 1903 - Bonham, Fannin Co., Texas
          d. 1963
      (3) Frieda Irene Berryhill
          b. 17 February 1906 - Bonham, Fannin Co., Texas
      (4) Evelyn Berryhill
          b. 2 July 1910 - Bonham, Fannin Co., Texas
          m. Odell Orton
          m. 2nd. William Williams
      (5) Dorothy Berryhill
          b. 6 October 1915 - Bonham, Fannin Co., Texas
          m. Russell Shoemaker
      (6) James Edwin Berryhill
          b. 7 November 1918 - Bonjam, Fannin Co., Texas

C. Benjamin Berryhill
b. 31 January 1870 approx. - Franklin Cl., Ala.

D. Melissa Clementine Berryhill - "Clemmie"
b. 31 January 1872 - Franklin Co., Ala.
d. 1943 - Texas
bur. Oak Ridge Cemetery - Ladonia, Texas
m. -?- Carter

E. Frances Bell Berryhill - "Fannie"
b. 7 February 1875 - Franklin Co., Ala.
bur. Oak Ridge Cemetery - Ladonia, Texas
m. -?- Carter

   (1) Herman Carter
       died young
       bur. Oakridge Cemetery - Ladonia, Texas

F. William Thomas Berryhill - "Tom"
b. 20 September 1877 - Franklin Co., Ala.

6. Martin Van Buren Berryhill
b. 1 October 1835 - N.C.
d. 2 October 1835 - N.C.
bur. N.C.
Since the earliest date shown any of this family was born in Ga.
was 1843, I think we can safely assume little Martin was born and
died in N.C.

7. James L. Berryhill
b. 11 December 1837 - N.C.
d. 1865 approx. - perhaps in the Civil War as his last child was
                 born in 1865.(Co. B, 13 Regt., Ala.)
m. Mary -?-
b. 1844 - Tenn.
d. living on the 1870 census

A. Harvey Berryhill
b. 1859 - Franklin Co., Ala.

B. Emily Berryhill
b. 1861 - Franklin Co., Ala.

C. Jennue Berryhill
b. 1865 - Franklin Co., Ala.

8. Lawrence Lee (or Leander) Berryhill
b. 18 May 1840 - Ga., perhaps Walker Co. - 1870 census says Leander
m. Julia -?-
b. 1843 - Tenn.

A. Lannes Moncey Berryhill
b. 14 March 1860 - Ala.
d. 1900/1901 - Clarksville, Texas. Died of pneumonia
bur. Fannin Co., Texas
m. Georgia Elizabeth Mays
   d. 1894/1985 approx. - Fannin Co., Texas
   dau. of John Mays

   (1) Gustie Berryhill
       b. 1888 approx.
   (2) Virgil Berryhill
       b. 5 September 1890
   (3) Curtis Odell Berryhill
       b. 23 June 1893
       bur. Mt. Olivet Cemetery - Hugo, Okla.
       m. Julit Davis
          b. 4 July 1897

(a) Charles Franklin Berryhill
   b. 5 September 1934 - Hugo, Choctaw Co., Okla.
   m. Harriet Eunice Kilcrease - 13 August 1956 - Hugo, OK
      b. 6 November 1937
      dau. of Simon Kilcrease (Killcrease), who is the
           Chickasaw Indian Agent, and Adelia Alta
           Griswold.

   1. Laura Lisa Berryhill
      b. 5 January 1958 - Oklahoma City, Okla.
   2. Shelli Suzanne Berryhill
      b. 15 January 1960 - Wewoka, Okla.
   3. Brian Kilcrease Berryhill
      b. 30 August 1961 - Dallas, Texas

(b) Ellen Jewel Berryhill
(c) Ralph Odell Berryhill
(d) Prentice Lee Berryhill
(e) Curtis Odell Berryhill, Jr.

(4) Lula Berryhill
   b. 1894/1895 approx.

Lannes M. Berryhill m. 2nd. 17 December 1896 - Fannin Co., Texas
m. Dora Lee Burnett
   b. 6 May 1882 - Smyra, Tenn.
   d. 17 July 1930 - Davis, Okla.
   bur. Green Hill Cemetery - Davis, Okla.
   dau. of Jim Burnett and Martha Duncan
           b. 1849 -   b. 1848
              Middle, Tenn.d. October 1905 - Fannin Co., Texas
              they married March 1905 - Fannin Co., Texas

(5) Annie Gertrude Berryhill
   b. 1 December 1887 - Honey Grove, Fannin Co., Texas
(6) Myrtle Viola Berryhill
   b. 14 July 1900 - Honey Grove, Fannin Co., Texas
   m. Wayne Barnett Mullins, Sr. - 28 November 1916

   (a) Barbara Mullins
       m. Joe Cunyus

B. Sarah Berryhill
   b. 1865 - Franklin Co., Ala.

C. Robert Berryhill
   b. 1868 - Franklin Co., Ala.

D. Nancy Berryhill
   b. April 1870 - Franklin Co., Ala.

9. Leroy R. Berryhill
   b. 12 February 1843 - Ga., possibly Walker Co.
   d. 6 July 1843 - Ga.
   bur. Ga.

10. Thomas K. F. Berryhill
   b. 24 June 1844 - Ga., possibly Walker Co.
   d. 3 May 1929 - Bonham, Fannin Co., Texas
   bur. Oak Ridge Cemetery - Ladonia, Texas
   m. Frances Spears
   Thomas served in Co. H, 16th Reg, Ala. Inf. - Pvt. - 17 years old.

A. Tom Berryhill
   b. 3 October 1866 - Franklin Co., Ala.
   d. 13 June 1937
   m. Harriet Pritchard - 2 June 1888

B. Catherine Permella Berryhill
   m. Jeff Hargrove

C. Molly Berryhill
   m. Louis Brown

D. Martin Berryhill
   bur. Dodd city, Texas
   m. Sid Payne - 25 August 1901

ADDENDA

Additional data on Daniel T. Berryhill and family. (See page 108)

(15) Daniel T. Berryhill
b. 15 Oct. 1897
d. 28 June 1952 - Hinds Co. Miss.
bur. Morrison Cemetery - Learned, Miss.
m. Josie Bush 22 Dec. 1945 - Hinds Co., Miss
b. 11 Nov. 1911 - Hinds Co., Miss
d. 29 March 1970 - bur. Morrison Ceme.

(a) Mary Jo Berryhill
b. 20 Sept. 1946
m. Robert Donald Nail - 20 Aug. 1965
b. 20 April 1941

1. Robert Danward Nail
b. 6 Feb. 1970
2. Darral Bush Nail
b. 9 July 1980

Additional data on family of Hughie Dennis Berryhill. (See page 109)

(a) Hughie Dennis Berryhill, Jr.
b. 10 Sept. 1926 - Hinds Co., Miss
m. Bettye Clara Boyd 18 Aug. 1951
b. 8 July 1933 - Hinds Co., Miss

1. Sherry Claire Berryhill
b. 10 Feb. 1953
m. Doyle Leon Jones 15 Oct. 1977
b. 6 July 1947

A. Anding Curtis Jones
b. 14 Dec. 1978 - Hinds Co., Miss
B. Katy Amanda Jones
b. 14 July 1981 - Hinds Co., Miss
2. Hughie Dennis Berryhill, III
b. 15 Sept. 1954
3. Tol Edward Berryhill
b. 5 March 1961

(b) Lois Lanelle Berryhill

b. 6 Jan. 1929 - Warren Co., Miss
m. James Edward Hudson 30 Nov. 1947
b. 12 March 1926 - Grant Parish, La.

1. Linda Lanelle Hudson
b. 6 Sept. 1949 - Warren Co., Miss
m. Thomas Louis Segrest 29 June 1969
b. 18 July 1946

A. Thomas James Segrest
b. 2 April 1974
B. Jeff Hudson Segrest
b. 4 Sept. 1976
C. Sarah Lauren Segrest
b. 22 May 1980
2. Jamie Nell Hudson
b. 9 Oct. 1951 - Warren Co., Miss
m. William Marcellus Banks Jr., 12 Mar. 1978
b. Aug. 22 1951 - Newton Co., Miss
3. Vivian Ann Hudson
b. 7 June 1955 - Warren Co., Miss
m. William Traylor Phelps 22 July 1978
b. Aug. 29, 1946

A. Jessica Hudson Phelps
b. Aug. 14, 1981 - Midland, Tex.

(c) Fay Laurin Berryhill
    b. 3 Oct. 1932 - Hinds Co., Miss
    m. Thomas Eugene Griffin Dec. 26 1953 [sic] ?
       b. 24 Nov. 1928 - Hinds Co., Miss

    1. Thomas Eugene Griffin, Jr.
       b. 24 Nov. 1953
       m. Valerie Dawn Howell 2 June 1973
          b. 5 Nov. 1954

       A. Jason Eugene Griffin - Hinds Co., Miss
          b. 3 Oct. 1974
       B. Shelby Dawn Griffin
          b. 12 March 1977
    2. Paula Elaine Griffin
       b. 12 May 1957
    3. Craig Franklin Griffin
       b. 24 June 1961
(d) Milton Horace Berryhill
    b. 25 Nov. 1933 - Hinds Co., Miss
    m. Charlene Fowler 3 June 1958
       b. 1 Oct. 1934 - Hinds Co., Miss

    1. Bradley Louis Berryhill
       b. 26 June 1960 - Hinds Co., Miss
    2. Robert Daniel Berryhill
       b. 21 July 1963 - Atlanta, Ga.

                        Contributed by:
                        H.D. Berryhill
                        Gen. Del.
                        Learned, Miss. 39093
                        Tel. 601-885-8314

Additional data on children of Della Frances Berryhill Ward
    (Daughter of Thaddeus Berryhill - see page 207)

    (a) Della Frances Berryhill
        b. Sept. 9, 1884 - Marion County, Alabama
        d. July 17, 1937
        bur. Moore Cemetery, Moore, Okla
        m. Benjamin Lester Ward Nov. 14, 1901 at Hamilton, Ala.
           d. 1968

        1. Earnestine Virginia Ward
           b. Sept. 2, 1902 - Winfield, Ala.
           d. June 15, 1972
           bur. Moore Cemetery, Moore, Okla.
           m. Chester Cecil Markham Jan. 17, 1924 Oklahoma
                City, Okla.
              b. Oct. 3, 1896 - Marion Co., Ala.
              d. Dec. 7, 1979 - Newcastle, Okla.
              bur. Moore, Okla

        A. Mary Lou Markham
           b. Aug. 2, 1925 - McClain Co., Okla
           m. Woodley H. Smith Aug. 11, 1943, Black River,NY
              b. Aug. 17, 1919 - Newton Co., Miss
           Resides at 2631 McArthur Dr., Columbus, Miss.

           (1) Virginia Anne Smith
               b. March 11, 1953 - Meridian, Miss
               m. Billy E. Smith June 10, 1973 Columbus, MS.
                  b. March 6, 1950 - Panola Co., Miss.
               Resides at Rt. 1, Box 113, Pope, Miss

               Twins
               a. John Markham Smith
                  b. May 15, 1979 - Memphis, Tenn.
               b. Elizabeth Anne Smith
                  b. May 15, 1979 - Memphis, Tenn.

b. Joy Melissa Smith
b. March 21, 1966 - Columbus, Miss
Resides - 2631 McArthur Dr., Columbus, Miss.
B. Joanne Markham
b. July 21, 1930 - McClain Co., Okla.
m. James C. McDonald at Newcastle, Okla.
June 10, 1948 at Newcastle, Okla.
b. Jan. 17, 1925

(1) Donna Lou McDonald
b. March 18, 1949 - Champaign, Ill.
m. Ronald W. Baker Feb. 15, 1969 at Wichita
Falls, Tex.
b. Aug. 15, 1947
Resides Rt. 1, Box 120-B, Glen Rose, Tex.

a. Amy Marie Baker
b. March 2, 1974 - Colorado City, Tex.
(2) David Carl McDonald
b. Nov. 10, 1973 - Wichita Falls, Tex.
Resides Rt. 1, Box 359, Wichita Falls, Tex.
C. Della Sue Markham
b. Nov. 16, 1936 - Oklahoma City, Okla.
m. Leo W. Robinson Oct., 1955 at Oklahoma City,
Okla.
b. July 21, 1936
Resides 2717 S.W. 87th St., Oklahoma City, Ok.

(1) Selena Jo Robinson
b. Aug. 5, 1958 - Tampa, Fla.
Resides Oklahoma State University, Stillwater, Okla.
(2) Mark Lyle Robinson
b. April 13, 1960 - Tampa, Fla.
Resides Oklahoma City, Okla.
2. Rulon Burr Ward
b. Sept. 23, 1904 - Winfield, Ala.
d. Jan. 10, 1935
bur. Moore Cemetery, Moore, Okla.
3. Raymond Walker Ward
b. March 24, 1907 - Winfield, Ala.
d. Oct. 13, 1964
bur. Resthaven Cemetery, Oklahoma City, Okla.
m. Louise Morris Nov. 8, 1930 at Oklahoma City, Okla.
b. Oct. 8, 1913

A. Doris Louise Ward
b. Oct. 2, 1932 - Oklahoma City, Okla
m. Col. John P. Bynum (Divorced)

a. Randolph Walker Bynum
b. Jeffrey Allen Bynum
c. Perry Bynum
d. Lisa Bynum

m. 2nd Dr. Andrew J. Mullen, resides at 333
Berkshire Pl., Shreveport, La.

B. Patricia Ann Ward
b. Feb. 27, 1939 - Oklahoma City, Okla.
m. Eddie Greggs
Resides 5720 N.W. 83rd, Oklahoma City, Okla.

a. Tracey Greggs
b. Corey Greggs
c. Sheri Greggs
4. Max Lester Ward
b. Dec 1, 1910 - Winfield, Ala.
m. Edna Thompson 1932 (Divorced)
A. Larry Bradford Ward (Bradford Lester Ward)
b. 1934
d. 1967
m. 2nd Nelsie Irene Gee 1940 Oklahoma City, Okla.
A. Carolyn Elaine Ward
b. March 22, 1943

```
                    b. Ronald Max Ward
                       b. June 22, 1948
        5. Alma Lee Ward
            b. Oct. 25, 1915 - Winfield, Ala.
            m. Charles Albert Keller Aug. 21, 1935 at Pauls
                    Valley, Okla.
            b. Jan. 2, 1913 - Wyoming, Ill
            Resides 3612 S. Goff, Oklahoma City, Okla.

            A. Dorothy Ann Keller
               b. July 15, 1936 - Oklahoma City, Okla
               m. Gary Long Dec. 3, 1954, Oklahoma City, Okla.
                  b. July 25, 1934 - Lindsay, Okla.
               Resides Rt. 1, Box 190, Blanchard, Okla.

               a. Gary Dewayne Long
                  b. Jan. 13, 1957 - Oklahoma City, Okla.
                  d. Feb. 1, 1976 at Kaiserlautern, Germ.
                  bur. Resthaven Gardens, Oklahoma City, Okla.
               b. Pamela Gail Long
                  b. Sept. 18, 1958 - Oklahoma City, Okla.
                  Resides 5550 Willow Cliff Rd., Apt. 366,
                          Oklahoma City, Okla.
               c. Jeffery Allen Long
                  b. Nov. 23, 1963 - Oklahoma City, Okla.
                  Resides Rt. 1, Box 190, Blanchard, Okla.
            B. Charlene M. Keller
               b. Jan. 23, 1940 - Oklahoma City, Okla.
               m. Charles J. Rector Nov. 16, 1957
                  b. June 11, 1936 - Frederick, Okla.
               Resides 5016 Buddy Lane, Oklahoma City, Okla.

               a. Marta Kay Rector
                  b. Oct. 13, 1958 - Shelby Co., Tenn.
                  m. Larry Smith March 27, 1981
                     b. July 28, 1953 - Oklahoma City, Okla.
                  Resides 1713 S.W. 15th, Oklahoma City, Okla.
               b. Charles Lee Rector
                  b. March 21, 1965 - Oklahoma City, Okla.
               Resides 5016 Buddy Lane, Oklahoma City, Okla.

            C. Robert Dewayne Rector
               b. Jan. 10, 1976 - Oklahoma City
               Resides at 5016 Buddy Lane, Oklahoma City

        6. Marilyn Ward
            b. Sept 20, 1918 - Winfield, Ala.
            m. Van Buren Quick Dec. 3, 1939 Calhoun City, Miss.
               b. June 10, 1917 - Cullman, Ala.
            Resides at 929 Nelson Place, Birmingham, Ala

            A. Van Buren Quick, Jr.
               b. Feb. 7, 1941 - Florala, Ala.
                  Career Officer in Army (Major).
               Resides in Atlanta, Ga.
               m. Madge Thigpen Jan. 23, 1965 at Bainbridge, Ga.
                  b. Dec. 22, 1943
               a. Charles Van Buren Quick
                  b. Sept. 10, 1971

            B. Marilyn Frances Quick
               b. Feb. 18, 1944 - Birmingham, Ala.
               m. William Samuel Looney June 23, 1962 Selma, Ala.
                  b. April 30, 1940
               Resides 3276 Tyrol Rd., Birmingham, Ala.

               a. Jeffery Glen Looney
                  b. May 26, 1963 - Selma, Ala.
               b. William Benjamin Looney
                  b. Dec. 28, 1966 - Pensacola, Fla.
```

Contributed by
Mrs. Woodley H. Smith   and   Max Ward
2631 McArthur Dr.   14766 Ash St.
Columbus, MS 39701   Hesperia, CA 92345

(5) Martha Elizabeth (Lizzie) Berryhill
    b. 3 November 1870 - Marion County, Alabama
    m. Will Henderson 24 Jan. 1891

    (a) Annie Margaret Henderson
        b. 7 November 1891 - Winfield, Alabama
        d. 24 December 1975, Corsicana, Tex.
        m. Robert Steve Flynn 10 Nov. 1909, Corsicana, Tex.
           b. 20 Oct. 1877 - Ft. Worth, Tex.
           d. 3 Oct. 1966

        1. Ruby Elizabeth Flynn
           b. 18 Sept. 1910 - Corsicana, Tex.
           m. Joe Brown, 30 Sept. 1925, Corsicana, Tex.
              b. 7 Aug. 1903 - Kaufman, Tex.
              d. 9 Feb. 1968

           A. Cecil Lloyd Brown
              b. 7 Sept. 1926 - Corsicana, Tex.
              m. Maggie Faye Brown 26 Nov. 1948, Corsicana,TX
                 b. 8 Feb. 1932 - Purdon, Tex.

              1. Robert Allen Brown
                 b. 1 Sept. 1949 - Corsicana, Tex.
                 m. Linda Sue Clevenger 17 Apr. 1970,
                       Dallas, Tex.
                    b. 5 Oct. 1950 - Dallas, Tex.

                 a. Kevin Todd Brown
                    b. 25 Aug. 1971 - Dallas, Tex.
                 b. Jason Allen Brown
                    b. 22 Feb. 1974 - Dallas, Tex.

              2. Curtis Lynn Brown
                 b. 9 March 1956 - Corsicana, Tex.
                 m. Shirley Elizabeth Cockerham 5 July 1974
                       Dallas, Tex.
                    b. 5 Sept. 1955 - Dallas, Tex.

           B. Billy Joe Brown
              b. 8 March 1939 - Powell, Tex.
              m. Anna Sue Lake 20 May 1961, Corsicana, Tex.
                 b. 10 March 1943 - Corsicana, Tex.

              1. Karla Jo Brown
                 b. 10 Oct. 1962 - Corsicana, Tex.
              2. Cary Earl Brown
                 b. 12 Oct. 1963 - Corsicana, Tex.

        2. William Robert Flynn
           b. 30 July 1913 - Corsicana, Tex.
           m. Edna Irene Bolen 7 June 1942, Stark, Fla.
              b. 5 Aug. 1913 - Purdon, Tex.

           A. Robert Larry Flynn
              b. 6 Jan. 1949 - Corsicana, Tex.
              m. Amy Virginia Awalt 15 Dec. 1972 Corsicana, Tx
                 b. 23 June 1952 - Grand Lake, Colo.

              1. Lari Rene Flynn
                 b. 2 Feb. 1974 - Corsicana, Tex.

           B. Donna Kay Flynn
              b. 25 Feb. 1951 - Corsicana, Tex.
              m. Johnny Turner 2 Feb. 1970, Dallas, Tex.

              1. Jennifer Lynn Turner
                 b. 23 Feb. 1974 - Corsicana, Tex.

3. Johnnie Carl Flynn
   b. 9 June 1916 - Corsicana, Tex.
   d. 22 Jan. 1972
   m. Dortha Nell Hardin 9 Nov. 1942, Corsicana, Tex.
      b. 17 March 1921 - Purdon, Tex.
   A. Johnnie Carl Flynn, Jr.
      b. 3 Oct. 1950 - Corsicana, Tex.
      m. Carolyn Elaine Duncan 30 Aug. 1975,
            Lubbock, Tex.
         b. 13 Sept. 1950 - Lamesa, Tex.

4. Steve L. Flynn
   b. 13 Jan. 1920 - Corsicana, Tex.
   m. Lillie Iola Keele 1 Nov. 1941, Fabens, Tex.
      b. 7 Oct. 1924

   A. Patsy Ann Flynn
      b. 18 Oct. 1943 - Corsicana, Tex.
      m. ?

      1. Paula Gail Parrott
         b. 28 March 1961 - Dallas, Tex.
      2. Steven Lynn Parrott
         b. 20 March 1965 - Dallas, Tex.

   B. Ricky Wayne Flynn
      b. 9 Dec. 1950 - Kernes, Tex.

5. Charlie Lee Flynn
   b. 6 June 1923 - Corsicana, Tex.
   m. Margie Faye French 21 June 1943, Corsicana, Tex.
      b. 8 Dec. 1922 - Irene, Tex. (Hill County)

   A. Ailsa Margette Flynn
      b. 23 Jan. 1948 - Corsicana, Tex.
      m. Guy Wilford Anderson, Jr. 23 May 1970
            Corsicana, Tex.
         b. 1 March 1943 - Gorman, Tex.

6. Annie Ruth Flynn
   b. 25 Apr. 1930 - Corsicana, Tex.
   m. Jackson J. Robinson 15 Dec. 1945 Corsicana, Tex.
      b. 21 June 1926 - Eureka, Tex.

   A. Judi Paulette Robinson
      b. 3 Feb. 1947 - Corsicana, Tex.
      m. Richard Earl Perry 17 July 1962, Corsicana,
            Tex.
         b. 18 Jan. 1944 - Eureka, Tex.

      1. Dana Lynn Perry
         b. 12 Sept. 1963 - Corsicana, Tex.
      2. Susan Michelle Perry
         b. 8 Oct. 1968 - Corsicana, Tex.

   B. Daniel Keith Robinson
      b. 3 Sept. 1953 - Corsicana, Tex.
      m. Brenda Roslyn Mason 2 Nov. 1973, Angus, Tex.
         b. 22 July 1956 - Roswell, NM

      1. Daniel Keith Robinson
         b. 10 May 1975 - Corsicana, Tex.

(b) Rufus Andrew Henderson
   b. 26 Jan. 1897 - Emhouse, Tex.
   m. Cora Lyons 5 April 1924, Corsicana, Tex.
      b. 26 Dec. 1904 - Roane, Tex.

   1. Rufus Clellon Henderson
      b. 2 Oct. 1927 - Mexia, Tex.
      m. Gloria Suggs 10 Dec. 1948, Dallas, Tex.
         b. 21 May 1930

      A. Peggy Gail Henderson
         b. 20 May 1954 - Dallas, Tex.
      B. Larry Don Henderson
         b. 26 Jan. 1959 - Dallas, Tex.

(c) Maudie Henderson
   b. 12 March 1901 - Navarro Co., Tex.
   d. 28 April 1974
   m. Clyde Barnes 20 Sept. 1923, Corsicana, Tex.
      b. ?
      d. 4 March 1958, Corsicana, Tex.

(d) Hattie Henderson
   (born after Maudie; no information on her; married
      and had one child.)

(e) Billie (Lily) Henderson
   b. 26 Sept. 1907 - Corsicana, Tex.

(f) Thelma Henderson
   b. 14 Sept. 1913 - Corsicana, Tex.
   d. 28 Sept. 1981
   m. Thomas Green Haynes 12 Dec. 1941, Corsicana, Tex.
      b. 11 Oct. 1911 - Corsicana, Tex.

   1. Thomas Allyn Haynes
      b. 25 April 1943 - Corsicana, Tex.
      m. Sherry Lajoun Clark 12 Sept. 1964, Corsicana, Tex.
         b. 21 Feb. 1945 - Corsicana, Tex.

      A. Rodney Allyn Haynes
         b. 17 March 1969 - Garland, Tex.
      B. Russell Shawn Haynes
         b. 4 Jan. 1971 - Garland, Tex.
   2. Jerry David Haynes
      b. 19 Oct. 1946 - Corsicana, Tex.
      m. Deborah Louise Farmer 6 May 1966, Corsicana, Tex.
         b. 14 Jan. 1951 - Corsicana, Tex.

      A. David Allan Haynes
         b. 23 Oct. 1966 - Corsicana, Tex.

Contributed by:
Mrs. Richard E. Day
14420-D Club Villa Dr.
Colorado Springs, CO 80908

Additional data on the family of Thomas Pricie Berryhill and
    Cynthia M. Todd. (See pp. 261-272)

   3. John H.W. Berryhill

   C. George Right Berryhill

      (1) Wallace Alexander Berryhill

         (b) Velma Fay Berryhill
            m. 14 June 1924
            d. 25 July 1964

            2. Betty Lou Wilcoxson

               A. Larry Harris
                  divorced Oct. 1974

                  1. Tracy Dawn Harris
                     b. 14 Sept. 1970

               B. Billy Wayne Harris
                  m. Connie Brannom 31 Dec. 1977

               C. Tyra Ann Harris
                  divorced June 1974
                  m. 2nd Jim Van Belle Nov. 1975

                  1. Casey Van Belle
                     b. 4 Sept. 1979

               E. Tonya Harris
                  m. Isaac Padilla 21 May 1977
                  divorced Mar. 1981

             1. Shay Miles Padilla
                b. ?
                d. 19 Jan. 1978

(c) Wallace Adrian Berryhill
    d. 18 Jan. 1972
    bur. Grants, N. Mex.

    1. Linda Joyce Berryhill
       m. James English - divorced
       d. 18 Jan. 1972
       bur. Grants, N. Mex.

    2. Ann Lee Berryhill
       bur. Grants, N. Mex.

(d) Edna Beatrice Berryhill

    1. Larry Joe Tietjen
       m. Beverly Ann Wilhelm
       divorced March 1965

    3. Thomas Jefferson Tietjen, Jr.

       E. Sandra Lee Tietjen
          b. 19 Apr. 1969 - Homer, Alaska

       F. Kenneth Ray Tietjen
          b. 17 June 1972 - Homer, Alaska

       G. Linda Joyce Tietjen
          b. 25 Apr. 1975 - Homer, Alaska

       H. Rodney Cliff Tietjen
          b. 11 July 1977 - Homer, Alaska

       I. Judy Ann Tietjen
          b. 7 May 1981 - Homer Alaska

    5. Jeryl Wayne Tietjen

       A. Ryan Lee Tietjen (adopted)
          b. 7 Apr. 1973 - Spokane, Wash.

       B. Maryah Lynn Tietjen
          b. 21 June 1975 - Tooele, Utah

       C. Flint Douglas Tietjen
          b. 21 Feb. 1977 - Gallup, N. Mex.

    6. Sheryl Ann Tietjen

       C. Alvin Scott Clawson
          b. 24 May 1969 - Homer, Alaska

       D. Dodie Susan Clawson
          b. 15 Nov. 1973 - Homer, Alaska

(e) Cecil Duane Berryhill
    d. 11 Aug. 1974
    m. Nelda Louise Elkins
    b. 26 May 1925
    bur. Grants, N. Mex

    1. Ina May Berryhill
       m. John Randolph Hoffman 6 June 1970 Grants,
          N. Mex.
         b. 18 April 1946 - Santa Ana, Calif.

       A. Caleb Randolph Hoffman
          b. 5 Oct. 1971 - Grants, N. Mex.

       B. Kyle Scott Hoffman
          b. 21 Apr. 1973 - Albuquerque, N. Mex.

       C. Brandon Lowell Hoffman
          b. 21 Feb. 1977 - Bountiful, Utah

    2. Nelda Rae Berryhill
       m. Jerry Ellis McPhaul 7 Nov. 1970
         b. 10 Sept. 1950 - Socorro, N. Mex.

    A. Nacona Naylynn McPhaul
       b. 12 Nov. 1971 - Gallup, N. Mex.

    B. Adrian Ellis McPhaul
       b. 20 Jan. 1975 - Gallup, N. Nex.

    C. Tawana Rae McPhaul
       b. 11 Aug. 1980 - Gallup, N. Mex.

3. Glenda Kae Berryhill
   m. Thomas Lee Bybee 8 Oct. 1977
      b. 2 May 1942 - Sheridan, Wyoming
   A. Chae Duane Bybee (adopted)
      b. 30 Apr. 1974 - Grants, N. Mex.

   B. Thomas Frank Bybee
      b. 24 Feb. 1979 - Buffalo, Wyoming

   C. Linda Louise Bybee
      b. 5 May 1980 - Gallup, N. Nex.

4. Duwana Gay Berryhill
   m. Danny Wayne Christensen 8 Mar. 1976,
      Grants, N. Mex. divorced
   m. 2nd Royal Paul Hopper 27 Jan. 1979

   A. Kindra Kaylynn Christensen
      b. 26 Oct. 1975 - Gallup, N. Mex.

   B. Royal Paul Hopper, Jr.
      b. 8 Aug. 1980 - Odessa, Tex.

2. Marvin Ollie Berryhill (See page 263)
   b. 4 Apr. 1886 - Zepher, Tex.

   (a) Ramon Berryhill
       b. 11 Aug. 1908 - Seminole, Tex.
       m. Loyce Huddleston 16 July 1932
          b. 26 Mar. 1912 - Snyder, Tex.

   1. Lowell Ray Berryhill
      b. 5 Nov. 1933 - Snyder, Tex.
      m. Donna Gene Wallis 21 Jan. 1956
         b. 30 June 1936 - Ballinger, Tex.

      A. Patricia Ray Berryhill
         b. 9 June 1958
         m. Monty Anderson 17 May 1980

      B. Dee Ann Berryhill
         b. 7 Oct. 1959

      C. Betsy Lea Berryhill
         b. 28 Dec. 1964

      D. Thomas Clay Berryhill
         b. 15 Feb. 1967

   2. Delphane Berryhill
      b. 14 Apr. 1936
      m. Bobby Lane Gray 30 Nov. 1956
         b. 26 Oct. 1933

      A. Tina Louise Gray
         b. 3 Aug. 1961

      B. Thomas Lane Gray
         b. 24 Oct. 1963

   3. Betty Louise Berryhill
      b. 18 Mar. 1938
      m. John Walter Duke 27 July 1957

      A. Douglas Alan Duke
         b. 14 Nov. 1960

      B. Diane Duke
         b. 12 Sept. 1962

```
            C. David Jeffery Duke
               b. 12 July 1965

    (b) I.B. Berryhill
            b. 27 May 1911 - Seminole, Texas
            m. Hazel Holcomb 22 Dec. 1937, Big Springs, Tex.
               b. 7 Mar. 1916; d. 30 Jan. 1960
               bur. Levelland, Tex.
            m. 2nd Marie Sones
            m. 3rd Emma Geffert
                  b. 7 Mar. 1921

            1. Vianna Kay Berryhill
               b. 1 Sept. 1938
               m. Fred Spears at Levelland, Tex.
                  b. 2 Aug. 1936

               A. Berry Dan Spears
                  b. 16 June 1957

               B. Troy Garth Spears
                  b. 25 July 1959

            2. Frantonya Berryhill
               b. 26 Jan. 1962

    (c) George Thomas Garth Berryhill
            b. 25 Jan. 1915 - Lubbock, Tex.
            m. Helen Morrow
               b. 31 Aug. 1921; d. 2 Feb. 1962
               bur. Levelland, Tex.
            m. 2nd Laverne Alford Jan. 1965
               b. 17 Apr. 1926

            1. Janice Marie Berryhill
               b. 6 July 1944
               m. Gary Smith

               A. Stacy Smith
                  b. 9 Oct. 1963

               B. Shawn Berryhill
                  b. 24 July 1959

    (d) Marguerite Berryhill
            b. 26 Dec. 1917
            d. 16 June 1920
            bur. Kenna, N. Mex.

    (e) Doris Berryhill (twin)
            b. 2 May 1920
            d. 2 May 1920
            bur. Kenna, N. Mex.

    (f) Coris Berryhill (twin)
            b. 2 May 1920
            d. 14 June 1920
            bur. Kenna, N. Mex.

    (g) Rudene Berryhill
            b. 1 Aug. 1921 - Lubbock, Tex.
            m. Wayne Gladson 12 Jan. 1940
               b. 11 Sept. 1918

            1. Sherene Gladson
               b. 28 Nov. 1941 - Los Angeles, Ca.
               m. Ted Lamb - Snyder, Tex.

               A. Stacy Sherene Lamb
                  b. 8 Sept. 1966

               B. Shelley Lamb
                  b. 14 May 1969

            2. Phyllis Lynn Gladson
               b. 29 Jan. 1947
               m. Paul Tidwell 30 Aug. 1968
```

                3. Denise Ozella Gladson
                   b. 25 Sept. 1957

        (h) Lafon Berryhill
            b. 22 May 1924 - Lubbock, Texas

        (i) LaNell Berryhill
            b. 18 July 1927 - Lubbock, Texas
            m. Jim Jr. Hogan
               b. 14 July 1925

            1. Jimmie Alton Hogan
               b. 2 Sept. 1947

            2. Kenneth Michael Hogan
               b. 24 Oct. 1949

        (j) Alvin Berryhill
            died at birth; no dates or places

        (k) James Berryhill
            died at birth; no dates or places

(5) Fred Bynum Berryhill

        (a) Laveta Berryhill

            1. Belva Lee Vaughan

                A. Jimmy Wayne Butterfield (adopted in 1963)
                   m. Rochelle Rae Larson 13 Oct. 1979,
                       Lincoln, Neb.
                   b. 2 May 1957 - Lincoln, Neb.

                B. Pamela Sue Butterfield (adopted in 1963)

        (e) Billie Jean Berryhill
            m. 3rd Robert M. Jones 9 Sept. 1974, Raton, N. Mex

            1. Ricky Dale Simmons
               m. Utunah Marie Hamilton Russell 11 Jan. 1973[sic]?
                   Hamilton, Ba.

                A. Janet Edwina Russell
                   b. 27 Oct. 1959
                   m. Lewis Melvin Coy, III

                    1. Samantha Kay Coy
                       b. 26 May 1979

                    2. Lewis Melvin Coy, IV
                       b. 2 May 1981

                B. John Edwin Russell
                   b. 3 May 1962

                C. Lanonda Marie Russell
                   b. 26 Apr. 1964

            2. Debbie Renae Simmons
               m. Edwin Greylon Wilson 4 Apr. 1975

                A. Shelly Renae Wilson
                   b. 25 Feb. 1976 - Wiesbaden, Ger.

        (f) Peggy Berryhill

            1. Vera Lynn Anthony
               m. Michael Gene Robertson 29 Dec. 1979
                   Boger, Texas
               b. 16 Oct. 1956 - Buffalo, Okla.

(7) Lillian Mellsenia Berryhill
    d. 24 Sept. 1970 - Bakersfield, Calif.
    m. Steven Lee Scott
    d. 7 June 1978 Bakersfield, Calif.

        (b) Earlagene Scott
            b. 3 Sept. 1928 - Bakersfield, Calif.
            m. Earl LeRoy Wilson 18 Jan. 1952 Bakersfield, Ca
               b. 4 Mar. 1924 - McLeod, Okla.

                1. Debra Kathleen Wilson (adopted)
                    b. 9 Nov. 1960 - Bakersfield, Ca.
                    m. Rodrick Bowman 28 Mar. 1981 Winston-Salem NC
                        b. 7 Nov. 1957 - Winston-Salem, NC

                2. Timothy Earl Wilson (adopted)
                    b. 13 Feb. 1968 - Inglewood, Calif.

        (c) Marion Decauter Scott
            b. 6 July 1932 - Bakersfield, Calif.
            m. Jeanne Leslie Rosske
                b. 26 Mar. 1933 - Fond du Lac, Wisc.
                Parents - Herbert & Lorraine Bonell Rosske

            1. Sharon Lorraine Scott
                b. 11 Sept. 1957 - San Diego, Calif.
                m. David Guy Coleman 7 Apr. 1979

            2. Stephen Marion Scott
                b. 2 Dec. 1958 - San Diego, Calif.

8. Lee Berryhill

    (b) Gary Royce Berryhill
        b. 23 July 1930 - Tatum, N. Mex.
        m. Wanda Linda Sue Autrey - 3 March 1953
            b. 13 Feb. 1932 - Clemscott, Okla.
                Parents - George Franklin & Eula Mattie
                        May Land Autrey

        1. Phillip Royce Berryhill
            b. 1 Nov. 1954 - Lea Co., Hobbs, N. Mex.
            m. Brenda Louise Black 2 Apr. 1977, Alamogordo,
                N. Mex.
                b. 13 Apr. 1957 - Alamogordo, N. Mex.
                    Parents - Rowland & Marie Carpenter Black

            A. Christopher Royce Berryhill
                b. 1 July 1980

        2. Brian Douglas Berryhill
            b. 2 Nov. 1960 - Alamogordo, N. Mex.

        3. Lisa Ann Berryhill
            b. 30 Mar. 1963 - Alamogordo, N. Mex.

        4. Brenda Eileen Berryhill
            b. 15 Nov. 1968 - Alamogordo, N. Mex.

9. Lue Artie Berryhill
    b. 27 Nov. 1902 - Gale, Tex.; d. 15 May 1891
    m. William Horace Belcher 20 Sept. 1919, Lovington,
            N. Mex.
        b. 8 May 1897, May, Texas
        d. Dec. 16, 1969
        bur. Slaton, Tex.
        Lue Artie bur. East Englewood Cem., Slaton, Tex.

    (a) Faye Oletha Belcher
        b. 23 Nov. 1920 - Plainview, N. Mex.
        d. 7 Dec. 1968
        bur. Slaton, Tex.
        m. Carl Frederick Payton 17 Mar. 1940, Roswell,
                N. Mex.
            b. 26 Sept. 1914 - Austin, Tex.
            d. 7 Dec. 1968
            bur. East Englewood Cem., Slaton, Tex.

        1. John William (JW) Payton
            b. 1 Mar. 1941 - Roswell, N. Mex.
            m. Breena Margaret Kass 10 Apr. 1966,
                    Treasure Island Naval Base, San Fran. Ca.
                    b. 3 April 1945
            A. Thomas Harlan (Tam) Payton
                b. 8 July 1967 - Lubbock, Tex.

B. Korren Ann (Korri) Payton
   b. 22 Dec. 1971 - Post, Tex.

2. Linda Joyce Payton
   b. 26 Oct. 1943 - Elida, N. M-x.
   m. Leon Earl Kenney 28 May 1962, Slaton, Tex.
   b. 14 Sept. 1941 - Levelland, Tex.

   A. Michael Douglas Kenney
      b. 26 Sept. 1966 - Warrick, Rhode Is.

   B. Timothy Miles Kenney
      b. 10 June 1968 - Leonard Town, Md.

   C. Leesha Lin Kenney (adopted Korean)
      b. 10 Mar. 1973 - Seol, Korea

   D. Jeremy Wade Kenney
      b. 5 Sept. 1974 - Pascagoula, Miss.

   E. Laura Lue Kenney (adopted)
      b. 31 Dec. 1976 - Mississippi

(b) (Baby boy) Belcher
    b. 23 Feb. 1926 - McDonald, N. Mex.
    d. 23 Feb. 1926
    bur. Tatum, N. Mex.

(c) Billie Evelyn Belcher
    b. 19 Dec. 1928 - Tatum, N. Mex.
    m. Ira Bruce Payton 14 June 1946 Maljarmar, N Mex.
    b. 6 June 1923 - Slaton, Tex.

1. Judy Sharon Payton
   b. 23 Aug. 1947 - Roswell, N. Mex.
   m. Linnell Gene Tisdale 31 May 1968 Bayfield,
        Colorado
      b. 26 Nov. 1945 - Littlefield, Tex.

   A. David Lynn Tisdale (adopted)
      b. 1 May 1972 - Ft. Worth, Tex.

   B. Deborah Michelle Tisdale (adopted)
      b. 10 Sept. 1974 - Ft. Worth, Tex.

2. William Douglas Payton
   b. 16 Aug. 1949 - Silaam Springs, Ark.
   m. Carol Ann France 8 Apr. 1971, Post, Tex.
   b. 1 Mar. 1949 - Massilon, Ohio

   A. Christopher Douglas Payton
      b. 26 July 1974 - Dallas, Tex.

   B. Brian Douglas Payton
      b. 11 May 1977 - Oklahoma City, Okla.

The Berryhill Family of America

I. A.E. Berryhill (Alexander), according to his Civil War Records,
    was born in Jones County, Georgia, moved to Mississippi and married
    Mary N. Liles in Rankin County on 31st March 1859. They had only
    one son listed in the Amite County records, William Harmon Berryhill.
    Alexander was enrolled in the Confederate Army August 24, 1861 at
    Grenada, Yallabusha County, Mississippi by General West. He was a
    private in Co. B., Sixth Regiment of Miss. (Fifteenth Regiment of
    Mississippi Infantry), 36 years old, five feet ten inches tall,
    Fair complexion, gray eyes, light hair, and by occupation a farmer.
    He died at Vicksburg, Mississippi on the 27th day of June, 1863.
    Mary N. Liles, Alexander Berryhill's wife was the daughter of
    Sarah (Mulholland) and Eli Liles. After her husband died, she
    moved back to Rankin County and was aided in making her application
    for pension by her uncle Henry Mulholland. She later married a
    Mr. Vance and had two children, one of whom was Leah Vance.

II. William Harmon Berryhill was reared in Rankin County with the Liles.
    He and Thomas Abraham Kelly married in a double wedding ceremony,
    Annie Elizabeth Berry, b. 29 Dec. 1860 and Katherine Verginia Berry,
    respectively, the only daughters of Mary Gitella (Robinson) and
    Halbert Berry on the 13th day of September, 1880. William Harmon
    and Annie Elizabeth (Berry) Berryhill had 10 children: Mary Ethel,
    Katherine (Kate), Annie Lee, Lorena Mae, Zula Hortense, Verna
    Berry, Hazel Augusta, Roy (William Roy) Holbert, Guy Robinson.

III. Mary Ethel (Ethel) (Berryhill) and Samuel Allen Baker were married
    on the 26th day of December, 1901. She was born in Brandon, and
    he was born in Pisgah, both in Rankin County, Mississippi. They
    had six children: Samuel Allen (S.A.), Ethel Marie, Hazel Eliza-
    beth, William Bertram (Bert), Dorothy May, and Katherine Lucile.
    They moved to Gulfport, Miss. in February of 1907 when Elizabeth
    Baker was one month old. Samuel Allen Baker Sr. was a Postmaster,
    and merchant at Pisgah before leaving.

    IV. Samuel Allen Baker, Jr. b. 18 Sept., 1903 m. Gertrude
    Cobb of Wiggins, and they had 5 children: Lillian Frances,
    Sam Allen, John Ware, Elizabeth Jane, and James Neil.

    V. Lillian Frances Baker, b. 12 Jan. 1929 m. H.R. Bond,
    in May, 1950. Their children are H. Ray Bond, b. May
    1951, Pat,Keith, Richard, and Cynthia (Cindy) b. Nov.
    1, 1965

    V. Sam Allen Baker III, b. Sept. 3, 1930 m. Vesta Eeds
    Dec. 31, 1932. Their children are Terry, Marilyn, Billy
    Joe, and David Wayne.

      VI. Terry Allen, b. June 3, 1954 m. Donna Monroe. Their
    two children are Alyssa and Jarrett.

      VI. Marilyn, b. June 1958 m. John Murray; one child,
    Michelle.

VI. Billy Joe, b. June 1962, not yet married
VI David Wayne, b. Dec. 1963
V. John Ware Baker, b. 8 Sept. 1937 m. Laverne Hegwood;
Their children are John Ware, Jr., Stevie, and Julia
Baker.
V. Elizabeth Jane Baker (Jane) b. 7 Jan. 1939 m. Bill
Byrd. Their children are Andrea Jane and Denise
Elizabeth.
V. James Neil Baker b. 31 Dec. 1939, m. Linda; His children
are James Edgar and Wanda.
IV. Ethel Marie Baker b. July 14, 1905 m. 1st Clifton Capers
and had one son, Archie Clifton Capers. Then she married
2nd Dan M. McKinnon b. 17 Jan. 1902 and they had girls,
Ethel Marie McKinnon, Janis Carol McKinnon, and Louise Rae
McKinnon.
V. Clifton Capers b. October 19, 1927 m. Maryon Roberts,
b. 31 July, 1927. They have four children: Clifton
Dennis (Butch) Capers b. 20 March 1952 and Dan Carley
(Dannie), b. May 6, 1954, Thomas Archie (Tommie, Capers
b. June 9, 1959 and Robert Glenn (Bob) b. 15 Mar. 1962.
V. Clifton Dennis m. Jaqueline Criser, b. February 7, 1953.
They have two children, Scott and Michael.
V. Dan Carley (Dannie) Capers m. Beth Bellman b. October
22, 1953. They have two children, Angie, a girl, and
Corley, a boy.
V. Thomas Archie (Tommie) b. 9 June 1959.
V. Robert Glenn (Bob) Capers, b. 15 March, 1962.
V. Ethel Marie McKinnon, b. 5 March 1936 m. Paul Davis
Yates b. 21 July 1928. They have 3 children:
VI. Paul Davis Yates b. 1 Aug. 1955 m., now divorced;
They have one child, Jennifer.
VI. Ethel Quinnette Yates, b. 31 July, 1958 m. Tony
Stevenson. They have one son, John.
VI.Dan Martin McKinnon Yates b. 27 Dec., 1960.
VI. Carol Marie Yates, b. 10 Sept., 1966.
V. Janis Carol McKinnon b. Aug. 29, 1940 m. Ralph Thomas
Rich. They live in Huntsville, Ala. and have two
children: Cynthia Michelle Rich, b. 5 Sept. 1968,
and Kendall, b. 4 April, 1971.
V. Louise Rae McKinnon b. 13 Dec. 1941 m. Gerald Lynn Jones
b. August 19, 1942. They married 10 October 1964.
They had two sons: Gerald Lynn Jones, Jr., b. 11 Oct.
1966, and Glenn Martin, b. 19 Oct. 1969.
IV. (Hazel) Elizabeth Baker, b. 17 Jan. 1907 m. Cyril Raymond
Haas on 30 Aug. 1941. They had two daughters Sarah Baker
Haas b. 27 Feb. 1945 and Elizabeth Ray Haas, b. Feb. 23,

1946. Both were born in Washington, D.C. but moved to the Coast later.

> V. Sarah Baker Haas, m. Dr. Atkinson Winan Longmire, b. June 1, 1945 in Gloster, Miss. Their children are Lela Darcy Longmire, b. April 6, 1973, Jerusha Elizabeth Longmire, b. 1 Sept., 1974 and Atkinson Garrett Longmire b. 6 Feb. 1978.
>
> V. Elizabeth Ray Haas, b. Feb. 23, 1946 m. 1st Daniel Joseph Wyatt. They had one daughter: Natalie Teresa (Wyatt), later changed to Bostick, b. 14 Oct. 1969; m. 2nd Lynn Bostick. They had two daughters: Tara Teneal Bostick, b. 19 Aug., 1976 and Katherine (Kay) Lynnelle, b. 25 Nov. 1977. Elizabeth Ray m. 3rd. James Edger (Ed) Maurer, b. 19 Sept. 1944. The child they are expecting will be named either Rebecca Elizabeth or Daniel Sheffield Maurer, depending upon its sex.

IV. William Bertram (Bert) Baker, b. July 29, 1909, m. Ellen Medora Henderson, b. 28 October, 1910. They have two children: William Bertram (Bill) Baker, Jr. and Virginia Virginia Ellen Baker.

> V. William Bertram (Bill) Baker, Jr., b. Feb. 2, 1940 m. Nancy Shirley Dunshee, b. Jan. 16, 1940. They m. May 25, 1962. Their two children are Steven Goodman Baker, b. 28 Aug. 1964 and Samuel Jackson Baker, b. 17 July 1967.
>
> V. Virginia Ellen Baker, b. April 17, 1948, m. John Joseph (Joe) Vidovich, (deceased), m. May 20, 1968.

IV. Dorothy May Baker, b. July 12, 1911 m. Ezra Winford Freeman, b. 1 Sept. 1910. Their two children are Elizabeth Ann Freeman, b. 23 Feb. 1939 and James Allen Freeman, b. 4 Aug. 1947.

> V. Elizabeth Ann Freeman m. Bill Clutter b. 15 Aug. 1931. No children.
>
> V. James Allen Freeman m. Mary Henderson b. 4 Nov. 1945; Their two children are James Allen Freeman, Jr. (Jaimie) b. Sept. 11, 1970 and an adopted son Jay Jack (J.J.) Freeman, b. 21 September, 1972.

IV. Katherine Lucile Baker, b. 19 October, 1914 m. Walter Lee Wood b. 9 June 1910. Their only child is Walter Lee Wood, Jr., b. 18 June 1942 m. 2 July 1966, Olivia Kemp b. 18 June, 1942.

> V. Walter Lee Wood, Jr. and Olivia Kemp have two daughters: Katherine Olivia Wood, b. 24 May, 1969 and Sarah Elizabeth Wood b. 17 December, 1973.

III. Katherine (Kate) Berryhill m. George Horne. They had one child
named Marguerite Horne.
    IV. Marguerite Horne m. 1st _____Babcock. They had two
    children: Phyllis Ann (Babcock) Norton and George Phillip
    Babcock (called Billy). They both have families. By
    her second husband she had one daughter: Margaret Catherine
    _____ who married Ralph H. Mims and has three children:
    Clayton Scott Mims, Leslie Ann Mims, and Donald Wayne Mims.

III. Annie Lee Berryhill m. William (Bill) Alman. They had two
daughters: Bernice Alman and Urmede Alman.
    IV. Bernice Alman m. John Gill. They had one son John Jr.
    who married and had one daughter.
    IV. Urmede Alman m. Jessie Broadus 1st, and had two daughters:
    Sharon Broadus and Vicki Broadus.
        V. Sharon Broadus m. Bobby Pate and had one daughter:
        Tonya Pate.
        V. Vicki Broadus m. Ronald Alan Gorham. Their only son
        is Lee Dillon Gorham.
    Urmede Alman m. 2nd John Martin.

III. Vorena Berryhill m. Bane Farr in Washington, D.C. They had
no children.

III. Verna Berry Berryhill b. Feb. 15, 1889 m. James Galloway. They
had two daughters: Elizabeth Galloway and Hazel Galloway.
Their home was Lucedale, Mississippi.
    IV. Elizabeth Galloway m. Ross Johnson. Their children are
    Lorena, Myrt, and Verna.
        V. Lorena m. Marvin Hutchins, Cottondale, Ala.
        V. Myrt m. James Brasher, Northport, Ala.
        V. Verna m. Bobbie Lee Windham, Duncanville, Ala.
        V. Linda Fay
    IV. Hazel Galloway m. a Mr. Barr in Lucedale, Miss.

III. William Roy Berryhill was in the Navy during World War I.
m. 1st Julie Louise Guard and had 3 children: Louise Berryhill,
William Roy, Jr. and Anna Catherine Berryhill. By his second
wife he had James Baxter Berryhill, Bain Benneyan, Guy Allen,
and Barbara Sue.
    IV. Louise Berryhill, b. 27 Nov. 1925
    IV. William Roy Berryhill, Jr. b. 8 March 1931 m. Delores
    Verleyen Berryhill and have two children, William Paul
    and Edward.
    IV. Anna Catherine b. 6 Sept. 1932 m. Henry Stafford.
    IV. James Baxter b. 31 July 1936
    IV. Bain Benneyan b. 24 July, 1937
    IV. Guy Allen b. 17 Jan. 1939
    IV. Barbara Sue b. 14 May 1941 m. David Alan Leary b. Sept.,
    1940. They have 3 children: David Alan Leary, Jr.,
    b. Feb. 10, 1961, Susan Michelle Leary b. Aug. 15, 1963
    and Mark ?, 1963.

III. Zula Hortense Berryhill m. William Smith in Virginia. Their children are: William Smith, Jr. and Zula Hortense Smith.

III. Hazel Augusta Berryhill m. Henry A. Guest and had two children: Anne Guest and Ray Guest.

    IV. Anne Guest m. Richard Suko, and they have two children: Diana b. Feb. 1955 and Scott b. 1963

    IV. Ray Guest.

III. Abraham Holbert (Holbert) Berryhill m. _____; children:

    IV. Holbert Berryhill

    IV. Peggy Berryhill

III. Isaac Guy (Guy) Robinson Berryhill b. Jan. 18, 1902, married twice - no children.

Compiled and researched by:

Elizabeth B. Haas
1203 Nelson Grove
Ocean Springs, Miss., 39564

The Family of William Thomas Berryhill, son of Marshall Henry Berryhill and Elsie Mae Zinn.

William Thomas Berryhill b May 31, 1911

    William Thomas Berryhill, Jr. b January 21, 1941

        Troy Thomas Berryhill Weir b February 23, 1964

W.T. Berryhill married Nancy A. Landers May 27, 1949

    Charlotte Berryhill b August 11, 1950

    John Marshall Berryhill b March 2 1954; m Adrianne Dyer October 31, 1976

        Judson Tanner Berryhill b July 31, 1981

    Robert Edward Berryhill b September 22, 1956; m. Debra Norris December 27, 1975

        Robert Jacob Berryhill b March 24, 1977

    Lois Ann Berryhill b December 1, 1960; m. Stephen Faught February 2, 1979

        Reagan Adair Faught b Sepbember 15, 1979

Contributed by:

Mr & Mrs W.T. Berryhill
Rt. 1, Box 269X
Brownwood, Tex. 76801

The Family of Frank and Gertha (Morrison) Berryhill

Frank Berryhill m. Gertha Morrison; They had one son:
Ira Lee Berryhill m. Dorothy Nell Jones, who had three children:
Darrell Dwaine Berryhill b 10 October 1943; m. Judith
Lynn Ater Nov. 29, 1963; They had two sons:
Parrish Leon Berryhill b. Sept. 28, 1964
Dale Dean Berryhill b. May 16, 1966
Darrell m. 2nd Doloras (Teaff) (Norris); he has two step-
children: a girl, Whitney Norris, b. Jan. 6, 1965,
and a boy, Rex Norris, b. Feb. 5, 1966
Patricia Darnell Berryhill, b. 12 June, 1947; m. Clinton
Alton Hassell Sept. 6, 1967; They have two children:
Clinton Alan Hassell, b. Aug. 22, 1977
Sharina Michell Hassell, b. June 13, 1980
Waymonn Lee Berryhill, b. 5 Sept., 1951; m. Tammie Irene
Jones Sept. 29, 1979. They have no children.

Contributed by:
I.L. and Dorothy Berryhill
Rt. 1
Purdon, Tex. 76679

The Family of William Howard Berryhill

William Howard Berryhill b. Sept. 16, 1872, Winfield, Ala.;
d. July 20, 1910; bur. in Corsicana, Tex.; m. Allie Langston
Sept. 13, 1908. She was b. Oct. 6, 1890, Blooming Grove, Tex;
d. 1971; bur. in San Diego, Calif.They had two children (twins):
Ira William Berryhill, b. Aug. 1, 1909; d. March 13, 1953;
bur. San Diego, Cal.; m. Ella Mae Montgomery. They had
no children.
Harvie Lillian Berryhill, b. Aug. 1, 1909; d. Oct 13, 1973;
bur. in Sardis, Tex.; m. 1st Robert Harvey Stafford;
They had two daughters:
Della Mae Stafford, b. April 7, 1931; m. Doyle J Kinney
Oct. 12, 1946; they had three children:
Doyle J Kinney, Jr., stillborn Jan. 4, 1948
Louis Glenn Kinney, b. Feb. 9, 1950; m. Brenda Gail
Guidry Nov. 1, 1970. They have one daughter:
Teresa Lynn Kinney, b. June 7, 1976
Edward Lee Kinney, b. 15 Aug. 1955, d. 11 March 1976
Edith Ruth Stafford, b. May 4, 1933; m. Colvin Crawford
Wallace, Jr. March 26, 1949. They had two children:
Dwayne Wallace stillborn Jan. 1, 1950
Glenda Sue Wallace, b. Oct. 28, 1951; m. Geoffrey
Paul Jones Dec. 19, 1970. Had two sons:
Geoffrey Paul Jones, II, b. July 6, 1979
Matthew John Jones, b. Dec. 3, 1981
Harvie Lillian Berryhill Stafford m. 2nd Joseph C. Chisholm

Issue of Charles and Mary McCullough - please add the marriage of Charles Wesley McCullough to Neena Jo Shoulty, b. Sept. 12, 1958.

Issue of Orilla Charlene Hudson Fotheringhouse: the marriage of #1 Jeffrey Wayne Hudson m. to Kelley Williams, b. June 6, 1959 and #4 Lisa Gay Hudson to Mark Lynn b. Feb. 24, 1960.

Contributed by:

Mary McCullough
1001 Phelps
Newburgh, IN   47630

BERRYHILL (cont.)
John Thomas 42, 49,
    96, 119, 154, 191,
    192, 215, 268
John W. 7, 130
John W. W. 6
John Walter 9, 115,
    118, 164
John William 102, 153
Johnnie 64
Johnnie Lynnwood 103
Johnnie May 140
Jonathan Lewis 153
Joseph 2, 3, 5, 199,
    200, 201, 246, 250,
    258
Joseph F. 258
Joseph Isaac 196
Joseph J. 10
Joseph J. N. C. 5, 13,
    16, 200
Joseph Roy 29
Joseph Troy 161
Joseph Vardaman 199
Josephine 257
Josh Robert 210
Josiah 79
Joy 144
Joyce 162
Joyce Adelle 188
Judith Ann 55
Judith Lynn 136
Judson Tanner 290
Judy 159
Judy K. 39
Judy Marolyn 159
Judy Zane 215
Julian Elizabeth 46
Julian Floyd 46
Julia -- 6, 270
Julia 207, 218, 259
Julia A. 245
June Elizabeth 46
Junius 246
Justina Louise 164
Karen 214
Kate 215
Katherine 65, 254,
    286, 289
Katherine Josephine
    214
Kathy 138
Kelly Marie 54
Kenneth Brian 216
Kenneth David 134
Kenneth Michael 65
Kenneth Ray 46, 157
Keri Tay 133
Kimalee, Ann 157
Kimberly, Leigh 138
Kuella 193
L. M. 10
Lafon 264, 283
Lane 259, 269
La Nell 264, 283
Lanelle 110
Lannes Moncey 270, 271
Lanta Mae 40
Laura 130
Laura Ann 9, 144
Laura Lisa 271
Laveta 283
La Vetta 265
La Von 265
Lavonne 52
Laurence 194
Laurence L. 260
Lawrence Leander (Lee)
    6
Lawrence Lee 270
Lawrence Moncey 270
Leah Mae 136
Leander 258, 259, 270

BERRYHILL (cont.)
Lee 82, 257, 267,
    284
Lena 151
Lensfield 6, 57, 99,
    201, 204, 207, 242
Leon John 29
Leon Nelson 54
Leona -- 162
Lenora Isabel 31
Leroy 271
Leroy R. 6, 260
Leslie Freeda 152
Letuis David 133, 134
Levi 258, 259, 261
Levi H. 6, 260, 269
Levi H. 2nd Sgt. 8
Lewis 242
Lexie Mae 37
Lila Rose 52
Lillian 148
Lillian Gertrude 53
Lillian Lucille 197
Lillian Mellsenia 267,
    283
Lillie 143
Lillie Ann 159
Limmie Washington 138
Lina 118
Linda 46, 118, 217
Linda Carolyn 159
Linda Joyce 262, 280
Linda Kay 29
Linda Sue 158, 159
Linwood John 29
Linzie Jefferson 137
Lisa 160
Lisa Ann 267, 284
Lisa Renee 139
Littleton 258
Lizzie 111
Lois 188
Lois Ann 290
Lois Lanella 273
Lois Regina 30
Lola Gay 153
Lola Lorene 212
Lona B. 144
Loney Love 258
Lonnie Haskel 138
Lorena Mae 255, 286
Lorena S. 99
Lou 268
Louisa 258
Louise 251, 256, 289
Lovella 207
Lowell Ray 264, 281
Loyd David 237
Lucy 258, 259
Lucy B. 259, 269
Lucinda -- 257
Lucinda 251
Lue Artie 284
Luella 193
Lula 271
Lula Lugene 212
Lulla 9, 169
Lurene 198
Lurie Marie 199
Luther 10
Luther Alton 144
M. A. (female) 4, 17,
    66
M. A. 18, 69
M. C. 10, 210
M. E. 9
M. F. 4
M. G. 9
M. J. 260
Mrs. M. M. 9
M. V. 7
M. V. Yancy 9
Maggie 42, 119

BERRYHILL (cont.)
Maggie Lou 216
Maggie M. 105
Malcum Otis 137
Marc Wayne 135
Margaret 3, 12, 57, 69,
    70, 115, 130, 154,
    177, 193, 250
Margaret A. 4, 15, 88
Margaret Ann 5, 15, 18,
    164, 191, 238
Margaret C. 5, 191
Margaret E. 4, 10, 111,
    248
Margaret Ellen 190
Margaret Emeline 110
Margaret Essie 163
Margaret Josephine 148
Margaret Louise 64
Margaret M. 9, 114,
    115, 258
Margaret Weeks 12, 13,
    15
Margaret Y. -- 5
Marguerite 264, 282
Maria Elizabeth 30
Marie 52
Marjorie 190, 257
Mark Wayne 46
Marsha 162
Marshall Henry 188,
    290
Martha -- 251, 257,
    258
Martha 5, 117, 200,
    201, 242, 246, 250,
    251
Martha A. 69
Martha Ann 4, 17, 47,
    69, 189, 191
Martha E. 56, 111
Martha Elizabeth 133,
    209, 277
Martha F. 4, 70, 112,
    129
Martha Frances 4, 89,
    194
Martha Jane 196, 247
Martha Yancey Virginia
    42, 119
Martin 250, 272
Martin V. 260
Martin Van Buren 6,
    270
Marvin Ollie 263, 281
Mary -- 6, 257, 269
Mary 2, 18, 23, 32,
    67, 69, 70, 81, 82,
    99, 130, 157, 207,
    218, 246, 247, 250,
    258, 259
Mary A. 5, 32, 99, 130,
    191, 250, 251
Mary Alabama 190
Mary Ann 4, 47, 67, 70,
    118, 129, 130, 154,
    207
Mary Ann (Polly) 6, 81,
    219, 241
Mary Darlene 158
Mary Doris 56
Mary E. 4, 5, 9, 112,
    129, 177, 178, 207,
    218
Mary Elizabeth 23, 83,
    87
Mary Emma 4
Mary Ethel 252, 286
Mary Florence 161
Mary Frances 145
Mary Imes 5
Mary Isabel 4, 16, 32
Mary Jane 9, 115, 158

BERRYHILL (cont.)
Robert Daniel 274
Robert Edward 290
Robert Grady 196
Robert Grady, Jr. 196
Robert Jacob 290
Robert L. 201
Robert Michael 196
Robert N. 245
Robert R. 81
Robert W. 4, 17, 18,
   129, 130, 152
Roberta Jean 56
Roger 81
Roger Dale 135, 217
Roland 147
Rolk D. 67
Rollie 119
Romie Lee 144
Ronald 215
Ronald H. 216
Ronald Raye 54
Rosa Lee 258
Rosa Belle 160
Rosalie 265
Rosie Belle 146
Roy Edward 216
Roy Grady 196
Roy M. 265
Roy Mayfield 158
Ruble Franklin 158
Ruby Dean 39
Ruby Elizabeth 151
Ruby Flora 26
Ruby Gladys 42
Ruby Jane Corilla 215
Ruby Mae 66
Ruby Olive 51, 189
Rudene 264, 282
Rudolph Dan 190
Rufus A. 99
Rufus Alsa 4, 129,
   130, 142
Rugus Gordan 216
Rufus "Ruffie" 100
Ruth Evelyn 117
Ruthie 152
S. L. 102
S. N. 11
Sallie 57, 258
Sally C. 218
Sam 251, 257
Sammie 23
Samuel Ensign 1
Samuel, Sergeant 1
Samuel 1, 2, 3, 32,
   205, 208, 246, 250,
   258, 260
Samuel Clyde 54
Samuel Darren 268
Samuel N. 111
Samuel Newton 10, 23,
   32, 186, 205
Samuel R. 9
Sandra Fay 136
Sandra June 118
Sara J. 4, 112, 129,
   130
Sarah 2, 258, 259, 271
Sarah Ann 5, 15, 18,
   20, 186
Sarah B. 12
Sarah C. 5, 214
Sarah Elizabeth 4, 10,
   69, 70, 88, 149,
   152
Sarah Jane 4, 112, 120,
   140
Sarah Lee 257
Savannah 123
Savannah Viola 137
Sharon Kay 118
Shawn 282

BERRYHILL (cont.)
Shelia Ann 54, 151
Shelia Merrie 118
Shelli Suzanna 271
Sheril G. 267
Sheri Lynn 59
Sherlene 267
Sherry Claire 109, 273
Shirley G. 151
Shirley Marie 216
Silas 250
Silla 177
Silliam 250
Simon 251, 258
Solon N. 99, 100
Sophie 251
Sophronia 245
Stanford 257
Stanley Norris 139
Stanley Wayne 157
Steven Curtis 134
Stormi Lynn 267
Sue Ellen 29
Sue Jean 151
Susie Rebecca 189
Susan -- 5, 200
Susan 5, 15, 112, 180,
   193, 195, 197, 201,
   242, 246, 247, 248
Susan C. 112, 237,
   238
Susan Catherine -- 4,
   69, 70, 71, 83,
   112, 121
Susan Flurry 5
Susan J. 177
Susan Jane 5, 183, 197
Susan M. 195
Susannah 257, 258
Susie 9, 196
Susie Ann 154
Susie Dane 29
Susie Foshee 4
Susie Jane 117
Susie Lee 29
Suzanne 134
Sylvia Ann 39
T. J. 8
T. N. 8
T. P. 258, 259
T. W., Jr. 188
Telsa 199
Thadious M. 207
Thaddeus 274
Thadius 228
Thelma 57
Thelma May 261
Theodocey (Doshia) 81,
   82
Theodore 258
Theodore F. 251
Theresa Youvonne 216
Thomas 3, 4, 5, 6, 7,
   12, 15, 16, 18, 36,
   69, 98, 99, 112,
   129, 164, 177, 193,
   202, 204, 207, 218,
   242, 245, 246, 250,
   258, 259
Thomas, Pvt. 7, 8
Thomas, Jr. 259, 260
Thomas A. 9
Thomas Alonzo 153
Thomas Alvin 37
Thomas Clay 281
Thomas E. 9, 147
Thomas E., Pvt. 7
Thomas Edward 136
Thomas G. 6, 260
Thomas Griffith 261
Thomas H. 258
Thomas J. 4, 129, 130,
   218

BERRYHILL (cont.)
Thomas J., Pvt. 8, 37
Thomas J. C. 5, 215,
   218
Thomas Jefferson 130,
   131, 257
Thomas K. F. 6, 259,
   260, 271
Thomas M. 38
Thomas Marshall 62
Thomas N. 250, 251
Thomas P. 259
Thomas Pricie 6, 249,
   259, 260, 261, 279
Thomas Raymond 49, 191
Thomas Winifred 188
Thurman Wallace 217
Timothy Joe 153
Tina Angela 108
Tiney Angela 108
Tishie 207
-- Todd 6
Tol Edward 109, 273
Tom 271
Tommie Lou 138
Tommy 152
Tommy Ray 101
Tony 63
Tony Edwin 135
Tracie Rachelle 133
Travis 46, 188
Travis Grady 217
Trilla 193
Troy 118
Troy Cleveland 161
Troy Thomas 290
Ura Linddell 156
Vanette Kay 104
Veldon 187
Velma Faye 261, 279
Velma Roena 162
Vergle E. 210
Verleyan 256
Verna Berry 255, 286,
   289
Vernon Washington 158
Vianna Kay 264, 282
Vickery 138
Vilantia Cantrell 5
Viola 5, 9, 199
Virgil 270
Virginia -- 52
Virginia Dianne 160
Virginia Estell 45
Virginia Pearl 133
Vorena 289
W. D. 52
W. H. 10, 111, 152
W. R. 10
W. S. 36
W. T. 290
Wallace 81
Wallace Adrian 262,
   280
Wallace Alexander 261,
   279
Wallace Jay 263
Walter 31, 64, 108
Walter A. 151
Walter Coleman 22
Walter Ray 251
Wanda 9
Wanda F. 151
Wanda Sue 54
Wannell 81
Warren 188
Waymond Lee 216
Waymonn Lee 291
Wayne 190
Wendy Arleen 163
Wesley Eugene 55
Whitney Norris 291
Wilford 9